PEARSON

ALWAYS LEARNING

Jonathan Berk • Peter DeMarzo • Jarrad Harford

Fundamentals of Corporate Finance

Third Custom Edition for Boston University FE 101

Taken from:
Fundamentals of Corporate Finance, Fourth Edition
by Jonathan Berk, Peter DeMarzo, and Jarrad Harford.

The Pearson Series in Finance

Berk/DeMarzo
*Corporate Finance**
*Corporate Finance: The Core**

Berk/DeMarzo/Harford
*Fundamentals of Corporate Finance**

Brooks
*Financial Management: Core Concepts**

Copeland/Weston/Shastri
Financial Theory and Corporate Policy

Dorfman/Cather
Introduction to Risk Management and Insurance

Eakins/McNally
*Corporate Finance Online**

Eiteman/Stonehill/Moffett
*Multinational Business Finance**

Fabozzi
Bond Markets: Analysis and Strategies

Foerster
*Financial Management: Concepts and Applications**

Frasca
Personal Finance

Gitman/Zutter
*Principles of Managerial Finance**
*Principles of Managerial Finance—Brief Edition**

Haugen
The Inefficient Stock Market: What Pays Off and Why
Modern Investment Theory

Holden
Excel Modeling in Corporate Finance
Excel Modeling in Investments

Hughes/MacDonald
International Banking: Text and Cases

Hull
Fundamentals of Futures and Options Markets
Options, Futures, and Other Derivatives

Keown
*Personal Finance: Turning Money into Wealth**

Keown/Martin/Petty
*Foundations of Finance: The Logic and Practice of Financial Management**

Madura
*Personal Finance**

Marthinsen
Risk Takers: Uses and Abuses of Financial Derivatives

McDonald
Derivatives Markets
Fundamentals of Derivatives Markets

Mishkin/Eakins
Financial Markets and Institutions

Moffett/Stonehill/Eiteman
Fundamentals of Multinational Finance

Pennacchi
Theory of Asset Pricing

Rejda/McNamara
Principles of Risk Management and Insurance

Smart/Gitman/Joehnk
*Fundamentals of Investing**

Solnik/McLeavey
Global Investments

Titman/Keown/Martin
*Financial Management: Principles and Applications**

Titman/Martin
Valuation: The Art and Science of Corporate Investment Decisions

Weston/Mitchell/Mulherin
Takeovers, Restructuring, and Corporate Governance

*denotes titles with MyFinanceLab.   Log onto **www.myfinancelab.com** to learn more.

To Rebecca, Natasha, and Hannah for the love and for being there. —J. B.

To Kaui, Pono, Koa, and Kai for all the love and laughter. —P. D.

To Katrina, Evan, and Cole for your love and support. —J. H.

Cover Art: Courtesy of Songquan Deng/123rf.com.

Taken from:

Fundamentals of Corporate Finance, Fourth Edition
by Jonathan Berk, Peter DeMarzo, and Jarrad Harford.
Copyright © 2018, 2015, 2012 by Pearson Education, Inc.
New York, New York 10013

This special edition published in cooperation with Pearson Education, Inc.

Pearson Education, Inc., 330 Hudson Street, New York, New York 10013
A Pearson Education Company
www.pearsoned.com

Printed in the United States of America

000200010272108387

JK

ISBN 10: 1-323-77255-3
ISBN 13: 978-1-323-77255-3

Brief Contents

Detailed Contents

About the Authors

Jonathan Berk, Peter DeMarzo, and Jarrad Harford

Jonathan Berk is the A.P. Giannini Professor of Finance at the Graduate School of Business, Stanford University and is a Research Associate at the National Bureau of Economic Research. Before coming to Stanford, he was the Sylvan Coleman Professor of Finance at Haas School of Business at the University of California, Berkeley. Prior to earning his PhD, he worked as an Associate at Goldman Sachs (where his education in finance really began).

Professor Berk's research interests in finance include corporate valuation, capital structure, mutual funds, asset pricing, experimental economics, and labor economics. His work has won a number of research awards including the TIAA-CREF Paul A. Samuelson Award, the Smith Breeden Prize, Best Paper of the Year in *The Review of Financial Studies*, and the FAME Research Prize. His paper, "A Critique of Size-Related Anomalies," was selected as one of the two best papers ever published in *The Review of Financial Studies*. In recognition of his influence on the practice of finance he has received the Bernstein-Fabozzi/Jacobs Levy Award, the Graham and Dodd Award of Excellence, and the Roger F. Murray Prize. He served two terms as an Associate Editor of the *Journal of Finance*, and a term as a director of the American Finance Association, the Western Finance Association, and academic director of the Financial Management Association. He is a Fellow of the Financial Management Association and a member of the advisory board of the *Journal of Portfolio Management*.

Born in Johannesburg, South Africa, Professor Berk is married, with two daughters, and is an avid skier and biker.

Peter DeMarzo is the Mizuho Financial Group Professor of Finance at the Graduate School of Business, Stanford University. He is the current Vice President of the American Finance Association and a Research Associate at the National Bureau of Economic Research. He teaches MBA and PhD courses in Corporate Finance and Financial Modeling. In addition to his experience at the Stanford Graduate School of Business, Professor DeMarzo has taught at the Haas School of Business and the Kellogg Graduate School of Management, and he was a National Fellow at the Hoover Institution.

Professor DeMarzo received the Sloan Teaching Excellence Award at Stanford, and the Earl F. Cheit Outstanding Teaching Award at U.C. Berkeley. Professor DeMarzo has served as an Associate Editor for *The Review of Financial Studies*, *Financial Management*, and the *B.E. Journals in Economic Analysis and Policy*, as well as a Director of the American Finance Association. He has served as Vice President and President of the Western Finance Association. Professor DeMarzo's research is in the area of corporate investment and financing, asset securitization, and contracting, as well as market structure and regulation. His recent work has examined issues of the optimal design of contracts and securities, leverage dynamics and the role of bank capital regulation, and the influence of information asymmetries on stock prices and corporate investment. He has received numerous awards including the Western Finance Association Corporate Finance Award and the Barclays Global Investors/Michael Brennan best-paper award from *The Review of Financial Studies*.

Professor DeMarzo was born in Whitestone, New York, and is married with three boys. He and his family enjoy hiking, biking, and skiing.

Jarrad Harford is the Paul Pigott - PACCAR Professor of Finance at the University of Washington. Prior to Washington, Professor Harford taught at the Lundquist College of Business at the University of Oregon. He received his PhD in Finance with a minor in Organizations and Markets from the University of Rochester. Professor Harford has taught the core undergraduate finance course, Business Finance, for over nineteen years, as well as an elective in Mergers and Acquisitions, and "Finance for Non-financial Executives" in the executive education program. He has won numerous awards for his teaching, including the UW Finance Professor of the Year (2010, 2012, 2016), Panhellenic/Interfraternity Council Business Professor of the Year Award (2011, 2013), ISMBA Excellence in Teaching Award (2006), and the Wells Fargo Faculty Award for Undergraduate Teaching (2005). Professor Harford is currently a Managing Editor of the *Journal of Financial and Quantitative Analysis*, and serves as an Associate Editor for the *Journal of Financial Economics*, and *Journal of Corporate Finance*. His main research interests are understanding the dynamics of merger and acquisition activity as well as the interaction of corporate cash management policy with governance, payout and global tax considerations. Professor Harford was born in Pennsylvania, is married, and has two sons. He and his family enjoy traveling, hiking, and skiing.

Bridging Theory and Practice

EXAMPLE 7.1
Stock Prices
and Returns

MyFinanceLab

PROBLEM

Suppose you expect Longs Drug Stores to pay an annual dividend of $0.56 per share in the coming year and to trade for $45.50 per share at the end of the year. If investments with equivalent risk to Longs' stock have an expected return of 6.80%, what is the most you would pay today for Longs' stock? What dividend yield and capital gain rate would you expect at this price?

SOLUTION

PLAN

We can use Eq. 7.1 to solve for the beginning price we would pay now (P_0) given our expectations about dividends ($Div_1 = \$0.56$) and future price ($P_1 = \$45.50$) and the return we need to expect to earn to be willing to invest ($r_E = 0.068$). We can then use Eq. 7.2 to calculate the dividend yield and capital gain rate.

EXECUTE

Using Eq. 7.1, we have

$$P_0 = \frac{Div_1 + P_1}{1 + r_E} = \frac{\$0.56 + \$45.50}{1.0680} = \$43.13$$

Referring to Eq. 7.2, we see that at this price, Longs' dividend yield is $Div_1/P_0 = 0.56/43.13 = 1.30\%$. The expected capital gain is $\$45.50 - \$43.13 = \$2.37$ per share, for a capital gain rate of $2.37/43.13 = 5.50\%$.

EVALUATE

At a price of $43.13, Longs' expected total return is $1.30\% + 5.50\% = 6.80\%$, which is equal to its equity cost of capital (the return being paid by investments with equivalent risk to Longs'). This amount is the most we would be willing to pay for Longs' stock. If we paid more, our expected return would be less than 6.8% and we would rather invest elsewhere.

PERSONAL FINANCE

EXAMPLE 4.5
Retirement Savings
Plan Annuity

MyFinanceLab

PROBLEM

Ellen is 35 years old and she has decided it is time to plan seriously for her retirement. At the end of each year until she is 65, she will save $10,000 in a retirement account. If the account earns 10% per year, how much will Ellen have in her account at age 65?

SOLUTION

PLAN

As always, we begin with a timeline. In this case, it is helpful to keep track of both the dates and Ellen's age:

Ellen's savings plan looks like an annuity of $10,000 per year for 30 years. (*Hint:* It is easy to become confused when you just look at age, rather than at both dates and age. A common error is to think there are only $65 - 36 = 29$ payments. Writing down both dates and age avoids this problem.)
    To determine the amount Ellen will have in her account at age 65, we'll need to compute the future value of this annuity.

EXECUTE

$$FV = \$10,000 \times \frac{1}{0.10}(1.10^{30} - 1)$$

$$= \$10,000 \times 164.49$$

$$= \$1.645 \text{ million at age 65}$$

Using a financial calculator or Excel:

	N	I/Y	PV	PMT	FV
Given:	30	10	0	−10,000	
Solve for:					1,644,940
Excel Formula: =FV(RATE,NPER, PMT, PV)=FV(0.10,30,−10000,0)					

EVALUATE

By investing $10,000 per year for 30 years (a total of $300,000) and earning interest on those investments, the compounding will allow Ellen to retire with $1.645 million.

Study Aids with a Practical Focus

To be successful, students need to master the core concepts and learn to identify and solve problems that today's practitioners face.

- The **Valuation Principle** is presented as the foundation of all financial decision making: The central idea is that a firm should take projects or make investments that increase the *value* of the *firm*. The tools of finance determine the impact of a project or investment on the firm's value by comparing the costs and benefits in equivalent terms. The Valuation Principle is first introduced in Chapter 3, revisited in the part openers, and integrated throughout the text.

- **Guided Problem Solutions (GPS)** are Examples that accompany every important concept using a consistent problem-solving methodology that breaks the solution process into three steps: *Plan*, *Execute*, and *Evaluate*. This approach aids student comprehension, enhances their ability to model the solution process when tackling problems on their own, and demonstrates the importance of interpreting the mathematical solution.

- **Personal Finance GPS** Examples showcase the use of financial analysis in everyday life by setting problems in scenarios, such as purchasing a new car or house and saving for retirement.

- **Common Mistake** boxes alert students to frequently made mistakes stemming from misunderstanding of core concepts and calculations—in the classroom and in the field.

COMMON MISTAKE

Summing Cash Flows Across Time

Once you understand the time value of money, our first rule may seem straightforward. However, it is very common, especially for those who have not studied finance, to violate this rule, simply treating all cash flows as comparable regardless of when they are received. One example is in sports contracts. In 2011, Albert Pujols signed a contract with the Los Angeles Angels that was repeatedly referred to as a "$240 million" contract. The $240 million comes from simply adding up all the payments Pujols would receive over the 10 years of the contract—treating dollars received in 10 years the same as dollars received today. The same thing occurred when Lionel Messi signed a contract extension with FC Barcelona in 2013, giving him a "$150 million" contract through 2018, and in 2015 when Giancarlo Stanton signed a "$325 million" 13-year contract with the Florida Marlins.

Applications That
Reflect Real Practice

Global Financial Crisis boxes reflect the reality of the recent financial crisis and sovereign debt crisis, noting lessons learned. Boxes interspersed through the book illustrate and analyze key details.

GLOBAL FINANCIAL CRISIS

2008–2009: A Very Cold IPO Market

The drop in IPO issues during the 2008 financial crisis was both global and dramatic. The bar graph shows the total worldwide dollar volume of IPO proceeds in billions of dollars (blue bars) and number of deals (red line) by quarter, from the last quarter of 2006 to the first quarter of 2009. Comparing the fourth quarter of 2007 (a record quarter for IPO issues) to the fourth quarter of 2008, dollar volume dropped a stunning 97% from $102 billion to just $3 billion. Things got even worse in the first quarter of 2009 with just $1.4 billion raised. The market for IPOs essentially dried up altogether.

During the 2008 financial crisis, IPO markets were not the only equity issue markets that saw a collapse in volume. Markets for seasoned equity offerings and leveraged buyouts also collapsed. The extreme market uncertainty at the time created a "flight to quality." Investors, wary of taking risk, sought to move their capital into risk-free investments like U.S. Treasury securities. The result was a crash in existing equity prices and a greatly reduced supply of new capital to risky asset classes.

Source: Shifting Landscape—Are You Ready? Global IPO Trends report 2009, Ernst & Young.

Practitioner Interviews from notable professionals featured in many chapters highlight leaders in the field and address the effects of the financial crisis.

INTERVIEW WITH KEVIN M. WARSH

Kevin M. Warsh, a lecturer at Stanford's Graduate School of Business and a distinguished visiting fellow at the Hoover Institution, was a Federal Reserve governor from 2006 to 2011, serving as chief liaison to the financial markets.

QUESTION: *What are the main policy instruments used by central banks to control the economy?*

ANSWER: The Federal Reserve (Fed) deploys several policy tools to achieve its goals of price stability, maximum sustainable employment, and financial stability. Lowering the federal funds short-term interest rate, the primary policy instrument, stimulates the economy. Raising the federal funds rate generally slows the economy. Buying and selling short-term U.S. Treasury securities through *open market operations* is standard practice. Prior to the 2007–2009 financial crisis, the Fed's balance sheet ranged from $700–$900 billion. But when the Fed was unable to lower interest rates further because rates were so close to zero already, it resorted to large-scale, longer-term open market operations to increase liquidity in the financial system in the hopes of stimulating the economy further, thus growing its balance sheet significantly. With *open mouth operations*, the Fed's announcements of its intent to buy or sell assets indicates its desired degree of future policy accommodation, often prompting markets to react by adjusting interest rates immediately. The Fed's Lender-of-Last-Resort authority allows it to lend money against good collateral to troubled institutions under certain conditions.

QUESTION: *What factors limit the effectiveness of Fed policy?*

ANSWER: Monetary policy does not act in isolation. Fiscal (taxing and spending), trade, and regulatory policies have huge consequence on the state of economic and financial conditions. In the short term, monetary policy can help buy time for an economy to improve, but it cannot cure structural failings of an economy in isolation or compensate for the country's growing indebtedness.

QUESTION: *What tools did the Fed create to address the 2007–2009 financial crisis?*

ANSWER: During the darkest days of the crisis, markets did not operate effectively, prices for securities did not clear, and banks and other financial institutions lacked clarity and confidence in the financial wherewithal of each other. One effective, innovative tool, the *Term Auction Facility (TAF)*, stimulated the economy by providing cheap and readily available term funding to banks, large and small, on the front lines of the economy, thus encouraging them to extend credit to businesses and consumers. After reducing the policy rate to near zero to help revive the economy, the Fed instituted two *Quantitative Easing (QE)* programs—special purchases of government and agency securities—to increase money supply, promote lending, and according to some proponents, increase prices of riskier assets.

The Fed also addressed the global financial crisis by establishing temporary *central bank liquidity swap lines* with the European Central Bank and other major central banks. Using this facility, a foreign central bank is able to obtain dollar funding for its customers by swapping euros for dollars or another currency and agreeing to reverse the swap at a later date. The Fed does not take exchange rate risk, but it is subject to the credit risk of its central bank counterparty.

QUESTION: *What tools is the European Central Bank (ECB) using to address the sovereign debt crisis? How does its approach compare to the Fed's approach to the 2007–2009 financial crisis?*

ANSWER: As a novel economic federation, the ECB finds itself in a more difficult position than the Fed. The underlying economies and competitiveness are markedly different across the Eurozone—in Germany versus Greece, for example. From 2007 until mid-2010, many European financiers and policymakers believed that global financial crisis was largely American-made, with some strains exported to the continent. By mid-2010, however, they recognized that it was indeed a global crisis. The ECB is formally charged with a single mandate of ensuring price stability, rather than the broader mandate of the Fed. Still, its actions ultimately mirrored many of those undertaken by the Fed: lowering the effective policy rate to record lows, providing direct liquidity to the Eurozone's financial institutions to avoid a potential run on the banking system, and instituting the Security Market Purchase program (buying sovereign credit of some of its distressed countries).

General Interest boxes highlight timely material from current financial events that shed light on business problems and real company practices.

 The Credit Crisis and Bond Yields

The financial crisis that engulfed the world's economies in 2008 originated as a credit crisis that first emerged in August 2007. At that time, problems in the mortgage market had led to the bankruptcy of several large mortgage lenders. The default of these firms, and the downgrading of many of the bonds backed by mortgages these firms had made, caused many investors to reassess the risk of other bonds in their portfolios. As perceptions of risk increased, and investors attempted to move into safer U.S. Treasury securities, the prices of corporate bonds fell and so their credit spreads rose relative to Treasuries, as shown in Figure 6.7. Panel (a) shows the yield spreads for long-term corporate bonds, where we can see that spreads of even the highest-rated Aaa bonds increased dramatically, from a typical level of 0.5% to over 2% by the fall of 2008. Panel (b) shows a similar pattern for the rate banks had to pay on short-term loans compared to the yields of short-term Treasury bills. This increase in borrowing costs made it more costly for firms to raise the capital needed for new investment, slowing economic growth. The decline in these spreads in early 2009 was viewed by many as an important first step in mitigating the ongoing impact of the financial crisis on the rest of the economy.

Teaching Every Student to Think Finance

Simplified Presentation of Mathematics

Because one of the hardest parts of learning finance for non-majors is mastering the jargon, math, and non-standardized notation, *Fundamentals of Corporate Finance* systematically uses:

- **Notation Boxes.** Each chapter begins with a Notation box that defines the variables and the acronyms used in the chapter and serves as a "legend" for students' reference.

Using a Financial Calculator

Financial calculators are programmed to perform most present and future value calculations. However, we recommend that you develop an understanding of the formulas before using the shortcuts. We provide a more extensive discussion of financial calculators on page 95 and in the appendix to Chapter 4, but we'll cover the relevant functions for this chapter here. To use financial calculator functions, you always enter the known values first and then the calculator solves for the unknown.

To answer Example 3.4 with a financial calculator, do the following:

Concept	Number of Periods	Interest Rate per Period	Recurring Payments	Future Value
Calculator Key	N	I/Y	PMT	FV
Enter	10	6	0	15000

Because you are solving for the present value (PV), press the **PV** key last (on an HP calculator), or press **CPT** then the **PV** key on a TI calculator. The calculator will return −8375.92. Note that the calculator balances inflows with outflows, so because the FV is positive (an inflow), it returns the PV as a negative (an outflow).

If you were solving for the future value instead, you would enter:

N	I/Y	PV	PMT
10	6	−8375.92	0

And finally, on an HP, press the **FV** key or on a TI, press **CPT** and then the **FV** key.

- **Numbered and Labeled Equations.** The first time a full equation is given in notation form it is numbered. Key equations are titled and revisited in the summary and in end papers.

- **Timelines.** Introduced in Chapter 3, timelines are emphasized as the important first step in solving *every* problem that involves cash flows over time.

- **Financial Calculator** instructions, including a box in Chapter 4 on solving for future and present values, and appendices to Chapters 4, 6, and 15 with keystrokes for HP-10BII and TI BAII Plus Professional calculators, highlight this problem-solving tool.

TABLE 18.18

Pro Forma Statement of Cash Flows for KMS, 2016–2021

	2016	2017	2018	2019	2020	2021
1 Year						
2 Statement of Cash Flows ($000s)						
3 Net Income		7,600	8,807	11,141	13,739	16,627
4 Depreciation		7,443	7,498	7,549	7,594	7,634
5 Changes in Working Capital						
6 Accounts Receivable		−2,561	−2,827	−3,144	−3,491	−3,872
7 Inventory		−2,696	−2,976	−3,309	−3,675	−4,076
8 Accounts Payable		2,157	2,381	2,647	2,940	3,261
9 Cash from Operating Activities		11,942	12,884	14,884	17,107	19,574
10 Capital Expenditures		−25,000	−8,000	−8,000	−8,000	−8,000
11 Other Investment		—	—	—	—	—
12 Cash from Investing Activities		−25,000	−8,000	−8,000	−8,000	−8,000
13 Net Borrowing		20,000	—	—	—	—
14 Dividends		−4,786	−2,503	−4,237	−6,167	−8,313
15 Cash from Financing Activities		15,214	−2,503	−4,237	−6,167	−8,313
16						
17 Change in Cash (9 + 12 + 15)		2,157	2,381	2,647	2,940	3,261

- **Spreadsheet Tables.** Select tables are available on MyFinanceLab as Excel® files, enabling students to change inputs and manipulate the underlying calculations. Icons in the text show students where spreadsheets are available in the eText.

USING EXCEL

Capital Budgeting Using a Spreadsheet Program

Capital budgeting forecasts and analysis are most easily performed in a spreadsheet program. Here, we highlight a few best practices when developing your own capital budgets.

Create a Project Dashboard

All capital budgeting analyses begin with a set of assumptions regarding future revenues and costs associated with the investment. Centralize these assumptions within your spreadsheet in a project dashboard so they are easy to locate, review, and potentially modify. Here, we show an example for the HomeNet project.

	A	B	C	D	E	F	G	H	I	J
1	HomeNet Capital Budget									
2	**Key Assumptions**									
3	Revenues & Costs			Year 0	Year 1	Year 2	Year 3	Year 4	Year 5	
4	HomeNet Units Sold				50	50	50	50		
5	HomeNet Ave. Price/Unit				$ 260.00	$ 260.00	$ 260.00	$ 260.00		
6	HomeNet Cost/Unit				$ 110.00	$ 110.00	$ 110.00	$ 110.00		
7	Operating Expenses									
8	Marketing, Support & Rent				(2,800)	(2,800)	(2,800)	(2,800)		
9	Capital Expenditures									
10	Purchase Equipment			(7,500)						
11	Other Assumptions									
12	Depreciation Schedule			0.0%	20.0%	20.0%	20.0%	20.0%	20.0%	
13	Corporate Tax Rate			40.9%	40.0%	40.0%	40.0%	40.0%	40.0%	
14	Receivables (% sales)			15.0%	15.0%	15.0%	15.0%	15.0%	15.0%	
15	Payables (% expenses)			15.0%	15.0%	15.0%	15.0%	15.0%	15.0%	
16										

- **Using Excel** boxes describe Excel techniques and include screenshots to serve as a guide for students using this technology.

Practice Finance to Learn Finance

MyFinanceLab

Here is what you should know after reading this chapter. MyFinanceLab will help you identify what you know, and where to go when you need to practice.

KEY POINTS AND EQUATIONS	KEY TERMS	ONLINE PRACTICE
4.1 Valuing a Stream of Cash Flows • The present value of a cash flow stream is: $$PV = C_0 + \frac{C_1}{(1+r)} + \frac{C_2}{(1+r)^2} + \cdots + \frac{C_N}{(1+r)^N} \quad (4.3)$$	stream of cash flows, p. 94	MyFinanceLab Study Plan 4.1
4.2 Perpetuities • A perpetuity is a stream of equal cash flows C paid every period, forever. The present value of a perpetuity is: $$PV(C \text{ in Perpetuity}) = \frac{C}{r} \quad (4.4)$$	consol, p. 98 perpetuity, p. 98	MyFinanceLab Study Plan 4.2
4.3 Annuities • An annuity is a stream of equal cash flows C paid every period for N periods. The present value of an annuity is: $$C \times \frac{1}{r}\left(1 - \frac{1}{(1+r)^N}\right) \quad (4.5)$$ • The future value of an annuity at the end of the annuity is: $$C \times \frac{1}{r}\left((1+r)^N - 1\right) \quad (4.6)$$	annuity, p. 101	MyFinanceLab Study Plan 4.3 Interactive Annuity Calculator Financial Calculator Tutorials: Calculating the Present Value of an Annuity and Solving for the Future Value of an Annuity

Working problems is the proven way to cement and demonstrate an understanding of finance.

- **Concept Check questions** at the end of each section enable students to test their understanding and target areas in which they need further review.

- **End-of-chapter problems written personally by Jonathan Berk, Peter DeMarzo, and Jarrad Harford** offer instructors the opportunity to assign first-rate materials to students for homework and practice with the confidence that the problems are consistent with the chapter content. All end-of-chapter problems are available in MyFinanceLab, the fully integrated homework and tutorial system. Both the problems and solutions, which were also prepared by the authors, have been class-tested and accuracy checked to ensure quality. Excel icons indicate the availability of instructor solutions and student templates in the Textbook Resources tab of MyFinanceLab.

End-of-Chapter Materials Reinforce Learning

Testing understanding of central concepts is crucial to learning finance.

- **MyFinanceLab Chapter Summary** presents the key points and conclusions from each chapter, provides a list of key terms with page numbers, and indicates online practice opportunities.

- **Data Cases** present in-depth scenarios in a business setting with questions designed to guide students' analysis. Many questions involve the use of Internet resources.

- **Integrative Cases** occur at the end of most parts and present a capstone extended problem for each part with a scenario and data for students to analyze based on that subset of chapters.

DATA CASE

This is your second interview with a prestigious brokerage firm for a job as an equity analyst. You survived the morning interviews with the department manager and the vice president of equity. Everything has gone so well that they want to test your ability as an analyst. You are seated in a room with a computer and a list with the names of two companies—Ford (F) and Microsoft (MSFT). You have 90 minutes to complete the following tasks:

1. Download the annual income statements, balance sheets, and cash flow statements for the last four fiscal years from Morningstar (www.morningstar.com). Enter each company's stock symbol and then go to "financials." Copy and paste the financial statements into Excel.

2. Find historical stock prices for each firm from Yahoo! Finance (finance.yahoo.com). Enter the stock symbol, click "Historical Prices" in the left column, and enter the proper date range to cover the last day of the month corresponding to the date of each financial statement. Use the closing stock prices (not the adjusted close). To calculate the firm's market capitalization at each date, multiply the number of shares outstanding by the firm's historic stock price. You can find the number of shares by using "Basic" under "Weighted average shares outstanding" at the bottom of the Income Statement.

Preface

Finance professors are united by their commitment to shaping future generations of financial professionals as well as instilling financial awareness and skills in non-majors. Our goal with *Fundamentals of Corporate Finance* is to provide an accessible presentation for both finance and non-finance majors. We know from experience that countless undergraduate students have felt that corporate finance is challenging. It is tempting to make finance *seem* accessible by de-emphasizing the core principles and instead concentrating on the results. In our over 50 years of combined teaching experience, we have found that emphasizing the core concepts in finance—which are clear and intuitive at heart—is what makes the subject matter accessible. What makes the subject challenging is that it is often difficult for a novice to distinguish between these core ideas and other intuitively appealing approaches that, if used in financial decision making, will lead to incorrect decisions.

The 2007–2009 financial crisis was fueled in part by many practitioners' poor decision making when they did not understand—or chose to ignore—the core concepts that underlie finance and the pedagogy in this book. With this point in mind, we present finance as one unified whole based on two simple, powerful ideas: (1) valuation drives decision making—the firm should take projects for which the value of the benefits exceeds the value of the costs, and (2) in a competitive market, market prices (rather than individual preferences) determine values. We combine these two ideas with what we call the *Valuation Principle*, and from it we establish all of the key ideas in corporate finance.

New to This Edition

All text discussions and figures, tables, and facts have been updated to accurately reflect exciting developments in the field of finance in the last three years. Specific highlights include the following:

- **New Interviews** with Frank Hatheway, Chief Economist and Senior VP for NASDAQ; Ruth Porat, Senior VP and CFO of Alphabet and Google; Kevin Laws, COO of Angel-List; and Douglas Kehring, Senior VP of Oracle.
- **Real-world examples** have been updated to reflect data through 2016.
- **New, Enhanced Media-Rich Pearson eText** includes Author Solution Videos that walk through the in-text examples using math, the financial calculator, and spreadsheets.
- **Using Excel boxes** have been updated and provide hands-on instruction of how to use Excel to solve financial problems and include screenshots to serve as a guide for students.
- **Added discussion of current issues** including negative interest rates, crowdfunding, new trading venues such as BATS and dark pools.

- Added and revised end-of-chapter problems throughout the book, once again personally writing and solving each one. In addition, every single problem is available in MyFinanceLab, the groundbreaking homework and tutorial system that accompanies the book.

- We updated Data Cases and Integrative Cases throughout the book, giving students a chance to apply the material with realistic data-analyzing exercises and problems that integrate material across chapters in each major part of the book.

Emphasis on Valuation

As painful as the financial crisis was, there is a silver lining: with the increasing focus on finance in the news, today's undergraduate students arrive in the classroom with an interest in finance. We strive to use that natural interest and motivation to overcome their fear of the subject and communicate time-tested core principles. Again, we take what has worked in the classroom and apply it to the text: By providing examples involving familiar companies such as Starbucks and Apple, making consistent use of real-world data, and demonstrating personal finance applications of core concepts, we strive to keep both non-finance and finance majors engaged.

By learning to apply the Valuation Principle, students develop the skills to make the types of comparisons—among loan options, investments, projects, and so on—that turn them into knowledgeable, confident financial consumers and managers. When students see how to apply finance to their personal lives and future careers, they grasp that finance is more than abstract, mathematically based concepts.

Table of Contents Overview

Fundamentals of Corporate Finance offers coverage of the major topical areas for introductory-level undergraduate courses. Our focus is on financial decision making related to the corporation's choice of which investments to make or how to raise the capital required to fund an investment. We designed the book with the need for flexibility and with consideration of time pressures throughout the semester in mind.

Part **1**	Introduction	
	Ch. 1: Corporate Finance and the Financial Manager	Introduces the corporation and its governance; updated to include comparison of traditional trading venues, new electronic exchanges, and how the market for trading stocks is changing
	Ch. 2: Introduction to Financial Statement Analysis	Introduces key financial statements; Coverage of financial ratios has been centralized to prepare students to analyze financial statements holistically
Part **2**	Interest Rates and Valuing Cash Flows	
	Ch. 3: Time Value of Money: An Introduction	Introduces the Valuation Principle and time value of money techniques for single-period investments
	Ch. 4: Time Value of Money: Valuing Cash Flow Streams	Introduces the mechanics of discounting; Includes examples with non-annual interest rates that provide time value of money applications in a personal loan context
	Ch. 5: Interest Rates	Presents how interest rates are quoted and compounding for all frequencies; Discusses key determinants of interest rates and their relation to the cost of capital; New discussion of negative interest rate

Ch. 22: Mergers and Acquisitions	Considers motives and methods for mergers and acquisitions, including leveraged buyouts
Ch. 23: International Corporate Finance	Analyzes the valuation of projects with foreign currency cash flows with integrated or segregated capital markets

Online Chapters
(on MyFinanceLab at www.myfinancelab.com)

Leasing	Opportunities for course customization with online-only chapter offerings
Insurance and Risk Management	
Corporate Governance	

A Complete Instructor and Student Support Package

MyFinanceLab

Not every student learns the same way or at the same rate. With the growing need for acceleration through many courses, it's more important than ever to meet students where they learn. Personalized learning in the MyFinanceLab gives you the flexibility to incorporate the approach that best suits your course and your students.

Study Plan

The **Study Plan** acts as a tutor, providing personalized recommendations for each of your students based on his or her ability to master the learning objectives in your course. This allows students to focus their study time by pinpointing the precise areas they need to review, and allowing them to use customized practice and learning aids—such as videos, eText, tutorials, and more—to get them back on track. Using the report available in the Gradebook, you can then tailor course lectures to prioritize the content where students need the most support—offering you better insight into classroom and individual performance.

Dynamic Study Modules

Dynamic Study Modules help students study effectively on their own by continuously assessing their activity and performance in real time. Here's how it works: students complete a set of questions with a unique answer format that also asks them to indicate their confidence level. Questions repeat until the student can answer them all correctly and confidently. Once completed, Dynamic Study Modules explain the concept using materials from the text. These are available as graded assignments prior to class, and accessible on smartphones, tablets, and computers. NEW! Instructors can now remove questions from Dynamic Study Modules to better fit their course.

Enhanced eText

The **Enhanced eText** keeps students engaged in learning on their own time, while helping them achieve greater conceptual understanding of course material. The worked examples bring learning to life, and algorithmic practice allows students to apply the very concepts they are reading about. Combining resources that illuminate content with accessible self-assessment, MyFinanceLab with Enhanced eText provides students with a complete digital learning experience—all in one place.

And with the **Pearson eText 2.0 mobile app** (available for select titles) students can now access the Enhanced eText and all of its functionality from their computer, tablet, or mobile phone. Because students' progress is synced across all of their devices, they can stop what they're doing on one device and pick up again later on another one—without breaking their stride.

Auto-Graded Excel Projects

Auto-graded Excel Projects allow instructors to seamlessly integrate Excel content into their course without having to manually grade spreadsheets. Students have the opportunity to practice important Finance skills in Microsoft Excel, helping them to master key concepts and gain proficiency with Excel.

Videos

Video clips available in MyFinanceLab profile well-known firms such as Boeing and Intel through interviews and analysis. The videos focus on core topical areas such as capital budgeting and risk and return. Author-created videos walk students through guided problem solutions for every in-text example.

Financial Calculator

The **Financial Calculator** is available as a smartphone application, as well as on a computer, and includes important functions such as cash flow, net present value, and internal rate of return. Fifteen helpful tutorial videos show the many ways to use the Financial Calculator in MyFinanceLab.

Interactive Figures

Select in-text graphs and figures have been digitally enhanced to allow students to interact with variables to affect outcomes and bring concepts to life.

Solutions Manual

The **Solutions Manual** provides students with detailed, accuracy-verified solutions to the problems in the book. The solutions, like the problems, were written by the authors themselves. Spreadsheet solutions in Excel, which allow the student to see the effect of changes in the input variables on the outcome, are also available to instructors for designated problems at the Instructor Resource Center (www.pearsonhighered.com/irc).

PowerPoint Presentations

The **PowerPoint Presentation**, authored by William Chittenden of Texas State University, is available in lecture form and includes art and tables from the book and additional examples. The PowerPoint presentation includes all tables and figures, examples, key terms, and spreadsheet tables from the textbook. All PowerPoint presentations are also available for download from the Instructor Resource Center at www.pearsonhighered.com/irc.

Test Bank

The **Test Bank** provides a wealth of accuracy-verified, algorithmic testing material. Each chapter offers a wide variety of true/false, short answer, and multiple-choice questions updated by Brian Nethercutt. Questions are verified by difficulty level and skill type, and correlated to the chapter topics. Numerical problems include step-by-step solutions and have been made algorithmic so they can be assigned for repeated practice.

TestGen

TestGen is a computerized test generation program, available exclusively from Pearson, that allows instructors to easily create and administer tests on paper, electronically, or online. Instructors can select test items from the publisher-supplied test bank, which is organized by chapter and based on the associated textbook material, or create their own questions from scratch. With both quick-and-simple test creation and flexible and robust editing tools, TestGen is a complete test generator system for today's educators.

Instructor's Manual

The **Instructor's Manual** was written by Mary R. Brown of the University of Illinois–Chicago, and contains annotated chapter outlines, lecture launchers, and questions for further class discussion. It also contains the solutions to the Data Cases and part-ending case problems, as well as answers to the end-of-chapter Critical Thinking questions in the book. As an additional resource to guide instructors with students who are planning to take the CFA exam, CFA learning outcomes met in each chapter are listed. A section also details how the end-of-chapter problems map to the accreditation standards set by the Association to Advance Collegiate Schools of Business (AACSB), so that instructors can track students' mastery of the AACSB standards. The Instructor's Manual is available for download as Microsoft Word files or as Adobe® PDF files from the Instructor Resource Center at www.pearsonhighered.com/irc.

Acknowledgments

Given the scope of this project, identifying the many people who made it happen is a tall order. This textbook was the product of the expertise and hard work of many talented colleagues. We are especially gratified with the work of those who developed the array of print supplements that accompany the book: William Chittenden for the PowerPoint presentations; Mary R. Brown, for the Instructor's Manual; James Linck, for serving as advisor for the videos; and our MyFinanceLab content development team, including Melissa Honig, Miguel Leonarte, Noel Lotz, and Sarah Peterson. We're also deeply appreciative of Susan White's contributions to the part-ending cases.

Creating a truly error-free text is a challenge we could not have lived up to without our team of expert error checkers. Jared Stanfield subjected the text and problem solutions to his exacting standards. We are also indebted to Jared for his adept research support throughout the writing process and Michael Wittry's assistance in providing updates.

At Pearson Education, we would like to single out Donna Battista, for her continued leadership and market insight; Kate Fernandes for her energy and fresh perspective as our new editor; Melissa Honig for her digital media expertise; and our production team, Meredith Gertz and especially Gillian Hall, for expertly managing the transformation of our files into a beautiful bound book. They were helped by Kalpana Arumugam at Spi Global, whose team provided the fantastic composition and artwork. We are truly thankful for the indispensable help provided by these and other professionals.

We are indebted to our colleagues for the time and expertise invested as manuscript reviewers, class testers, and focus group participants. We list all of these contributors on the following pages, but want to single out one group, our First Edition editorial board, for special notice: Tom Berry, *DePaul University*; Elizabeth Booth, *Michigan State University*; Julie Dahlquist, the *University of Texas–San Antonio*; Michaël Dewally, *Marquette University*; Robert M. Donchez, the *University of Colorado–Boulder*; Belinda Mucklow, the *University of Wisconsin–Madison*; Coleen Pantalone, *Northeastern University*; and Susan White, the *University of Maryland*. We strived to incorporate every contributor's input and are truly grateful for each comment and suggestion. The book has benefited enormously from this input.

Reviewers

Pankaj Agrrawal, *University of Maine*
Daniel Ahern, *California State University–Chico*
Paul Asabere, *Temple University*
Ajeyo Banerjee, *University of Colorado–Denver*
Tom Berry, *DePaul University*
Karan Bhanot, *University of Texas–San Antonio*
Rafiqul Bhuyan, *California State University–San Bernardino*
Eugene Bland, *Texas A&M University–Corpus Christi*
Matej Blasko, *University of Georgia*
Elizabeth Booth, *Michigan State University*
Mary Brown, *University of Illinois–Chicago*
Bill Brunsen, *Eastern New Mexico University*
David G. Cazier, *Brigham Young University–Provo*
Leo Chan, *Delaware State University*
Cindy Chen, *California State University–Long Beach*
Haiyu Chen, *Youngstown State University*
James F. Cotter, *Wake Forest University*
Vicentiu Covrig, *California State University–Northridge*
Julie Dahlquist, *University of Texas–San Antonio*
Pieter de Jong, *University of Texas–Arlington*
Andrea L. DeMaskey, *Villanova University*
Xiaohui Deng, *California State University–Fresno*
Michaël Dewally, *Marquette University*
Robert M. Donchez, *University of Colorado Boulder*
Gang Dong, *Rutgers University*
Dean Drenk, *Montana State University*
Robert Dubil, *University of Utah*
Hsing Fang, *California State University–Los Angeles*
David O. Fricke, *University of North Carolina–Pembroke*
Scott Fung, *California State University–East Bay*
Sharon Garrison, *University of Arizona*
Rakesh Gupta, *Central Queensland University*
Joseph D. Haley, *St. Cloud State University*
Thomas Hall, *Christopher Newport University*
Karen Hallows, *University of Maryland*
Karen L. Hamilton, *Georgia Southern University*
Robert Hanson, *Eastern Michigan University*
Mahfuzul Haque, *Indiana State University*
Edward C. Howell, *Northwood University*
Ping Hsiao, *San Francisco State University*
Xiaoqing Hu, *University of Illinois at Chicago*
Pankaj Jain, *University of Memphis*
Robert James, *Boston College*
Susan Ji, *Baruch College, City University of New York*
Domingo Joaquin, *Illinois State University*
Fred R. Kaen, *University of New Hampshire*
Terrill Keasler, *Appalachian State University*
Howard Keen, *Temple University*
Brett A. King, *University of North Alabama*
Daniel Klein, *Bowling Green State University*

Gregory Kuhlemeyer, *Carroll University*
Rose Neng Lai, *University of Macau*
Keith Lam, *University of Macau*
Reinhold P. Lamb, *University of North Florida*
Douglas Lamdin, *University of Maryland–Baltimore County*
Mark J. Laplante, *University of Georgia*
Sie Ting Lau, *Nanyang Technological University*
Richard LeCompte, *Wichita State University*
Adam Y.C. Lei, *Midwestern State University*
Qian Li, *Midwestern State University*
Chang Liu, *Washington State University*
Wei Liu, *Texas A&M University*
Hugh Marble III, *University of Vermont*
James Milanese, *University of North Carolina at Greensboro*
Sunil K. Mohanty, *University of St. Thomas*
Ted Moorman, *Northern Illinois University*
James Morris, *University of Colorado–Denver*
Belinda Mucklow, *University of Wisconsin–Madison*
Rick Nelson, *University of Minnesota*
Tom C. Nelson, *University of Colorado–Boulder*
Curtis Nicholls, *Bucknell University*
Anthony C. Ng, *Hong Kong Polytechnic University*
Coleen Pantalone, *Northeastern University*
Daniel Park, *Azusa Pacific University*
Janet Payne, *Texas State University*
Jay Peroni, *College of Charleston*
Lynn Pi, *Hong Kong University of Science and Technology*
J. Michael Pinegar, *Brigham Young University*
Annette Poulsen, *University of Georgia*
Eric Powers, *University of South Carolina*
Rose M. Prasad, *Central Michigan University*
Shoba Premkumar, *Iowa State University*
Mark K. Pyles, *College of Charleston*
A.A.B. Resing, *Hogeschool Van Amsterdam*
Greg Richey, *California State University, San Bernardino*
Scott Roark, *Boise State University*
David L. Robbins, *University of New Mexico*
Andrew Samwick, *Dartmouth College*
Salil K. Sarkar, *University of Texas–Arlington*
Oliver Schnusenberg, *University of North Florida*
Kenneth Scislaw, *University of Alabama–Huntsville*
Roger Severns, *Minnesota State University–Mankato*
Tatyana Sokolyk, *University of Wyoming*
Andrew C. Spieler, *Hofstra University*
Timothy G. Sullivan, *Bentley College*
Janikan Supanvanij, *St. Cloud State University*
Hugo Tang, *Purdue University*
Oranee Tawatnuntachai, *Pennsylvania State University–Harrisburg*
Robert Terpstra, *University of Macau*

Thomas Thomson, *University of Texas–San Antonio*
Olaf J. Thorp, *Babson College*
Ed Tiryakian, *Duke University*
Emery Trahan, *Northeastern University*
Joe Ueng, *University of St. Thomas*
Mo Vaziri, *California State University–San Bernardino*
Premal P. Vora, *Pennsylvania State University–Harrisburg*
Hefei Wang, *University of Illinois–Chicago*
Gwendolyn Webb, *Baruch College*
Paul M. Weinstock, *Ohio State University*
Susan White, *University of Maryland*
Annie Wong, *Western Connecticut State University*
Xiaoyan Xu, *San Jose State University*
Zhong-gou Zhou, *California State University–Northridge*
Kermit C. Zieg, Jr., *Florida Institute of Technology*

Focus Group Participants

Anne-Marie Anderson, *Lehigh University*
Sung Bae, *Bowling Green State University*
H. Kent Baker, *American University*
Steven Beach, *Radford University*
Rafiqul Bhuyan, *California State University–San Bernardino*
Deanne Butchey, *Florida International University*
Leo Chan, *Delaware State University*
George Chang, *Grand Valley State University*
Haiwei Chen, *California State University–San Bernardino*
Haiyu Chen, *Youngstown State University*
Massimiliano De Santis, *Dartmouth College*
Jocelyn Evans, *College of Charleston*
Kathleen Fuller, *University of Mississippi*
Xavier Garza Gomez, *University of Houston–Victoria*
William Gentry, *Williams College*
Axel Grossmann, *Radford University*
Pankaj Jain, *University of Memphis*
Zhenhu Jin, *Valparaiso University*
Steve Johnson, *University of Northern Iowa*
Steven Jones, *Samford University*
Yong-Cheol Kim, *University of Wisconsin–Milwaukee*
Robert Kiss, *Eastern Michigan University*
Ann Marie Klingenhagen, *DePaul University*
Thomas J. Krissek, *Northeastern Illinois University*
Olivier Maisondieu Laforge, *University of Nebraska–Omaha*
Douglas Lamdin, *University of Maryland–Baltimore County*
D. Scott Lee, *Texas A&M University*
Stanley A. Martin, *University of Colorado–Boulder*

Jamshid Mehran, *Indiana University, South Bend*
Sunil Mohanty, *University of St. Thomas*
Karyn L. Neuhauser, *State University of New York–Plattsburgh*
Thomas O'Brien, *University of Connecticut*
Hyuna Park, *Minnesota State University–Mankato*
G. Michael Phillips, *California State University–Northridge*
Wendy Pirie, *Valparaiso University*
Antonio Rodriguez, *Texas A&M International University*
Camelia S. Rotaru, *St. Edward's University*
Salil Sarkar, *University of Texas at Arlington*
Mark Sunderman, *University of Wyoming*
Chu-Sheng Tai, *Texas Southern University*
Oranee Tawatnuntachai, *Pennsylvania State University–Harrisburg*
Benedict Udemgba, *Alcorn State University*
Rahul Verma, *University of Houston–Downtown*
Angelo P. Vignola, *Loyola University–Chicago*
Premal Vora, *Pennsylvania State University–Harrisburg*
Eric Wehrly, *Seattle University*
Yan A. Xie, *University of Michigan–Dearborn*
Fang Zhao, *Siena College*
Sophie Zong, *California State University–Stanislaus*

Class Testers

Tom Berry, *DePaul University*
Eugene Bland, *Texas A&M University–Corpus Christi*
Charles Blaylock, *Murray State University*
Mary Brown, *University of Illinois–Chicago*
Bill Brunsen, *Eastern New Mexico University*
Sarah Bryant Bower, *Shippensburg University of Pennsylvania*
Alva Wright Butcher, *University of Puget Sound*
David G. Cazier, *Brigham Young University–Provo*
Asim G. Celik, *University of Nevada–Reno*
Michaël Dewally, *Marquette University*
Richard Gaddis, *Oklahoma Wesleyan University*
TeWhan Hahn, *Auburn University–Montgomery*
Matthew Hood, *University of Southern Mississippi*
Zhenhu Jin, *Valparaiso University*
Travis Jones, *Florida Gulf Coast University*
Francis E. Laatsch, *Bowling Green State University*
Diane Lander, *Saint Michael's College*
Vance Lesseig, *Texas State University*
Frances Maloy, *University of Washington*
Jamshid Mehran, *Indiana University–South Bend*
Belinda Mucklow, *University of Wisconsin–Madison*
Kuo-Chung Tseng, *California State University–Fresno*
Kermit C. Zieg, Jr., *Florida Institute of Technology*

Introduction

Valuation Principle Connection. What is *corporate finance*? No matter what your role in a corporation, an understanding of why and how financial decisions are made is essential. The focus of this book is how to make optimal corporate financial decisions. In Part 1, we lay the foundation for our study of corporate finance. In Chapter 1, we begin by introducing the corporation and related business forms. We then examine the role of financial managers and outside investors in decision making for the firm. To make optimal decisions, a decision maker needs information. As a result, in Chapter 2, we review and analyze an important source of information for corporate decision making—the firm's accounting statements. These chapters will introduce us to the role and objective of the financial manager and some of the information the financial manager uses in applying the Valuation Principle to make optimal decisions. Then, in Part 2, we will introduce and begin applying the Valuation Principle.

1

Corporate Finance and the Financial Manager

LEARNING OBJECTIVES

- Grasp the importance of financial information in both your personal and business lives

- Understand the important features of the four main types of firms and see why the advantages of the corporate form have led it to dominate economic activity

- Explain the goal of the financial manager and the reasoning behind that goal, as well as understand the three main types of decisions a financial manager makes

- Know how a corporation is managed and controlled, the financial manager's place in it, and some of the ethical issues financial managers face

- Understand the importance of financial markets, such as stock markets, to a corporation and the financial manager's role as liaison to those markets

- Recognize the role that financial institutions play in the financial cycle of the economy

This book focuses on how people in corporations make financial decisions. Despite its name, much of what we discuss in corporate finance applies to the financial decisions made within any organization, including not-for-profit entities such as charities and universities. In this chapter, we introduce the four main types of firms. We stress corporations, however, because they represent 85% of U.S. business revenue. We also highlight the financial manager's critical role inside any business enterprise. What products to launch, how to pay to develop those products, what profits to keep and how to return profits to investors—all of these decisions and many more fall within corporate finance. The financial manager makes these decisions with the goal of maximizing the value of the business, which is determined in the financial markets. In this chapter and throughout the book, we will focus on this goal, provide you with the tools to make financial management decisions, and show you how the financial markets provide funds to a corporation and produce market prices that are key inputs to any financial manager's investment analysis.

1.1   Why Study Finance?

Finance and financial thinking are everywhere in our daily lives. Consider your decision to go to college. You surely weighed alternatives, such as starting a full-time job immediately, and then decided that college provided you with the greatest net benefit. More and more, individuals are taking charge of their personal finances with decisions such as:

- When to start saving and how much to save for retirement.
- Whether a car loan or lease is more advantageous.
- Whether a particular stock is a good investment.
- How to evaluate the terms of a home mortgage.

Our career paths have become less predictable and more dynamic. In previous generations, it was common to work for one employer your entire career. Today, that would be highly unusual. Most of us will instead change jobs, and possibly even careers, many times. With each new opportunity, we must weigh all the costs and benefits, financial and otherwise.

Some financial decisions, such as whether to pay $2.00 for your morning coffee, are simple, but most are more complex. In your business career, you may face questions such as:

- Should your firm launch a new product?
- Which supplier should your firm choose?
- Should your firm produce a part of the product or outsource production?
- Should your firm issue new stock or borrow money instead?
- How can you raise money for your start-up firm?

In this book, you will learn how all of these decisions in your personal life and inside a business are tied together by one powerful concept, the *Valuation Principle*. The Valuation Principle shows how to make the costs and benefits of a decision comparable so that we can weigh them properly. Learning to apply the Valuation Principle will give you the skills to make the types of comparisons—among loan options, investments, and projects—that will turn you into a knowledgeable, confident financial consumer and manager.

From 2007 to 2009 we witnessed a credit freeze, a severe stock market decline, and the failures of well-known financial institutions. Attempts to understand these elements of the crisis, their origins, and how they affect our businesses and personal finances have highlighted the need for learning core financial principles and concepts.

Whether you plan to major in finance or simply take this one course, you will find the fundamental financial knowledge gained here to be essential in your personal and business lives.

1.2   The Four Types of Firms

We begin our study of corporate finance by examining the types of firms that financial managers run. As shown in Figure 1.1, There are four major types of firms: sole proprietorships, partnerships, limited liability companies, and corporations. We explain each organizational form in turn, but our primary focus is on the most important form—the corporation.

Sole Proprietorships

sole proprietorship A
business owned and run
by one person.

A **sole proprietorship** is a business owned and run by one person. Sole proprietorships are usually very small with few, if any, employees. Although they do not account for much sales revenue in the economy, they are the most common type of firm in the world. In 2012, an estimated 72% of businesses in the United States were sole proprietorships, although they generated only 3% of the revenue.[1]

We now consider the key features of a sole proprietorship.

1. Sole proprietorships have the advantage of being straightforward to set up. Consequently, many new businesses use this organizational form.

2. The principal limitation of a sole proprietorship is that there is no separation between the firm and the owner—the firm can have only one owner who runs the business. If there are other investors, they cannot hold an ownership stake in the firm.

3. The owner has unlimited personal liability for the firm's debts. That is, if the firm defaults on any debt payment, the lender can (and will) require the owner to repay the loan from personal assets. An owner who cannot afford to repay a loan for which he or she is personably liable must declare personal bankruptcy.

4. The life of a sole proprietorship is limited to the life of the owner. It is also difficult to transfer ownership of a sole proprietorship.

For most growing businesses, the disadvantages of a sole proprietorship outweigh the advantages. As soon as the firm reaches the point at which it can borrow without the owner agreeing to be personally liable, the owners typically convert the business into another form. Conversion also has other benefits that we will consider as we discuss the other forms below.

FIGURE 1.1

Types of U.S. Firms

There are four major types of firms in the United States. As (a) and (b) show, although the majority of U.S. firms are sole proprietorships, they generate only a small fraction of total revenue, in contrast to corporations.

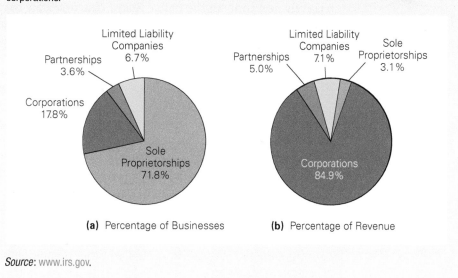

(a) Percentage of Businesses   **(b)** Percentage of Revenue

Source: www.irs.gov.

---

[1]U.S. Census Bureau National Data Book.

Partnerships

A **partnership** is a business owned and run by more than one owner. Key features include the following:

1. *All* partners are liable for the firm's debt. That is, a lender can require *any* partner to repay all the firm's outstanding debts.
2. The partnership ends in the event of the death or withdrawal of any single partner.
3. Partners can avoid liquidation if the partnership agreement provides for alternatives such as a buyout of a deceased or withdrawn partner.

Some old and established businesses remain as partnerships or sole proprietorships. Often these firms are the types of businesses in which the owners' personal reputations are the basis for the businesses. For example, law firms, medical practices, and accounting firms are frequently organized as partnerships. For such enterprises, the partners' personal liability increases the confidence of the firm's clients that the partners will strive to maintain the firm's reputation.

A **limited partnership** is a partnership with two kinds of owners: general partners and limited partners. In this case, the general partners have the same rights and privileges as partners in any general partnership—they are personally liable for the firm's debt obligations. Limited partners, however, have **limited liability**—that is, their liability is limited to their investment. Their private property cannot be seized to pay off the firm's outstanding debts. Furthermore, the death or withdrawal of a limited partner does not dissolve the partnership, and a limited partner's interest is transferable. However, a limited partner has no management authority and cannot legally be involved in the managerial decision making for the business.

Limited Liability Companies

A **limited liability company (LLC)** is like a limited partnership but without a general partner. That is, all the owners (referred to as *members*) have limited liability, but unlike limited partners, they can also run the business (as managing members). The LLC is a relatively new entity in the United States. The first state to pass a statute allowing the creation of an LLC was Wyoming in 1977; the last was Hawaii in 1997. Internationally, companies with limited liability are much older and established. LLCs first rose to prominence in Germany over 100 years ago as a *Gesellschaft mit beschränkter Haftung* (GmbH) and then in other European and Latin American countries. An LLC is known in France as a Société à responsabilité limitée (SAR), and by similar names in Italy (SRL) and Spain (SL).

Corporations

A **corporation** is a legally defined, artificial being (a legal entity), separate from its owners. As such, it has many of the legal powers that people have. It can enter into contracts, acquire assets, and incur obligations, and it enjoys protection under the U.S. Constitution against the seizure of its property. Because a corporation is a legal entity separate and distinct from its owners, it is solely responsible for its own obligations. Consequently, the owners of a corporation (or its employees, customers, etc.) are not liable for any obligations the corporation enters into. Similarly, the corporation is not liable for any personal obligations of its owners.

In the same way that it is difficult to imagine modern business life without e-mail and cell phones, the corporation revolutionized the economy. On February 2, 1819, the U.S. Supreme Court established the legal precedent that the property of a corporation, similar to that of a person, is private and entitled to protection under the U.S. Constitution.[2] This decision led to dramatic growth in the number of U.S. corporations from fewer than 1000 in 1830 to 50,000 in 1890. Today, the corporate structure is ubiquitous, not only in the United States (where it is responsible for 85% of business revenue), but all over the world.

Formation of a Corporation. A corporation must be legally formed, which means that the state in which it is incorporated must formally give its consent to the incorporation by chartering it. Setting up a corporation is therefore considerably more costly than setting up a sole proprietorship. The state of Delaware has a particularly attractive legal environment for corporations, so many corporations choose to incorporate there. For jurisdictional purposes, a corporation is a citizen of the state in which it is incorporated. Most firms hire lawyers to create a corporate charter that includes formal articles of incorporation and a set of bylaws. The corporate charter specifies the initial rules that govern how the corporation is run.

stock The ownership or equity of a corporation divided into shares.

equity The collection of all the outstanding shares of a corporation.

shareholder (also stockholder or equity holder) An owner of a share of stock or equity in a corporation.

dividend payments Payments made at the discretion of the corporation to its equity holders.

Ownership of a Corporation. There is no limit to the number of owners a corporation can have. Because most corporations have many owners, each owner owns only a fraction of the corporation. The entire ownership stake of a corporation is divided into shares known as **stock**. The collection of all the outstanding shares of a corporation is known as the **equity** of the corporation. An owner of a share of stock in the corporation is known as a **shareholder, stockholder, or equity holder**. Shareholders are entitled to **dividend payments**; that is, payments made at the discretion of the corporation to its equity holders. Shareholders usually receive a share of the dividend payments that is proportional to the amount of stock they own. For example, a shareholder who owns 25% of the firm's shares would be entitled to 25% of the total dividend payment.

An important feature of a corporation is that there is no limitation on who can own its stock. That is, an owner of a corporation need not have any special expertise or qualification. This feature allows free and anonymous trade in the shares of the corporation and provides one of the most important advantages of organizing a firm as a corporation. Corporations can raise substantial amounts of capital because they can sell ownership shares to anonymous outside investors.

The availability of outside funding has enabled corporations to dominate the economy. Let's look at one of the world's largest firms, Microsoft Corporation, as an example. Microsoft reported annual revenue of $93.6 billion over the 12 months from July 2014 through June 2015. The total value of the company (the owners' collective wealth in the company) as of June 2015 was $354 billion. The company employed 118,000 people. Putting these numbers into perspective, treating the sales of $93.6 billion as gross domestic product (GDP) in 2014 would rank Microsoft (just behind Slovak Republic) as the 62nd richest *country* (out of almost 200).[3] The Slovak Republic has almost 5.4 million people, about 45 times as many people as employees at Microsoft. Indeed, if the number of Microsoft employees were used as the "population" of the corporation, Microsoft would rank just above Curacao as the 28th least populous country on Earth!

---

[2]The case was Dartmouth v. Woodward and the full text of John Marshall's decision can be found at www.constitution.org/dwebster/dartmouth_decision.htm.

[3]World Development Indicators database, April 11, 2016. For quick reference tables on GDP, go to http://data.worldbank.org/indicator/NY.GDP.MKTP.CD.

Tax Implications for Corporate Entities

An important difference among the types of corporate organizational forms is the way they are taxed. Because a corporation is a separate legal entity, a corporation's profits are subject to taxation separate from its owners' tax obligations. In effect, shareholders of a corporation pay taxes twice. First, the corporation pays tax on its profits, and then when the remaining profits are distributed to the shareholders, the shareholders pay their own personal income tax on this income. This system is sometimes referred to as *double taxation*.

EXAMPLE 1.1

Taxation of
Corporate Earnings

MyFinanceLab

PROBLEM

You are a shareholder in a corporation. The corporation earns $5.00 per share before taxes. After it has paid taxes, it will distribute the rest of its earnings to you as a dividend (we make this simplifying assumption, but should note that most corporations retain some of their earnings for reinvestment). The dividend is income to you, so you will then pay taxes on these earnings. The corporate tax rate is 40% and your tax rate on dividend income is 15%. How much of the earnings remains after all taxes are paid?

SOLUTION

PLAN

Earnings before taxes: $5.00   Corporate tax rate: 40%   Personal dividend tax rate: 15%

To calculate the corporation's earnings after taxes, first we subtract the taxes paid at the corporate level from the pretax earnings of $5.00. The taxes paid will be 40% (the corporate tax rate) of $5.00. Since all of the after-corporate tax earnings will be paid to you as a dividend, you will pay taxes of 15% on that amount. The amount leftover is what remains after all taxes are paid.

EXECUTE

$5.00 per share × 0.40 = $2.00 in taxes at the corporate level, leaving $5.00 − $2.00 = $3.00 in after-corporate tax earnings per share to distribute.

You will pay $3.00 × $2.00 = $0.45 in taxes on that dividend, leaving you with $2.55 from the original $5.00 after all taxes.

EVALUATE

As a shareholder, you keep $2.55 of the original $5.00 in earnings; the remaining $2.00 + $0.45 = $2.45 is paid as taxes. Thus, your total effective tax rate is 2.45/5 = 49%.

S corporations Those corporations that elect subchapter S tax treatment and are exempted by the U.S. Internal Revenue Service's tax code from double taxation.

S Corporations. The corporate organizational structure is the only organizational structure subject to double taxation. However, the U.S. Internal Revenue Code exempts **S corporations** from double taxation because they elect subchapter S tax treatment. Under subchapter S tax regulations, the firm's profits (and losses) are not subject to corporate taxes, but instead are allocated directly to shareholders based on their ownership share. The shareholders must include these profits as income on their individual tax returns (even if no money is distributed to them). However, after the shareholders have paid income taxes on these profits, no further tax is due.

 Corporate Taxation Around the World

Most countries offer investors in corporations some relief from double taxation. Thirty countries make up the Organization for Economic Co-operation and Development (OECD), and of these countries, only Ireland offers no relief whatsoever. A few countries, including Australia, Finland, Mexico, New Zealand, and Norway, offer complete relief by effectively not taxing dividend income. The United States offers partial relief by having a lower tax rate on dividend income than on other sources of income. As of 2016, qualified dividends are taxed at 15% or 20%, depending on the investor's tax bracket, rates significantly below their personal income tax rate.

EXAMPLE 1.2

Taxation of S
Corporation Earnings

MyFinanceLab

PROBLEM

Rework Example 1.1, assuming the corporation in that example has elected subchapter S tax treatment and your tax rate on non-dividend income is 30%.

SOLUTION

PLAN

Earnings before taxes: $5.00   Corporate tax rate: 0%   Personal tax rate: 30%

In this case, the corporation pays no taxes. It earned $5.00 per share. In an S corporation, all income is treated as personal income to you, whether or not the corporation chooses to distribute or retain this cash. As a result, you must pay a 30% tax rate on those earnings.

EXECUTE

Your income taxes are $0.30 \times \$5.00 = \$1.50$, leaving you with $\$5.00 - \$1.50 = \$3.50$ in after-tax earnings.

EVALUATE

The $1.50 in taxes that you pay is substantially lower than the $2.45 you paid in Example 1.1. As a result, you are left with $3.50 per share after all taxes instead of $2.55. However, note that in a C corporation, you are only taxed when you receive the income as a dividend, whereas in an S corporation, you pay taxes on the income immediately regardless of whether the corporation distributes it as a dividend or reinvests it in the company.

C corporations
Corporations that have no restrictions on who owns their shares or the number of shareholders; they cannot qualify for subchapter S tax treatment and are subject to direct taxation.

C Corporations. The government places strict limitations on the qualifications for subchapter S tax treatment. In particular, the shareholders of such corporations must be individuals who are U.S. citizens or residents, and there can be no more than 100 of them. Because most corporations have no restrictions on who owns their shares or the number of shareholders, they cannot qualify for subchapter S tax treatment. Thus, most corporations are **C corporations**, which are corporations subject to corporate taxes.

As we have discussed, there are four main types of firms: sole proprietorships, partnerships (general and limited), limited liability companies, and corporations ("S" and "C"). To help you see the differences among them, Table 1.1 compares and contrasts the main characteristics of each.

TABLE 1.1

Characteristics of the
Different Types of Firms

	Number of Owners	Liability for Firm's Debts	Owners Manage the Firm	Ownership Change Dissolves Firm	Taxation
Sole Proprietorship	One	Yes	Yes	Yes	Personal
Partnership	Unlimited	Yes; each partner is liable for the entire amount	Yes	Yes	Personal
Limited Partnership	At least one general partner (GP), no limit on limited partners (LP)	GP-Yes LP-No	GP-Yes LP-No	GP-Yes LP-No	Personal
Limited Liability Company	Unlimited	No	Yes	No*	Personal
S Corporation	At most 100	No	No (but they legally may)	No	Personal
C Corporation	Unlimited	No	No (but they legally may)	No	Double

*However, most LLCs require the approval of the other members to transfer your ownership.

1.3 The Financial Manager

As of December 2015, Apple, Inc. had over 5.5 *billion* shares of stock held by 26,000 owners.[4] Because there are many owners of a corporation, each of whom can freely trade their stock, it is often not feasible for the owners of a corporation to have direct control of the firm. It falls to the financial manager to make the financial decisions of the business for the stockholders. Within the corporation, the financial manager has three main tasks:

1. Make investment decisions.
2. Make financing decisions.
3. Manage short-term cash needs.

We will discuss each of these in turn, along with the financial manager's overarching goal.

Making Investment Decisions

The financial manager's most important job is to make the firm's investment decisions. The financial manager must weigh the costs and benefits of each investment or project and decide which ones qualify as good uses of the money stockholders have invested in the firm. These investment decisions fundamentally shape what the firm does and whether it will add value for its owners. For example, it may seem hard to imagine now, but there was a time when Apple's financial managers were evaluating whether to invest in the development of the first iPhone. They had to weigh the substantial development and production costs against uncertain future sales. Their analysis indicated that it was a good investment, and the rest is history. In this book, you will learn all the tools necessary to make these investment decisions.

GLOBAL FINANCIAL CRISIS

The Dodd-Frank Act

In response to the 2008 financial crisis, the U.S. federal government reevaluated its role in the control and management of financial institutions and private corporations. Signed into law on July 21, 2010, the **Dodd-Frank Wall Street Reform and Consumer Protection Act** brought a sweeping change to financial regulation in response to widespread calls for financial regulatory system reform after the near collapse of the world's financial system in the fall of 2008 and the ensuing global credit crisis. History indeed repeats itself: It was in the wake of the 1929 stock market crash and subsequent Great Depression that Congress passed the Glass-Steagall Act establishing the Federal Deposit Insurance Corporation (FDIC) and instituted significant bank reforms to regulate transactions between commercial banks and securities firms.

The Dodd-Frank Act aims to (1) promote U.S. financial stability by "improving accountability and transparency in the financial system," (2) put an end to the notion of "too big to fail," (3) "protect the American taxpayer by ending bailouts," and (4) "protect consumers from abusive financial services practices." Time will tell whether the Act will actually achieve these important goals.

Implementing the wide-ranging financial reforms in the Dodd-Frank Act requires the work of many federal agencies, either through rulemaking or other regulatory actions. As of mid-2015, five years since Dodd-Frank's passage, 247 of the reforms have been finalized, providing a clear picture of the Dodd-Frank regulatory framework. But another 143 rules or actions await completion. While only two-thirds of the rules have been finalized, many of the core reforms have been or are nearing completion. For instance, the Volcker Rule, which bars banks that take government-insured deposits from making speculative investments, took full effect in late July of 2015.

---

[4]Apple, Inc., Notice of 2016 Annual Meeting of Shareholders, December 28, 2015.

Making Financing Decisions

Once the financial manager has decided which investments to make, he or she also decides how to pay for them. Large investments may require the corporation to raise additional money. The financial manager must decide whether to raise more money from new and existing owners by selling more shares of stock (equity) or to borrow the money instead (bonds and other debt). A bond is a security sold by governments and corporations to raise money from investors today in exchange for a promised future payment. It can be viewed as a loan from those investors to the issuer. In this book, we will discuss the characteristics of each source of money and how to decide which one to use in the context of the corporation's overall mix of debt and equity.

Managing Short-Term Cash Needs

The financial manager must ensure that the firm has enough cash on hand to meet its obligations from day to day. This job, also commonly known as *managing working capital*,[5] may seem straightforward, but in a young or growing company, it can mean the difference between success and failure. Even companies with great products require a lot of money to develop and bring those products to market. Consider the costs to Starbucks of launching their VIA instant coffee, which included developing the instant coffee crystals and creating a big marketing campaign for them, or the costs to Boeing of producing the 787—billions of dollars were spent before the first 787 finally left the ground in December 2009. A company typically burns through a significant amount of cash before the sales of the product generate income. The financial manager's job is to make sure that limited access to cash does not hinder the firm's success.

The Goal of the Financial Manager

All of these decisions by the financial manager are made within the context of the overriding goal of financial management—*to maximize the wealth of the owners, the stockholders*. The stockholders have invested in the corporation, putting their money at risk to become the owners of the corporation. Thus, the financial manager is a caretaker of the stockholders' money, making decisions in their interests. Many corporations have thousands of owners (shareholders). These shareholders vary from large institutions to small first-time investors, from retirees living off their investments to young employees just

starting to save for retirement. Each owner is likely to have different interests and priorities. Whose interests and priorities determine the goals of the firm? You might be surprised to learn that the interests of shareholders are aligned for many, if not most, important decisions. Regardless of their own personal financial position and stage in life, all the shareholders will agree that they are better off if the value of their investment in the corporation is maximized. For example, suppose the decision concerns whether to develop a new product that will be a profitable investment for the corporation. All shareholders will very likely agree that developing this product is a good idea. Returning to our iPhone example, by October 2010, Apple shares were worth three times as much as they were in January 2007, when the first iPhone was introduced. All Apple shareholders at the time of the development of

---

[5]*Working capital* refers to things such as cash on hand, inventories, raw materials, loans to suppliers, and payments from customers—the grease that keeps the wheels of production moving. We will discuss working capital in more detail in Chapter 2 and devote all of Chapter 19 to working capital management.

the first iPhone are clearly much better off because of it, whether they have since sold their shares of Apple to pay for retirement, or are still holding those shares in their retirement savings account.

Even when all the owners of a corporation agree on the goals of the corporation, these goals must be implemented. In the next section, we will discuss the financial manager's place in the corporation and how owners exert control over the corporation.

Shareholder Value Versus Stakeholder Value

While the goal of a financial manager is to increase the value of the firm to its shareholders, this responsibility does not imply that the impact of the firm's decisions on other stakeholders, such as employees or customers, can be ignored. By creating additional value for customers, the firm can raise prices and increase profits.

Similarly, if the firm makes decisions that benefit employees (for example, increasing their job security), it will be able to offer lower wages or benefit from increased productivity. On the other hand, if customers or employees anticipate that the firm is likely to exploit them, they will demand lower prices or higher wages. Thus, to maximize shareholder value, the financial manager must consider the impact of her decision on all stakeholders of the firm.

CONCEPT CHECK

3. What are the main types of decisions that a financial manager makes?
4. What is the goal of the financial manager?

1.4 The Financial Manager's Place in the Corporation

We've established that the stockholders own the corporation but rely on financial managers to actively manage the corporation. The *board of directors* and the management team headed by the *chief executive officer* possess direct control of the corporation. In this section, we explain how the responsibilities for the corporation are divided between these two entities and describe conflicts that arise between stockholders and the management team.

The Corporate Management Team

board of directors A group of people elected by shareholders who have the ultimate decision-making authority in the corporation.

The shareholders of a corporation exercise their control by electing a **board of directors**, a group of people who have the ultimate decision-making authority in the corporation. In most corporations, each share of stock gives a shareholder one vote in the election of the board of directors, so investors with more shares have more influence. When one or two shareholders own a very large proportion of the outstanding stock, these shareholders might either be on the board of directors themselves, or they may have the right to appoint a number of directors.

chief executive officer (CEO) The person charged with running the corporation by instituting the rules and policies set by the board of directors.

The board of directors makes rules on how the corporation should be run (including how the top managers in the corporation are compensated), sets policy, and monitors the performance of the company. The board of directors delegates most decisions that involve the day-to-day running of the corporation to its management. The **chief executive officer (CEO)** is charged with running the corporation by instituting the rules and policies set by the board of directors. The size of the rest of the management team varies from corporation to corporation. In some corporations, the separation of powers between the board of directors and CEO is not always distinct. In fact, the CEO can also be the chairman of the board of directors. The most senior financial manager is the chief financial officer (CFO), often reporting directly to the CEO. Figure 1.2 presents part of a typical organizational chart for a corporation, highlighting the positions a financial manager may take.

FIGURE 1.2

The Financial Functions Within a Corporation

The board of directors, representing the stockholders, controls the corporation and hires the top management team. A financial manager might hold any of the green-shaded positions, including the Chief Financial Officer (CFO) role. The controller oversees accounting and tax functions. The treasurer oversees more traditional finance functions, such as capital budgeting (making investment decisions), risk management (managing the firm's exposure to movements in the financial markets), and credit management (managing the terms and policies of any credit the firm extends to its customers).

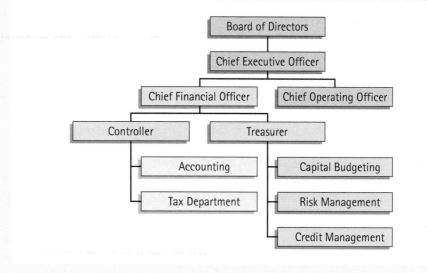

Ethics and Incentives in Corporations

A corporation is run by a management team, separate from its owners. How can the owners of a corporation ensure that the management team will implement their goals?

Agency Problems. Many people claim that because of the separation of ownership and control in a corporation, managers have little incentive to work in the interests of the shareholders when this means working against their self-interest. Economists call this an **agency problem**—when managers, despite being hired as the agents of shareholders, put their self-interest ahead of the interests of those shareholders. Managers face the ethical dilemma of whether to adhere to their responsibility to put the interests of shareholders first, or to do what is in their personal best interests. This problem is commonly addressed in practice by minimizing the number of decisions managers make that require putting their self-interest against the interests of the shareholders. For example, managers' compensation contracts are designed to ensure that most decisions in the shareholders' interest are also in the managers' interests; shareholders often tie the compensation of top managers to the corporation's profits or perhaps to its stock price. There is, however, a limitation to this strategy. By tying compensation too closely to performance, shareholders might be asking managers to take on more risk than they are comfortable taking. As a result, the managers may not make decisions that shareholders want them to, or it might be hard to find talented managers willing to accept the job. For example, biotech firms take big risks on drugs that fight cancer, AIDS, and other widespread diseases. The market for a successful drug is huge, but the risk of failure is high. Investors who put only some of their money in biotech may be comfortable with this risk, but managers who have all of their compensation tied to the success of such a drug might opt to develop a less risky drug that has a smaller market.

agency problem When managers, despite being hired as the agents of shareholders, put their self-interest ahead of the interests of those shareholders.

The Dodd-Frank Act on Corporate Compensation and Governance

Compensation is one of the most important conflicts of interest between corporate executives and shareholders. To limit senior corporate executives' influence over their own compensation and prevent excessive compensation, the Act directs the SEC to adopt new rules that:

- Mandate the independence of a firm's compensation committee and its advisers.
- Provide shareholders the opportunity to approve—in a non-binding, advisory vote—the compensation of executive officers at least once every three years (referred to as a "Say-on-Pay" vote).
- Require firm disclosure and shareholder approval of large bonus payments (so-called "golden parachutes") to ousted senior executives as the result of a takeover.
- Require disclosure of the relationship of executive pay to the company's performance, as well as the ratio between the CEO's total compensation and that of the median employee.
- Create "clawback" provisions that allow firms to recoup compensation paid based on erroneous financial results.

Further potential for conflicts of interest and ethical considerations arise when some stakeholders in the corporation benefit and others lose from a decision. Shareholders and managers are two stakeholders in the corporation, but others include the regular employees and the communities in which the company operates, for example. Managers may decide to take the interests of other stakeholders into account in their decisions, such as keeping a loss-generating factory open because it is the main provider of jobs in a small town, paying above local market wages to factory workers in a developing country, or operating a plant at a higher environmental standard than local law mandates.

In some cases, these actions that benefit other stakeholders may also benefit the firm's shareholders by creating a more dedicated workforce, generating positive publicity with customers, or other indirect effects. In other instances, when these decisions benefit other stakeholders at shareholders' expense, they represent a form of corporate charity. Indeed, many if not most corporations explicitly donate (on behalf of their shareholders) to local and global causes. Shareholders often approve of such actions, even though they are costly and so reduce their wealth. While it is the manager's job to make decisions that maximize shareholder value, shareholders—who own the firm—also want the firm's actions to reflect their moral and ethical values. Of course, shareholders may not have identical preferences in these matters, leading to potential sources of conflict.

The CEO's Performance. Another way shareholders can encourage managers to work in the interests of shareholders is to discipline them if they do not. If shareholders are unhappy with a CEO's performance, they could, in principle, pressure the board to oust the CEO. Disney's Michael Eisner, Hewlett-Packard's Carly Fiorina, and Home Depot's Robert Nardelli were all forced to resign by their boards. Despite these high-profile examples, directors and top executives are rarely replaced through a grassroots shareholder uprising. Instead, dissatisfied investors often choose to sell their shares. Of course, somebody must be willing to buy the shares from the dissatisfied shareholders. If enough shareholders are dissatisfied, the only way to entice investors to buy (or hold) the shares is to offer them a low price. Similarly, investors who see a well-managed corporation, will want to purchase shares, which drives the stock price up. Thus, the stock price of the corporation

Citizens United v. Federal Election Commission

On January 21, 2010, the U.S. Supreme Court ruled on what some scholars have argued is the most important First Amendment case in many years. In *Citizens United v. Federal Election Commission*, the Court held, in a controversial 5–4 decision, that the First Amendment allows corporations and unions to make political expenditures in support of a particular candidate. This ruling overturned existing restrictions on political campaigning by corporations. Because it is highly unlikely that all shareholders of a corporation would unanimously support a particular candidate, allowing such activities effectively guarantees a potential conflict of interest.

is a barometer for corporate leaders that continuously gives them feedback on the shareholders' opinion of their performance.

When the stock performs poorly, the board of directors might react by replacing the CEO. In some corporations, however, the senior executives might be entrenched because boards of directors do not have the independence or motivation to replace them. Often, the reluctance to fire results when the board is comprised of people who are close friends of the CEO and lack objectivity. In corporations in which the CEO is entrenched and doing a poor job, the expectation of continued poor performance will cause the stock price to be low. Low stock prices create a profit opportunity. In a **hostile takeover**, an individual or organization—sometimes known as a *corporate raider*—purchases a large fraction of a company's stock and in doing so gets enough votes to replace the board of directors and the CEO. With a new superior management team, the stock is a much more attractive investment, which would likely result in a price rise and a profit for the corporate raider and the other shareholders. Although the words "hostile" and "raider" have negative connotations, corporate raiders provide an important service to shareholders. The mere threat of being removed as a result of a hostile takeover is often enough to discipline bad managers and motivate boards of directors to make difficult decisions. Consequently, the fact that a corporation's shares can be publicly traded creates a "market for corporate control" that encourages managers and boards of directors to act in the interests of their shareholders.

hostile takeover
A situation in which an individual or organization—sometimes referred to as a *corporate raider*—purchases a large fraction of a company's stock and in doing so gets enough votes to replace the board of directors and its CEO.

CONCEPT CHECK

5. How do shareholders control a corporation?

6. What types of jobs would a financial manager have in a corporation?

7. What ethical issues could confront a financial manager?

1.5 The Stock Market

stock market (also stock exchange or bourse) Organized market on which the shares of many corporations are traded.

liquid Describes an investment that can be easily turned into cash because it can be sold immediately at a competitive market price.

In Section 1.3, we established the goal of the financial manager: to maximize the wealth of the owners, the stockholders. The value of the owners' investments in the corporation is determined by the price of a share of the corporation's stock. Corporations can be private or public. A private corporation has a limited number of owners and there is no organized market for its shares, making it hard to determine the market price of its shares at any point in time. A public corporation has many owners and its shares trade on an organized market, called a **stock market** (or **stock exchange** or **bourse**). These markets provide *liquidity* for a company's shares and determine the market price for those shares. An investment is **liquid** if it can be easily turned into cash by selling it immediately at a competitive market price. An investor in a public company values the ability to turn his investment into cash easily and quickly by simply selling his shares on one of these markets. In this section, we provide an overview of the functioning of the major stock markets. The analysis and trading by participants in these markets provides an evaluation of the financial managers' decisions that determines the stock price and provides essential feedback to the managers on their decisions.

The Largest Stock Markets

The best known U.S. stock market and one of the largest stock markets in the world is the New York Stock Exchange (NYSE). Billions of dollars of stock are exchanged every day on the NYSE. The other well-known U.S. stock market is the NASDAQ (the National Association of Security Dealers Automated Quotation). Most other countries have at least one stock market. The biggest stock markets are the Shanghai and Shenzhen Stock Exchanges in China. Figure 1.3 ranks the world's largest stock exchanges by trading volume and reflects the recent rise in importance of electronic exchanges such as BATS Global Markets and BATS Chi-x, which we discuss later in this section.

FIGURE 1.3

Worldwide Stock Markets Ranked by Volume of Trade

The bar graph shows the 10 biggest stock markets in the world ranked by total value of shares traded on exchange in 2015.

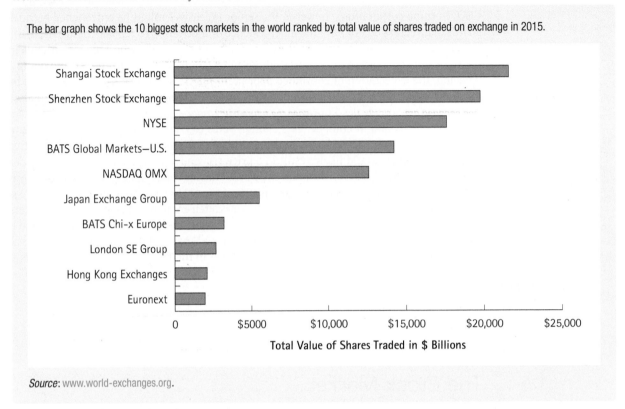

Source: www.world-exchanges.org.

primary market When a corporation issues new shares of stock and sells them to investors.

secondary market Markets, such as NYSE or NASDAQ, where shares of a corporation are traded between investors without the involvement of the corporation.

market makers Individuals or companies at an exchange who match buyers with sellers.

specialists market makers at the NYSE.

bid price The price at which a market maker is willing to buy a security.

ask price The price at which a market maker is willing to sell a security.

Primary Versus Secondary Markets

All of the markets in Figure 1.3 are secondary markets. The **primary market** refers to a corporation issuing new shares of stock and selling them to investors. After this initial transaction between the corporation and investors, the shares continue to trade in a **secondary market** between investors without the involvement of the corporation. For example, if you wish to buy 100 shares of Starbucks Coffee, you could place an order on the NASDAQ, where Starbucks trades under the ticker symbol SBUX. You would buy your shares from someone who already held shares of Starbucks, not from Starbucks itself. Because firms only occasionally issue new shares, secondary market trading accounts for the vast majority of trading in the stock market.

Traditional Trading Venues

Historically, firms would choose one stock exchange to list their stock, and almost all trade in the stock would occur on that exchange. In the U.S., the two most important exchanges are the New York Stock Exchange (NYSE) and the National Association of Security Dealers Automated Quotation (NASDAQ).

Prior to 2005, almost all trade on the NYSE took place on the exchange's trading floor in lower Manhattan. **Market makers** (known then on the NYSE as **specialists**) matched buyers and sellers. They posted two prices for every stock they made a market in: the price they stood willing to buy the stock at (the **bid price**) and the price they stood willing to sell the stock for (the **ask price**). When a customer arrived wanting to make a trade at these prices, they would honor the price (up to a limited number of shares) and would make the trade even if they did

FRANK HATHEWAY

As Chief Economist and Senior Vice President for NASDAQ, Dr. Frank Hatheway leads a team of 20 professionals who serve as an internal consultancy for the NASDAQ markets. Their work includes designing new features, evaluating operations markets, and advising on strategic initiatives.

QUESTION: *Compared to 15 years ago, the number of potential trading venues for investors has changed dramatically. Who have these changes benefited?*

ANSWER: The number of trading venues has increased dramatically. In 2000 you placed an order on NASDAQ or the NYSE, and the majority of trading activity in that stock occurred on the same market as your order. That's not the case anymore. Your trade may be executed on the National Stock Exchange, BATS, or one of 10 other exchanges. To deal with the soaring number of venues, trading became highly automated and highly competitive, benefiting both individual and institutional investors. A fast retail trade in the 1980s took about three minutes and cost over $100 (in 1980s money). Now it's a mouse click, browser refresh, and maybe $20 (in 2016 money). Trading costs for individual investors are down over 90 percent since 2000. Institutional-size block orders are also cheaper and easier to trade today.

Automation has virtually removed traditional equity traders like the market makers, specialists, and floor brokers at the exchanges. As the head of the trading desk for a major firm quipped around 2006, "I used to have 100 traders and 10 IT guys. I now have 100 IT guys and 10 traders." The once bustling New York Stock Exchange floor is now essentially a TV studio.

QUESTION: *How have these changes affected market liquidity?*

ANSWER: Liquidity is very transitory. The computer algorithms controlling trading constantly enter orders into the market and remove orders if the order fails to trade or if market conditions change. The algorithms quickly re-enter removed orders into the market, leading to rapidly changing prices and quantities. Also, numerous studies show that there is more liquidity in the market today. To control an order 15 years ago, you phoned your broker with your instructions. Today, the algorithm you selected controls the order and can change the order almost instantly. Because computers have more control over orders than human traders did, there is less risk associated with placing an order. Consequently there are more orders and greater liquidity.

QUESTION: *How has NASDAQ been affected by these changes and what does the future hold?*

ANSWER: NASDAQ has become an innovative, technologically savvy company—much like the companies we list. Fifteen years ago we operated a single stock market in the United States. Thanks to increased technological efficiency, today we operate three stock markets, three listed-options markets, and a futures market. Operating these seven markets requires less than half the personnel required for a single market 15 years ago. To compete in this environment, NASDAQ had to develop a better trading system to handle our increased order volume. Order volume that took an entire day to process 15 years ago, today takes a few seconds. We've also transformed our culture from supporting an industry based on human traders to one based on algorithmic traders and the IT professionals who design those algorithms.

QUESTION: *Is High Frequency Trading a cause for concern in the market? Should it be limited?*

ANSWER: Specific concerns about High Frequency Trading are generally about market disruptions and manipulation, and cases center around the operation of trading algorithms. I believe market oversight is evolving to appropriately address disruptive or manipulative activity.

These days essentially every order in the United States is handled by a computer trading algorithm. Simply put, we are all High Frequency Traders. Consequently, limiting High Frequency Trading should not be a policy objective. What should be a policy objective is making sure that equity markets benefit investors and issuers by ensuring that the algorithms do not disrupt the markets and that they operate in a manner that is fair to investors. The market exists to support capital formation and economic growth. Market operators such as NASDAQ work with regulators and others to look after the interests of investors and issuers.

---

liquidity Extent to which the market for an asset is liquid, meaning that assets can be easily turned into cash because they can be sold immediately at competitive market prices.

bid-ask spread The amount by which the ask price exceeds the bid price.

not have another customer willing to take the other side of the trade. In this way, they provided **liquidity** by ensuring market participants that they always had somebody to trade with.

In contrast to the NYSE, the NASDAQ market never had a trading floor. Instead all trades were completed over the phone or on a computer network. An important difference between the NYSE and NASDAQ was that on the NYSE, each stock had only one market maker. On NASDAQ, stocks had multiple market makers who competed with each other. Each market maker posted bid and ask prices in the NASDAQ network which were viewed by all participants.

Market makers make money because ask prices exceed bid prices. This difference is called the **bid-ask spread**. Customers always buy at the ask (the higher price) and sell at

FIGURE 1.4

Distribution of trading volume for NYSE-listed (left panel) and NASDAQ-listed (right panel) stocks. NYSE Arca is the electronic trading platform of the NYSE. BATS and Direct Edge merged in 2014; these new electronic exchanges now handle about 20% of all trades. Other venues, including internal dealer platforms and so called "dark pools," accounted for almost 40% of all trades in 2015.

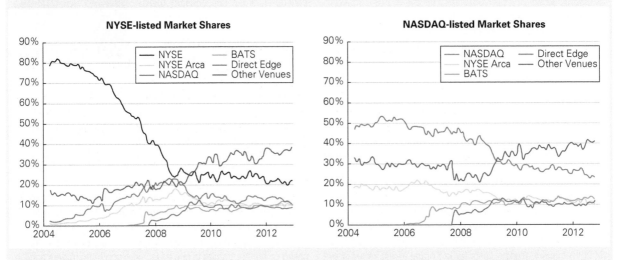

Source: J. Angel, L. Harris, and C. Spatt, "Equity Trading in the 21st Century: An Update," *Quarterly Journal of Finance* 5 (2015): 1–39.

transaction cost In most markets, an expense such as a broker commission and the bid-ask spread investors must pay in order to trade securities.

the bid (the lower price). The bid-ask spread is a **transaction cost** investors pay in order to trade. Because specialists on the NYSE took the other side of the trade from their customers, this cost accrued to them as a profit. This was the compensation they earned for providing a liquid market by standing ready to honor any quoted price. Investors also paid other forms of transactions costs like commissions.

New Competition and Market Changes

Stock markets have gone through enormous changes in the last decade. In 2005, the NYSE and NASDAQ exchanges accounted for over 75% of all trade in U.S. stocks. Since that time, however, they have faced increasing competition from new fully electronic exchanges as well as alternative trading systems. As Figure 1.4 shows, today these new entrants handle more than 50% of all trades.

With this change in market structure, the role of an official market maker has largely disappeared. Because all transactions occur electronically with computers matching buy and sell orders, anybody can make a market in a stock by posting a **limit order**. A limit order is an order to buy or sell a set amount at a fixed price. For example, an order to buy 100 shares of IBM at a price of $138/share is a limit buy order. The bid-ask spread of a stock is determined by the outstanding limit orders. The limit sell order with the lowest price is the ask price. The limit buy order with the highest price is the bid price. Traders make the market in the stock by posting limit buy and sell orders. The collection of all limit orders is known as the **limit order book**. Exchanges make their limit order books public so that investors (or their brokers) can see the best bid and ask prices when deciding where to trade.

Traders who post limit orders provide liquidity to the market. On the other hand, traders who place **market orders**—orders that trade immediately at the best outstanding limit order—are said to be "takers" of liquidity. Providers of liquidity earn the bid-ask spread, but in doing so they risk the possibility that their orders will become stale: When news about the stock arrives that causes the price of the stock to move, smart traders will quickly take advantage of the existing limit orders by executing trades at the old prices. To protect

limit order Order to buy or sell a set amount of a security at a fixed price.

limit order book Collection of all current limit orders for a given security.

market orders Orders to trade immediately at the best outstanding limit order available.

themselves against this possibility, liquidity providers need to constantly monitor the market, cancelling old orders and posting new orders when appropriate. So called **high frequency traders** (**HFTs**) are a class of traders who, with the aid of computers, place, update, cancel, and execute trades many times per second in response to new information as well as other orders, profiting by both providing liquidity and taking advantage of stale limit orders.

high frequency traders (HFTs) Traders who place, update, cancel, and execute trades many times per second.

Dark Pools

When trading on an exchange, investors are guaranteed the opportunity to trade immediately at the current bid or ask price, and transactions are visible to all traders when they occur. In contrast, alternative trading systems called **dark pools** do not make their limit order books visible. Instead, these dark pools offer investors the ability to trade at a better price (for example, the average of the bid and ask, thus saving the bid-ask spread) with the tradeoff that their order might not be filled if an excess of either buy or sell orders is received. Trading on a dark pool is therefore attractive to traders who do not want to reveal their demand and who are willing to sacrifice the guarantee of immediacy for potential price improvement.

dark pools Trading venues in which the size and price of orders are not disclosed to participants. Prices are within the best bid and ask prices available in public markets, but traders face the risk their orders may not be filled if an excess of either buy or sell orders is received.

When dark pools are included, researchers estimate that in the U.S. alone there could be as many 50 venues to trade stocks. These venues compete with one another for order volume. Because traders value liquid markets, an important area of competition is liquidity—exchanges try to ensure that their limit order books are deep, that is, contain many orders. As a result exchanges have been experimenting with different rules designed to encourage traders who provide liquidity and discourage traders who take advantage of stale limit orders. For example, some trading venues pay traders to post limit orders and charge traders who place market orders. Others pay for volume from retail investors, and impose additional charges on high frequency trading. The proliferation of exchange venues has generated a wide variety of different compensation schemes. Indeed, BATS (which stands for Better Alternative Trading System) operates different markets with different rules, essentially tailoring their markets to the perceived needs of their customers. It is highly unlikely that we have seen the end of these changes. Stock markets remain in a state of flux, and only time will tell what the eventual shakeout will look like.

Listing Standards

listing standards Outlines of the requirements a company must meet to be traded on the exchange.

Each exchange has its own **listing standards**, outlines of the requirements a company must meet to be traded on the exchange. These standards usually require that the company has enough shares outstanding for shareholders to have a liquid market and to be of interest to a broad set of investors. The NYSE's standards are more stringent than those of NASDAQ; traditionally, there has been a certain pride in being listed on the NYSE. Many companies would start on the NASDAQ and then move to the NYSE as they grew. However, NASDAQ has retained many big, successful companies such as Starbucks, Apple, and Microsoft. The two exchanges compete actively over listings of larger companies (NASDAQ landed Facebook and the NYSE won Twitter's listing) and the decision of where to list often comes down to which exchange the company's board believes will give its stockholders the best execution and liquidity for their trades.

Other Financial Markets

Of course, stock markets are not the only financial markets. There are markets to trade practically anything—some of them are physical places like the NYSE and others are purely electronic, like the NASDAQ. Two of the largest financial markets in the world, the bond market and the foreign exchange market, are simply networks of dealers connected by phone and computer. We will discuss these markets in more detail in later chapters (Chapters 6 and 15 for bonds and Chapter 23 for foreign exchange). Commodities like oil, wheat, and soybeans are traded on physical exchanges like the New York Mercantile Exchange. *Derivative securities*, which are complicated financial products used to hedge risks, are traded in locations like the Chicago Board Options Exchange (discussed in Chapter 21).

NYSE, BATS, DJIA, S&P 500: Awash in Acronyms

With all of these acronyms floating around, it's easy to get confused. You may have heard of the "Dow Jones" or "Dow Jones (Industrial) Average" and the "S&P 500" on news reports about the stock markets. The NYSE, BATS, and NASDAQ are all stock markets where the prices of stocks are determined through trading. However, when commentators talk about whether stocks are up or down in general in a given day, they often refer to the Dow Jones Industrial Average (DJIA) and the Standard and Poor's 500 (S&P 500). The DJIA and S&P 500 are simply measures of the aggregate price level of collections of preselected stocks—30 in the case of the DJIA and 500 in the case of the S&P 500. These stocks were selected by Dow Jones (the publisher of the *Wall Street Journal*) or Standard & Poor's as representative of

the overall market. The S&P 500 consists of 500 of the highest-valued U.S. companies. While fewer in number, the 30 stocks in the DJIA include companies such as Microsoft, Walmart, Boeing, and 3M, and are selected to cover the important sectors in the U.S. economy. The table below shows the 30 stocks in the DJIA as of August 2016. Dow Jones editors choose these stocks to reflect the overall U.S. economy. The membership of the index has changed over time to reflect the U.S. economy's transition from being industrial-driven to being more services and technology based. For example, they added Chevron in 2008 to capture the growing importance of energy. In 2012, they added UnitedHealth, the United States' largest insurer, to reflect the importance of healthcare for an aging U.S. population. Both the DJIA and S&P 500 include stocks that are traded on the NYSE and stocks that are traded on NASDAQ and so are distinct from the exchanges themselves.

Composition of the Dow Jones Industrial Average (DJIA) as of October 2016

3M Co.	General Electric Co.	Nike Inc.
American Express Co.	Goldman Sachs Group Inc.	Pfizer Inc.
Apple Inc.	Home Depot Inc.	Procter & Gamble Co.
Boeing Co.	Intel Corp.	Travelers Co.
Caterpillar Inc.	International Business Machines	UnitedHealth Group Inc.
Chevron Corp.	Johnson & Johnson	United Technologies Corp.
Cisco Systems Inc.	J.P. Morgan Chase & Co.	Verizon Communications Inc.
Coca-Cola Co.	McDonald's Corp.	Visa Inc.
Du Pont	Merck & Co.	Walmart Stores Inc.
Exxon Mobil Co.	Microsoft Corp.	Walt Disney Co.

Source: djindexes.com.

CONCEPT CHECK

8. What advantage does a stock market provide to corporate investors? To financial managers?
9. What are the important changes that have occurred in stock markets over the last decade?

1.6   Financial Institutions

financial institutions
Entities that provide financial services, such as taking deposits, managing investments, brokering financial transactions, or making loans.

The spread of the 2008 financial crisis from subprime mortgages to Wall Street to traditional banks and businesses drew everyone's attention to *financial institutions* and their role in the economy. In general, **financial institutions** are entities that provide financial services, such as taking deposits, managing investments, brokering financial transactions, or making loans. In this section, we describe the key types of financial institutions and their functions.

The Financial Cycle

Keeping the names and roles of the different types of financial institutions straight can be challenging. It is helpful to think of the basic financial cycle, depicted in Figure 1.5, as context. In the financial cycle, (1) people invest and save their money, (2) that money, through loans and stock, flows to companies who use it to fund growth through new

FIGURE 1.5

The Financial Cycle

This figure depicts the basic financial cycle, which matches funds from savers to companies that have projects requiring funds and then returns the profits from those projects back to the savers and investors.

products, generating profits and wages, and (3) the money then flows back to the savers and investors. All financial institutions play a role at some point in this cycle of connecting money with ideas and returning the profits back to the savers and investors.

Types of Financial Institutions

Table 1.2 lists the major categories of financial institutions, provides examples of representative firms, and summarizes the institutions' sources and uses of funds.

Financial conglomerates, sometimes referred to as *financial services firms*, combine more than one type of institution. Examples include Bank of America, JPMorgan Chase, and Deutsche Bank, all of which engage in commercial banking (like Wells Fargo) as well as investment banking. Investment banking refers to the business of advising companies in major financial transactions. Examples include buying and selling companies or divisions, and raising new capital by issuing stock or bonds. Goldman Sachs and Morgan Stanley are financial institutions that are focused on investment banking activities.

Role of Financial Institutions

Financial institutions have a role beyond moving funds from those who have extra funds (savers) to those who need funds (borrowers and firms): They also move funds through time. For example, suppose you need a $20,000 car loan. You need $20,000 now, but do not have it. However, you will have it in the future as you earn a salary. The financial institution, in this case a bank or credit union, helps transfer your future salary into funds today by issuing you a loan.

Financial institutions also help spread out risk-bearing. Insurance companies essentially pool premiums together from policyholders and pay the claims of those who have an accident, fire, medical need, or who die. This process spreads the financial risk of these events out across a large pool of policyholders and the investors in the insurance company. Similarly, mutual funds and pension funds take your savings and spread them out among the stocks and bonds of many different companies, limiting your risk exposure to any one company.

TABLE 1.2

Financial Institutions
and Their Roles in the
Financial Cycle

Institution	Source of Money	Use of Money
Banks and Credit Unions Examples: *Wells Fargo, SunTrust*	Deposits (savings)	Loans to people and businesses
Insurance Companies Examples: *Liberty Mutual, Allstate*	Premiums and investment earnings	Invests mostly in bonds and some stocks, using the investment income to pay claims
Mutual Funds Examples: *Vanguard, Fidelity*	People's investments (savings)	Buys stocks, bonds, and other financial instruments on behalf of its investors
Pension Funds Examples: *CalPERS, REST*	Retirement savings contributed through the workplace	Similar to mutual funds, except with the purpose of providing retirement income
Hedge Funds Examples: *Bridgewater, Citadel*	Investments by wealthy individuals and endowments	Invests in any kind of investment in an attempt to maximize returns
Venture Capital Funds Examples: *Kleiner Perkins, Sequoia Capital*	Investments by wealthy individuals and endowments	Invests in start-up, entrepreneurial firms
Private Equity Funds Examples: *TPG Capital, KKR*	Investments by wealthy individuals and endowments	Purchases whole companies by using a small amount of equity and borrowing the rest

While you may have seen coverage of the stock markets and discussion of financial institutions on the news, it is unlikely that you have been exposed to the finance function within a firm. In this chapter, we provided a sense of what corporate finance is all about, what a financial manager does, and the importance of stock markets and financial institutions. In upcoming chapters, you will learn how to make financial management decisions and how to use financial market information. We will explore the tools of financial analysis hand-in-hand with a clear understanding of when to apply them and why they work.

CONCEPT CHECK

10. What is the basic financial cycle?

11. What are the three main roles financial institutions play?

MyFinanceLab

Here is what you should know after reading this chapter. MyFinanceLab will help you identify what you know, and where to go when you need to practice.

KEY POINTS AND EQUATIONS	KEY TERMS	ONLINE PRACTICE

1.1 Why Study Finance?
- Finance and financial decisions are everywhere in our daily lives.
- Many financial decisions are simple, but others are complex. All are tied together by the Valuation Principle—the foundation for financial decision making—which you will learn in this book.

1.2 The Four Types of Firms

- There are four types of firms in the United States: sole proprietorships, partnerships, limited liability companies, and corporations.
- Firms with unlimited personal liability include sole proprietorships and partnerships.
- Firms with limited liability include limited partnerships, limited liability companies, and corporations.
- A corporation is a legally defined artificial being (a judicial person or legal entity) that has many of the legal powers people have. It can enter into contracts, acquire assets, and incur obligations, and it enjoys protection under the U.S. Constitution against the seizure of its property.
- The shareholders in a C corporation effectively must pay tax twice. The corporation pays tax once and then investors must pay personal tax on any funds that are distributed. S corporations are exempt from the corporate income tax.
- The ownership of a corporation is divided into shares of stock collectively known as equity. Investors in these shares are called shareholders, stockholders, or equity holders.

C corporations, p. 9
corporation, p. 6
dividend payments,
    p. 7
equity, p. 7
equity holder, p. 7
limited liability, p. 6
limited liability company
    (LLC), p. 6
limited partnership,
    p. 6
partnership, p. 6
S corporations, p. 8
shareholder, p. 7
sole proprietorship, p. 5
stock, p. 7
stockholder, p. 7

MyFinanceLab
Study Plan 1.2

1.3 The Financial Manager

- The financial manager makes investing, financing, and cash flow management decisions.
- The goal of the financial manager is to maximize the wealth of the shareholders (maximize the stock price).

MyFinanceLab
Study Plan 1.3

1.4 The Financial Manager's Place in the Corporation

- The ownership and control of a corporation are separate. Shareholders exercise their control indirectly through the board of directors.

agency problem, p. 13
board of directors, p. 12
chief executive officer
    (CEO), p. 12
hostile takeover, p. 15

MyFinanceLab Study
Plan 1.4

1.5 The Stock Market

- The shares of public corporations are traded on stock markets. The shares of private corporations do not trade on a stock market.
- When a firm sells shares to investors, that is a primary market. The stock markets, such as NYSE and NASDAQ, are secondary markets where investors trade shares among each other.
- Traders provide liquidity in stock markets by posting limit orders.
- The bid-ask spread is determined by the best bid and offer prices in the limit order book.

ask price, p. 16
auction market, p. 18
bid-ask spread, p. 17
bid price, p. 16
bourse, p. 15
dark pools, p. 19
high frequency traders
    (HFTs), p. 19
limit order, p. 18
limit order book, p. 18
liquid, p. 15
liquidity, p.17
listing standards, p. 19
market makers, p. 16
market orders, p. 18

MyFinanceLab
Study Plan 1.5

	primary market, p. 16	
	secondary market, p. 16	
	specialists, p. 16	
	stock exchange, p. 15	
	stock market, p. 15	
	transaction cost, p. 18	

1.6 Financial Institutions • In the basic financial cycle, money flows from savers and investors to companies and entrepreneurs with ideas, and then back to the savers and investors in the form of profits and interest. • Financial institutions all play some role in this cycle. • Financial institutions also help move money through time (e.g., loans against future wages) and spread risk across large investor bases.	financial institutions, p. 20	MyFinanceLab Study Plan 1.6

PROBLEMS   *All problems are available in MyFinanceLab.*

The Four Types of Firms

1. What is the most important difference between a corporation and *all* other organizational forms?

2. What does the phrase *limited liability* mean in a corporate context?

3. Which organizational forms give their owners limited liability?

4. What are the main advantages and disadvantages of organizing a firm as a corporation?

5. Explain the difference between an S and a C corporation.

6. You are a shareholder in a C corporation. The corporation earns $2.00 per share before taxes. Once it has paid taxes it will distribute the rest of its earnings to you as a dividend. Assume the corporate tax rate is 40% and the personal tax rate on (both dividend and non-dividend) income is 30%. How much is left for you after all taxes are paid?

7. Repeat Problem 6 assuming the corporation is an S corporation.

The Financial Manager

8. What is the most important type of decision that the financial manager makes?

9. Why do all shareholders agree on the same goal for the financial manager?

The Financial Manager's Place in the Corporation

10. Corporate managers work for the owners of the corporation. Consequently, they should make decisions that are in the interests of the owners, rather than in their own interests. What strategies are available to shareholders to help ensure that managers are motivated to act this way?

11. Recall the last time you ate at an expensive restaurant where you paid the bill. Now think about the last time you ate at a similar restaurant, but your parents paid the bill. Did you order more food (or more expensive food) when your parents paid? Explain how this relates to the agency problem in corporations.

12. Suppose you are considering renting an apartment. You, the renter, can be viewed as an agent while the company that owns the apartment can be viewed as the principal. What agency conflicts do you anticipate? Suppose, instead, that you work for the apartment company. What features would you put into the lease agreement that would give the renter incentives to take good care of the apartment?

13. You are the CEO of a company and you are considering entering into an agreement to have your company buy another company. You think the price might be too high, but you will be the CEO of the combined, much larger company. You know that when the company gets bigger, your pay and prestige will increase. What is the nature of the agency conflict here and how is it related to ethical considerations?

14. You are a financial manager in a public corporation. One of your engineers says that they can increase the profit margin on your flagship product by using a lower quality vendor. However, the product is likely to fail more often and will generally not last as long. Will taking your engineer's suggestion necessarily make shareholders better off? Why or why not?

15. You sit on the board of a public corporation. Your CEO has proposed taking steps to offset the carbon impact of your company's manufacturing process. Doing so will add to the company's overall expenses. Your CEO argues, however, that this action will actually increase the stock price, maximizing shareholder wealth. Why might socially-responsible activities also be value-maximizing?

The Stock Market

16. What is the difference between a public and a private corporation?

17. What is the difference between a primary and a secondary market?

18. How are limit orders and market orders different?

19. Explain why the bid-ask spread is a transaction cost.

20. What are the tradeoffs in using a dark pool?

21. The following quote on Yahoo! stock appeared on April 11, 2016, on Yahoo! Finance:

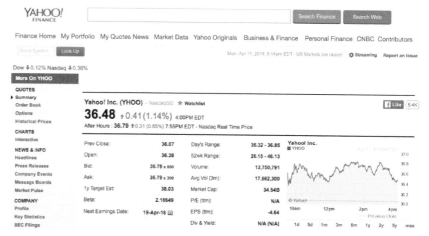

Reproduced with permission of Yahoo. © 2016 Yahoo. YAHOO! and the YAHOO! logo are registered trademarks of Yahoo.

If you wanted to buy Yahoo!, what price would you pay per share? How much would you receive per share if you wanted to sell Yahoo!?

Financial Institutions

22. What is the financial cycle?

23. How do financial institutions help with risk-bearing?

24. What role do investment banks play in the economy?

25. What are some of the similarities and differences among mutual funds, pension funds, and hedge funds?

2

Introduction to Financial Statement Analysis

LEARNING OBJECTIVES

- Know why the disclosure of financial information through financial statements is critical to investors

- Understand the function of the balance sheet

- Understand how the income statement is used

- Interpret a statement of cash flows

- Understand the management's discussion and analysis and the statement of stockholders' equity

- Analyze a firm through its financial statements, including using the DuPont Identity

- Understand the main purpose and aspects of the Sarbanes-Oxley reforms following Enron and other financial scandals

As we discussed in Chapter 1, anyone with money to invest is a potential investor who can own shares in a corporation. As a result, corporations are often widely held, with investors ranging from individuals who hold one share to large financial institutions that own millions of shares. For example, at the end of 2015, Microsoft Corporation had almost 8 billion shares outstanding held by hundreds of thousands of stockholders. Although the corporate organizational structure greatly facilitates the firm's access to investment capital, it also means that stock ownership is most investors' sole tie to the company. How, then, do investors learn enough about a company to know whether or not they should invest in it? One way firms evaluate their performance and communicate this information to investors is through their *financial statements*. Financial statements also enable financial managers to assess the success of their own firm and compare it to competitors.

Firms regularly issue financial statements to communicate financial information to the investment community. A detailed description of the preparation and analysis of these statements is sufficiently complicated that to do it justice would require an entire book. In this chapter, we briefly review the subject, emphasizing only the material that investors and corporate financial managers need in order to make the corporate finance decisions we discuss in the text.

We review the four main types of financial statements, present examples of these statements for a firm, and discuss where an investor or manager might find various types of information about the company. We also discuss some of the financial ratios used to assess a firm's performance and value. We close the chapter with a look at financial reporting abuses and the Sarbanes-Oxley regulatory response.

27

2.1

Firms' Disclosure of Financial Information

financial statements
Accounting reports issued by a firm quarterly and/or annually that present past performance information and a snapshot of the firm's assets and the financing of those assets.

Financial statements are accounting reports issued by a firm periodically (usually quarterly and annually) that present past performance information and a snapshot of the firm's assets and the financing of those assets. Public companies in the United States are required to file their financial statements with the U.S. Securities and Exchange Commission (SEC) on a quarterly basis on form *10-Q* and annually on form *10-K*.[1] They must also send an **annual report (10-K)** with their financial statements to their shareholders each year. Often, private companies also prepare financial statements, but they usually do not have to disclose these reports to the public. Financial statements are important tools with which investors, financial analysts, and other interested outside parties (such as creditors) obtain information about a corporation. They are also useful for managers within the firm as a source of information for the corporate financial decisions we discussed in Chapter 1. In this section, we examine the guidelines for preparing financial statements and introduce the different types of financial statements.

annual report (10-K) The yearly summary of business, accompanying or including financial statements, sent by U.S. public companies to their shareholders.

Generally Accepted Accounting Principles (GAAP) A common set of rules and a standard format for public companies to use when they prepare their financial reports.

Preparation of Financial Statements

Reports about a company's performance must be understandable and accurate. In the United States, the Financial Accounting Standards Board (FASB) establishes **Generally Accepted Accounting Principles (GAAP)** to provide a common set of rules and a standard format for public companies to use when they prepare their reports. This standardization also makes it easier to compare the financial results of different firms.

International Financial Reporting Standards

Generally Accepted Accounting Principles (GAAP) differ among countries. As a result, companies face tremendous accounting complexities when they operate internationally. Investors also face difficulty interpreting financial statements of foreign companies, which discourages them from investing abroad. As companies and capital markets become more global, however, interest in harmonization of accounting standards across countries has increased.

The most important harmonization project began in 1973 when representatives of 10 countries (including the United States) established the International Accounting Standards Committee. This effort led to the creation of the International Accounting Standards Board (IASB) in 2001, with headquarters in London. Now the IASB has issued a set of International Financial Reporting Standards (IFRS).

The IFRS are taking root throughout the world. The European Union (EU) approved an accounting regulation in 2002 requiring all publicly traded EU companies to follow IFRS in their consolidated financial statements starting in 2005. As of 2016, more than 130 jurisdictions either require or permit the use of IFRS, including the EU, Australia, Brazil, Canada, Russia, Hong Kong, Taiwan, and Singapore. China, India, and Japan will soon follow suit. In fact,

currently all major stock exchanges around the world accept IFRS except the United States and Japan, which maintain their local GAAP.

The main difference between U.S. GAAP and IFRS is conceptual—U.S. GAAP are based primarily on accounting rules with specific guidance in applying them, whereas IFRS are based more on principles requiring professional judgment by accountants, and specific guidance in application is limited. Even so, some differences in rules also exist. For example, U.S. GAAP generally prohibit the upward revaluation of non-financial assets, whereas the IFRS allow the revaluation of some such assets to fair value. U.S. GAAP also rely more heavily on historical cost, as opposed to "fair value," to estimate the value of assets and liabilities.

Effort to achieve convergence between U.S. GAAP and IFRS was spurred by the Sarbanes-Oxley Act of 2002 in the United States. It included a provision that U.S. accounting standards move toward international convergence on high-quality accounting standards. Currently, SEC regulations still require public U.S. firms to report using U.S. GAAP. That said, modifications to both IFRS and U.S. GAAP have brought the two closer together, with the key remaining differences in the areas of revenue recognition, impairment charges, leasing, insurance, and the treatment of financial instruments. As of the early 2016, the SEC looks likely to allow U.S. companies to use IFRS to provide supplemental information, but will still require them to file their financials in accordance with U.S. GAAP.

---

[1]The Securities and Exchange Commission was established by Congress in 1934 to regulate securities (for example, stocks and bonds) issued to the public and the financial markets (exchanges) on which those securities trade.

INTERVIEW WITH RUTH PORAT

Ruth Porat is Senior Vice President and Chief Financial Officer of Alphabet and Google. Previously she spent 27 years at Morgan Stanley, where she last was Executive Vice President and Chief Financial Officer. As Morgan Stanley's Vice Chairman of Investment Banking and Global Head of the Financial Institutions Group, she advised the U.S. Treasury and the New York Federal Reserve Bank.

QUESTION: *What best practices do you recommend for financial managers?*

ANSWER:

1. *Maintain a tight financial control environment with respect to accounting controls and process.* Incorporate a strategic approach to IT architecture to ensure data integrity, consistency, and process controls while reducing reliance on human, manual processes—a source of risk and errors.

2. *Ensure a robust budgeting and capital allocation process built on a strong Financial Planning & Analysis team that is well integrated into the business.* Push data transparency to business leaders. They are best positioned to make difficult tradeoffs in the budgeting process, but often lack data granularity to make those choices (and to see the imperative).

3. *Culture matters.* A culture of honest, frank debate that challenges the status quo and avoids homogeneity of thought makes the job more fun and leads to better results. A broad range of experience, and even some "battle scars," ensures the organization recognizes patterns to foresee emerging risks. In that regard, a diverse team with respect to gender, race, and socioeconomic background brings differentiated perspectives, contributing to effective risk management.

4. *Make tough calls early and, ideally, once.* Lead.

QUESTION: *How has the crisis shaped the role of the CFO, or your view of it?*

ANSWER: In financial services, it redefined the perception of a CFO. Beyond focusing on accounting and external reporting functions, the CFO is now also the firm's most senior global manager for guardianship and risk management. Guardianship includes accounting (the controller function) and overseeing a comprehensive approach to IT systems. Risk management requires identifying sources of vulnerability, stress testing, and planning against them. The CFO has become a trusted adviser to the CEO, board

and business leaders, which includes budgeting, capital allocation, and sensitivity analyses. Finally, in certain industries the CFO is the point person with regulators.

QUESTION: *What key lessons did you take from the financial crisis? What advice would you give future CFOs?*

ANSWER: I have three key takeaways from the financial crisis, relevant in both good and bad markets as well as across industries:

1. *Understand your greatest sources of vulnerability and defend against them.* For financial services, liquidity (access to cash) was a weak spot. In that period, we often said, "Liquidity is oxygen for a financial system: without it, you choke." Without sufficient liquidity, banks were forced into a negative cycle of selling assets to raise cash. As Morgan Stanley's CFO, I managed liquidity with the maxim that it was sacrosanct. We invested substantially in the amount and durability of the company's liquidity reserve. Similarly, regulators coming out of the crisis appropriately demanded higher capital, lower leverage, better liquidity, more durable funding, and rigorous stress testing, which imposed transparency on the banks and exposed their weaknesses.

2. *Build a robust control infrastructure ahead of needs, including financial and risk management controls, systems, and processes.* Just as one shouldn't drive a car at 100 mph with mud on the windshield, business leaders must have visibility about their business from accurate, insightful, and timely data consistent with strong financial controls. Rapid growth industries need to invest in infrastructure early because the business requirements continue to grow so rapidly.

3. *Recognize that time is your enemy.* Treasury Secretary Paulson told me during the financial crisis that you must have the will and the means to solve problems; too often, by the time you have the will, you no longer have the means. He was talking about policy, but that rule applies to any decision maker. The glaring examples, in retrospect, were the clear signs of crisis in August 2007 and the March 2008 collapse of Bear Stearns, but reactions were slow or nonexistent. Even in good times, business leaders must focus on resource optimization to maximize the potential for highest returns on investment.

auditor A neutral third party, which corporations are required to hire, that checks a firm's annual financial statements to ensure they are prepared according to GAAP, and provides evidence to support the reliability of the information.

Investors also need some assurance that the financial statements are prepared accurately. Publicly traded corporations are required to hire a neutral third party, known as an **auditor**, to check the annual financial statements, ensure they are prepared according to GAAP, and provide evidence to support the reliability of the information.

Types of Financial Statements

Every public company is required to produce four financial statements: the *balance sheet*, the *income statement*, the *statement of cash flows*, and the *statement of stockholders' equity*. These financial statements provide investors and creditors with an overview of the firm's financial performance. In the sections that follow, we take a close look at the content of these financial statements.

CONCEPT CHECK

1. What is the role of an auditor?
2. What are the four financial statements that all public companies must produce?

2.2 The Balance Sheet

balance sheet (or statement of financial position) A list of a firm's assets and liabilities that provides a snapshot of the firm's financial position at a given point in time.

assets The cash, inventory, property, plant, and equipment, and other investments a company has made.

liabilities A firm's obligations to its creditors.

shareholders' equity, stockholders' equity An accounting measure of a firm's net worth that represents the difference between the firm's assets and its liabilities.

common stock and paid-in surplus The amount that stockholders have directly invested in the firm through purchasing stock from the company.

retained earnings Profits made by the firm, but retained within the firm and reinvested in assets or held as cash.

The **balance sheet**, or **statement of financial position**,[2] lists the firm's *assets* and *liabilities*, providing a snapshot of the firm's financial position at a given point in time. Table 2.1 shows the balance sheet for a fictitious company, Global Corporation. Notice that the balance sheet is divided into two parts ("sides") with the assets on the left side and the liabilities on the right side.

1. The **assets** list the firm's cash, inventory, property, plant and equipment, and any other investments the company has made.
2. The **liabilities** show the firm's obligations to its creditors.
3. Also shown with liabilities on the right side of the balance sheet is the *stockholders' equity*. **Stockholders' equity** (also called **shareholders' equity**), the difference between the firm's assets and liabilities, is an accounting measure of the firm's net worth. For Global, the stockholders' equity has two parts: (1) **common stock and paid-in surplus**, the amount that stockholders have directly invested in the firm through purchasing stock from the company and (2) **retained earnings**, which are profits made by the firm, but retained within the firm and reinvested in assets or held as cash. We will take a more detailed look at retained earnings in our discussion of the statement of cash flows later in this chapter.

The assets on the left side show how the firm uses its capital (its investments), and the information on the right side summarizes the sources of capital, or how the firm raises the money it needs. Because of the way stockholders' equity is calculated, the left and right sides must balance:

The Balance Sheet Identity

$$\text{Assets} = \text{Liabilities} + \text{Stockholders' Equity} \qquad (2.1)$$

In Table 2.1, total assets for 2016 ($170.1 million) are equal to total liabilities ($147.9 million) plus stockholders' equity ($22.2 million).

Let's examine Global's assets, liabilities, and stockholders' equity in more detail.

---

[2]In IFRS and recent U.S. GAAP pronouncements, the balance sheet is referred to as the *statement of financial position*.

TABLE 2.1

Global Corporation Balance Sheet for 2016 and 2015 ($ millions)

Assets	2016	2015	Liabilities and Stockholders' Equity	2016	2015
Current Assets			Current Liabilities		
Cash	23.2	20.5	Accounts payable	29.2	26.5
Accounts receivable	18.5	13.2	Notes payable/short-term debt	5.5	3.2
Inventories	15.3	14.3			
Total current assets	57.0	48.0	Total current liabilities	34.7	29.7
Long-Term Assets			Long-Term Liabilities		
Net property, plant, and equipment	113.1	80.9	Long-term debt	113.2	78.0
Total long-term assets	113.1	80.9	Total long-term liabilities	113.2	78.0
			Total Liabilities	147.9	107.7
			Stockholders' Equity		
			Common stock and paid-in surplus	8.0	8.0
			Retained earnings	14.2	13.2
			Total Stockholders' Equity	22.2	21.2
Total Assets	170.1	128.9	Total Liabilities and Stockholders' Equity	170.1	128.9

current assets Cash or assets that can be converted into cash within one year.

marketable securities Short-term, low-risk investments that can be easily sold and converted to cash.

accounts receivable Amounts owed to a firm by customers who have purchased goods or services on credit.

inventories A firm's raw materials as well as its work-in-progress and finished goods.

long-term assets Assets that produce tangible benefits for more than one year.

depreciation A yearly deduction a firm makes from the value of its fixed assets (other than land) over time, according to a depreciation schedule that depends on an asset's life span.

book value The acquisition cost of an asset less its accumulated depreciation.

Assets

In Table 2.1, Global's assets are divided into *current* and *long-term assets*. We discuss each in turn.

Current Assets. **Current assets** are either cash or assets that can be converted into cash within one year. This category includes:

1. Cash and other **marketable securities**, which are short-term, low-risk investments that can be easily sold and converted to cash (such as money market investments, like government debt, that mature within a year);

2. **Accounts receivable**, which are amounts owed to the firm by customers who have purchased goods or services on credit;

3. **Inventories**, which are composed of raw materials as well as work-in-progress and finished goods; and

4. Other current assets, which is a catch-all category that includes items such as prepaid expenses (such as rent or insurance).

Long-Term Assets. Assets such as real estate or machinery that produce tangible benefits for more than one year are called **long-term assets**. If Global spends $2 million on new equipment, this $2 million will be included with net property, plant, and equipment under long-term assets on the balance sheet. Because equipment tends to wear out or become obsolete over time, Global will reduce the value recorded for this equipment through a yearly deduction called **depreciation** according to a depreciation schedule that depends on an asset's life span. Depreciation is not an actual cash expense that the firm pays; it is a way of recognizing that buildings and equipment wear out and thus become less valuable the older they get. The **book value** of an asset, which is the value shown in the firm's financial statements, is equal to its acquisition cost less accumulated depreciation. The figures for net property, plant, and equipment show the total book value of these assets.

Other long-term assets can include such items as property not used in business operations, start-up costs in connection with a new business, trademarks and patents, and property held for sale. The sum of all the firms' assets is the total assets at the bottom of the left side of the balance sheet in Table 2.1.

Liabilities

We now examine the liabilities, shown on the right side of the balance sheet, which are divided into *current* and *long-term liabilities*.

Current Liabilities. Liabilities that will be satisfied within one year are known as **current liabilities**. They include:

current liabilities Liabilities that will be satisfied within one year.

accounts payable The amounts owed to creditors for products or services purchased with credit.

notes payable, short-term debt Loans that must be repaid in the next year.

1. **Accounts payable**, the amounts owed to suppliers for products or services purchased with credit.
2. **Notes payable** and **short-term debt**, loans that must be repaid in the next year. Any repayment of long-term debt that will occur within the next year would also be listed here as current maturities of long-term debt.
3. Accrual items, such as salary or taxes, that are owed but have not yet been paid, and deferred or unearned revenue, which is revenue that has been received for products or services that have not yet been delivered.

net working capital The difference between a firm's current assets and current liabilities that represents the capital available in the short term to run the business.

The difference between current assets and current liabilities is the firm's **net working capital**, the capital available in the short term to run the business. While notes payable and short-term debt are included in current liabilities, they are different from accounts payable and accrual items. Notes payable and short-term debt are related to financing decisions of the firm, while accounts payable and accruals arise from operating decisions of the firm. This distinction is important later when we see that financial managers generally try to keep these two decisions (operating and financing) separate.

$$\text{Net Working Capital} = \text{Current Assets} - \text{Current Liabilities} \tag{2.2}$$

For example, in 2016, Global's net working capital totaled $22.3 million ($57.0 million in current assets − $34.7 million in current liabilities). Firms with low (or negative) net working capital may face a shortage of funds. In such cases, the liabilities due in the short term exceed the company's cash and expected payments on receivables.

long-term debt Any loan or debt obligation with a maturity of more than a year.

Long-Term Liabilities. Long-term liabilities are liabilities that extend beyond one year. When a firm needs to raise funds to purchase an asset or make an investment, it may borrow those funds through a long-term loan. That loan would appear on the balance sheet as **long-term debt**, which is any loan or debt obligation with a maturity of more than a year.

Stockholders' Equity

book value of equity The difference between the book value of a firm's assets and its liabilities; also called *shareholders' equity* and *stockholders' equity*, it represents the net worth of a firm from an accounting perspective.

The sum of the current liabilities and long-term liabilities is total liabilities. The difference between the firm's assets and liabilities is the *stockholders' equity*; it is also called the **book value of equity** or *shareholders' equity*. As we stated earlier, it represents the net worth of the firm from an accounting perspective. The two main components are common stock and paid-in surplus and retained earnings. These two components form the book value of stockholders' ownership claims, stemming from their direct investment and reinvestment of profits.

Ideally, the balance sheet would provide us with an accurate assessment of the true value of the firm's equity. Unfortunately, this is unlikely to be the case. First, many of the assets listed on the balance sheet are valued based on their historical cost rather than their true value today. For example, an office building is listed on the balance sheet according to its historical cost less its accumulated depreciation. But the actual value of the office building today may be very different than this amount; in fact, if real estate prices went up it will be worth *more* than the amount the firm paid for it years ago. The same is true for other property, plant, and equipment: The true value today of an asset may be very different from, and even exceed, its book value. A second, and probably more important, problem is that *many of the firm's valuable assets are not captured on the balance sheet.* Consider, for example, the expertise of the firm's employees, the firm's reputation in the marketplace, the relationships with customers and suppliers, and the quality of the management team. All these assets add to the value of the firm but do not appear on the balance sheet. Although the book value of a firm's equity is not a good estimate of its true value as an ongoing firm, it is sometimes used as an estimate of the **liquidation value** of the firm, the value that would be left after its assets were sold and liabilities paid.

liquidation value The value of a firm after its assets are sold and liabilities paid.

Market Value Versus Book Value

For these reasons, the book value of equity is an inaccurate assessment of the actual value of the firm's equity. Thus, it is not surprising that it will often differ substantially from the amount investors are willing to pay for the equity. The total market value of a firm's equity equals the market price per share times the number of shares, referred to as the company's **market capitalization**. The market value of a stock does not depend on the historical cost of the firm's assets; instead, it depends on what investors expect those assets to produce in the future. To see the difference, think about what happens when a company like Boeing unveils a new plane. Investors' expectations about future cash flows from selling those planes increase the stock price immediately, elevating the market value of Boeing. However, the revenue from selling the planes will only be reflected in Boeing's financial statements when it actually sells them.

market capitalization The total market value of equity; equals the market price per share times the number of shares.

Finally, we note that the book value of equity can be negative (liabilities exceed assets), and that a negative book value of equity is not necessarily an indication of poor

---

EXAMPLE 2.1

Market Versus
Book Value

MyFinanceLab

PROBLEM

If Global has 3.6 million shares outstanding, and these shares are trading for a price of $10.00 per share, what is Global's market capitalization? How does the market capitalization compare to Global's book value of equity?

SOLUTION

PLAN

Market capitalization is equal to price per share times shares outstanding. We can find Global's book value of equity at the bottom of the right side of its balance sheet.

EXECUTE

Global's market capitalization is ($10.00/share) × (3.6 million shares) = $36 million. This market capitalization is significantly higher than Global's book value of equity of $22.2 million.

EVALUATE

Global must have sources of value that do not appear on the balance sheet. These include potential opportunities for growth, the quality of the management team, relationships with suppliers and customers, etc.

performance. Successful firms are often able to borrow in excess of the book value of their assets because creditors recognize that the market value of the assets is far higher. For example, in June 2005 Amazon.com had total liabilities of $2.6 billion and a book value of equity of −$64 million. At the same time, the market value of its equity was over $15 billion. Clearly, investors recognized that Amazon's assets were worth far more than the book value reported on the balance sheet. By 2016, several years of strong growth had brought its book value of equity to over $13 billion and its market value of equity to around $300 billion!

Market-to-Book Ratio

market-to-book ratio (price-to-book [P/B] ratio) The ratio of a firm's market (equity) capitalization to the book value of its stockholders' equity.

In Example 2.1, we compared the market and book values of Global's equity. A common way to make this comparison is to compute the **market-to-book ratio** (also called the **price-to-book [P/B] ratio**), which is the ratio of a firm's market capitalization to the book value of stockholders' equity.

$$\text{Market-to-Book Ratio} = \frac{\text{Market Value of Equity}}{\text{Book Value of Equity}} \qquad (2.3)$$

It is one of many financial ratios used to evaluate a firm. The market-to-book ratio for most successful firms substantially exceeds 1, indicating that the value of the firm's assets when put to use exceeds their historical cost (or liquidation value). The ratio will vary across firms due to differences in fundamental firm characteristics as well as the value added by management. Thus, this ratio is one way a company's stock price provides feedback to its managers on the market's assessment of their decisions.

In early-2016, AmeriServ Financial, Inc. (ASRV) had a market-to-book ratio of 0.57, a reflection of investors' assessment that many of AmeriServ's assets were unlikely to be profitable and were worth less than their book value. Citigroup's market-to-book ratio of 0.59 tells a similar story. Figure 2.1 shows that at the same time, the average market-to-book ratio for the financial services industry was about 1.9 and for large U.S. firms it was close to 3. In contrast, consider that Amazon.com, Inc. (AMZN) had a market-to-book ratio of over 20, and the average for technology firms was over 8. Analysts often classify firms with low market-to-book ratios as **value stocks**, and those with high market-to-book ratios as **growth stocks**.

value stocks Firms with low market-to-book ratios.

growth stocks Firms with high market-to-book ratios.

Enterprise Value

enterprise value The total market value of a firm's equity and debt, less the value of its cash and marketable securities. It measures the value of the firm's underlying business.

A firm's market capitalization measures the market value of the firm's equity, or the value that remains after the firm has paid its debts. So it includes any cash the firm holds. But what if you are interested in just the value of the business itself? The **enterprise value** of a firm assesses the value of the underlying business assets, unencumbered by debt and separate from any cash and marketable securities. We compute it as follows:

$$\text{Enterprise Value} = \text{Market Value of Equity} + \text{Debt} - \text{Cash} \qquad (2.4)$$

For example, given its market capitalization from Example 2.1, Global's enterprise value in 2016 is 36 + 118.7 − 23.2 = $131.5 million. We can interpret the enterprise value as the cost to take over the business. That is, it would cost 36 + 118.7 = $154.7 million to buy all of Global's equity and pay off its debts. Because we would acquire Global's $23.2 million in cash (which can be used to pay off Global's debt), the net cost is only 154.7 − 23.2 = $131.5 million.

FIGURE 2.1

Market-to-Book
Ratios in 2016

This figure presents market-to-book ratios of different firms and groups of firms in 2016. Firms that might be classified as value stocks (low market-to-book ratios) are in red and those that might be classified as growth stocks (high market-to-book ratios) are in blue.

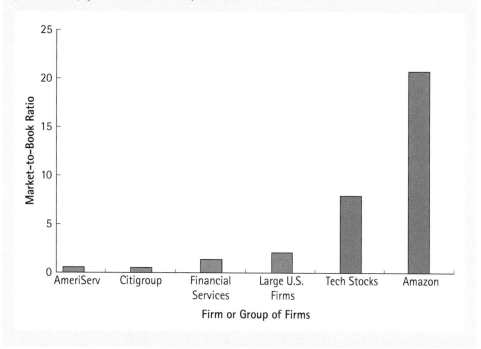

EXAMPLE 2.2

Computing
Enterprise Value

MyFinanceLab

PROBLEM

In June 2013, H.J. Heinz Co. (HNZ) had 320.7 million shares outstanding, a share price of $72.36, a book value of debt of $4.98 billion, and cash of $1.1 billion. What was Heinz's market capitalization (its market value of equity)? What was its enterprise value?

SOLUTION

PLAN

Share Price	$72.36
Shares Outstanding	320.7 million
Cash	$1.10 billion
Debt (book)	$4.98 billion

We will solve the problem using Eq. 2.4: Enterprise Value = Market Value of Equity + Debt − Cash. We can compute the market capitalization by multiplying the share price times the number of shares outstanding. We are given the amount of cash and the amount of debt.

EXECUTE

Heinz had a market capitalization of $72.36/share × 320.7 million shares = $23.21 billion. Thus, Heinz's enterprise value was 23.21 + 4.98 − 1.10 = $27.09 billion.

EVALUATE

The value of Heinz's underlying business, separate from any cash it holds, should be equal to the total value of the financial claims (equity and debt) on that business, which is its enterprise value of $27.09 billion.

3. What is depreciation designed to capture?

4. The book value of a company's assets usually does not equal the market value of those assets. What are some reasons for this difference?

2.3   The Income Statement

income statement A list of a firm's revenues and expenses over a period of time.

net income or earnings The last or "bottom" line of a firm's income statement that is a measure of the firm's income over a given period of time.

When you want someone to get to the point, you might ask them for the "bottom line." This expression comes from the *income statement*. The **income statement** lists the firm's revenues and expenses over a period of time. The last or "bottom" line of the income statement shows the firm's **net income**, which is a measure of its profitability during the period. The income statement is sometimes called a *profit and loss* or *P&L statement*, and the net income is also referred to as the firm's **earnings**. In this section, we examine the components of the income statement in detail and introduce ratios we can use to analyze this data.

Earnings Calculations

Whereas the balance sheet shows the firm's assets and liabilities at a given point in time, the income statement shows the flow of revenues and expenses generated by those assets and liabilities between two dates. Table 2.2 shows Global's income statement for 2016 and 2015. We examine each category on the statement.

gross profit The third line of an income statement that represents the difference between a firm's sales revenues and its costs.

Gross Profit. The first two lines of the income statement list the revenues from sales of products and the costs incurred to make and sell the products. Note that in accounting, the terms *revenues* and *net sales* are equivalent. Net sales is simply gross sales minus any returns, discounts, and allowances. We will simply use the term *sales* from here forward. The third line is **gross profit**, the difference between sales revenues and the cost of sales.

TABLE 2.2

Global Corporation's Income Statement Sheet for 2016 and 2015

GLOBAL CORPORATION Income Statement Year ended December 31 (in $ millions)		
	2016	**2015**
Net sales	186.7	176.1
Cost of sales	−153.4	−147.3
Gross Profit	33.3	28.8
Selling, general, and administrative expenses	−13.5	−13
Research and development	−8.2	−7.6
Depreciation and amortization	−1.2	−1.1
Operating Income	10.4	7.1
Other income	—	—
Earnings Before Interest and Taxes (EBIT)	10.4	7.1
Interest income (expense)	−7.7	−4.6
Pretax Income	2.7	2.5
Taxes	−0.7	−0.6
Net Income	2.0	1.9
Earnings per share:	$0.56	$0.53
Diluted earnings per share:	$0.53	$0.50

Operating Expenses. The next group of items is operating expenses. These are expenses from the ordinary course of running the business that are not directly related to producing the goods or services being sold. They include administrative expenses and overhead, salaries, marketing costs, and research and development expenses. The third type of operating expense, depreciation and amortization (a charge that captures the change in value of acquired assets), represents an estimate of the costs that arise from wear and tear or obsolescence of the firm's assets.[3] It is not an actual cash expense. The firm's gross profit less its operating expenses is called **operating income**.

operating income
A firm's gross profit less its operating expenses.

Earnings Before Interest and Taxes. We next include other sources of income or expenses that arise from activities that are not the central part of a company's business. Cash flows from the firm's financial investments are one example of other income that would be listed here. After we have adjusted for other sources of income or expenses, we have the firm's earnings before interest and taxes, or **EBIT**.

EBIT A firm's earnings before interest and taxes are deducted.

Pretax and Net Income. From EBIT, we deduct the interest paid on outstanding debt to compute Global's pretax income, and then we deduct corporate taxes to determine the firm's net income.

Net income represents the total earnings of the firm's equity holders. It is often reported on a per-share basis as the firm's **earnings per share (EPS)**, which we compute by dividing net income by the total number of shares outstanding:

earnings per share (EPS) A firm's net income divided by the total number of shares outstanding.

$$\text{EPS} = \frac{\text{Net Income}}{\text{Shares Outstanding}} = \frac{\$2.0 \text{ million}}{3.6 \text{ million shares}} = \$0.56 \text{ per share} \qquad (2.5)$$

Although Global has only 3.6 million shares outstanding as of the end of 2016 (from Example 2.1), the number of shares outstanding may grow if Global has made commitments that would cause it to issue more shares. Consider these two examples:

stock options The right to buy a certain number of shares of stock by a specific date at a specific price.

1. Suppose Global compensates its employees or executives with **stock options** that give the holder the right to buy a certain number of shares by a specific date at a specific price. If employees "exercise" these options, the company issues new stock and the number of shares outstanding would grow.

2. The number of shares may also grow if the firm issues **convertible bonds**, a form of debt that can be converted into shares of common stock.

convertible bonds Corporate bonds with a provision that gives the bondholder an option to convert each bond owned into a fixed number of shares of common stock.

In the cases of stock options and convertible bonds, because there will be more total shares to divide the same earnings, this growth in the number of shares is referred to as **dilution**. Firms disclose the potential for dilution from options they have awarded by reporting **diluted EPS**, which shows the earnings per share the company would have if the stock options were exercised. For example, if Global has awarded options for 200,000 shares of stock to its key executives, its diluted EPS is $2.0 million/3.8 million shares = $0.53.

dilution An increase in the total number of shares that will divide a fixed amount of earnings.

diluted EPS The earnings per share a company would have based on the total number of shares including the effects of all stock options and convertible bonds.

EBITDA

As will become clear when we discuss the Statement of Cash Flows in the next section, neither EBIT nor net income are the same as the firm's cash flow. So, financial analysts often compute a firm's earnings before interest, taxes, depreciation, and amortization, or **EBITDA**. Because depreciation and amortization are not cash expenses for the firm,

---

[3]Only certain types of amortization are deductible as a pretax expense (e.g., amortization of the cost of an acquired patent). Amortization of goodwill is not a pretax expense and is generally included as an extraordinary item after taxes are deducted.

EBITDA A computation of a firm's earnings before interest, taxes, depreciation, and amortization are deducted.

EBITDA reflects the cash a firm has earned from its operations. If we add back Global's depreciation and amortization to its EBIT, we find that its EBITDA in 2016 was $10.4 + 1.2 = \$11.6$ million.

CONCEPT CHECK

5. What do a firm's earnings measure?
6. What is dilution?

2.4   The Statement of Cash Flows

The income statement provides a measure of the firm's profit over a given time period. However, it does not indicate the amount of *cash* the firm has earned. There are two reasons that net income does not correspond to cash earned. First, there are non-cash entries on the income statement, such as depreciation and amortization. Second, certain uses, such as the purchase of a building or expenditures on inventory, and sources of cash, such as the collection of accounts receivable, are not reported on the income statement. The firm's **statement of cash flows** utilizes the information from the income statement and balance sheet to determine how much cash the firm has generated, and how that cash has been allocated, during a set period. Cash is important: It is needed to pay bills and maintain operations and is the source of any return of investment for investors. Thus, from the perspective of an investor attempting to value the firm or a financial manager concerned about cash flows (vs. earnings), the statement of cash flows provides what may be the most important information of the four financial statements.

statement of cash flows An accounting statement that shows how a firm has used the cash it earned during a set period.

The statement of cash flows is divided into three sections: operating activities, investment activities, and financing activities. These sections roughly correspond to the three major jobs of the financial manager.

1. *Operating activities* starts with net income from the income statement. It then adjusts this number by adding back all non-cash entries related to the firm's operating activities.
2. *Investment activities* lists the cash used for investment.
3. *Financing activities* shows the flow of cash between the firm and its investors.

Global's statement of cash flows is shown in Table 2.3. In this section, we take a close look at each component of the statement of cash flows.

Operating Activity

The first section of Global's statement of cash flows adjusts net income by all non-cash items related to operating activity. For instance, depreciation is deducted when computing net income, but it is not an actual cash expense. Thus, we add it back to net income when determining the amount of cash the firm has generated. Similarly, we add back any other non-cash expenses (for example, deferred taxes).

Next, we adjust for changes to net working capital that arise from changes to accounts receivable, accounts payable, or inventory. When a firm sells a product, it records the revenue as income even though it may not receive the cash from that sale immediately. Instead, it may grant the customer credit and let the customer pay in the future. The customer's obligation adds to the firm's accounts receivable. We use the following guidelines to adjust for changes in working capital:

1. Accounts receivable: When a sale is recorded as part of net income, but the cash has not yet been received from the customer, we must adjust the cash flows by *deducting* the increases in accounts receivable. This increase represents additional lending by the firm to its customers and it reduces the cash available to the firm.

2. Accounts payable: We *add* increases in accounts payable. Accounts payable represents borrowing by the firm from its suppliers. This borrowing increases the cash available to the firm.

3. Inventory: Finally, we *deduct* increases in inventory. Increases in inventory are not recorded as an expense and do not contribute to net income (the cost of the goods are only included in net income when the goods are actually sold). However, the cost of increasing inventory is a cash expense for the firm and must be deducted.

Working capital adjustments address the difference between the time when sales and costs are recorded on the income statement and when the cash actually goes in and out of the firm. For example, Table 2.3 shows that in 2016 we *subtracted* the $5.3 million increase in accounts receivable from net income as part of the operating cash flow calculation. What happened? From Table 2.2, we see that Global had $10.6 million more in sales in 2016 than

TABLE 2.3

Global Corporation's Statement of Cash Flows for 2016 and 2015

GLOBAL CORPORATION **Statement of Cash Flows** **Year ended December 31 (in $ millions)**		
	2016	**2015**
Operating activities		
Net income	2.0	1.9
Depreciation and amortization	1.2	1.1
Cash effect of changes in		
Accounts receivable	−5.3	−0.3
Accounts payable	2.7	−0.5
Inventory	−1.0	−1.0
Cash from operating activities	−0.4	1.2
Investment activities		
Capital expenditures	−33.4	−4.0
Acquisitions and other investing activity	—	—
Cash from investing activities	−33.4	−4.0
Financing activities		
Dividends paid	−1.0	−1.0
Sale or purchase of stock	—	—
Increase in short-term borrowing	2.3	3.0
Increase in long-term borrowing	35.2	2.5
Cash from financing activities	36.5	4.5
Change in cash and cash equivalents	2.7	1.7

in 2015. However, from Table 2.1, we also see that Global's accounts receivable increased from $13.2 million in 2015 to $18.5 million in 2016. So, even though Global's sales were up considerably, it has not yet collected all the cash flow for those sales—instead, Global's customers owe it $5.3 million more at the end of 2016 than they did at the end of 2015. Because the statement of cash flows starts with net income, which includes sales for which Global has not yet been paid, we deduct the additional $5.3 million in sales Global is still owed when computing the actual cash flows it generated.

We must make a similar adjustment for inventory. Global does not record the cost of the inventory until it is sold, when it is included in the cost of goods sold. However, when it actually pays for the inventory, cash has flowed out of Global, decreasing operating cash flow. The opposite is true for accounts payable—Global has recorded additional expenses without actually paying for them yet. Those expenses reduce net income, but do not represent cash outflows.

Finally, we add depreciation to net income before calculating operating cash flow. Depreciation is an accounting adjustment to book value that is an expense, but not a cash outflow. That is, when Global's property, plant, and equipment depreciate by $1.2 million, it does not literally cost Global $1.2 million in cash flow. Because this is an expense that reduces net income, but not an actual cash outflow, we must add it back to calculate cash flow. We will talk more about depreciation when we do capital budgeting in Chapter 9. All these adjustments mean that cash flow can be very different from net income. Although Global showed positive net income on the income statement, it actually had a negative $0.4 million cash flow from operating activity, in large part because of the increase in accounts receivable.

EXAMPLE 2.3 The Impact of Depreciation on Cash Flow MyFinanceLab	## PROBLEM Suppose Global had an additional $1 million depreciation expense in 2016. If Global's tax rate on pretax income is 26%, what would be the impact of this expense on Global's earnings? How would it impact Global's cash at the end of the year? ## SOLUTION ### PLAN Depreciation is an operating expense, so Global's operating income, EBIT, and pretax income would be affected. With a tax rate of 26%, Global's tax bill will decrease by 26 cents for every dollar that pretax income is reduced. In order to determine how Global's cash would be impacted, we have to determine the effect of the additional depreciation on cash flows. Recall that depreciation is not an actual cash outflow, even though it is treated as an expense, so the only effect on cash flow is through the reduction in taxes. ### EXECUTE Global's operating income, EBIT, and pretax income would fall by $1 million because of the $1 million in additional operating expense due to depreciation. This $1 million decrease in pretax income would reduce Global's tax bill by 26% × $1 million = $0.26 million. Therefore, net income would fall by $1 − $0.26 = $0.74 million. On the statement of cash flows, net income would fall by $0.74 million, but we would add back the additional depreciation of $1 million because it is not a cash expense. Thus, cash from operating activities would rise by −$0.74 + 1 = $0.26 million. Therefore, Global's cash balance at the end of the year would increase by $0.26 million, the amount of the tax savings that resulted from the additional depreciation deduction. ### EVALUATE The increase in cash balance comes completely from the reduction in taxes. Because Global pays $0.26 million less in taxes even though its cash expenses have not increased, it has $0.26 million more in cash at the end of the year.

Investment Activity

capital expenditures
Purchases of new property, plant, and equipment.

The next section of the statement of cash flows shows the cash required for investment activities. Purchases of new property, plant, and equipment are **capital expenditures**. Recall that capital expenditures do not appear immediately as expenses on the income statement. Instead, the firm depreciates these assets and deducts depreciation expenses over time. To determine the firm's cash flow, we already added back depreciation because it is not an actual cash expense. Now, we subtract the actual capital expenditure that the firm made. Similarly, we also deduct other assets purchased or investments made by the firm, such as acquisitions. In Table 2.3, we see that in 2016, Global spent $33.4 million in cash on investing activities. This can be confirmed by adding the depreciation amount of $1.2 from Table 2.2 to the change in long-term assets of ($113.1 – $80.9) from Table 2.1.

Financing Activity

The last section of the statement of cash flows shows the cash flows from financing activities. Dividends paid to shareholders are a cash outflow. Global paid $1 million to its shareholders as dividends in 2016.

The difference between a firm's net income and the amount it spends on dividends is referred to as the firm's retained earnings for that year:

$$\text{Retained Earnings} = \text{Net Income} - \text{Dividends} \qquad (2.6)$$

payout ratio The ratio of a firm's dividends to its net income.

Global retained $2 million – $1 million = $1 million, or 50% of its earnings in 2016. This makes its *payout ratio* for 2016 equal to 50%. A firm's **payout ratio** is the ratio of its dividends to its net income:

$$\text{Payout Ratio} = \frac{\text{Dividends}}{\text{Net Income}} \qquad (2.7)$$

Also listed under financing activity is any cash the company received from the sale of its own stock, or cash spent buying (repurchasing) its own stock. Global did not issue or repurchase stock during this period.

The last items to include in this section result from changes to Global's short-term and long-term borrowing. Global raised money by issuing debt, so the increases in short-term and long-term borrowing represent cash inflows. The last line of the statement of cash flows combines the cash flows from these three activities to calculate the overall change in the firm's cash balance over the period of the statement. In this case, Global had cash inflows of $2.7 million in 2016, which matches the change in cash from 2015 to 2016 shown earlier in the balance sheet. By looking at the statement in Table 2.3 as a whole, we can determine that Global chose to borrow (mainly in the form of long-term debt) to cover the cost of its investment and operating activities. Although the firm's cash balance has increased, Global's negative operating cash flows and relatively high expenditures on investment activities might give investors some reasons for concern. If this pattern continues, Global will need to raise new external capital to remain in business.

CONCEPT CHECK

7. Why does a firm's net income not correspond to cash earned?
8. What are the components of the statement of cash flows?

2.5 Other Financial Statement Information

The most important elements of a firm's financial statements are the balance sheet, income statement, and the statement of cash flows, which we have already discussed. Several other pieces of information contained in the financial statements warrant brief mention: the *statement of stockholders' equity*, the *management discussion and analysis*, and *notes to the financial statements*.

Statement of Stockholders' Equity

statement of stockholders' equity An accounting statement that breaks down the stockholders' equity computed on the balance sheet into the amount that came from issuing new shares versus retained earnings.

The **statement of stockholders' equity** breaks down the stockholders' equity computed on the balance sheet into the amount that came from issuing shares (par value plus paid-in capital) versus retained earnings. Because the book value of stockholders' equity is not a useful assessment of value for financial purposes, financial managers use the statement of stockholders' equity infrequently (so we will skip the computational details here). We can, however, determine the change in stockholders' equity using information from the firm's other financial statements as follows:[4]

$$\text{Change in Stockholders' Equity} = \text{Retained Earnings} + \text{Net Sales of Stock}$$
$$= \text{Net Income} - \text{Dividends} + \text{Sales of Stock}$$
$$- \text{Repurchases of Stock} \qquad (2.8)$$

For example, because Global had no stock sales or repurchases, its stockholders' equity increased by the amount of its retained earnings, or $1.0 million, in 2016. Note that this result matches the change in stockholders' equity shown earlier on Global's balance sheet.

Management Discussion and Analysis

management discussion and analysis (MD&A) A preface to the financial statements in which a company's management discusses the recent year (or quarter), providing a background on the company and any significant events that may have occurred.

The **management discussion and analysis (MD&A)** is a preface to the financial statements in which the company's management discusses the recent year (or quarter), providing a background on the company and any significant events that may have occurred. Management may also discuss the coming year, and outline goals and new projects.

Management must also discuss any important risks that the firm faces or issues that may affect the firm's liquidity or resources. Management is also required to disclose any **off-balance sheet transactions**, which are transactions or arrangements that can have a material impact on the firm's future performance yet do not appear on the balance sheet. For example, if a firm has made guarantees that it will compensate a buyer for losses related to an asset purchased from the firm, these guarantees represent a potential future liability for the firm that must be disclosed as part of the MD&A.

off-balance sheet transactions Transactions or arrangements that can have a material impact on a firm's future performance yet do not appear on the balance sheet.

Notes to the Financial Statements

In addition to the four financial statements, companies provide extensive notes with additional details on the information provided in the statements. For example, the notes document important accounting assumptions that were used in preparing the statements. They often provide information specific to a firm's subsidiaries or its separate product lines. They show the details of the firm's stock-based compensation plans for employees and the different types of debt the firm has outstanding. Details of acquisitions, spin-offs, leases, taxes, and risk management activities are also given. The information provided in the notes is often very important to a full interpretation of the firm's financial statements.

CONCEPT CHECK

9. Where do off-balance sheet transactions appear in a firm's financial statements?
10. What information do the notes to financial statements provide?

2.6 Financial Statement Analysis

Investors often use accounting statements to evaluate a firm in one of two ways:

1. Compare the firm with itself by analyzing how the firm has changed over time.
2. Compare the firm to other similar firms using a common set of financial ratios.

---

[4]Sales of stock would also include any stock-based compensation.

In this section, we will describe the most commonly used ratios—related to profitability, liquidity, asset efficiency, working capital, interest coverage, leverage, valuation, and operating returns—and explain how each one is used in practice.

Profitability Ratios

We introduce three profitability ratios: *gross margin*, *operating margin*, and *net profit margin*.

gross margin The ratio of gross profit to revenues (sales), it reflects the ability of the company to sell a product for more than the sum of the direct costs of making it.

Gross Margin. The **gross margin** of a firm is the ratio of gross profit to revenues (sales):

$$\text{Gross Margin} = \frac{\text{Gross Profit}}{\text{Sales}} \qquad (2.9)$$

The gross margin simply reflects the ability of the company to sell a product for more than the sum of the direct costs of making it. All of the firm's other expenses of doing business (those not directly related to producing the goods sold) must be covered by this margin. In 2016, Global's gross profit was $33.3 million and its sales were $186.7 million, for a gross margin of 33.3/186.7 = 17.84%.

operating margin The ratio of operating income to revenues, it reveals how much a company has earned from each dollar of sales before deducting interest and taxes.

Operating Margin. Because operating income reflects all of the expenses of doing business, another important profitability ratio is the **operating margin**, the ratio of operating income to revenues:

$$\text{Operating Margin} = \frac{\text{Operating Income}}{\text{Sales}} \qquad (2.10)$$

The operating margin reveals how much a company earns before interest and taxes from each dollar of sales. Global's operating margin in 2016 was 10.4/186.7 = 5.57%, an increase from its 2015 operating margin of 7.1/176.1 = 4.03%. By comparing operating margins across firms within an industry, we can assess the relative efficiency of firms' operations. For example, in 2015, United Continental Holdings (UAL) had an operating margin of 13.64% (i.e., they gained 13.64 cents for each dollar in revenues). However, competitor Alaska Air Group (ALK) had an operating margin of 23.19%.

Differences in operating margins can also result from differences in strategy. For example, in 2016, Walmart Stores had an operating margin of 5% while higher-end retailer Macy's had an operating margin of 9%. In this case, Walmart's lower operating margin is not a result of its inefficiency but is part of its strategy of offering lower prices to sell common products in high volume. Indeed, Walmart's sales were more than 17 times higher than those of Macy's.

net profit margin The ratio of net income to revenues, it shows the fraction of each dollar in revenues that is available to equity holders after the firm pays its expenses, plus interest and taxes.

Net Profit Margin. A firm's **net profit margin** is the ratio of net income to revenues:

$$\text{Net Profit Margin} = \frac{\text{Net Income}}{\text{Sales}} \qquad (2.11)$$

The net profit margin shows the fraction of each dollar in revenues that is available to equity holders after the firm pays its expenses, interest, and taxes. Global's net profit margin in 2016 was 2.0/186.7 = 1.07%. Differences in net profit margins can be due to differences in efficiency, but they can also result from differences in leverage (the firm's reliance on debt financing), which determines the amount of interest payments.

Liquidity Ratios

current ratio The ratio of current assets to current liabilities.

Creditors often compare a firm's current assets and current liabilities to assess whether the firm has sufficient working capital to meet its short-term needs. This comparison is sometimes summarized in the firm's **current ratio**, the ratio of current assets to current liabilities. A more stringent test of the firm's liquidity is the **quick ratio ("acid-test" ratio)**, which compares only cash and "near cash" assets, such as short-term investments and accounts receivable, to current liabilities.

quick ratio ("acid-test ratio") The ratio of current assets other than inventory to current liabilities.

$$\text{Current Ratio} = \frac{\text{Current Assets}}{\text{Current Liabilities}} \qquad (2.12)$$

$$\text{Quick Ratio} = \frac{\text{Current Assets} - \text{Inventory}}{\text{Current Liabilities}} \qquad (2.13)$$

In 2016, Global's quick ratio was $(57.0 - 15.3)/34.7 = 1.20$. A higher current or quick ratio implies less risk of the firm experiencing a cash shortfall in the near future. A reason to exclude inventory is that an increase in the current ratio that results from an unusual increase in inventory could be an indicator that the firm is having difficulty selling its products.

Ultimately, firms need cash to pay employees and meet other obligations. Running out of cash can be very costly for a firm, so firms often gauge their cash position by calculating the **cash ratio**, which is the most stringent liquidity ratio:

cash ratio The ratio of cash to current liabilities.

$$\text{Cash Ratio} = \frac{\text{Cash}}{\text{Current Liabilities}} \qquad (2.14)$$

Asset Efficiency

asset turnover The ratio of sales to total assets.

A financial manager can use the combined information in the firm's income statement and balance sheet to gauge how efficiently his or her firm is utilizing its assets. A first broad measure of efficiency is **asset turnover**, the ratio of sales to total assets:

$$\text{Asset Turnover} = \frac{\text{Sales}}{\text{Total Assets}} \qquad (2.15)$$

Low values of asset turnover indicate that the firm is not generating much revenue (sales) per dollar of assets. In 2016, Global's $170.1 million in assets generated $186.7 million in sales, for an asset turnover ratio of 1.1 (= $186.7/$170.1). Since total assets includes assets, such as cash, that are not directly involved in generating sales, Global's manager might also look at Global's fixed asset turnover, which is equal to sales divided by fixed assets:

$$\text{Fixed Asset Turnover} = \frac{\text{Sales}}{\text{Fixed Assets}} \qquad (2.16)$$

accounts receivable days (average collection period or days sales outstanding) An expression of a firm's accounts receivable in terms of the number of days' worth of sales that the accounts receivable represents.

Global's fixed assets in 2016 were $113.1 million worth of property, plant, and equipment, yielding a fixed asset turnover of 1.7 (= $186.7/$113.1). Low asset turnover ratios indicate that the firm is generating relatively few sales given the amount of assets it employs.

Working Capital Ratios

Global's managers might be further interested in how efficiently they are managing their net working capital. We can express the firm's accounts receivable in terms of the number of days' worth of sales that it represents, called the **accounts receivable days, average collection period**, or **days sales outstanding:**[5]

$$\text{Accounts Receivable Days} = \frac{\text{Accounts Receivable}}{\text{Average Daily Sales}} \qquad (2.17)$$

accounts payable days An expression of a firm's accounts payable in terms of the number of days' worth of cost of goods sold that the accounts payable represents.

Given average daily sales of $186.7 million/365 = $0.51 million in 2016, Global's receivables of $18.5 million represent 18.5/0.51 = 36 days' worth of sales. In other words, Global takes a little over one month to collect payment from its customers, on average. In 2015, Global's accounts receivable represented only 27.5 days worth of sales. Although the number of receivable days can fluctuate seasonally, a significant unexplained increase could be a cause for concern (perhaps indicating the firm is doing a poor job collecting from its customers or is trying to boost sales by offering generous credit terms). Similar ratios exist for accounts payable and inventory. Those ratios are called **accounts payable days** (accounts payable divided by average daily cost of goods sold) and **inventory days** (inventory divided by average daily cost of goods sold).

inventory days An expression of a firm's inventory in terms of the number of days' worth of cost of goods sold that the inventory represents.

We can also compute how efficiently firms use inventory. The **inventory turnover ratio** is equal to the cost of goods sold divided by either the latest cost of inventory or the average inventory over the year. We use the cost of goods sold because that is how inventory costs are reflected on the income statement. It is also common to use sales in the numerator to make the ratio more like the asset turnover ratios.

inventory turnover ratio The cost of goods sold divided by either the latest cost of inventory or the average inventory over the year, it shows how efficiently companies turn their inventory into sales.

$$\text{Inventory Turnover} = \frac{\text{Cost of Goods Sold}}{\text{Inventory}} \qquad (2.18)$$

As with the other ratios in this section, a normal level for this ratio can vary substantially for different industries, although a higher level (more dollars of sales per dollar of inventory) is generally better.

EXAMPLE 2.4

Computing Working Capital Ratios

MyFinanceLab

PROBLEM

Compute Global's accounts payable days, inventory days, and inventory turnover for 2016.

SOLUTION

PLAN AND ORGANIZE

Working capital ratios require information from both the balance sheet and the income statement. For these ratios, we need inventory and accounts payable from the balance sheet and cost of goods sold from the income statement (often listed as cost of sales).

Inventory = 15.3, Accounts payable = 29.2, Cost of goods sold (cost of sales) = 153.4

EXECUTE

$$\text{Accounts payable days} = \frac{\text{Accounts Payable}}{\text{Average Daily Cost of Goods Sold}} = \frac{29.2}{(153.4/365)} = 69.48$$

$$\text{Inventory days} = \frac{\text{Inventory}}{\text{Average Daily Cost of Goods Sold}} = \frac{15.3}{(153.4/365)} = 36.40$$

$$\text{Inventory turnover} = \frac{\text{Cost of Goods Sold}}{\text{Inventory}} = \frac{153.4}{15.3} = 10.03$$

(Continued)

---

[5]Accounts receivable days can also be calculated based on the average accounts receivable at the end of the current and prior years.

EVALUATE

Assuming that Global's accounts payable at year-end on its balance sheet is representative of the normal amount during the year, Global is able, on average, to take about 69.5 days to pay its suppliers. This compares well with the 27.5 days we calculated that it waits on average to be paid (its accounts receivable days). Global typically takes 36 days to sell its inventory. Note that inventory turnover and inventory days tell us the same thing in different ways—if it takes Global about 36 days to sell its inventory, then it turns over its inventory about 10 times per 365-day year. In Chapter 19 on working capital management, we'll see how a company's receivable, inventory, and payable days make up its operating cycle.

Interest Coverage Ratios

interest coverage ratio or times interest earned (TIE) ratio An assessment by lenders of a firm's leverage, it is equal to a measure of earnings divided by interest.

Lenders often assess a firm's leverage by computing an **interest coverage ratio**, also known as a **times interest earned (TIE) ratio**, which is equal to a measure of earnings divided by interest. Financial managers watch these ratios carefully because they assess how easily the firm will be able to cover its interest payments. There is no one accepted measure of earnings for these ratios; it is common to consider operating income, EBIT, or EBITDA as a multiple of the firm's interest expenses. When this ratio is high, it indicates that the firm is earning much more than is necessary to meet its required interest payments.

EXAMPLE 2.5

Computing Interest Coverage Ratios

MyFinanceLab

PROBLEM

Assess Global's ability to meet its interest obligations by calculating interest coverage ratios using both EBIT and EBITDA.

SOLUTION

PLAN AND ORGANIZE

Gather the EBIT, depreciation, and amortization and interest expense for each year from Global's income statement.

$$2015: \text{EBIT} = 7.1, \quad \text{EBITDA} = 7.1 + 1.1, \quad \text{Interest expense} = 4.6$$

$$2016: \text{EBIT} = 10.4, \quad \text{EBITDA} = 10.4 + 1.2, \quad \text{Interest expense} = 7.7$$

EXECUTE

In 2015 and 2016, Global had the following interest coverage ratios:

$$2015: \frac{\text{EBIT}}{\text{Interest}} = \frac{7.1}{4.6} = 1.54 \quad \text{and} \quad \frac{\text{EBITDA}}{\text{Interest}} = \frac{7.1 + 1.1}{4.6} = 1.78$$

$$2016: \frac{\text{EBIT}}{\text{Interest}} = \frac{10.4}{7.7} = 1.35 \quad \text{and} \quad \frac{\text{EBITDA}}{\text{Interest}} = \frac{10.4 + 1.2}{7.7} = 1.51$$

EVALUATE

The coverage ratios indicate that Global is generating enough cash to cover its interest obligations. However, Global's low—and declining—interest coverage could be a source of concern for its creditors.

Leverage Ratios

leverage A measure of the extent to which a firm relies on debt as a source of financing.

Another important piece of information that we can learn from a firm's balance sheet is the firm's **leverage**, or the extent to which it relies on debt as a source of financing. The **debt-equity ratio** is a common ratio used to assess a firm's leverage that we calculate by

debt-equity ratio The ratio of a firm's total amount of short- and long-term debt (including current maturities) to the value of its equity, which may be calculated based on market or book values.

dividing the total amount of short- and long-term debt (including current maturities) by the total stockholders' equity:

$$\text{Debt-Equity Ratio} = \frac{\text{Total Debt}}{\text{Total Equity}} \qquad (2.19)$$

We can calculate this ratio using either book or market values for equity and debt. From Table 2.1, Global's debt in 2016 includes notes payable ($5.5 million) and long-term debt ($113.2 million), for a total of $118.7 million. Therefore, using the book value of equity, its *book* debt-equity ratio is 118.7/22.2 = 5.3. Note the large increase from 2015, when the book debt-equity ratio was only (3.2 + 78)/21.2 = 3.8.

Because of the difficulty interpreting the book value of equity, the book debt-equity ratio is not especially useful. It is more informative to compare the firm's debt to the market value of its equity. Global's debt-equity ratio in 2016, using the market value of equity (from Example 2.1), is 118.7/36 = 3.3, which means Global's debt is a bit more than triple the market value of its equity.[6] As we will see later in the text, a firm's *market* debt-equity ratio has important consequences for the risk and return of its stock.

debt-to-capital ratio The ratio of total debt to total debt plus total equity.

We can also calculate the fraction of the firm financed by debt in terms of its **debt-to-capital ratio**:

$$\text{Debt-to-Capital Ratio} = \frac{\text{Total Debt}}{\text{Total Equity} + \text{Total Debt}} \qquad (2.20)$$

Again, this ratio can be computed using book or market values.

While leverage increases the risk to the firm's equity holders, firms may also hold cash reserves in order to reduce risk. Thus, another useful measure to consider is the firm's **net debt**, or debt in excess of its cash reserves:

net debt Debt in excess of a firm's cash reserves.

$$\text{Net Debt} = \text{Total Debt} - \text{Excess Cash \& Short-Term Investments} \qquad (2.21)$$

To understand why net debt may be a more relevant measure of leverage, consider a firm with more cash than debt outstanding: Because such a firm could pay off its debts immediately using its available cash, it has not increased its risk and has no effective leverage.

Analogous to the debt-to-capital ratio, we can use the concept of net debt to compute the firm's **debt-to-enterprise value ratio**:

debt-to-enterprise value ratio The ratio of a firm's net debt to its enterprise value.

$$\text{Debt-to-Enterprise Value Ratio} = \frac{\text{Net Debt}}{\text{Market Value of Equity} + \text{Net Debt}}$$

$$= \frac{\text{Net Debt}}{\text{Enterprise Value}} \qquad (2.22)$$

Given Global's 2016 cash balance of $23.2 million, and total long- and short-term debt of $118.7 million, its net debt is 118.7 − 23.2 = $95.5 million.[7] Given its market value of equity of $36.0 million, Global's enterprise value in 2016 is 36.0 + 95.5 = $131.5 million, and thus its debt-to-enterprise value ratio is 95.5/131.5 = 72.6%. That is, 72.6% of Global's underlying business activity is financed via debt.

---

[6]In this calculation, we have compared the market value of equity to the book value of debt. Strictly speaking, it would be best to use the market value of debt. But because the market value of debt is generally not very different from its book value, this distinction is often ignored in practice.

[7]While net debt should ideally be calculated by deducting cash in excess of the firm's operating needs, absent additional information, it is typical in practice to deduct all cash on the balance sheet.

equity multiplier A
measure of leverage equal
to total assets divided by
total equity.

A final measure of leverage is a firm's **equity multiplier**, measured in book value terms as Total Assets/Book Value of Equity. As we will see shortly, this measure captures the amplification of the firm's accounting returns that results from leverage. The market value equity multiplier, which is generally measured as Enterprise Value/Market Value of Equity, indicates the amplification of shareholders' financial risk that results from leverage.

Valuation Ratios

**price-earnings ratio
(P/E)** The ratio of the
market value of equity to
the firm's earnings, or its
share price to its earnings
per share.

Analysts and investors use a number of ratios to gauge the market value of a firm. The most important is the firm's **price-earnings ratio (P/E)**:

$$\text{P/E Ratio} = \frac{\text{Market Capitalization}}{\text{Net Income}} = \frac{\text{Share Price}}{\text{Earnings per Share}} \qquad (2.23)$$

That is, the P/E ratio is the ratio of the value of equity to the firm's earnings, either on a total basis or on a per-share basis. Following Eq. 2.23, Global's P/E ratio in 2016 was $36/2.0 = 10/0.56 = 18$. The P/E ratio is a simple measure that is often used to assess whether a stock is over- or under-valued, based on the idea that the value of a stock should be proportional to the level of earnings it can generate for its shareholders. P/E ratios can vary widely across industries and tend to be higher for industries with high growth rates. For example, in 2016, the average large U.S. firm had a P/E ratio of about 25. But software firms, which tend to have above-average growth rates, had an average P/E ratio of 38. One way to capture the idea that a higher P/E ratio can be justified by a higher growth rate is to compare it to the company's expected earnings growth rate. For example, if Global's expected growth rate is 18%, then it would have a P/E to Growth, or **PEG ratio**, of 1. Some investors consider PEG ratios of 1 or below as indicating the stock is fairly priced, but would question whether the company is potentially overvalued if the PEG is higher than 1.

PEG ratio The ratio of a
firm's P/E to its expected
earnings growth rate.

The P/E ratio considers the value of the firm's equity and so depends on its leverage. Recall that the amount of assets controlled by the equity holders can be increased through the use of leverage. To assess the market value of the underlying business, it is common to consider valuation ratios based on the firm's enterprise value. Typical ratios include the ratio of enterprise value to revenue, or enterprise value to operating income, or EBITDA. These ratios compare the value of the business to its sales, operating profits, or cash flow. Similar to the P/E ratio, managers use these ratios to make intra-industry comparisons of how firms are priced in the market.

COMMON MISTAKE

Mismatched Ratios

When considering valuation (and other) ratios, be sure that the items you are comparing both represent amounts related to the entire firm or that both represent amounts related solely to equity holders. For example, a firm's share price and market capitalization are values associated with the firm's equity. Thus, it makes sense to compare them to the firm's earnings per share or net income, which are amounts to equity holders after interest has been paid to debt holders. We must be careful, however, if we compare a firm's market capitalization to its revenues, operating income, or EBITDA. These amounts are related to the whole firm, and both debt and equity holders have a claim to them. Therefore, it is better to compare revenues, operating income, or EBITDA to the enterprise value of the firm, which includes both debt and equity.

The P/E ratio is not useful when the firm's earnings are negative. In this case, it is common to look at the firm's enterprise value relative to sales. The risk in doing so, however, is that earnings might be negative because the firm's underlying business model is fundamentally flawed, as was the case for many Internet firms in the late 1990s.

EXAMPLE 2.6

Computing Profitability and Valuation Ratios

MyFinanceLab

PROBLEM

Consider the following data for Walmart Stores and Target Corporation ($ billions):

	Walmart Stores (WMT)	**Target Corporation (TGT)**
Sales	469	73
Operating Income	28	5
Net Income	17	3
Market Capitalization	222	38
Cash	8	1
Debt	54	18

Compare Walmart's and Target's operating margin, net profit margin, P/E ratio, and the ratio of enterprise value to operating income and sales.

SOLUTION

PLAN

The table contains all of the raw data, but we need to compute the ratios using the inputs in the table.

> Operating Margin = Operating Income/Sales
> Net Profit Margin = Net Income/Sales
> P/E Ratio = Price/Earnings = Market Capitalization/Net Income
> Enterprise Value to Operating Income = Enterprise Value/Operating Income
> Enterprise Value to Sales = Enterprise Value/Sales

EXECUTE

Walmart had an operating margin of 28/469 = 6.0%, a net profit margin of 17/469 = 3.6%, and a P/E ratio of 222/17 = 13.1. Its enterprise value was 222 + 54 − 8 = $268 billion. Its ratio to operating income is 268/28 = 9.6, and its ratio to sales is 268/469 = 0.57.

Target had an operating margin of 5/73 = 6.8%, a net profit margin of 3/73 = 4.1%, and a P/E ratio of 38/3 = 12.7. Its enterprise value was 38 + 18 − 1 = $55 billion. Its ratio to operating income is 55/5 = 11, and its ratio to sales is 55/73 = 0.75.

EVALUATE

Target has a slightly higher operating margin, net profit margin, and enterprise value ratio, but a slightly lower P/E ratio. This suggests that the market expects similar growth rates from Target and Walmart, despite large differences in size.

Operating Returns

Analysts and financial managers often evaluate the firm's return on investment by comparing its income to its investment using ratios such as the firm's **return on equity (ROE):**[8]

return on equity (ROE) The ratio of a firm's net income to the book value of its equity.

$$\text{Return on Equity} = \frac{\text{Net Income}}{\text{Book Value of Equity}} \quad (2.24)$$

Global's ROE in 2016 was 2.0/22.2 = 9.0%. The ROE provides a measure of the return that the firm has earned on its past investments. A high ROE may indicate the firm is able to find investment opportunities that are very profitable. Of course, one weakness of this measure is the difficulty in interpreting the book value of equity.

---

[8]Because net income is measured over the year, the ROE can also be calculated based on the average book value of equity at the end of the current and prior years.

return on assets (ROA) The ratio of net income plus interest expense to the total book value of the firm's assets.

Another common measure is the **return on assets (ROA)**, which is net income plus interest expense divided by the total assets. The ROA calculation includes interest expense in the numerator because the assets in the denominator have been funded by both debt and equity investors. A firm must earn both a positive ROE and ROA to grow.

As a performance measure, ROA has the benefit that it is less sensitive to leverage than ROE. However, it is sensitive to working capital—for example, an equal increase in the firm's receivables and payables will increase total assets and thus lower ROA. To avoid this problem, we can consider the firm's **return on invested capital (ROIC)**:

return on invested capital (ROIC) The ratio of the after-tax profit before interest to the book value of invested capital not being held as cash (book equity plus net debt).

$$\text{Return on Invested Capital} = \frac{\text{EBIT} \, (1 - \text{Tax Rate})}{\text{Book Value of Equity} + \text{Net Debt}} \qquad (2.25)$$

The return on invested capital measures the after-tax profit generated by the business itself, excluding any interest expenses (or interest income), and compares it to the capital raised from equity and debt holders that has already been deployed (i.e., is not held as cash). Of the three measures of operating returns, ROIC is the most useful in assessing the performance of the underlying business.

EXAMPLE 2.7

Computing Operating Returns

MyFinanceLab

PROBLEM

Assess how Global's ability to use its assets effectively has changed in the last year by computing the change in its return on assets.

SOLUTION

PLAN AND ORGANIZE

In order to compute ROA, we need net income, interest expense, and total assets.

	2015	2016
Net Income	1.9	2.0
Interest Expense	4.6	7.7
Total Assets	128.9	170.1

EXECUTE

In 2016, Global's ROA was $(2.0 + 7.7)/170.1 = 5.7\%$, compared to an ROA in 2015 of $(1.9 + 4.6)/128.9 = 5.0\%$.

EVALUATE

The improvement in Global's ROA from 2015 to 2016 suggests that Global was able to use its assets more effectively and increase its return over this period.

The DuPont Identity

Global's financial manager will need to know that its ROE is 9%, but that financial manager would also need to understand the drivers of his or her firm's return on equity. High margins, efficient use of assets, or even simply high leverage could all lead to a higher return on equity. By delving deeper into the sources of return on equity, the financial manager can gain a clear sense of the firm's financial picture. One common tool for doing so is the **DuPont Identity**, named for the company that popularized it, which expresses return on equity as the product of profit margin, asset turnover, and a measure of leverage.

DuPont Identity Expresses return on equity as the product of profit margin, asset turnover, and a measure of leverage.

To understand the DuPont Identity, we start with ROE and decompose it in steps into the drivers identified in the identity. First, we simply multiply ROE by (sales/sales), which is just 1, and rearrange terms:

$$\text{ROE} = \left(\frac{\text{Net Income}}{\text{Total Equity}}\right)\left(\frac{\text{Sales}}{\text{Sales}}\right) = \left(\frac{\text{Net Income}}{\text{Sales}}\right)\left(\frac{\text{Sales}}{\text{Total Equity}}\right) \qquad (2.26)$$

This expression says that ROE can be thought of as net income per dollar of sales (profit margin) times the amount of sales per dollar of equity. For example, Global's ROE comes from its profit margin of 1.07% multiplied by its sales per dollar of equity (186.7/22.2 = 8.41): 1.07% × 8.41 = 9%. We can take the decomposition further by multiplying Eq. 2.26 by (total assets/total assets), which again is just 1, and rearranging the terms:

DuPont Identity

$$\text{ROE} = \left(\frac{\text{Net Income}}{\text{Sales}}\right)\left(\frac{\text{Sales}}{\text{Total Equity}}\right)\left(\frac{\text{Total Assets}}{\text{Total Assets}}\right)$$

$$= \left(\frac{\text{Net Income}}{\text{Sales}}\right)\left(\frac{\text{Sales}}{\text{Total Assets}}\right)\left(\frac{\text{Total Assets}}{\text{Total Equity}}\right) \qquad (2.27)$$

This final expression says that ROE is equal to net income per dollar of sales (profit margin) times sales per dollar of assets (asset turnover) times assets per dollar of equity (equity multiplier). Equation 2.27 is the DuPont Identity, expressing return on equity as the product of profit margin, asset turnover, and the equity multiplier. Turning to Global, its equity multiplier is 7.7(=170.1/22.2). A financial manager at Global looking for ways to increase ROE could assess the drivers behind its current ROE with the DuPont Identity. With a profit margin of 1.07%, asset turnover of 1.1, and an equity multiplier of 7.7, we have:

$$\text{ROE} = 9\% = (1.07\%)(1.1)(7.7)$$

This decomposition of ROE shows that leverage is already high (confirmed by the fact that the book debt-to-equity ratio shows that Global's debt is more than five times its equity). However, Global is operating with only 1% profit margins and relatively low asset turnover. Thus, Global's managers should focus on utilizing the firm's existing assets more efficiently and lowering costs to increase the profit margin.[9]

EXAMPLE 2.8

DuPont Analysis

MyFinanceLab

PROBLEM

The following table contains information about Walmart (WMT) and Nordstrom (JWN). Compute their respective ROEs and then determine how much Walmart would need to increase its profit margin in order to match Nordstrom's ROE.

	Profit Margin	**Asset Turnover**	**Equity Multiplier**
Walmart	3.6%	2.3	2.7
Nordstrom	6.1%	1.5	4.2

(Continued)

---

[9]Although the DuPont Identity makes it look like you can increase ROE just by increasing leverage, it is not quite that simple. An increase in leverage will increase your interest expense, decreasing your profit margin.

SOLUTION

PLAN AND ORGANIZE

The table contains all the relevant information to use the DuPont Identity to compute the ROE. We can compute the ROE of each company by multiplying together its profit margin, asset turnover, and equity multiplier. In order to determine how much Walmart would need to increase its profit margin to match Nordstrom's ROE, we can set Walmart's ROE equal to Nordstrom's, keep its turnover and equity multiplier fixed, and solve for the profit margin.

EXECUTE

Using the DuPont Identity, we have:

$$ROE_{WMT} = 3.6\% \times 2.3 \times 2.7 = 22.4\%$$
$$ROE_{JWN} = 6.1\% \times 1.5 \times 4.2 = 38.4\%$$

Now, using Nordstrom's ROE, but Walmart's asset turnover and equity multiplier, we can solve for the profit margin that Walmart needs to achieve Nordstrom's ROE:

$$38.4\% = \text{Margin} \times 2.3 \times 2.7$$
$$\text{Margin} = 38.4\%/6.21 = 6.2\%$$

EVALUATE

Walmart would have to increase its profit margin from 3.6% to 6.2% in order to match Nordstrom's ROE. It would be able to achieve Nordstrom's ROE with much lower leverage and around the same profit margin as Nordstrom (6.2% vs. 6.1%) because of its higher turnover.

Table 2.4 summarizes financial ratios and provides typical values of those ratios for the manufacturing, retail, and service sectors along with the 500 firms in the S&P 500 index. Because many companies with debt also held high levels of cash over the period, leverage ratios based on Net Debt are much lower than those based on Total Debt.

TABLE 2.4

A Summary of Key Financial Ratios

Ratio	Formula	Manufacturing	Retail	Service	S&P 500
Profitability Ratios					
Gross Margin	Gross Profit / Sales	33.8%	30.1%	51.4%	39.0%
Operating Margin	Operating Income / Sales	8.1%	7.3%	12.2%	16.2%
Net Profit Margin	Net Income / Sales	1.3%	2.6%	2.5%	4.5%
Liquidity Ratios					
Current Ratio	Current Assets / Current Liabilities	2.6	1.5	1.8	2.1
Quick Ratio	Current Assets − Inventory / Current Liabilities	1.9	0.8	1.7	1.6
Cash Ratio	Cash / Current Liabilities	0.9	0.3	0.9	0.7
Efficiency and Working Capital Ratios					
Accounts Receivable Days	Accounts Receivable / Average Daily Sales	57.6	7.8	63.0	60.2
Fixed Asset Turnover	Sales / Fixed Assets	5.4	6.6	10.6	4.8

Ratio	Formula	Manufacturing	Retail	Service	S&P 500
Total Asset Turnover	$\dfrac{\text{Sales}}{\text{Total Assets}}$	0.7	1.7	0.6	0.5
Inventory Turnover	$\dfrac{\text{Cost of Goods Sold}}{\text{Inventory}}$	4.2	6.9	26.9	5.7
Interest Coverage Ratios					
EBIT/Interest Coverage	$\dfrac{\text{EBIT}}{\text{Interest Expense}}$	3.2	5.5	2.3	3.9
EBITDA/Interest Coverage	$\dfrac{\text{EBITDA}}{\text{Interest Expense}}$	6.0	9.3	5.3	6.7
Leverage Ratios					
Book Debt-to-Equity Ratio	$\dfrac{\text{Total Debt}}{\text{Book Value of Total Equity}}$	27.1%	44.2%	21.5%	46.6%
Market Debt-to-Equity Ratio	$\dfrac{\text{Total Debt}}{\text{Market Value of Total Equity}}$	10.0%	17.2%	6.2%	21.8%
Debt-to-Capital Ratio	$\dfrac{\text{Total Debt}}{\text{Total Equity} + \text{Total Debt}}$	20.9%	30.6%	17.6%	32.0%
Debt-to-Enterprise Value	$\dfrac{\text{Net Debt}}{\text{Enterprise Value}}$	0.0%	4.7%	0.0%	2.0%
Equity Multiplier	$\dfrac{\text{Total Assets}}{\text{Total Equity}}$	1.8	2.4	1.98	2.4
Operating Returns					
Return on Equity	$\dfrac{\text{Net Income}}{\text{Book Value of Equity}}$	4.2%	10.4%	3.6%	7.1%
Return on Assets	$\dfrac{\text{Net Income} + \text{Interest Expense}}{\text{Total Assets}}$	3.6%	5.8%	3.3%	4.1%
Return on Invested Capital (ROIC)	$\dfrac{\text{EBIT}(1 - \text{Tax Rate})}{\text{Book Value of Equity} + \text{Net Debt}}$	18.0%	20.1%	18.3%	17.0%
Valuation Ratios					
Market-to-Book Ratio	$\dfrac{\text{Market Value of Equity}}{\text{Book Value of Equity}}$	2.7	2.7	3.5	2.1
Price-to-Earnings Ratio	$\dfrac{\text{Share Price}}{\text{Earnings per Share}}$	21.5	21.6	28.8	21.2
Enterprise Value Ratios (typical values shown are based on EV/EBITDA)	$\dfrac{\text{Enterprise Value}}{\text{EBIT or EBITDA or Sales}}$	8.3	11.7	10.5	12.1

Source: Standard and Poors' Compustat based on averages of fiscal years 2012 to 2015.

CONCEPT CHECK

11. What does a high debt-to-equity ratio tell you?

12. What is a firm's enterprise value?

13. How can a financial manager use the DuPont Identity to assess the firm's ROE?

14. How do you use the price-earnings (P/E) ratio to gauge the market value of a firm?

2.7   Financial Reporting in Practice

The various financial statements we have examined are of critical importance to investors and financial managers alike. Even with safeguards such as GAAP and auditors, financial reporting abuses unfortunately do take place. We now review one of the most infamous recent examples and offer some concluding thoughts to guide financial managers through the complexities of financial statements.

Enron

Enron is the most well-known of the accounting scandals of the early 2000s. Enron started as an operator of natural gas pipelines but evolved into a global trader dealing in a range of products including gas, oil, electricity, and even broadband Internet capacity. A series of events unfolded that led Enron to file what was at the time the largest bankruptcy filing in U.S. history in December 2001. By the end of 2001, the market value of Enron's shares had fallen by over $60 billion.

Interestingly, throughout the 1990s and up to late 2001, Enron was touted as one of the most successful and profitable companies in America. *Fortune* rated Enron "The Most Innovative Company in America" for six straight years, from 1995 to 2000. But while many aspects of Enron's business were successful, subsequent investigations suggest that Enron executives had been manipulating Enron's financial statements to mislead investors and artificially inflate the price of Enron's stock and to maintain its credit rating. In 2000, for example, 96% of Enron's reported earnings were the result of accounting manipulation.[10]

Although the accounting manipulation that Enron used was quite sophisticated, the essence of most of the deceptive transactions was surprisingly simple. Enron sold assets at inflated prices to other firms (or, in many cases, business entities that Enron's CFO Andrew Fastow had created), together with a promise to buy back those assets at an even higher future price. Thus, Enron was effectively borrowing money, receiving cash today in exchange for a promise to pay more cash in the future. But Enron recorded the incoming cash as revenue and then hid the promises to buy the assets back in a variety of ways.[11] In the end, much of their revenue growth and profits in the late 1990s were the result of this type of manipulation.

The Sarbanes-Oxley Act

Accurate and up-to-date financial statements are essential to investors evaluating investment opportunities. In 2002, Congress passed the **Sarbanes-Oxley Act (SOX)**. While SOX contains many provisions, the overall intent of the legislation was to improve the accuracy of information given to both boards and shareholders. SOX attempted to achieve this goal in three ways: (1) by overhauling incentives and independence in the auditing process, (2) by stiffening penalties for providing false information, and (3) by forcing companies to validate their internal financial control processes.

Many of the problems at Enron and elsewhere were kept hidden from boards and shareholders until it was too late. In the wake of these scandals, many people felt that the

Sarbanes-Oxley Act (SOX) Legislation passed by Congress in 2002, intended to improve the accuracy of financial information given to both boards and shareholders.

---

[10]John R. Kroger, "Enron, Fraud and Securities Reform: An Enron Prosecutor's Perspective," *University of Colorado Law Review*, December 2005, pp. 57–138.

[11]In some cases, these promises were called "price risk management liabilities" and hidden with other trading activities; in other cases they were off-balance sheet transactions that were not fully disclosed.

accounting statements of these companies, while often remaining true to the letter of GAAP, did not present an accurate picture of the financial health of the companies.

Auditing firms are supposed to ensure that a company's financial statements accurately reflect the financial state of the firm. In reality, most auditors have a long-standing relationship with their audit clients; this extended relationship and the auditors' desire to keep the lucrative auditing fees make auditors less willing to challenge management. More importantly, perhaps, most accounting firms have developed large and extremely profitable consulting divisions. Obviously, if an audit team refuses to accommodate a request by a client's management, that client will be less likely to choose the accounting firm's consulting division for its next consulting contract. SOX addressed this concern by putting strict limits on the amount of non-audit fees (consulting or otherwise) that an accounting firm can earn from the same firm that it audits. It also required that audit partners rotate every five years to limit the likelihood that auditing relationships become too cozy over time. Finally, SOX called on the SEC to force companies to have audit committees that are dominated by outside directors, and required that at least one outside director has a financial background.

SOX also stiffened the criminal penalties for providing false information to shareholders. It required both the CEO and the CFO to personally attest to the accuracy of the financial statements presented to shareholders and to sign a statement to that effect. Penalties for providing false or misleading financial statements were increased under SOX—fines of as much as $5 million and imprisonment of a maximum of 20 years are permitted. Further, CEOs and CFOs must return bonuses or profits from the sale of stock or the exercise of options during any period covered by statements that are later restated.

Finally, Section 404 of SOX requires senior management and the boards of public companies to attest to the effectiveness and validity of the process through which funds are allocated and controlled, and outcomes monitored throughout the firm. Section 404 has arguably garnered more attention than any other section in SOX because of the potentially enormous burden it places on every firm to validate its entire financial control system. When the SEC estimated the cost of implementing Section 404, its staff economists put the total cost at $1.24 billion. In 2005, surveys by Financial Executives International and the American Electronics Association predicted that the actual cost would be between $20 billion and $35 billion.[12] The burden of complying with this provision is greater, as a fraction of revenue, for smaller companies. The surveys cited earlier found that multibillion-dollar companies would pay less than 0.05% of their revenues to comply, whereas small companies with less than $20 million in revenues would pay more than 3% of their revenues to comply.

Dodd-Frank Act

To mitigate the compliance burden on small firms, the Dodd-Frank Wall Street Reform and Consumer Protection Act passed in 2010 exempts firms with less than $75 million in publicly held shares from the SOX Section 404 requirements. It also requires the SEC to study how it might reduce cost for medium-sized firms with a public float of less than $250 million, and to assess whether such measures would encourage more firms to list on U.S. exchanges.

Dodd-Frank also broadened the whistleblower provisions of SOX, so that an individual who provides "information related to a possible violation of the federal securities laws (including any rules or regulations thereunder)" that results in penalties or recoveries by the SEC or agencies is eligible to receive from 10 to 30% of that penalty or recovery.

---

[12]American Electronics Association, "Sarbanes-Oxley Section 404: The 'Section' of Unintended Consequences and Its Impact on Small Business" (2005).

GLOBAL FINANCIAL CRISIS

Bernard Madoff's Ponzi Scheme

"It's only when the tide goes out that you learn who's been swimming naked."
—Warren Buffett

On December 11, 2008, federal agents arrested Bernie Madoff, one of the largest and most successful hedge fund managers. It turned out that the $65 billion[13] fund he ran was in fact a fraud. His spectacular performance of the last 17 years, generating consistent annual returns between 10% and 15%, was actually a complete fabrication. Madoff had been running the world's largest Ponzi scheme: That is, he used the capital contributed by new investors to pay off old investors. His strategy was so successful that for more than a decade investors ranging from Steven Spielberg to New York University, as well as a number of large banks and investment advisors, lined up to invest with him. Indeed, Madoff quite likely would have been able to hide the fraud until his deathbed had not the global financial crisis spurred many investors to seek to withdraw funds from their Madoff accounts in order to raise cash and cover losses elsewhere in their portfolios. In addition, the financial crisis meant there were fewer new investors with both the cash and the willingness to invest. As a result, Madoff did not have enough new capital to pay off the investors who wanted to withdraw their capital, and the scheme finally collapsed.

How was Madoff able to hide perhaps the largest fraud of all time for so long? Rather than simply manipulate his accounting statements, Madoff *made them up* with the assistance of a virtually unknown accounting firm with only one active accountant. Although many investors may have questioned why such a large fund, with $65 billion in assets, would choose an unknown and tiny audit firm, not enough of them recognized this choice as a potential red flag. In addition, because Madoff's firm was private, it was not subject to the strict regulatory requirements for public companies (such as the Sarbanes-Oxley Act) and so had weak reporting requirements. As this case makes clear, when making an investment decision, it is important not only to review the firm's financial statements, but also to consider the reliability and reputation of the auditors who prepared them.

The Financial Statements: A Useful Starting Point

In this chapter, we have highlighted the role of the financial statements in informing outside analysts, investors, and the financial managers themselves about the performance, position, and financial condition of the firm. However, especially from the financial manager's perspective, financial statements are only a starting point. For example, we have emphasized the importance of market values over book values. We have also shown that while much can be learned through ratio analysis, these ratios are only markers that point the financial manager toward areas where the firm is doing well or where he or she needs to focus an effort toward improvement. No single ratio tells the whole story. However, by studying all of the financial statements and considering ratios that assess profitability, leverage, and efficiency, you should be able to develop a clear sense of the health and performance of the firm. Finally, the usefulness of the financial statements to investors relies on the ethics of those constructing them. However, even in cases of deception, an informed reader of the financial statements could have spotted the warning signs by focusing on the statement of cash flows and carefully reading the notes to the financial statements.

CONCEPT CHECK

15. Describe the transactions Enron used to increase its reported earnings.

16. What is the Sarbanes-Oxley Act?

---

[13]$65 billion is the total amount Madoff had reported to his investors, including (fictitious) returns; investigators are still trying to determine the exact amount that investors had actually contributed to the fund, but it appears to be in excess of $17 billion (see www.madoff.com).

MyFinanceLab

Here is what you should know after reading this chapter. MyFinanceLab will help you identify what you know, and where to go when you need to practice.

KEY POINTS AND EQUATIONS	KEY TERMS	ONLINE PRACTICE

2.1 Firms' Disclosure of Financial Information
• Financial statements are accounting reports that a firm issues periodically to describe its past performance.
• Investors, financial analysts, managers, and other interested parties, such as creditors, rely on financial statements to obtain reliable information about a corporation.
• The main types of financial statements are the balance sheet, the income statement, the statement of cash flows, and the statement of stockholders' equity.
• While the U.S. maintains its own GAAP, most countries in the world are standardizing their accounting systems around International Financial Reporting Standards.
	annual report (10-K), p. 28
	auditor, p. 30
	financial statements, p. 28
	Generally Accepted
	   Accounting Principles
	   (GAAP), p. 28
		MyFinanceLab
		Study Plan 2.1

2.2 The Balance Sheet
• The balance sheet shows the current financial position (assets, liabilities, and stockholders' equity) of the firm at a single point in time.
• The two sides of the balance sheet must balance:
 	
  Assets = Liabilities + Stockholders' Equity (2.1)
 	
• Stockholders' equity is the book value of the firm's equity. It differs from the market value of the firm's equity, its market capitalization, because of the way assets and liabilities are recorded for accounting purposes.
• A successful firm's market-to-book ratio typically exceeds 1.
• The enterprise value of a firm is the total value of its underlying business operations:
 	
  Enterprise Value = Market Value of Equity
                 + Debt − Cash (2.4)
	accounts payable, p. 32
	accounts receivable, p. 31
	assets, p. 30
	balance sheet, p. 30
	book value, p. 31
	book value of equity, p. 32
	common stock and paid-in
	   surplus, p. 30
	current assets, p. 31
	current liabilities, p. 32
	depreciation, p. 31
	enterprise value, p. 34
	growth stocks, p. 34
	inventories, p. 31
	liabilities, p. 30
	liquidation value, p. 33
	long-term assets, p. 31
	long-term debt, p. 32
	market capitalization, p. 33
	marketable securities, p. 31
	market-to-book ratio (price-
	   to-book [P/B] ratio), p. 34
	net working capital, p. 32
	notes payable, p. 32
	retained earnings, p. 30
	shareholders' equity, p. 30
	short-term debt, p. 32
	statement of financial
	   position, p. 30
	stockholders' equity, p. 30
	value stocks, p. 34
		MyFinanceLab
		Study Plan 2.2

2.3 The Income Statement

- The income statement reports the firm's revenues and expenses, and it computes the firm's bottom line of net income, or earnings.
- Net income is often reported on a per-share basis as the firm's earnings per share:

Earnings per Share (EPS) = Net Income/ Shares Outstanding   (2.5)

- We compute diluted EPS by adding to the number of shares outstanding the possible increase in the number of shares from the exercise of stock options the firm has awarded.

convertible bonds, p. 37
diluted EPS, p. 37
dilution, p. 37
earnings per share (EPS), p. 37
EBIT, p. 37
EBITDA, p. 38
gross profit, p. 36
income statement, p. 36
net income or earnings, p. 36
operating income, p. 37
stock options, p. 37

MyFinanceLab
Study Plan 2.3

2.4 The Statement of Cash Flows

- The statement of cash flows reports the sources and uses of the firm's cash. It shows the adjustments to net income for non-cash expenses and changes to net working capital, as well as the cash used (or provided) from investing and financing activities.

capital expenditures, p. 41
payout ratio, p. 41
statement of cash flows, p. 38

MyFinanceLab
Study Plan 2.4

2.5 Other Financial Statement Information

- The management discussion and analysis section of the financial statement contains management's overview of the firm's performance, as well as disclosure of risks the firm faces, including those from off-balance sheet transactions.
- The statement of stockholders' equity breaks down the stockholders' equity computed on the balance sheet into the amount that came from issuing new shares versus retained earnings. It is not particularly useful for financial valuation purposes.
- The notes to a firm's financial statements generally contain important details regarding the numbers used in the main statements.

management discussion and analysis (MD&A), p. 42
off-balance sheet transactions, p. 42
statement of stockholders' equity, p. 42

MyFinanceLab
Study Plan 2.5

2.6 Financial Statement Analysis

- Profitability ratios show the firm's operating or net income as a fraction of sales, and they are an indication of a firm's efficiency and its pricing strategy.
- Liquidity ratios help creditors assess whether the firm has enough cash to meet its short-term needs.
- Asset efficiency ratios assess how efficiently the firm is using its assets by showing how many dollars of revenues the firm produces per dollar of assets.
- Working capital ratios express the firm's working capital as a number of days of sales (for receivables) or cost of sales (for inventory or payables).

accounts payable days, p. 45
accounts receivable days, p. 44
asset turnover, p. 44
average collection period or days sales outstanding, p. 44
cash ratio, p. 44
current ratio, p. 44
debt-equity ratio, p. 47
debt-to-capital ratio, p. 47
debt-to-enterprise value ratio, p. 47
DuPont Identity, p. 50
equity multiplier, p. 48
gross margin, p. 43
interest coverage ratio, p. 46

MyFinanceLab
Study Plan 2.6

- Interest coverage ratios indicate the ratio of the firm's income or cash flows to its interest expenses, and they are a measure of financial strength.
- A common ratio used to assess a firm's leverage is:

$$\text{Debt-Equity Ratio} = \frac{\text{Total Debt}}{\text{Total Equity}} \quad (2.19)$$

- This ratio is most informative when computed using the market value of equity. It indicates the degree of leverage of the firm.
- Valuation ratios compute market capitalization or enterprise value of the firm relative to its earnings or operating income.
- The P/E ratio computes the value of a share of stock relative to the firm's EPS. P/E ratios tend to be high for fast-growing firms.
- When comparing valuation ratios, it is important to be sure both the numerator and denominator match in terms of whether they include debt.
- ROE and ROA are typical operating return ratios. ROE expresses the firm's net income as a return on the book value of its equity. ROA expresses net income plus interest as a return on total assets.
- The DuPont Identity says that

$$\text{ROE} = \left(\frac{\text{Net Income}}{\text{Sales}}\right) \times \left(\frac{\text{Sales}}{\text{Total Assets}}\right)$$
$$\times \left(\frac{\text{Total Assets}}{\text{Total Equity}}\right) \quad (2.27)$$

2.7 Financial Reporting in Practice

- Recent accounting scandals have drawn attention to the importance of financial statements. New legislation has increased the penalties for fraud, and tightened the procedures firms must use to ensure that statements are accurate.

CRITICAL THINKING

1. Why do firms disclose financial information?

2. Who reads financial statements? List at least three different categories of people. For each category, provide an example of the type of information they might be interested in and discuss why?

3. What is the purpose of the balance sheet?

4. What is the purpose of the income statement?

5. How does the statement of cash flows differ from the income statement?

6. Can a firm with positive net income run out of cash? Explain.

7. How can you use the balance sheet to assess the health of a firm?

8. How are the balance sheet and the income statement related?

9. What is the DuPont Identity and how can a financial manager use it?

10. What can you learn from the management's discussion in the financial statements or the notes to the financial statements?

11. How did accounting fraud contribute to the collapse of Enron?

PROBLEMS

All problems are available in MyFinanceLab. *The* ⊞ *icon indicates problems that are easier to solve using Excel and have data in an Excel format available in* MyFinanceLab. *An asterisk * indicates problems with a higher level of difficulty.*

Firms' Disclosure of Financial Information

1. What four financial statements can be found in a firm's 10-K filing? What checks are there on the accuracy of these statements?

2. What is GAAP and who oversees it?

3. Confirm that you can find the most recent financial statements for Starbucks Corporation (SBUX) using the following sources:
   a. From the company's Web page. (*Hint*: Search their Web site for "investor relations.")
   b. From the SEC Web site (www.sec.gov). (*Hint*: Search for company filings in the EDGAR database.)
   c. From the Yahoo! Finance Web site (finance.yahoo.com).
   d. From at least one other source. (*Hint*: Enter "SBUX 10K" at www.bing.com.)

The Balance Sheet

4. Consider the following potential events that might have occurred to Global on December 30, 2016. For each one, indicate which line items in Global's balance sheet would be affected and by how much. Also indicate the change to Global's book value of equity.
   a. Global used $20 million of its available cash to repay $20 million of its long-term debt.
   b. A warehouse fire destroyed $5 million worth of uninsured inventory.
   c. Global used $5 million in cash and $5 million in new long-term debt to purchase a $10 million building.
   d. A large customer owing $3 million for products it already received declared bankruptcy, leaving no possibility that Global would ever receive payment.
   e. Global's engineers discover a new manufacturing process that will cut the cost of its flagship product by more than 50%.
   f. A key competitor announces a radical new pricing policy that will drastically undercut Global's prices.

5. What was the change in Global's book value of equity from 2015 to 2016 according to Table 2.1? Does this imply that the market price of Global's shares increased in 2016? Explain.

6. Use EDGAR (www.sec.gov) to find Qualcomm's 10K filing for 2014. From the balance sheet, answer the following questions:
   a. How much did Qualcomm have in cash and short-term investments?
   b. What were Qualcomm's total accounts receivable?
   c. What were Qualcomm's total assets?
   d. What were Qualcomm's total liabilities? How much of this was long-term debt?
   e. What was the book value of Qualcomm's equity?

7. Find the annual 10-K report for Costco Wholesale Corporation (COST) for fiscal year 2015 (filed in October 2015). Answer the following questions from its balance sheet:
   a. How much cash did Costco have?
   b. What were Costco's total assets?
   c. What were Costco's total liabilities? How much debt did Costco have?
   d. What was the book value of Costco equity?

Income Statement

8. Find online the annual 10-K report for Costco Wholesale Corporation (COST) for fiscal year 2015 (filed in October 2015). Answer the following questions from the income statement:
   a. What were Costco revenues for 2015? By what percentage did revenues grow from the prior year?
   b. What were Costco operating and net profit margins in 2015? How do they compare with its margins in the prior year?
   c. What were Costco diluted earnings per share in 2015? What number of shares is this EPS based on?

TABLE 2.5

2012–2016 Financial Statement Data and Stock Price Data for Mydeco Corp.

Mydeco Corp. 2012–2016	(All data as of fiscal year end; $ in millions)				
Income Statement	**2012**	**2013**	**2014**	**2015**	**2016**
Revenue	404.3	363.8	424.6	510.7	604.1
Cost of Goods Sold	(188.3)	(173.8)	(206.2)	(246.8)	(293.4)
Gross Profit	215.9	190.0	218.3	263.9	310.7
Sales and Marketing	(66.7)	(66.4)	(82.8)	(102.1)	(120.8)
Administration	(60.6)	(59.1)	(59.4)	(66.4)	(78.5)
Depreciation & Amortization	(27.3)	(27.0)	(34.3)	(38.4)	(38.6)
EBIT	61.3	37.4	41.8	57.0	72.8
Interest Income (Expense)	(33.7)	(32.9)	(32.2)	(37.4)	(39.4)
Pretax Income	27.7	4.5	9.6	19.6	33.4
Income Tax	(9.7)	(1.6)	(3.4)	(6.9)	(11.7)
Net Income	18.0	2.9	6.2	12.7	21.7
Shares Outstanding (millions)	55.0	55.0	55.0	55.0	55.0
Earnings per Share	$0.33	$0.05	$0.11	$0.23	$0.39
Balance Sheet	**2012**	**2013**	**2014**	**2015**	**2016**
Assets					
Cash	48.8	68.8	86.2	77.4	84.9
Accounts Receivable	88.6	69.8	69.8	76.9	86.1
Inventory	33.7	30.9	28.4	31.7	35.3
Total Current Assets	171.1	169.4	184.4	186.1	206.3
Net Property, Plant, & Equipment	245.3	243.2	308.9	345.5	347.0
Goodwill & Intangibles	361.7	361.7	361.7	361.7	361.7
Total Assets	778.1	774.3	855.0	893.3	914.9

(Continued)

Mydeco Corp. 2012–2016		(All data as of fiscal year end; $ in millions)			
Balance Sheet (continued)	2012	2013	2014	2015	2016
Liabilities & Stockholders' Equity					
Accounts Payable	18.7	17.9	22.0	26.8	31.7
Accrued Compensation	6.7	6.4	7.0	8.1	9.7
Total Current Liabilities	25.5	24.2	29.0	34.9	41.4
Long-Term Debt	500.0	500.0	575.0	600.0	600.0
Total Liabilities	525.5	524.2	604.0	634.9	641.4
Stockholders' Equity	252.6	250.1	251.0	258.3	273.5
Total Liabilities & Stock-holders' Equity	778.1	774.3	855.0	893.3	914.9
Statement of Cash Flows	2012	2013	2014	2015	2016
Net Income	18.0	2.9	6.2	12.7	21.7
Depreciation & Amortization	27.3	27.0	34.3	38.4	38.6
Change in Accounts Receivable	3.9	18.8	(0.0)	(7.2)	(9.1)
Change in Inventory	(2.9)	2.9	2.5	(3.3)	(3.6)
Change in Payables & Accrued Compensation	2.2	(1.3)	4.8	5.9	6.5
Cash from Operations	48.4	50.4	47.8	46.6	54.0
Capital Expenditures	(25.0)	(25.0)	(100.0)	(75.0)	(40.0)
Cash from Investing Activities	(25.0)	(25.0)	(100.0)	(75.0)	(40.0)
Dividends Paid	(5.4)	(5.4)	(5.4)	(5.4)	(6.5)
Sale (or Purchase) of Stock	—	—	—	—	—
Debt Issuance (Pay Down)	—	—	75.0	25.0	—
Cash from Financing Activities	(5.4)	(5.4)	69.6	19.6	(6.5)
Change in Cash	18.0	20.0	17.4	(8.8)	7.5
Mydeco Stock Price	*$7.90*	*$3.29*	*$5.23*	*$8.70*	*$10.87*

9. See Table 2.5 showing financial statement data and stock price data for Mydeco Corp.
   a. By what percentage did Mydeco's revenues grow each year from 2013–2016?
   b. By what percentage did net income grow each year?
   c. Why might the growth rates of revenues and net income differ?

10. See Table 2.5 showing financial statement data and stock price data for Mydeco Corp. Suppose Mydeco repurchases 2 million shares each year from 2013–2016. What would its earnings per share be in 2016?

11. See Table 2.5 showing financial statement data and stock price data for Mydeco Corp. Suppose Mydeco had purchased additional equipment for $12 million at the end of 2013, and this equipment was depreciated by $4 million per year in 2014, 2015, and 2016. Given Mydeco's tax rate of 35%, what impact would this additional purchase have had on Mydeco's net income in years 2013–2016?

12. See Table 2.5 showing financial statement data and stock price data for Mydeco Corp. Suppose Mydeco's costs and expenses had been the same fraction of revenues in 2013–2016 as they were in 2012. What would Mydeco's EPS have been each year in this case?

13. Suppose a firm's tax rate is 35%.
    a. What effect would a $10 million operating expense have on this year's earnings? What effect would it have on next year's earnings?
    b. What effect would a $10 million capital expense have on this year's earnings if the capital is depreciated at a rate of $2 million per year for five years? What effect would it have on next year's earnings?

*14. Quisco Systems has 6.5 billion shares outstanding and a share price of $18. Quisco is considering developing a new networking product in house at a cost of $500 million. Alternatively, Quisco can acquire a firm that already has the technology for $900 million worth (at the current price) of Quisco stock. Suppose that absent the expense of the new technology, Quisco will have EPS of $0.80.
    a. Suppose Quisco develops the product in house. What impact would the development cost have on Quisco's EPS? Assume all costs are incurred this year and are treated as an R&D expense, Quisco's tax rate is 35%, and the number of shares outstanding is unchanged.
    b. Suppose Quisco does not develop the product in house but instead acquires the technology. What effect would the acquisition have on Quisco's EPS this year? (Note that acquisition expenses do not appear directly on the income statement. Assume the firm was acquired at the start of the year and has no revenues or expenses of its own, so that the only effect on EPS is due to the change in the number of shares outstanding.)
    c. Which method of acquiring the technology has a smaller impact on earnings? Is this method cheaper? Explain.

The Statement of Cash Flows

15. Find online the annual 10-K report for Costco Wholesale Corporation (COST) for fiscal year 2015 (filed in October 2015). Answer the following questions from its cash flow statement:
    a. How much cash did Costco generate from operating activities in 2015?
    b. What was Costco depreciation expense in 2015?
    c. How much cash was invested in new property and equipment (net of any sales) in 2015?
    d. How much did Costco raise from the sale of shares of its stock (net of any purchases) in 2015?

16. See the cash flow statement below (all values in thousands of dollars) (*see* MyFinanceLab *for the data in Excel format*):
    a. What were the company's cumulative earnings over these four quarters? What were its cumulative cash flows from operating activities?

Quarter	4	3	2	1
Net income	276,710	228,964	194,062	218,532
Operating Activities, Cash Flows Provided by or Used in				
Depreciation	69,997	75,733	74,570	73,173
Adjustments to net income	14,359	(13,142)	48,826	(47,993)
Changes in accounts receivable	(38,869)	(53,218)	100,732	(84,711)
Changes in liabilities	82,816	(111,577)	201,725	39,949
Changes in inventories	(195,186)	(114,121)	85,028	57,681
Changes in other operating activities	17,675	(26,574)	12,692	(2,097)

(*Continued*)

Quarter	4	3	2	1
Total Cash Flow from Operating Activities	227,502	(13,935)	717,635	254,534
Investing Activities, Cash Flows Provided by or Used in				
Capital expenditures	(82,584)	(41,634)	(100,109)	(69,170)
Investments	(5,465)	5,465	(93,153)	(48,330)
Other cash flows from investing activities	(108,903)	732	(58,069)	20,652
Total Cash Flows from Investing Activities	(196,952)	(35,437)	(251,331)	(96,848)
Financing Activities, Cash Flows Provided by or Used in				
Dividends paid	(131,483)	(131,333)	(119,452)	(121,404)
Sale purchase of stock	78,774	1,210	(76,807)	(79,288)
Net borrowings	515,709	114,766	(283,696)	64,885
Other cash flows from financing activities	(282)	2,000	(46,234)	39,763
Total Cash Flows from Financing Activities	462,718	(13,357)	(526,189)	(96,044)
Effect of exchange rate changes	(119,960)	(610)	32,807	6,890
Change in Cash and Cash Equivalents	$373,308	(63,339)	(27,078)	$68,532

b. What fraction of the cash from operating activities was used for investment over the four quarters?

c. What fraction of the cash from operating activities was used for financing activities over the four quarters?

17. Suppose your firm receives a $5 million order on the last day of the year. You fill the order with $2 million worth of inventory. The customer picks up the entire order the same day and pays $1 million up front in cash; you also issue a bill for the customer to pay the remaining balance of $4 million within 40 days. Suppose your firm's tax rate is 0% (i.e., ignore taxes). Determine the consequences of this transaction for each of the following:

a. Revenues

b. Earnings

c. Receivables

d. Inventory

e. Cash

18. Nokela Industries purchases a $40 million cyclo-converter. The cyclo-converter will be depreciated by $10 million per year over four years, starting this year. Suppose Nokela's tax rate is 40%.

a. What impact will the cost of the purchase have on earnings for each of the next four years?

b. What impact will the cost of the purchase have on the firm's cash flow for the next four years?

Financial Statement Analysis

19. In December 2015, General Electric (GE) had a book value of equity of $98 billion, 9.4 billion shares outstanding, and a market price of $31 per share. GE also had cash of $102 billion, and total debt of $199 billion.
    a. What was GE's market capitalization? What was GE's market-to-book ratio?
    b. What was GE's book debt-equity ratio? What was GE's market debt-equity ratio?
    c. What was GE's enterprise value?

20. In December 2015, Apple had cash of $38.07 billion, current assets of $76.22 billion, and current liabilities of $76.09 billion. It also had inventories of $2.45 billion.
    a. What was Apple's current ratio?
    b. What was Apple's quick ratio?
    c. In January 2016, Hewlett-Packard had a quick ratio of 0.66 and a current ratio of 0.90. What can you say about the asset liquidity of Apple relative to Hewlett-Packard?

21. In early-2016, the following information was true about Abercrombie and Fitch (ANF) and The Gap (GPS), both clothing retailers. Values (except price per share) are in millions of dollars.

	Book Equity	Price per Share	Number of Shares (millions)
ANF	1,291	26.35	67.59
GPS	2,545	24.74	397.14

    a. What is the market-to-book ratio of each company?
    b. What conclusions do you draw from comparing the two ratios?

22. In fiscal year 2015, Walmart Stores. (WMT) had revenue of $485.65 billion, gross profit of $120.57 billion, and net income of $16.36 billion. Costco Wholesale Corporation (COST) had revenue of $116.20 billion, gross profit of $15.13 billion, and net income of $2.38 billion.
    a. Compare the gross margins for Walmart and Costco.
    b. Compare the net profit margins for Walmart and Costco.
    c. Which firm was more profitable in 2015?

23. Local Co. has sales of $10 million and cost of sales of $6 million. Its selling, general, and administrative expenses are $500,000 and its research and development is $1 million. It has annual depreciation charges of $1 million and a tax rate of 35%.
    a. What is Local's gross margin?
    b. What is Local's operating margin?
    c. What is Local's net profit margin?

24. If Local Co., the company in Problem 23, had an increase in selling expenses of $300,000, how would that affect each of its margins?

25. If Local Co., the company in Problem 23, had interest expense of $800,000, how would that affect each of its margins?

26. Chutes & Co. has interest expense of $1 million and an operating margin of 10% on total sales of $30 million. What is Chutes' interest coverage ratio?

27. Ladders, Inc. has a net profit margin of 5% on sales of $50 million. It has book value of equity of $40 million and total liabilities with a book value of $30 million. What is Ladders' ROE? ROA?

28. JPJ Corp has sales of $1 million, accounts receivable of $50,000, total assets of $5 million (of which $3 million are fixed assets), inventory of $150,000, and cost of goods sold of $600,000. What is JPJ's accounts receivable days? Fixed asset turnover? Total asset turnover? Inventory turnover?

29. If JPJ Corp (the company in Problem 28) is able to increase sales by 10% but keep its total and fixed asset growth to only 5%, what will its new asset turnover ratios be?

*30. Suppose that in 2016, Global launched an aggressive marketing campaign that boosted sales by 15%. However, their operating margin fell from 5.57% to 4.50%. Suppose that they had no other income, interest expenses were unchanged, and taxes were the same percentage of pretax income as in 2015.
   a. What was Global's EBIT in 2016?
   b. What was Global's income in 2016?
   c. If Global's P/E ratio and number of shares outstanding remained unchanged, what was Global's share price in 2016?

31. You are analyzing the leverage of two firms and you note the following (all values in millions of dollars):

	Debt	Book Equity	Market Equity	Operating Income	Interest Expense
Firm A	500	300	400	100	50
Firm B	80	35	40	8	7

   a. What is the market debt-to-equity ratio of each firm?
   b. What is the book debt-to-equity ratio of each firm?
   c. What is the interest coverage ratio of each firm?
   d. Which firm will have more difficulty meeting its debt obligations?

32. For 2015, Walmart and Target had the following information (all values are in millions of dollars):

	Sales (Income Statement)	Cost of Goods Sold (Income Statement)	Accounts Receivable (Balance Sheet)	Inventory (Balance Sheet)
Walmart	482,130	360,984	5,624	44,469
Target	73,785	51,997	779	8,601

   a. What is each company's accounts receivable days?
   b. What is each company's inventory turnover?
   c. Which company is managing its accounts receivable and inventory more efficiently?

33. In January 2016, United Airlines (UAL) had a market capitalization of $20.6 billion, debt of $11.9 billion, and cash of $5.2 billion. United Airlines had revenues of $37.9 billion. Southwest Airlines (LUV) had a market capitalization of $27.5 billion, debt of $3.2 billion, cash of $3.0 billion, and revenues of $19.8 billion.
   a. Compare the market capitalization-to-revenue ratio (also called the price-to-sales ratio) for United Airlines and Southwest Airlines.
   b. Compare the enterprise value-to-revenue ratio for United Airlines and Southwest Airlines.
   c. Which of these comparisons is more meaningful? Explain.

34. Consider a retail firm with a net profit margin of 3.5%, a total asset turnover of 1.8, total assets of $44 million, and a book value of equity of $18 million.
    a. What is the firm's current ROE?
    b. If the firm increased its net profit margin to 4%, what would its ROE be?
    c. If, in addition, the firm increased its revenues by 20% (while maintaining this higher profit margin and without changing its assets or liabilities), what would its ROE be?

*35. Find online the annual 10-K report for Costco Wholesale Corporation (COST) for fiscal year 2015 (filed in October 2015).
    a. Compute Costco's net profit margin, total asset turnover, and equity multiplier.
    b. Verify the DuPont Identity for Costco ROE.
    c. If Costco managers wanted to increase its ROE by 1 percentage point, how much higher would their asset turnover need to be?

36. Repeat the analysis from parts a and b in Problem 35 using Walmart Stores (WMT) instead. Specifically, use Walmart's 2015 fiscal data, filed in October 2015. Based on the DuPont Identity, what explains the difference between the two firms' ROEs?

Other Financial Statement Information

37. Some balance sheet information is shown here (all values in millions of dollars) (*see* MyFinanceLab *for the data in Excel format*):

Balance Sheet: Assets	31-Mar-16	31-Dec-15	30-Sep-15	30-Jun-15
Assets				
Current Assets				
Cash and cash equivalents	293	300	255	232
Net receivables	401	362	385	460
Inventory	374	342	437	306
Other current assets	60	43	53	45
Total Current Assets	1,128	1,047	1,130	1,043
Long-term investments	128	97	—	200
Property, plant, and equipment	979	991	995	1,052
Goodwill	744	748	736	742
Other assets	777	827	911	797
Total Assets	3,756	3,710	3,772	3,834
Liabilities				
Current Liabilities				
Accounts payable	876	1,467	922	980
Short/current long-term debt	410	2	173	288
Other current liabilities	—	—	—	—
Total Current Liabilities	1,286	1,469	1,095	1,268
Long-term debt	2,381	2,124	474	475
Other liabilities	435	574	559	551
Total Liabilities	4,102	4,167	2,128	2,294
Total Stockholder Equity	−346	−457	1,644	1,540
Total Liabilities and Stockholder Equity	$3,756	$3,710	$3,772	$3,834

    a. What change in the book value of the company's equity took place at the end of 2015?

    b. Is the company's market-to-book ratio meaningful? Is its book debt-equity ratio meaningful? Explain.

    c. Find the company's other financial statements from that time online. What was the cause of the change to its book value of equity at the end of 2015?

    d. Does the company's book value of equity in 2016 imply that it is unprofitable? Explain.

Financial Reporting in Practice

38. Find online the annual 10-K report for Costco Wholesale Corporation (COST) for fiscal year 2015 (filed in October 2015).

    a. Which auditing firm certified the financial statements?

    b. Which officers of Costco certified the financial statements?

DATA CASE

This is your second interview with a prestigious brokerage firm for a job as an equity analyst. You survived the morning interviews with the department manager and the vice president of equity. Everything has gone so well that they want to test your ability as an analyst. You are seated in a room with a computer and a list with the names of two companies—Ford (F) and Microsoft (MSFT). You have 90 minutes to complete the following tasks:

1. Download the annual income statements, balance sheets, and cash flow statements for the last four fiscal years from Morningstar (www.morningstar.com). Enter each company's stock symbol and then go to "financials." Copy and paste the financial statements into Excel.

2. Find historical stock prices for each firm from Yahoo! Finance (finance.yahoo.com). Enter the stock symbol, click "Historical Prices" in the left column, and enter the proper date range to cover the last day of the month corresponding to the date of each financial statement. Use the closing stock prices (not the adjusted close). To calculate the firm's market capitalization at each date, multiply the number of shares outstanding by the firm's historic stock price. You can find the number of shares by using "Basic" under "Weighted average shares outstanding" at the bottom of the Income Statement.

3. For each of the four years of statements, compute the following ratios for each firm:

   Valuation Ratios
   Price-earnings ratio (for EPS use diluted EPS total)
   Market-to-book ratio
   Enterprise value-to-EBITDA
   (For debt, include long-term and short-term debt; for cash, include marketable securities.)

   Profitability Ratios
   Operating margin
   Net profit margin
   Return on equity

   Financial Strength Ratios
   Current ratio
   Book debt–equity ratio
   Market debt–equity ratio
   Interest coverage ratio (EBIT ÷ interest expense)

4. Obtain industry averages for each firm from Reuters (www.reuters.com/finance/stocks). Enter the stock symbol at the top of the page in the "Symbol lookup" and then click the "Financials" button, and then click "Search."

   a. Scroll down to "Valuation Ratios," and compare each firm's ratios to the available industry ratios for the most recent year. (Ignore the "Company" column as your calculations will be different.)

   b. Analyze the performance of each firm versus the industry and comment on any trends in each individual firm's performance. Identify any strengths or weaknesses you find in each firm.

5. Examine the market-to-book ratios you calculated for each firm. Which, if either, of the two firms can be considered "growth firms" and which, if either, can be considered "value firms"?

6. Compare the valuation ratios across the two firms. How do you interpret the difference between them?

7. Consider the enterprise value of both firms for each of the four years. How have the values of both firms changed over the time period?

3

Time Value of Money: An Introduction

LEARNING OBJECTIVES

- Identify the roles of financial managers and competitive markets in decision making

- Understand the Valuation Principle, and how it can be used to identify decisions that increase the value of the firm

- Assess the effect of interest rates on today's value of future cash flows

- Calculate the value of distant cash flows in the present and of current cash flows in the future

notation

r	interest rate		C	cash flow
PV	present value		n	number of periods
FV	future value			

In 2011, Amazon.com managers decided to more directly compete in the tablet market with the launch of the Kindle Fire, and they priced it at $199, which by some estimates was either at or below the cost to build it. How did Amazon's managers decide this was the right decision for the company? Similarly, how did Apple's managers decide to enter the wearable technology market with the Apple Watch in 2015?

Every decision has future consequences that will affect the value of the firm. These consequences will generally include both benefits and costs. For example, in addition to the up-front cost of developing its own mobile phone and software, Amazon will also incur ongoing costs associated with future software and hardware development for the Fire, marketing efforts, and customer support. The benefits to Amazon include the revenues from the sales as well as additional content purchased through the device. This decision will increase Amazon's value if these benefits outweigh the costs.

More generally, a decision is good for the firm's investors if it increases the firm's value by providing benefits whose value exceeds the costs. But how do we compare costs and benefits that occur at different points in time, or are in different currencies, or have different risks associated with them? To make a valid comparison, we must use the tools of finance to express all costs and benefits in common terms. We convert all costs and benefits into a common currency and common point of time, such as dollars today. In this chapter, we learn (1) how to use market information to evaluate costs and benefits and (2) why market prices are so important. Then, we will start to build the critical tools relating to the time value of money. These tools will allow you to correctly compare the costs and benefits of a decision no matter when they occur.

3.1   Cost-Benefit Analysis

The first step in decision making is to identify the costs and benefits of a decision. In this section, we look at the role of financial managers in evaluating costs and benefits and the tools they use to quantify them.

Role of the Financial Manager

A financial manager's job is to make decisions on behalf of the firm's investors. Our objective in this book is to explain how to make decisions that increase the value of the firm to its investors. In principle, the idea is simple and intuitive: For good decisions, the benefits exceed the costs. Of course, real-world opportunities are usually complex and the costs and benefits are often difficult to quantify. Quantifying them often means using skills from other management disciplines, as in the following examples:

Marketing: to determine the increase in revenues resulting from an advertising campaign

Economics: to determine the increase in demand from lowering the price of a product

Organizational Behavior: to determine the effect of changes in management structure on productivity

Strategy: to determine a competitor's response to a price increase

Operations: to determine production costs after the modernization of a manufacturing plant

For the remainder of this text, we will assume we can rely on experts in these areas to provide this information so the costs and benefits associated with a decision have already been identified. With that task done, the financial manager's job is to compare the costs and benefits and determine the best decision for the value of the firm.

Quantifying Costs and Benefits

Any decision in which the value of the benefits exceeds the costs will increase the value of the firm. To evaluate the costs and benefits of a decision, we must value the options in the same terms—cash today. Let's make this concrete with a simple example.

Suppose a jewelry manufacturer has the opportunity to trade 200 ounces of silver for 10 ounces of gold today. An ounce of silver differs in value from an ounce of gold. Consequently, it is incorrect to compare 200 ounces to 10 ounces and conclude that the larger quantity is better. Instead, to compare the cost of the silver and the benefit of the gold, we first need to quantify their values in equivalent terms—cash today.

Consider the silver. What is its cash value today? Suppose silver can be bought and sold for a current market price of $20 per ounce. Then the 200 ounces of silver we would give up has a cash value of:[1]

$$(\text{200 ounces of silver}) \times (\text{\$20/ounce of silver}) = \$4000$$

If the current market price for gold is $1000 per ounce, then the 10 ounces of gold we would receive has a cash value of

$$(\text{10 ounces of gold}) \times (\text{\$1000/ounce of gold}) = \$10,000$$

We have now quantified the decision. The jeweler's opportunity has a benefit of $10,000 and a cost of $4000. The net benefit of the decision is $10,000 − $4000 = $6000 today.

---

[1]You might wonder whether commissions and other transactions costs need to be included in this calculation. For now, we will ignore transactions costs, but we will discuss their effect in later chapters.

The net value of the decision is positive, so by accepting the trade, the jewelry firm will be richer by $6000.

Role of Competitive Market Prices. Suppose the jeweler works exclusively on silver jewelry or thinks the price of silver should be higher. Should his decision change? The answer is no—he can always make the trade and then buy silver at the current market price. Even if he has no use for the gold, he can immediately sell it for $10,000, buy back the 200 ounces of silver at the current market price of $4000, and pocket the remaining $6000. Thus, independent of his own views or preferences, the value of the silver to the jeweler is $4000.

competitive market
A market in which a good can be bought *and* sold at the same price.

Because the jeweler can both buy and sell silver at its current market price, his personal preferences or use for silver and his opinion of the fair price are irrelevant in evaluating the value of this opportunity. This observation highlights an important general principle related to goods trading in a **competitive market**, a market in which a good can be bought *and* sold at the same price. Whenever a good trades in a competitive market, that price determines the value of the good. This point is one of the central and most powerful ideas in finance. It will underlie almost every concept we develop throughout the text.

EXAMPLE 3.1
Competitive Market
Prices Determine Value

MyFinanceLab

PROBLEM

You have just won a radio contest and are disappointed to learn that the prize is four tickets to the Def Leppard reunion tour (face value $40 each). Not being a fan of 1980s power rock, you have no intention of going to the show. However, the radio station offers you another option: two tickets to your favorite band's sold-out show (face value $45 each). You notice that, on eBay, tickets to the Def Leppard show are being bought and sold for $30 apiece and tickets to your favorite band's show are being bought and sold at $50 each. What should you do?

SOLUTION

PLAN

Market prices, not your personal preferences (or the face value of the tickets), are relevant here:

    4 Def Leppard tickets at $30 apiece

    2 of your favorite band's tickets at $50 apiece

You need to compare the market value of each option and choose the one with the highest market value.

EXECUTE

The Def Leppard tickets have a total value of $120 $(4 \times \$30)$ versus the $100 total value of the other 2 tickets $(2 \times \$50)$. Instead of taking the tickets to your favorite band, you should accept the Def Leppard tickets, sell them on eBay, and use the proceeds to buy 2 tickets to your favorite band's show. You'll even have $20 left over to buy a T-shirt.

EVALUATE

Even though you prefer your favorite band, you should still take the opportunity to get the Def Leppard tickets instead. As we emphasized earlier, whether this opportunity is attractive depends on its net value using market prices. Because the value of Def Leppard tickets is $20 more than the value of your favorite band's tickets, the opportunity is appealing.

CONCEPT CHECK

1. When costs and benefits are in different units or goods, how can we compare them?

2. If crude oil trades in a competitive market, would an oil refiner that has a use for the oil value it differently than another investor would?

› **3.2** Market Prices and the Valuation Principle

In the previous examples, the right decisions for the firms were clear because the costs and benefits were easy to evaluate and compare. They were easy to evaluate because we were able to use current market prices to convert them into equivalent cash values. Once we can express costs and benefits in terms of cash today, it is a straightforward process to compare them and determine whether the decision will increase the firm's value.

The Valuation Principle

Our discussion so far establishes competitive market prices as the way to evaluate the costs and benefits of a decision in terms of cash today. Once we do this, it is a simple matter to determine the best decision for the firm. The best decision makes the firm and its investors wealthier, because the value of its benefits exceeds the value of its costs. We call this idea the Valuation Principle:

The Valuation Principle:

The value of a commodity or an asset to the firm or its investors is determined by its competitive market price. The benefits and costs of a decision should be evaluated using those market prices. When the value of the benefits exceeds the value of the costs, the decision will increase the market value of the firm.

The Valuation Principle provides the basis for decision making throughout this text. In the remainder of this chapter, we apply it to decisions whose costs and benefits occur at different points in time.

EXAMPLE 3.2

Applying the Valuation Principle

MyFinanceLab

PROBLEM

You are the operations manager at your firm. Due to a pre-existing contract, you have the opportunity to acquire 200 barrels of oil and 3000 pounds of copper for a total of $25,000. The current market price of oil is $90 per barrel and for copper is $3.50 per pound. You are not sure that you need all the oil and copper, so you are wondering whether you should take this opportunity. How valuable is it? Would your decision change if you believed the value of oil or copper would plummet over the next month?

SOLUTION

PLAN

We need to quantify the costs and benefits using market prices. We are comparing $25,000 with:

  200 barrels of oil at $90 per barrel

  3000 pounds of copper at $3.50 per pound

EXECUTE

Using the competitive market prices we have:

$$(200 \text{ barrels of oil}) \times (\$90/\text{barrel today}) = \$18,000 \text{ today}$$
$$(3000 \text{ pounds of copper}) \times (\$3.50/\text{pound today}) = \$10,500 \text{ today}$$

The value of the opportunity is the value of the oil plus the value of the copper less the cost of the opportunity, or $18,000 + $10,500 − $25,000 = $3500 today. Because the value is positive, we should take it. This value depends only on the *current* market prices for oil and copper. If we do not need all of the oil and copper, we can sell the excess at current market prices. Even if we thought the value of oil or copper was about to plummet, the value of this investment would be unchanged. (We can always exchange them for dollars immediately at the current market prices.)

EVALUATE

Since we are transacting today, only the current prices in a competitive market matter. Our own use for or opinion about the future prospects of oil or copper do not alter the value of the decision today. This decision is good for the firm and will increase its value by $3500.

Why There Can Be Only One Competitive Price for a Good

The Valuation Principle and finance in general rely on using a competitive market price to value a cost or benefit. We cannot have two different competitive market prices for the same good—otherwise we would arrive at two different values. Fortunately, powerful market forces keep competitive prices the same. To illustrate, imagine what you would do if you saw gold simultaneously trading for two different prices. You and everyone else who noticed the difference would buy at the low price and sell at the high price for as many ounces of gold as possible, making instant risk-free profits. The flood of buy and sell orders would push the two prices together until the profit was eliminated. These forces establish the **Law of One Price**, which states that in competitive markets, the same good or securities must have the same price. More generally, securities that produce exactly the same cash flows must have the same price.

Law of One Price In competitive markets, securities with the same cash flows must have the same price.

In general, the practice of buying and selling equivalent goods in different markets to take advantage of a price difference is known as **arbitrage**. We refer to any situation in which it is possible to make a profit without taking any risk or making any investment as an **arbitrage opportunity**. Because an arbitrage opportunity's benefits are more valuable than its costs, whenever an arbitrage opportunity appears in financial markets, investors will race to take advantage of it and their trades will eliminate the opportunity.

arbitrage The practice of buying and selling equivalent goods to take advantage of a price difference.

arbitrage opportunity Any situation in which it is possible to make a profit without taking any risk or making any investment.

Retail stores often quote different prices for the same item in different countries. *The Economist* magazine has long compared prices for a McDonald's Big Mac around the world. Here, we compare Big Mac prices from January 2016. The price in the local currency and converted to U.S. dollars is listed. Of course, these prices are not examples of competitive market prices, because you can only buy a Big Mac at these prices. Hence, they do not present an arbitrage opportunity. Even if shipping were free, you could buy as many Big Macs as you could get your hands on in Venezuela but you would not be able to sell those rotten Big Macs in Switzerland for a profit!

Country	Local Cost	U.S. Dollar Cost
Switzerland	6.50 Swiss francs	$6.44
Sweden	45 Swedish Krona	$5.23
United States	4.93 US dollars	$4.93
Britain	2.89 pounds	$4.22
Canada	5.84 Canadian dollars	$4.14
Australia	5.30 Australian dollars	$3.74
U.A.E.	13 dirhams	$3.54
Brazil	13.50 reals	$3.35
Japan	370 yen	$3.12
Mexico	49 pesos	$2.81
China	17.60 yuan	$2.68
Hong Kong	19.20 HK dollars	$2.48
Poland	960 zlotys	$2.37
Indonesia	30,500 rupiahs	$2.19
Russia	114 rubles	$1.53
Venezuela	132 bolivares fuertes	$0.66

Source: Economist.com.

CONCEPT CHECK

3. How do investors' profit motives keep competitive market prices correct?

4. How do we determine whether a decision increases the value of the firm?

3.3   The Time Value of Money and Interest Rates

Unlike the examples presented so far, most financial decisions have costs and benefits that occur at different points in time. For example, typical investment projects incur costs up front and provide benefits in the future. In this section, we show how to account for this time difference when using the Valuation Principle to make a decision.

The Time Value of Money

Your company has an investment opportunity with the following cash flows:

Cost: $100,000 today
Benefit: $105,000 in one year

Both are expressed in dollar terms, but are the cost and benefit directly comparable? No. Calculating the project's net value as $105,000 − $100,000 = $5000 is incorrect because it ignores the *timing* of the costs and benefits. That is, it treats money today as equivalent to money in one year. In general, a dollar received today is worth *more* than a dollar received in one year: If you have $1 today, you can invest it now and have more money in the future. For example, if you deposit it in a bank account paying 10% interest, you will have $1.10 at the end of one year. We call the difference in value between money today and money in the future the **time value of money**.

time value of money The difference in value between money received today and money received in the future; also, the observation that two cash flows at two different points in time have different values.

Figure 3.1 illustrates how we use competitive market prices and interest rates to convert between dollars today and other goods, or dollars in the future. Just like silver and gold, money today and money tomorrow are not the same thing. We compare them just like we did with silver and gold—using competitive market prices. But in the case of money, what is the price? It is the interest rate, the price for exchanging money today for money in a year. We can use the interest rate to determine values in the same way we used competitive market prices. Once we quantify all the costs and benefits of an investment

FIGURE 3.1

Converting Between
Dollars Today and Gold
or Dollars in the Future

We can convert dollars today to different goods or points in time by using the competitive market price or interest rate. Once values are in equivalent terms, we can use the Valuation Principle to make a decision.

in terms of dollars today, we can rely on the Valuation Principle to determine whether the investment will increase the firm's value.

The Interest Rate: Converting Cash Across Time

We now develop the tools needed to value our $100,000 investment opportunity correctly. By depositing money into a savings account, we can convert money today into money in the future with no risk. Similarly, by borrowing money from the bank, we can exchange money in the future for money today. Suppose the current annual interest rate is 10%. By investing $1 today we can convert this $1 into $1.10 in one year. Similarly, by borrowing at this rate, we can exchange $1.10 in one year for $1 today. More generally, we define the **interest rate**, r, for a given period as the interest rate at which money can be borrowed or lent over that period. In our example, the interest rate is 10% and we can exchange 1 dollar today for $(1 + .10)$ dollars in one year. In general, we can exchange 1 dollar today for $(1 + r)$ dollars in one year, and vice versa. We refer to $(1 + r)$ as the **interest rate factor** for cash flows; it defines how we convert cash flows across time, and has units of "$ in one year/$ today."

> **interest rate** The rate at which money can be borrowed or lent over a given period.

> **interest rate factor** One plus the interest rate, it is the rate of exchange between dollars today and dollars in the future. It has units of "$ in the future/$ today."

Like other market prices, the interest rate ultimately depends on supply and demand. In particular, the interest rate equates the supply of savings to the demand for borrowing. But regardless of how it is determined, once we know the interest rate, we can apply the Valuation Principle and use it to evaluate other decisions in which costs and benefits are separated in time.

Value of $100,000 Investment in One Year. Let's reevaluate the investment we considered earlier, this time taking into account the time value of money. If the interest rate is 10%, then your company faces a choice: use $1 today, or deposit it and have $1.10 in one year. That means we can think of $1.10 as the cost of every dollar used today. So, we can express the cost of the investment as:

$$\text{Cost} = (\$100,000 \text{ today}) \times \left(\frac{\$1.10 \text{ in one year}}{\$1 \text{ today}} \right)$$

$$= \$110,000 \text{ in one year}$$

Think of this amount as the opportunity cost of spending $100,000 today: The firm gives up the $110,000 it would have had in one year if it had left the money in the bank. Alternatively, by borrowing the $100,000 from the same bank, the firm would owe $110,000 in one year.

	Today	One Year
Investment	−$100,000	+$105,000
Bank	−$100,000	+$110,000

We have used a market price, the interest rate, to put both the costs and benefits in terms of "dollars in one year," so now we can use the Valuation Principle to compare them and compute the investment's net value by subtracting the cost of the investment from the benefit in one year:

$$\$105,000 - \$110,000 = -\$5000 \text{ in one year}$$

In other words, the firm could earn $5000 more in one year by putting the $100,000 in the bank rather than making this investment. Because the net value is negative, we should reject the investment: If we took it, the firm would be $5000 poorer in one year than if we didn't.

Value of $100,000 Investment Today. The preceding calculation expressed the value of the costs and benefits in terms of dollars in one year. Alternatively, we can use the interest rate factor to convert to dollars today. Consider the benefit of $105,000 in one year. What is the equivalent amount in terms of dollars today? That is, how much would we need to have in the bank today so we end up with $105,000 in the bank in one year? We find this amount by dividing $105,000 by the interest rate factor:

$$\text{Benefit} = (\$105,000 \text{ in one year}) \div \left(\frac{\$1.10 \text{ in one year}}{\$1 \text{ today}} \right)$$

$$= \$95,454.55 \text{ today}$$

This is also the amount the bank would lend to us today if we promised to repay $105,000 in one year.[2] Thus, it is the competitive market price at which we can "buy" or "sell" today an amount of $105,000 in one year.

	Today	One Year
Value of Cost Today	−$100,000	+$105,000
Value of Benefit Today	+$95,454.55 ← $\frac{105,000}{1.10}$ ←	+$105,000

Now we are ready to compute the net value of the investment today (as opposed to its net value in one year) by subtracting the cost from the benefit:

$$\$95,454.55 - \$100,000 = -\$4545.45 \text{ today}$$

Because this net value is calculated in terms of dollars today (in the present), it is typically called the *net present value*. We will formally introduce this concept in Chapter 8. Once again, the negative result indicates that we should reject the investment. Taking the investment would make the firm $4,545.45 poorer today because it gave up $100,000 for something worth only $95,454.55.

---

[2]We are assuming the bank is willing to lend at the same 10% interest rate, which would be the case if there were no risk associated with the cash flow.

Present Versus Future Value. This calculation demonstrates that our decision is the same whether we express the value of the investment in terms of dollars in one year or dollars today: We should reject the investment. Indeed, if we convert from dollars today to dollars in one year,

$$(-\$4545.45 \text{ today}) \times (\$1.10 \text{ in one year}/\$1 \text{ today}) = -\$5000 \text{ in one year}$$

we see that the two results are equivalent, but expressed as values at different points in time. When we express the value in terms of dollars today, we call it the **present value (PV)** of the investment. If we express it in terms of dollars in the future, we call it the **future value (FV)** of the investment.

present value (PV) The value of a cost or benefit computed in terms of cash today.

future value (FV) The value of a cash flow that is moved forward in time.

discount factor The value today of a dollar received in the future.

discount rate The appropriate rate to discount a cash flow to determine its value at an earlier time.

Discount Factors and Rates. In the preceding calculation, we can interpret

$$\frac{1}{1 + r} = \frac{1}{1.10} = 0.90909$$

as the *price* today of $1 in one year. In other words, for just under 91 cents, you can "buy" $1 to be delivered in one year. Note that the value is less than $1—money in the future is worth less today, so its price reflects a discount. Because it provides the discount at which we can purchase money in the future, the amount $1/(1 + r)$ is called the one-year **discount factor**. The interest rate is also referred to as the **discount rate** for an investment.

EXAMPLE 3.3

Comparing Revenues at Different Points in Time

MyFinanceLab

PROBLEM

The launch of Sony's PlayStation 3 was delayed until November 2006, giving Microsoft's Xbox 360 a full year on the market without competition. Sony did not repeat this mistake in 2013 when PS4 launched at the same time as Xbox One. Imagine that it is November 2005 and you are the marketing manager for the PlayStation. You estimate that if PlayStation 3 were ready to be launched immediately, you could sell $2 billion worth of the console in its first year. However, if your launch is delayed a year, you believe that Microsoft's head start will reduce your first-year sales by 20% to $1.6 billion. If the interest rate is 8%, what is the cost of a delay of the first year's revenues in terms of dollars in 2005?

SOLUTION

PLAN

Revenues if released today: $2 billion   Revenue if delayed: $1.6 billion   Interest rate: 8%

We need to compute the revenues if the launch is delayed and compare them to the revenues from launching today. However, in order to make a fair comparison, we need to convert the future revenues of the PlayStation if they are delayed into an equivalent present value of those revenues today.

EXECUTE

If the launch is delayed to 2006, revenues will drop by 20% of $2 billion, or $400 million, to $1.6 billion. To compare this amount to revenues of $2 billion if launched in 2005, we must convert it using the interest rate of 8%:

$$\$1.6 \text{ billion in } 2006 \div (\$1.08 \text{ in } 2006/\$1 \text{ in } 2005) = \frac{\$1.6 \text{ billion}}{(1.08)} = \$1.481 \text{ billion in } 2005$$

Therefore, the cost of a delay of one year is

$$\$2 \text{ billion} - \$1.481 \text{ billion} = \$0.519 \text{ billion } (\$519 \text{ million}).$$

(Continued)

EVALUATE

Delaying the project for one year was equivalent to giving up $519 million in cash. In this example, we focused only on the effect on the first year's revenues. However, delaying the launch delays the entire revenue stream by one year, so the total cost would be calculated in the same way by summing the cost of delay for each year of revenues.

Timelines

timeline A linear representation of the timing of (potential) cash flows.

Our visual representation of the cost and benefit of the $100,000 investment in this section is an example of a **timeline**, a linear representation of the timing of the expected cash flows. Timelines are an important first step in organizing and then solving a financial problem. We use them throughout this text.

Constructing a Timeline. To understand how to construct a timeline, assume a friend owes you money. He has agreed to repay the loan by making two payments of $10,000 at the end of each of the next two years. We represent this information on a timeline as follows:

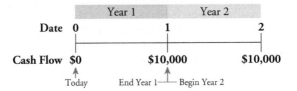

Identifying Dates on a Timeline. To track cash flows, we interpret each point on the timeline as a specific date. The space between date 0 and date 1 represents the first year of the loan. Date 0 is today, the beginning of the first year, and date 1 is the end of the first year. The $10,000 cash flow below date 1 is the payment you will receive at the end of the first year. Similarly, date 1 is the beginning of the second year, date 2 is the end of the second year, and the $10,000 cash flow below date 2 is the payment you will receive at the end of the second year. Note that date 1 signifies *both* the end of year 1 *and* the beginning of year 2, which makes sense since those dates are effectively the same point in time.[3]

Distinguishing Cash Inflows from Outflows. In this example, both cash flows are inflows. In many cases, however, a financial decision will include inflows and outflows. To differentiate between the two types of cash flows, we assign a different sign to each: Inflows (cash flows received) are positive cash flows, whereas outflows (cash flows paid out) are negative cash flows.

To illustrate, suppose you have agreed to lend your brother $10,000 today. Your brother has agreed to repay this loan with interest by making payments of $6000 at the end of each of the next two years. The timeline is:

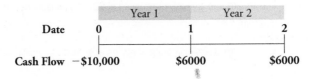

---

[3]That is, there is no real time difference between a cash flow paid at 11:59 P.M. on December 31 and one paid at 12:01 A.M. on January 1, although there may be some other differences such as taxation, which we will overlook for now.

Notice that the first cash flow at date 0 (today) is represented as −$10,000 because it is an outflow. The subsequent cash flows of $6000 are positive because they are inflows.

Representing Various Time Periods. So far, we have used timelines to show the cash flows that occur at the end of each year. Actually, timelines can represent cash flows that take place at any point in time. For example, if you pay rent each month, you could use a timeline such as the one in our first example to represent two rental payments, but you would replace the "year" label with "month."

Many of the timelines included in this chapter are simple. Consequently, you may feel that it is not worth the time or trouble to construct them. As you progress to more difficult problems, however, you will find that timelines identify events in a transaction or investment that are easy to overlook. If you fail to recognize these cash flows, you will make flawed financial decisions. Therefore, approach *every* problem by drawing the timeline as we do in this chapter and the next.

CONCEPT CHECK

5. How is an interest rate like a price?

6. Is the value today of money to be received in one year higher when interest rates are high or when interest rates are low?

3.4 Valuing Cash Flows at Different Points in Time

The example of the $100,000 investment in the previous section laid the groundwork for how we will compare cash flows that happen at different points in time. In this section, we will generalize from the example by introducing three important rules central to financial decision making that allow us to compare or combine values across time.

Rule 1: Comparing and Combining Values

Our first rule is that it is only possible to compare or combine values at the same point in time. This rule restates a conclusion from the last section: Only cash flows in the same units can be compared or combined. A dollar today and a dollar in one year are not equivalent. Having money now is more valuable than having money in the future; if you have the money today you can invest it and earn interest.

To compare or combine cash flows that occur at different points in time, you first need to convert the cash flows into the same units by moving them to the same point in time. The next two rules show how to move the cash flows on the timeline.

COMMON MISTAKE

Summing Cash Flows Across Time

Once you understand the time value of money, our first rule may seem straightforward. However, it is very common, especially for those who have not studied finance, to violate this rule, simply treating all cash flows as comparable regardless of when they are received. One example is in sports contracts. In 2011, Albert Pujols signed a contract with the Los Angeles Angels that was repeatedly referred to as a "$240 million" contract. The $240 million comes from simply adding up all the payments Pujols would receive over the 10 years of the contract—treating dollars received in 10 years the same as dollars received today. The same thing occurred when Lionel Messi signed a contract extension with FC Barcelona in 2013, giving him a "$150 million" contract through 2018, and in 2015 when Giancarlo Stanton signed a "$325 million" 13-year contract with the Florida Marlins.

Rule 2: Compounding

Suppose we have $1000 today, and we wish to determine the equivalent amount in one year's time. If the current market interest rate is 10%, we saw in the last section that we can use that rate as an exchange rate, meaning the rate at which we exchange money today for money in one year, to move the cash flow forward in time. That is:

$$(\$1000 \text{ today}) \times (\$1.10 \text{ in one year}/\$1 \text{ today}) = \$1100 \text{ in one year}$$

In general, if the market interest rate for the year is r, then we multiply by the interest rate factor, $(1 + r)$ to move the cash flow from the beginning to the end of the year. We multiply by $(1 + r)$ because at the end of the year you will have $(1 \times \text{your original investment})$ plus interest in the amount of $(r \times \text{your original investment})$. This process of moving forward along the timeline to determine a cash flow's value in the future (its future value) is known as **compounding**. *Our second rule stipulates that to calculate a cash flow's future value, you must compound it.*

compounding Computing the return on an investment over a long horizon by multiplying the return factors associated with each intervening period.

We can apply this rule repeatedly. Suppose we want to know how much the $1000 is worth in two years' time. If the interest rate for year 2 is also 10%, then we convert as we just did:

$$(\$1100 \text{ in one year}) \times (\$1.10 \text{ in two years}/\$1 \text{ in one year}) = \$1210 \text{ in two years}$$

Let's represent this calculation on a timeline:

Given a 10% interest rate, all of the cash flows—$1000 at date 0, $1100 at date 1, and $1210 at date 2—are equivalent. They have the same value but are expressed in different units (different points in time). An arrow that points to the right indicates that the value is being moved forward in time—that is, compounded.

In the preceding example, $1210 is the future value of $1000 two years from today. Note that the value grows as we move the cash flow further in the future. In the last section, we defined the time value of money as the difference in value between money today and money in the future. Here, we can say that $1210 in two years is equivalent to $1000 today. The reason money is more valuable to you today is that you have opportunities to invest it. As in this example, by having money sooner, you can invest it (here at a 10% return) so that it will grow to a larger amount in the future. Note also that the equivalent amount grows by $100 the first year, but by $110 the second year. In the second year, we earn interest on our original $1000, plus we earn interest on the $100 interest we received in the first year. This effect of earning interest on both the original principal plus the accumulated interest, so that you are earning "interest on interest," is known as **compound interest**. Figure 3.2 shows how over time the amount of money you earn from interest on interest grows so that it will eventually exceed the amount of money that you earn as interest on your original deposit.

compound interest The effect of earning "interest on interest."

How does the future value change in the third year? Continuing to use the same approach, we compound the cash flow a third time. Assuming the competitive market interest rate is fixed at 10%, we get:

$$\$1000 \times (1.10) \times (1.10) \times (1.10) = \$1000 \times (1.10)^3 = \$1331$$

FIGURE 3.2

The Composition of Interest over Time

This bar graph shows how the account balance and the composition of the interest changes over time when an investor starts with an original deposit of $1000, represented by the red area, in an account earning 10% interest over a 20-year period. The green (middle) bars show the effect of **simple interest**, interest earned only on the initial deposit. The blue (top) bars show the effect of compound interest, where interest is also earned on prior interest payments. Over time, the effect of compounding is more pronounced, and by year 20, simple interest is only $2000, whereas interest on interest is $3727.50.

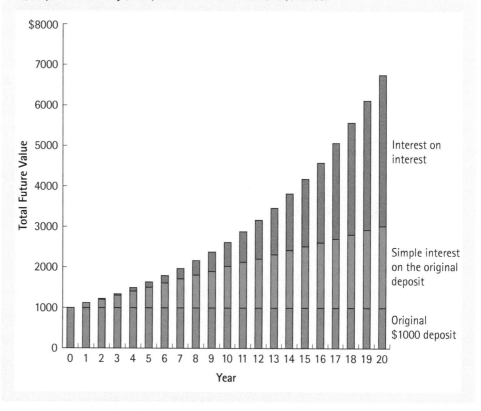

simple interest Interest earned only on the initial deposit

In general, to compute a cash flow C's value n periods into the future, we must compound it by the n intervening interest rate factors. If the interest rate r is constant, this calculation yields:

Future Value of a Cash Flow

$$FV_n = C \times \underbrace{(1 + r) \times (1 + r) \times \cdots \times (1 + r)}_{n \text{ times}} = C \times (1 + r)^n \quad (3.1)$$

 Rule of 72

Another way to think about the effect of compounding is to consider how long it will take your money to double given different interest rates. Suppose you want to know how many years it will take for $1 to grow to a future value of $2. You want the number of years, n, to solve:

$$FV_n = \$1 \times (1 + r)^n = \$2$$

If you solve this formula for different interest rates, you will find the following approximation:

Years to double $\approx 72 \div$ (interest rate in percent)

This simple "Rule of 72" is fairly accurate (that is, within one year of the exact doubling time) for interest rates higher than 2%. For example, if the interest rate is 9%, the doubling time should be about $72 \div 9 = 8$ years. Indeed, $1.09^8 = 1.99$! So, given a 9% interest rate, your money will approximately double every 8 years.

Rule 3: Discounting

The third rule describes how to put a value today on a cash flow that comes in the future. Suppose you would like to compute the value today of $1000 that you anticipate receiving in one year. If the current market interest rate is 10%, you can compute this value by converting units as we did in the last section:

$$(\$1000 \text{ in one year}) \div (\$1.10 \text{ in one year/} \$1 \text{ today}) = \$909.09 \text{ today}$$

That is, to move the cash flow back along the timeline, we divide it by the interest rate factor, $(1 + r)$, where r is the interest rate. This process of finding the equivalent value today of a future cash flow is known as **discounting**. *Our third rule stipulates that to calculate the value of a future cash flow at an earlier point in time, we must discount it.*

discounting Finding the equivalent value today of a future cash flow by multiplying by a discount factor, or equivalently, dividing by 1 plus the discount rate.

Suppose that you anticipate receiving the $1000 two years from today rather than in one year. If the interest rate for both years is 10%, you can prepare the following timeline:

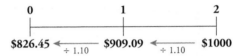

When the interest rate is 10%, all of the cash flows—$826.45 at date 0, $909.09 at date 1, and $1000 at date 2—are equivalent. They represent the same value in different units (different points in time). The arrow points to the left to indicate that the value is being moved backward in time or discounted. Note that the value decreases the further in the future is the original cash flow.

The value of a future cash flow at an earlier point on the timeline is its present value at the earlier point in time. That is, $826.45 is the present value at date 0 of $1000 in two years. Recall that the present value is the "do-it-yourself" price to produce a future cash flow. Thus, if we invested $826.45 today for two years at 10% interest, we would have a future value of $1000, using the second rule of valuing cash flows:

Suppose the $1000 were three years away and you wanted to compute the present value. Again, if the interest rate is 10%, we have:

That is, the present value today of a cash flow of $1000 in three years is given by:

$$\$1000 \div (1.10) \div (1.10) \div (1.10) = \$1000 \div (1.10)^3 = \$751.31$$

In general, to compute the present value of a cash flow C that comes n periods from now, we must discount it by the n intervening interest rate factors. If the interest rate r is constant, this yields:

Present Value of a Cash Flow

$$PV = C \div (1 + r)^n = \frac{C}{(1 + r)^n} \tag{3.2}$$

PERSONAL FINANCE

EXAMPLE 3.4
Present Value
of a Single Future
Cash Flow

MyFinanceLab

PROBLEM

You are considering investing in a savings bond that will pay $15,000 in 10 years. If the competitive market interest rate is fixed at 6% per year, what is the bond worth today?

SOLUTION

PLAN

First, set up your timeline. The cash flows for this bond are represented by the following timeline:
Thus, the bond is worth $15,000 in 10 years. To determine the value today, we compute the present value using Equation 3.2 and our interest rate of 6%.

EXECUTE

$$PV = \frac{15{,}000}{1.06^{10}} = \$8375.92 \text{ today}$$

EVALUATE

The bond is worth much less today than its final payoff because of the time value of money.

As we've seen in this section, we can compare cash flows at different points in time as long as we follow the Three Rules of Valuing Cash Flows, summarized in Table 3.1. Armed with these three rules, a financial manager can compare an investment's costs and benefits that are spread out over time and apply the Valuation Principle to make the right decision. In Chapter 4, we will show you how to apply these rules to situations involving multiple cash flows at different points in time.

TABLE 3.1

The Three Rules of
Valuing Cash Flows

Rule	Formula
1: Only values at the same point in time can be compared or combined.	None
2: To calculate a cash flow's future value, we must compound it.	Future value of a cash flow: $FV_n = C \times (1 + r)^n$
3: To calculate the present value of a future cash flow, we must discount it.	Present value of a cash flow: $PV = C \div (1 + r)^n = \dfrac{C}{(1 + r)^n}$

**CONCEPT
CHECK**

7. Can you compare or combine cash flows at different times?

8. What do you need to know to compute a cash flow's present or future value?

Using a Financial Calculator

Financial calculators are programmed to perform most present and future value calculations. However, we recommend that you develop an understanding of the formulas before using the shortcuts. We provide a more extensive discussion of financial calculators on page 95 and in the appendix to Chapter 4, but we'll cover the relevant functions for this chapter here. To use financial calculator functions, you always enter the known values first and then the calculator solves for the unknown.

To answer Example 3.4 with a financial calculator, do the following:

Concept	Number of Periods	Interest Rate per Period	Recurring Payments	Future Value
Calculator Key	N	I/Y	PMT	FV
Enter	10	6	0	15000

Because you are solving for the present value (PV), press the PV key last (on an HP calculator), or press CPT then the PV key on a TI calculator. The calculator will return −8375.92. Note that the calculator balances inflows with outflows, so because the FV is positive (an inflow), it returns the PV as a negative (an outflow).

If you were solving for the future value instead, you would enter:

N	I/Y	PV	PMT
10	6	−8375.92	0

And finally, on an HP, press the FV key or on a TI, press CPT and then the FV key.

MyFinanceLab

Here is what you should know after reading this chapter. MyFinanceLab will help you identify what you know, and where to go when you need to practice.

KEY POINTS AND EQUATIONS	KEY TERMS	ONLINE PRACTICE
3.1 Cost-Benefit Analysis • To evaluate a decision, we must value the incremental costs and benefits associated with that decision. A good decision is one for which the value of the benefits exceeds the value of the costs. • To compare costs and benefits that occur at different points in time we must put all costs and benefits in common terms. Typically, we convert costs and benefits into cash today. • A competitive market is one in which a good can be bought and sold at the same price. We use prices from competitive markets to determine the cash value of a good.	competitive market, p. 75	MyFinanceLab Study Plan 3.1

3.2 Market Prices and the Valuation Principle
- Arbitrage is the process of trading to take advantage of equivalent goods that have different prices in different competitive markets.
- If equivalent goods or securities trade simultaneously in different competitive markets, they will trade for the same price in each market. This is equivalent to saying that no arbitrage opportunities should exist.
- The Valuation Principle states that the value of a commodity or an asset to the firm or its investors is determined by its competitive market price. The benefits and costs of a decision should be evaluated using those market prices. When the value of the benefits exceeds the value of the costs, the decision will increase the market value of the firm.

arbitrage, p. 77
arbitrage opportunity, p. 77
Law of One Price, p. 77

MyFinanceLab Study Plan 3.2

3.3 The Time Value of Money and Interest Rates
- The time value of money is the difference in value between money today and money in the future.
- The rate at which we can exchange money today for money in the future by borrowing or investing is the current market interest rate.
- The present value (PV) of a cash flow is its value in terms of cash today.
- Timelines are a critical first step in organizing the cash flows in a financial problem.

discount factor, p. 81
discount rate, p. 81
future value (FV), p. 81
interest rate, p. 79
interest rate factor, p. 79
present value (PV), p. 81
time value of money, p. 78
timeline, p. 82

MyFinanceLab Study Plan 3.3

3.4 Valuing Cash Flows at Different Points in Time
- There are three rules of valuing cash flows:
  a. Only cash flows that occur at the same point in time can be compared or combined.
  b. To calculate a cash flow's future value, you must compound it.
  c. To calculate a cash flow's present value, you must discount it.
- The future value in n years of a cash flow C today is:
$$C \times (1 + r)^n \qquad (3.1)$$
- The present value today of a cash flow C received in n years is:
$$C \div (1 + r)^n \qquad (3.2)$$

compounding, p. 84
compound interest, p. 84
discounting, p. 86
simple interest, p. 85

MyFinanceLab Study Plan 3.4

Financial Calculator Tutorials: Calculating the Future Value of a Lump Sum and Solving for the Present Value of a Single Future Cash Flow

CRITICAL THINKING

1. What makes an investment decision a good one?
2. How important are our personal preferences in valuing an investment decision?
3. Why are market prices useful to a financial manager?
4. Why is arbitrage important to competitive market prices?
5. How does the Valuation Principle help a financial manager make decisions?
6. Can we directly compare dollar amounts received at different points in time?
7. Why is a cash flow in the future worth less than the same amount today?

8. What is a discount rate?

9. What is compound interest?

10. What is the intuition behind the geometric growth in interest?

PROBLEMS

All problems are available in MyFinanceLab. An asterisk * indicates problems with a higher level of difficulty.

Cost-Benefit Analysis

1. Honda Motor Company is considering offering a $2000 rebate on its minivan, lowering the vehicle's price from $30,000 to $28,000. The marketing group estimates that this rebate will increase sales over the next year from 40,000 to 55,000 vehicles. Suppose Honda's profit margin with the rebate is $6000 per vehicle. If the change in sales is the only consequence of this decision, what are its costs and benefits? Is it a good idea?

2. You are an international shrimp trader. A food producer in the Czech Republic offers to pay you 2 million Czech koruna today in exchange for a year's supply of frozen shrimp. Your Thai supplier will provide you with the same supply for 3 million Thai baht today. If the current competitive market exchange rates are 25.50 koruna per dollar and 41.25 baht per dollar, what is the value of this exchange to you?

3. Suppose your employer offers you a choice between a $5000 bonus and 100 shares of the company's stock. Whichever one you choose will be awarded today. The stock is currently trading at $63 per share.
   a. Suppose that if you receive the stock bonus, you are free to trade it. Which form of the bonus should you choose? What is its value?
   b. Suppose that if you receive the stock bonus, you are required to hold it for at least one year. What can you say about the value of the stock bonus now? What will your decision depend on?

4. Suppose Big Bank offers an interest rate of 5.5% on both savings and loans, and Bank Enn offers an interest rate of 6% on both savings and loans.
   a. What profit opportunity is available?
   b. Which bank would experience a surge in the demand for loans? Which bank would receive a surge in deposits?
   c. What would you expect to happen to the interest rates the two banks are offering?

5. If the cost of buying a CD and ripping the tracks to your iPod (including your time) is $25, what is the most Apple could charge on iTunes for a whole 15-track CD?

6. Some companies cross-list their shares, meaning that their stock trades on more than one stock exchange. For example, Restaurant Brands International (QSR), the parent company of Burger King and Tim Hortons, trades on both the Toronto Stock Exchange and NYSE. If its price in Toronto is 50 Canadian dollars per share and anyone can exchange Canadian dollars for U.S. dollars at the rate of US$0.85 per C$1.00, what must QSR's price be on NYSE?

Market Prices and the Valuation Principle

7. Bubba is a shrimp farmer. In an ironic twist, Bubba is allergic to shellfish, so he cannot eat any shrimp. Each day he has a one-ton supply of shrimp. The market price of shrimp is $10,000 per ton.
   a. What is the value of a ton of shrimp to him?
   b. Would this value change if he were not allergic to shrimp? Why or why not?

8. Brett has almond orchards, but he is sick of almonds and prefers to eat walnuts instead. The owner of the walnut orchard next door has offered to swap this year's crop with him. Assume he produces 1000 tons of almonds and his neighbor produces 800 tons of walnuts. If the market price of almonds is $100 per ton and the market price of walnuts is $110 per ton:
   a. Should he make the exchange?
   b. Does it matter whether he prefers almonds or walnuts? Why or why not?

The Time Value of Money and Interest Rates

9. You have $100 and a bank is offering 5% interest on deposits. If you deposit the money in the bank, how much will you have in one year?

10. You expect to have $1000 in one year. A bank is offering loans at 6% interest per year. How much can you borrow today?

11. Due to your good credit, your bank reduces the interest rate on your $12,000 loan from 9% to 7.5% per year. Thanks to the change, how much will you save in interest this year?

12. A friend asks to borrow $55 from you and in return will pay you $58 in one year. If your bank is offering a 6% interest rate on deposits and loans:
   a. How much would you have in one year if you deposited the $55 instead?
   b. How much money could you borrow today if you pay the bank $58 in one year?
   c. Should you loan the money to your friend or deposit it in the bank?

13. What is the discount factor that is equivalent to a 6% discount rate?

14. If your discount factor is 0.9009, what is your discount rate?

15. You plan to borrow $1000 from a bank. In exchange for $1000 today, you promise to pay $1080 in one year. What does the cash flow timeline look like from your perspective? What does it look like from the bank's perspective?

16. The local electronics store is offering a promotion "1-year: same as cash," meaning that you can buy a TV now, and wait a year to pay (with no interest). So, if you take home a $1000 TV today, you will owe them $1000 in one year. If your bank is offering 4% interest, what is the true cost of the TV to you today?

Valuing Cash Flows at Different Points in Time

17. Suppose the interest rate is 4%.
   a. Having $200 today is equivalent to having what amount in one year?
   b. Having $200 in one year is equivalent to having what amount today?
   c. Which would you prefer, $200 today or $200 in one year? Does your answer depend on when you need the money? Why or why not?

18. You are considering a savings bond that will pay $100 in 10 years. If the interest rate is 2%, what should you pay today for the bond?

19. If your bank pays you 1.5% interest and you deposit $500 today, what will your balance be in 5 years?

20. Consider the following alternatives:
   i. $100 received in one year
   ii. $200 received in 5 years
   iii. $300 received in 10 years
   a. Rank the alternatives from most valuable to least valuable if the interest rate is 10% per year.
   b. What is your ranking if the interest rate is only 5% per year?
   c. What is your ranking if the interest rate is 20% per year?

*21. Suppose you invest $1000 in an account paying 8% interest per year.
   a. What is the balance in the account after 3 years? How much of this balance corresponds to "interest on interest"?
   b. What is the balance in the account after 25 years? How much of this balance corresponds to "interest on interest"?

22. Calculate the future value of $2000 in
   a. 5 years at an interest rate of 5% per year.
   b. 10 years at an interest rate of 5% per year.
   c. 5 years at an interest rate of 10% per year.
   *d. Why is the amount of interest earned in part (a) less than half the amount of interest earned in part (b)?

23. What is the present value of $10,000 received
   a. 12 years from today when the interest rate is 4% per year?
   b. 20 years from today when the interest rate is 8% per year?
   c. 6 years from today when the interest rate is 2% per year?

24. Your brother has offered to give you either $5000 today or $10,000 in 10 years. If the interest rate is 7% per year, which option is preferable?

25. Your bank pays 2.5% interest per year. You put $1000 in the bank today and $500 more in the bank in one year. How much will you have in the bank in 2 years?

26. Your cousin is currently 12 years old. She will be going to college in 6 years. Your aunt and uncle would like to have $100,000 in a savings account to fund her education at that time. If the account promises to pay a fixed interest rate of 4% per year, how much money do they need to put into the account today to ensure that they will have $100,000 in 6 years?

27. Your mom is thinking of retiring. Her retirement plan will pay her either $250,000 immediately on retirement or $350,000 five years after the date of her retirement. Which alternative should she choose if the interest rate is
   a. 0% per year?
   b. 8% per year?
   c. 20% per year?

28. You just won a prize that comes with two payout choices. The first option is to get $100,000 right now and nothing hereafter. The second option is to get $94,000 right now and $10,000 three years from now (and nothing after that). If your discount rate is 8%, which should you take?

29. You are planning to invest $5000 in an account earning 9% per year for retirement.
   a. If you put the $5000 in an account at age 23, and withdraw it 42 years later, how much will you have?
   b. If you wait 10 years before making the deposit, so that it stays in the account for only 32 years, how much will you have at the end?

*30. Your grandfather put some money in an account for you on the day you were born. You are now 18 years old and are allowed to withdraw the money for the first time. The account currently has $3996 in it and pays an 8% interest rate.
   a. How much money would be in the account if you left the money there until your 25th birthday?
   b. What if you left the money until your 65th birthday?
   c. How much money did your grandfather originally put in the account?

4

Time Value of Money: Valuing Cash Flow Streams

LEARNING OBJECTIVES

- Value a series of many cash flows

- Value a perpetual series of regular cash flows called a *perpetuity*

- Value a common set of regular cash flows called an *annuity*

- Value both perpetuities and annuities when the cash flows grow at a constant rate

- Compute the number of periods, cash flow, or rate of return of a loan or investment

- Value cash flow streams with non-annual payments

notation		
C	cash flow	
C_n	cash flow at date n	
FV	future value	
FV_n	future value on date n	
g	growth rate	

N	date of the last cash flow in a stream of cash flows	
P	initial principal or deposit, or equivalent present value	
PV	present value	
r	interest rate or rate of return	

As we have discussed, to evaluate a project a financial manager must compare its costs and benefits. In most cases, the cash flows in financial investments involve more than one future period. Thus, the financial manager is faced with the task of trading off a known up-front cost against a series of uncertain future benefits. We learned to value those costs and benefits by computing their cash values today—their present values.

In financial management, as well as your personal finances, you will need to evaluate series of cash flows occurring across time. In this chapter, we build on the tools we developed in Chapter 3 to value any series of cash flows. We will develop shortcuts for valuing *annuities*, *perpetuities*, and other special cases of assets with cash flows that follow regular patterns.

In Chapter 5, we will learn how interest rates are quoted and determined. Once we understand how interest rates are quoted, it will be straightforward to extend the tools of this chapter to cash flows that occur more frequently than once per year.

Valuing a Stream of Cash Flows

stream of cash flows
A series of cash flows
lasting several periods.

We refer to a series of cash flows lasting several periods as a **stream of cash flows**. As with single cash flows, we can represent a stream of cash flows on a timeline. In this chapter, we will continue to use timelines and the rules of cash flow valuation introduced in Chapter 3 to organize and then solve financial problems.

Applying the Rules of Valuing Cash Flows to a Cash Flow Stream

Most investment opportunities have multiple cash flows that occur at different points in time. In Chapter 3, we learned the rules to value such cash flows:

Rule 1: Only values at the same point in time can be compared or combined.

Rule 2: To calculate a cash flow's future value, we must compound it using Eq. 3.1 from Chapter 3.

$$FV_n = C \times (1 + r)^n \tag{4.1}$$

Rule 3: To calculate the present value of a future cash flow, we must discount it using Eq. 3.2 from Chapter 3.

$$PV = C \div (1 + r)^n = \frac{C}{(1 + r)^n} \tag{4.2}$$

The rules of cash flow valuation allow us to compare and combine cash flows that occur at different points in time. Suppose we plan to save $1000 today and $1000 at the end of each of the next two years. If we earn a fixed 10% interest rate on our savings, how much will we have three years from today?

Again, we start with a timeline:

The timeline shows the three deposits we plan to make. We need to compute their value at the end of three years.

We can use the cash flow valuation rules in a number of ways to solve this problem. First, we can take the deposit at date 0 and move it forward to date 1. Because it is then in the same time period as the date 1 deposit, we can combine the two amounts to find out the total in the bank on date 1:

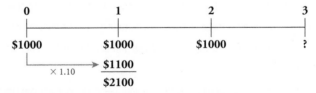

Using the first two rules, we find that our total savings on date 1 will be $2100. Continuing in this fashion, we can solve the problem as follows:

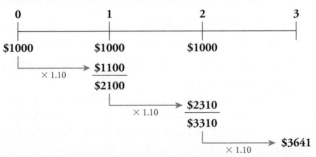

The total amount we will have in the bank at the end of three years is $3641. This amount is the future value of our $1000 savings deposits.

Another approach to the problem is to compute the future value in year 3 of each cash flow separately. Once all three amounts are in year 3 dollars, we can then combine them.

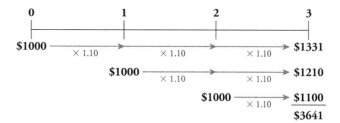

Both calculations give the same future value of $3641. As long as we follow the rules, we get the same result. The order in which we apply the rules does not matter. The calculation we choose depends on which is more convenient for the problem at hand.

Now we formalize this approach by deriving a general formula for valuing a stream of cash flows.

Consider a stream of cash flows: C_0 at date 0, C_1 at date 1, and so on, up to C_N at date N. We represent this cash flow stream on a timeline as follows:

$$
\begin{array}{ccccc}
0 & 1 & 2 & & N \\
\vert & \vert & \vert & \cdots & \vert \\
C_0 & C_1 & C_2 & & C_N
\end{array}
$$

Using the rules of cash flow valuation, we compute the present value of this cash flow stream in two steps. First, we compute the present value of each individual cash flow. Then, once the cash flows are in common units of dollars today, we can combine them.

For a given interest rate r, we represent this process on the timeline as follows:

This timeline provides the general formula for the present value of a cash flow stream:

$$PV = C_0 + \frac{C_1}{(1+r)} + \frac{C_2}{(1+r)^2} + \cdots + \frac{C_N}{(1+r)^N} \tag{4.3}$$

That is, the present value of the cash flow stream is the sum of the present values of each cash flow. Recall from Chapter 3 that we defined the present value as the dollar amount you would need to invest today to produce the single cash flow in the future. The same idea holds in this context. The present value is the amount you need to invest today to generate the cash flows stream $C_0, C_1, \ldots, C_N$. That is, receiving those cash flows is equivalent to having their present value in the bank today.

EXAMPLE 4.1
Present Value of a Stream of Cash Flows

MyFinanceLab

PROBLEM

You have just graduated and need money to buy a new car. Your rich Uncle Henry will lend you the money as long as you agree to pay him back within four years, and you offer to pay him the rate of interest that he would otherwise get by putting his money in a savings account. Based on your earnings and living expenses, you think you will be able to pay him $5000 in one year, and then $8000 each year for the next three years. If Uncle Henry would otherwise earn 6% per year on his savings, how much can you borrow from him?

SOLUTION

PLAN

The cash flows you can promise Uncle Henry are as follows:

How much money should Uncle Henry be willing to give you today in return for your promise of these payments? He should be willing to give you an amount that is equivalent to these payments in present value terms. This is the amount of money that it would take him to produce these same cash flows. We will (1) solve the problem using Eq. 4.3 and then (2) verify our answer by calculating the future value of this amount.

EXECUTE

1. We can calculate the PV as follows:

$$PV = \frac{5000}{1.06} + \frac{8000}{1.06^2} + \frac{8000}{1.06^3} + \frac{8000}{1.06^4}$$
$$= 4716.98 + 7119.97 + 6716.95 + 6336.75$$
$$= \$24{,}890.65$$

Now suppose that Uncle Henry gives you the money, and then deposits your payments to him in the bank each year. How much will he have four years from now?

We need to compute the future value of the annual deposits. One way to do this is to compute the bank balance each year:

2. To verify our answer, suppose your uncle kept his $24,890.65 in the bank today earning 6% interest. In four years he would have:
$$FV = \$24{,}890.65 \times (1.06)^4 = \$31{,}423.87 \text{ in 4 years}$$

We get the same answer both ways (within a penny, which is due to rounding).

EVALUATE

Thus, Uncle Henry should be willing to lend you $24,890.65 in exchange for your promised payments. This amount is less than the total you will pay him ($5000 + $8000 + $8000 + $8000 = $29,000) due to the time value of money.

Example 4.1 illustrates that if you want to compute the future value of a stream of cash flows, you can do it directly (the first approach), or you can first compute the present value and then move it to the future (the second approach). As always, we use Eq. 4.1 to calculate the future value of any present value. Because we obey the rules of valuing cash flows in both cases, we get the same result.

Using a Financial Calculator: Solving for Present and Future Values of Cash Flow Streams

So far, we have used formulas to compute present values and future values of cash flow streams. As we discussed at the end of Chapter 3, both financial calculators and spreadsheets have these formulas preprogrammed to quicken the process. In this box, we focus on financial calculators, but spreadsheets such as Excel have very similar shortcut functions.

Financial calculators have a set of functions that perform the calculations that finance professionals do most often. These functions are all based on the following timeline, which among other things can handle most types of loans:

0	1	2		NPER
PV	PMT	PMT	$\cdots$	$PMT + FV$

There are a total of five variables: number of periods (N or $NPER$), present value (PV), cash flow or "payment" (PMT), future value (FV), and the interest rate, denoted I/Y. Each function takes four of these variables as inputs and returns the value of the fifth one that ensures that the sum of the present value of the cash flows is zero.

By setting the recurring payments equal to 0, you could compute present and future values of single cash flows such as we have done above using Eqs. 4.2 and 4.1. In the examples shown in Sections 4.2 through 4.4, we will calculate cash flows using the **PMT** button. The best way to learn to use a financial calculator is by practicing. We present one example below. We will also show the calculator buttons for any additional examples in this chapter that can be solved with financial calculator functions. Finally, the appendix to this chapter contains step-by-step instructions for using the two most popular financial calculators.

Example

Suppose you plan to invest $20,000 in an account paying 8% interest. You will invest an additional $1000 at the end of each year for 15 years. How much will you have in the account in 15 years? We represent this problem with the following timeline:

0	1	2		NPER = 15
$PV = -\$20,000$	$PMT = -\$1000$	$-\$1000$	$\cdots$	$FV = ?$

To compute the solution, we enter the four variables we know, $N = 15$, $I/Y = 8$, $PV = -20,000$, $PMT = -\$1000$, and solve for the one we want to determine: FV. Specifically, for the HP-10BII or TI-BAII Plus calculators:

1. Enter 15 and press the **N** button.
2. Enter 8 and press the **I/Y** button (**I/YR** for the HP calculator).
3. Enter −20,000 and press the **PV** button.
4. Enter −$1000 and press the **PMT** button.
5. Press the **FV** button (for the Texas Instruments calculator, press **CPT** and then **FV**).

	N	**I/Y**	**PV**	**PMT**	**FV**
Given:	15	8	−20,000	−1000	
Solve for:					90,595.50
	Excel Formula: =FV(0.08,15,−1000,−20000)				

The calculator then shows a future value of $90,595.50.

Note that we entered PV and PMT as negative numbers (the amounts we are putting *into* the bank), and FV is shown as a positive number (the amount we can take *out* of the bank). It is important to use signs correctly to indicate the direction in which the money is flowing when using the calculator functions. You will see more examples of getting the sign of the cash flows correct throughout the chapter.

Excel has the same functions, but it calls "N," "NPER" and "I/Y," "RATE." *Also, it is important to note that you enter an interest rate of 8% as "8" in a financial calculator, but as "0.08" in Excel.*

PERSONAL FINANCE

EXAMPLE 4.2
Computing the
Future Value

MyFinanceLab

PROBLEM

Let's revisit the savings plan we considered earlier: We plan to save $1000 today and at the end of each of the next two years. At a fixed 10% interest rate, how much will we have in the bank three years from today?

SOLUTION

PLAN

We'll start with the timeline for this savings plan:

Let's solve this problem in a different way than we did in the text, while still following the rules we established. First, we'll compute the present value of the cash flows. Then, we'll compute its value three years later (its future value).

EXECUTE

There are several ways to calculate the present value of the cash flows. Here, we treat each cash flow separately and then combine the present values.

Saving $2735.54 today is equivalent to saving $1000 per year for three years. Now let's compute future value in year 3 of that $2735.54:

EVALUATE

This answer of $3641 is precisely the same result we found earlier. As long as we apply the three rules of valuing cash flows, we will always get the correct answer.

CONCEPT
CHECK

1. How do you calculate the present value of a cash flow stream?

2. How do you calculate the future value of a cash flow stream?

4.2 Perpetuities

The formulas we have developed so far allow us to compute the present or future value of any cash flow stream. In this section and the next one, we consider two types of cash flow streams, *perpetuities* and *annuities*, and learn shortcuts for valuing them. These shortcuts are possible because the cash flows follow a regular pattern.

Perpetuities

perpetuity A stream of equal cash flows that occurs at regular intervals and lasts forever.

consol A bond that promises its owner a fixed cash flow every year, forever.

A **perpetuity** is a stream of equal cash flows that occur at regular intervals and last forever. One example is the British government bond called a **consol** (or *perpetual bond*). Consol bonds promise the owner a fixed cash flow every year, forever.

Here is the timeline for a perpetuity:

Note from the timeline that the first cash flow does not occur immediately; *it arrives at the end of the first period.* This timing is sometimes referred to as *payment in arrears* and is a standard convention in loan payment calculations and elsewhere, so we adopt it throughout this text.

Using the formula for the present value, the present value of a perpetuity with payment C and interest rate r is given by:

$$PV = \frac{C}{(1+r)} + \frac{C}{(1+r)^2} + \frac{C}{(1+r)^3} + \cdots$$

Notice that all the cash flows (C in the formula) are the same because the cash flow for a perpetuity is constant. Also, because the first cash flow is in one period, there is no cash flow at time 0 ($C_0 = 0$).

To find the value of a perpetuity by discounting one cash flow at a time would take forever—literally! You might wonder how, even with a shortcut, the sum of an infinite number of positive terms could be finite. The answer is that the cash flows in the future are discounted for an ever-increasing number of periods, so their contribution to the sum eventually becomes negligible.

To derive the shortcut, we calculate the value of a perpetuity by creating our own perpetuity. The Valuation Principle tells us that the value of a perpetuity must be the same as the cost we incurred to create our own identical perpetuity. To illustrate, suppose you could invest $100 in a bank account paying 5% interest per year, forever. At the end of one year, you will have $105 in the bank—your original $100 plus $5 in interest. Suppose you withdraw the $5 interest and reinvest the $100 for a second year. Again, you will have $105 after one year, and you can withdraw $5 and reinvest $100 for another year. By doing this year after year, you can withdraw $5 every year in perpetuity:

By investing $100 in the bank today, you can, in effect, create a perpetuity paying $5 per year. Because the bank will "sell" us (allow us to create) the perpetuity for $100, the present value of the $5 per year in perpetuity is this "do-it-yourself" cost of $100.

Now let's generalize this argument. Suppose we invest an amount P in a bank account with an interest rate r. Every year we can withdraw the interest we have earned, $C = r \times P$, leaving the principal, P, in the bank. Because our cost for creating the perpetuity is only the initial investment of principal (P), the value of receiving C in perpetuity is therefore the upfront cost P. Rearranging $C = r \times P$ to solve for P we have $P = C/r$. Therefore:

Present Value of a Perpetuity

$$PV(C \text{ in Perpetuity}) = \frac{C}{r} \tag{4.4}$$

By depositing the amount $\dfrac{C}{r}$ today, we can withdraw interest of $\dfrac{C}{r} \times r = C$ each period in perpetuity.

Note the logic of our argument. To determine the present value of a cash flow stream, we computed the "do-it-yourself" cost of creating those same cash flows at the bank. This is an extremely useful and powerful approach—and is much simpler and faster than summing those infinite terms![1]

Historical Examples of Perpetuities

Companies sometimes issue bonds that they call perpetuities, but in fact are not really perpetuities. For example, in mid-2010, Europe's largest bank, HSBC, sold $3.4 billion of "perpetual" bonds that promise investors a fixed amount each year with no maturity date. But while the bonds have no fixed maturity, they are not exactly true perpetuities as HSBC has the right to pay off the bonds after 5½ years. Thus, the bond's payments might not last forever. Perpetual bonds were some of the first bonds ever issued. The oldest perpetuities that are still making interest payments were issued in 1624 by the *Hoogheemraadschap Lekdijk Bovendams*, a seventeenth-century Dutch water board responsible for upkeep of the local dikes. To verify that these bonds continue to pay interest, two finance professors at Yale University,

William Goetzmann and Geert Rouwenhorst, purchased one of these bonds on July 1, 2003, and collected 26 years of back interest. On its issue date in 1648, this bond originally paid interest in Carolus guilders. Over the next 355 years, the currency of payment changed to Flemish pounds, Dutch guilders, and most recently euros. Recently, the bond was paying interest of €11.34 annually.

Although the Dutch bonds are the oldest perpetuities still in existence, the first perpetuities date from much earlier times. For example, *cencus agreements* and *rentes*, which were forms of perpetuities and annuities, were issued in the twelfth century in Italy, France, and Spain. They were initially designed to circumvent the usury laws of the Catholic Church: Because they did not require the repayment of principal, in the eyes of the church they were not considered loans.

PERSONAL FINANCE

EXAMPLE 4.3

Endowing a Perpetuity

MyFinanceLab

PROBLEM

You want to endow an annual graduation party at your alma mater. You want the event to be memorable, so you budget $30,000 per year forever for the party. If the university earns 8% per year on its investments, and if the first party is in one year's time, how much will you need to donate to endow the party?

SOLUTION

PLAN

The timeline of the cash flows you want to provide is:

This is a standard perpetuity of $30,000 per year. The funding you would need to give the university in perpetuity is the present value of this cash flow stream.

EXECUTE

Use the formula for a perpetuity:

$$PV = C/r = \$30,000/0.08 = \$375,000 \text{ today}$$

EVALUATE

If you donate $375,000 today, and if the university invests it at 8% per year forever, then the graduates will have $30,000 every year to fund their graduation party.

---

[1]Another mathematical derivation of this result exists (see the online appendix), but it is less intuitive.

COMMON MISTAKE

Discounting One Too Many Times

The perpetuity formula assumes that the first payment occurs at the end of the first period (at date 1). Sometimes perpetuities have cash flows that start later. In this case, we can adapt the perpetuity formula to compute the present value, but we need to do so carefully to avoid a common mistake.

To illustrate, consider the graduation party described in Example 4.3. Rather than starting in one year, suppose the first party will be held two years from today. How would this delay change the amount of the donation required?

Now the timeline looks like this:

We need to determine the present value of these cash flows, as it tells us the amount of money needed in the bank today to finance the future parties. We cannot apply the perpetuity formula directly, however, because these cash flows are not *exactly* a perpetuity as we defined it. Specifically, the cash flow in the first period is "missing." But consider the situation on date 1—at that

point, the first party is one period away and then the cash flows occur regularly. From the perspective of date 1, this *is* a perpetuity, and we can apply the formula. From the preceding calculation, we know we need $375,000 on date 1 to have enough to start the parties on date 2. We rewrite the timeline as follows:

Our goal can now be restated more simply: How much do we need to invest today to have $375,000 in one year? This is a simple present value calculation:

$$PV = \$375,000/1.08 = \$347,222 \text{ today}$$

A common mistake is to discount the $375,000 twice because the first party is in two periods. *Remember—the present value formula for the perpetuity already discounts the cash flows to one period prior to the first cash flow.* Keep in mind that this common mistake may be made with perpetuities, annuities, and all the other special cases discussed in this chapter. All these formulas discount the cash flows to one period prior to the first cash flow.

CONCEPT CHECK

3. What are some examples of perpetuities?

4. What is the intuition behind the fact that an infinite stream of cash flows has a finite present value?

4.3   Annuities

annuity A stream of equal cash flows arriving at a regular interval and ending after a specified time period.

An **annuity** is a stream consisting of a fixed number of equal cash flows paid at regular intervals. So the difference between an annuity and a perpetuity is that an annuity ends after some fixed number of payments whereas a perpetuity continues forever. Most car loans, mortgages, and some bonds are annuities. We represent the cash flows of an annuity on a timeline as follows:

Note that just as with the perpetuity, we adopt the convention that the first payment takes place at date 1, one period from today. The present value of an N-period annuity with payment C and interest rate r is:

$$PV = \frac{C}{(1+r)} + \frac{C}{(1+r)^2} + \frac{C}{(1+r)^3} + \cdots + \frac{C}{(1+r)^N}$$

Present Value of an Annuity

To find a simpler formula, we use the same approach we followed with the perpetuity: Find a way to create your own annuity. To illustrate, suppose you invest $100 in a bank account paying 5% interest. At the end of one year, you will have $105 in the bank—your original

$100 plus $5 in interest. Using the same strategy as you did for calculating the value of a perpetuity, suppose you withdraw the $5 interest and reinvest the $100 for a second year. Once again you will have $105 after one year. You can repeat the process, withdrawing $5 and reinvesting $100, every year. For a perpetuity, you left the principal in the bank forever. Alternatively, you might decide after 20 years to close the account and withdraw the principal. In that case, your cash flows will look like this:

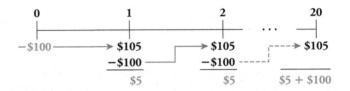

With your initial $100 investment, you have created a 20-year annuity of $5 per year, plus you will receive an extra $100 at the end of 20 years. The Valuation Principle's Law of One Price tells us that things that produce exactly the same cash flows must have the same value. Because it only took an initial investment of $100 to create the cash flows on the timeline, the present value of these cash flows is $100, or:

$$\$100 = PV(\text{20-year annuity of \$5 per year}) + PV(\$100 \text{ in 20 years})$$

So if we invest $100 now, we can receive $5 per year for 20 years as well as $100 in the 20th year, representing the following cash flows:

0	1	2		20
−$100	$5	$5	...	$5 + $100

Rearranging the equation above shows that the cost of a 20-year annuity of $5 per year is $100 minus the present value of $100 in 20 years.

$$PV(\text{20-year annuity of \$5 per year}) = \$100 - PV(\$100 \text{ in 20 years})$$

$$= 100 - \frac{100}{(1.05)^{20}} = \$100 - \$37.69 = \$62.31$$

0	1	2		20
−$100	$5	$5	...	$5 + $100

Removing the $100 in 20 years and its present value ($37.69) leaves the following cash flows:

−$62.31	$5	$5	...	$5

So the present value of $5 for 20 years is $62.31. Intuitively, the value of the annuity is the initial investment in the bank account minus the present value of the principal that will be left in the account after 20 years.

The $5 we receive every year is the interest on the $100 and can be written as $100(.05) = $5. Rearranging this equation, we have $100 = $5/.05. If we substitute $5/.05 into our formula above, we can represent the PV of the annuity as a function of its cash flow ($5), the discount rate (5%) and the number of years (20):

$$PV(\text{20-year annuity of \$5 per year}) = \frac{\$5}{.05} - \frac{\frac{\$5}{.05}}{(1.05)^{20}} = \frac{\$5}{.05}\left(1 - \frac{1}{(1.05)^{20}}\right)$$

$$= \$5 \times \frac{1}{.05}\left(1 - \frac{1}{(1.05)^{20}}\right)$$

This method is very useful because we will most often want to know the PV of the annuity given its cash flow, discount rate, and number of years. We can write this as a general formula for the present value of an annuity of C for N periods:

Present Value of an Annuity

$$PV(\text{Annuity of } C \text{ for } N \text{ Periods with Interest Rate } r) = C \times \frac{1}{r}\left(1 - \frac{1}{(1+r)^N}\right) \qquad (4.5)$$

PERSONAL FINANCE

EXAMPLE 4.4
Present Value of
a Lottery Prize
Annuity

MyFinanceLab

PROBLEM

You are the lucky winner of a $30 million state lottery. You can take your prize money either as (a) 30 payments of $1 million per year (starting today), or (b) $15 million paid today. If the interest rate is 8%, which option should you choose?

SOLUTION

PLAN

Option (a) provides $30 million in prize money but paid over time. To evaluate it correctly, we must convert it to a present value. Here is the timeline:

```
    0              1              2                   29
    |              |              |         . . .      |
$1 million     $1 million     $1 million           $1 million
```

Because the first payment starts today, the last payment will occur in 29 years (for a total of 30 payments).[2] The $1 million at date 0 is already stated in present value terms, but we need to compute the present value of the remaining payments. Fortunately, this case looks like a 29-year annuity of $1 million per year, so we can use the annuity formula.

EXECUTE

We use the annuity formula:

$$PV(\text{29-year annuity of \$1 million at 8\% annual interest}) = \$1 \text{ million} \times \frac{1}{0.08}\left(1 - \frac{1}{1.08^{29}}\right)$$

$$= \$1 \text{ million} \times 11.16$$

$$= \$11.16 \text{ million today}$$

(Continued)

---

[2]An annuity in which the first payment occurs immediately is sometimes called an *annuity due*. Throughout this text, we always use the term "annuity" to mean one that is paid in arrears.

Thus, the total present value of the cash flows is $1 million + $11.16 million = $12.16 million. In timeline form:

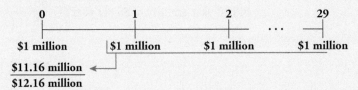

Option (b), $15 million upfront, is more valuable—even though the total amount of money paid is half that of option (a).

Financial calculators or Excel can handle annuities easily—just enter the cash flow in the annuity as the PMT:

	N	I/Y	PV	PMT	FV
Given:	29	8		1,000,000	0
Solve for:			−11,158,406		
Excel Formula: =PV(RATE,NPER,PMT,FV)=PV(0.08,29,1000000,0)					

Both the financial calculator and Excel will give you the PV of the 29 payments ($11,158,406, or 11.16 million), to which you must add the first payment of $1 million just as shown.

EVALUATE

The reason for the difference is the time value of money. If you have the $15 million today, you can use $1 million immediately and invest the remaining $14 million at an 8% interest rate. This strategy will give you $14 million × 8% = $1.12 million per year in perpetuity! Alternatively, you can spend $15 million − $11.16 million = $3.84 million today, and invest the remaining $11.16 million, which will still allow you to withdraw $1 million each year for the next 29 years before your account is depleted.

Future Value of an Annuity

Now that we have derived a simple formula for the present value of an annuity, it is easy to find a simple formula for the future value. If we want to know the value N years in the future, we move the present value N periods forward on the timeline.

$$PV = \frac{C}{r}\left(1 - \frac{1}{(1+r)^N}\right) \longrightarrow FV = \frac{C}{r}\left(1 - \frac{1}{(1+r)^N}\right) \times (1 + r)^N$$

As the timeline shows, we compound the present value for N periods at interest rate r:

Future Value of an Annuity

$$FV(\text{Annuity}) = PV \times (1 + r)^N$$

$$= \frac{C}{r}\left(1 - \frac{1}{(1 + r)^N}\right) \times (1 + r)^N$$

$$= C \times \frac{1}{r}\left((1 + r)^N - 1\right) \tag{4.6}$$

This formula is useful if we want to know how a savings account will grow over time if the investor deposits the same amount every period.

PERSONAL FINANCE

EXAMPLE 4.5

Retirement Savings
Plan Annuity

MyFinanceLab

PROBLEM

Ellen is 35 years old and she has decided it is time to plan seriously for her retirement. At the end of each year until she is 65, she will save $10,000 in a retirement account. If the account earns 10% per year, how much will Ellen have in her account at age 65?

SOLUTION

PLAN

As always, we begin with a timeline. In this case, it is helpful to keep track of both the dates and Ellen's age:

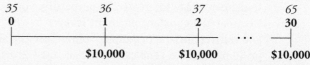

Ellen's savings plan looks like an annuity of $10,000 per year for 30 years. (*Hint*: It is easy to become confused when you just look at age, rather than at both dates and age. A common error is to think there are only 65 − 36 = 29 payments. Writing down both dates and age avoids this problem.)

To determine the amount Ellen will have in her account at age 65, we'll need to compute the future value of this annuity.

EXECUTE

$$FV = \$10,000 \times \frac{1}{0.10}(1.10^{30} - 1)$$

$$= \$10,000 \times 164.49$$

$$= \$1.645 \text{ million at age 65}$$

Using a financial calculator or Excel:

	N	I/Y	PV	PMT	FV
Given:	30	10	0	−10,000	
Solve for:					1,644,940

Excel Formula: =FV(RATE,NPER, PMT, PV)=FV(0.10,30,−10000,0)

EVALUATE

By investing $10,000 per year for 30 years (a total of $300,000) and earning interest on those investments, the compounding will allow Ellen to retire with $1.645 million.

CONCEPT
CHECK

5. What are some examples of annuities?

6. What is the difference between an annuity and a perpetuity?

4.4 Growing Cash Flows

So far, we have considered only cash flow streams that have the same cash flow every period. If, instead, the cash flows are expected to grow at a constant rate in each period, we can also derive a simple formula for the present value of the future stream.

Growing Perpetuity

growing perpetuity
A stream of cash flows
that occurs at regular
intervals and grows at a
constant rate forever.

A **growing perpetuity** is a stream of cash flows that occur at regular intervals and grow at a constant rate forever. For example, a growing perpetuity with a first payment of $100 that grows at a rate of 3% has the following timeline:

To derive the formula for the present value of a growing perpetuity, we follow the same logic used for a regular perpetuity: Compute the amount you would need to deposit today to create the perpetuity yourself. In the case of a regular perpetuity, we created a constant payment forever by withdrawing the interest earned each year and reinvesting the principal. To increase the amount we can withdraw each year, the principal that we reinvest each year must grow. Therefore, we withdraw less than the full amount of interest earned each period, using the remaining interest to increase our principal.

Let's consider a specific case. Suppose you want to create a perpetuity growing at 2%, so you invest $100 in a bank account that pays 5% interest. At the end of one year, you will have $105 in the bank—your original $100 plus $5 in interest. If you withdraw only $3, you will have $102 to reinvest—2% more than the amount you had initially. This amount will then grow to $102 × 1.05 = $107.10 in the following year, and you can withdraw $3 × 1.02 = $3.06, which will leave you with principal of $107.10 − $3.06 = $104.04. Note that $102 × 1.02 = $104.04. That is, both the amount you withdraw and the principal you reinvest grow by 2% each year. On a timeline, these cash flows look like this:

By following this strategy, you have created a growing perpetuity that starts at $3 and grows 2% per year. This growing perpetuity must have a present value equal to the cost of $100.

We can generalize this argument. If we want to increase the amount we withdraw from the bank each year by g, then the principal in the bank will have to grow by the same factor g. That is, instead of reinvesting P in the second year, we should reinvest $P(1+g) = P + gP$. In order to increase our principal by gP, we need to leave gP of the interest in the account, so of the total interest of rP, we can only withdraw $rP − gP = P(r − g)$. We demonstrate this for the first year of our example:

Initial amount deposited	$100	P
Interest earned	(.05)($100)	rP
Amount needed to increase principal	(.02)($100)	gP
Amount withdrawn	(.05)($100) − (.02)($100)	$rP − gP$
	= $100(.05 − .02)	= $P(r − g)$

Denoting our withdrawal as C, we have $C = P(r - g)$. Solving this equation for P, the initial amount deposited in the bank account, gives the present value of a growing perpetuity with initial cash flow C:[3]

Present Value of a Growing Perpetuity

$$PV(\text{Growing Perpetuity}) = \frac{C}{r - g} \qquad (4.7)$$

To understand intuitively the formula for a growing perpetuity, start with the formula for a perpetuity. In the earlier case, you had to put enough money in the bank to ensure that the interest earned matched the cash flows of the regular perpetuity. In the case of a growing perpetuity, you need to put more than that amount in the bank because you have to finance the growth in the cash flows. How much more? If the bank pays interest at a rate of 5%, then all that is left to take out, if you want to make sure the principal grows 2% per year, is the difference: 5% − 2% = 3%. So instead of the present value of the perpetuity being the first cash flow divided by the interest rate, it is now the first cash flow divided by the *difference* between the interest rate and the growth rate.

PERSONAL FINANCE

EXAMPLE 4.6

Endowing a Growing Perpetuity

MyFinanceLab

PROBLEM

In Example 4.3, you planned to donate money to your alma mater to fund an annual $30,000 graduation party. Given an interest rate of 8% per year, the required donation was the present value of:

$$PV = \$30,000/0.08 = \$375,000 \text{ today}$$

Before accepting the money, however, the student association has asked that you increase the donation to account for the effect of inflation on the cost of the party in future years. Although $30,000 is adequate for next year's party, the students estimate that the party's cost will rise by 4% per year thereafter. To satisfy their request, how much do you need to donate now?

SOLUTION

PLAN

The cost of the party next year is $30,000, and the cost then increases 4% per year forever. From the timeline, we recognize the form of a growing perpetuity and can value it that way.

EXECUTE

To finance the growing cost, you need to provide the present value today of:

$$PV = \$30,000/(0.08 - 0.04) = \$750,000 \text{ today}$$

EVALUATE

You need to double the size of your gift!

---

[3]Suppose $g \geq r$. Then the cash flows grow even faster than they are discounted; each term in the sum of discounted cash flows gets larger, rather than smaller. In this case, the sum is infinite! What does an infinite present value mean? Remember that the present value is the "do-it-yourself" cost of creating the cash flows. An infinite present value means that no matter how much money you start with, it is *impossible* to sustain a growth rate of g forever and reproduce those cash flows on your own. Growing perpetuities of this sort cannot exist in practice because no one would be willing to offer one at any finite price. A promise to pay an amount that forever grew faster than the interest rate is also unlikely to be kept (or believed by any savvy buyer). The only viable growing perpetuities are those where the perpetual growth rate is less than the interest rate, so we assume that $g < r$ for a growing perpetuity.

Growing Annuity

growing annuity A stream of cash flows, growing at a constant rate and paid at regular intervals, that end after a specified number of periods.

A **growing annuity** is a stream of N growing cash flows, paid at regular intervals. It is a growing perpetuity that eventually comes to an end. The following timeline shows a growing annuity with initial cash flow C, growing at rate g every period until period N:

The conventions used earlier still apply: (1) The first cash flow arrives at the end of the first period and (2) the first cash flow is before growth. The last cash flow therefore reflects only $N - 1$ periods of growth.

The present value of an N-period growing annuity with initial cash flow C, growth rate g, and interest rate r is given by

Present Value of a Growing Annuity

$$PV = C \times \frac{1}{r-g}\left(1 - \left(\frac{1+g}{1+r}\right)^{N}\right) \tag{4.8}$$

Because the annuity has a finite number of terms, Eq. 4.8 also works when $g > r$.[4] The process of deriving this simple expression for the present value of a growing annuity is the same as for a regular annuity. Interested readers may consult the online appendix for details.

EXAMPLE 4.7

Retirement Savings with a Growing Annuity

MyFinanceLab

PROBLEM

In Example 4.5, Ellen considered saving $10,000 per year for her retirement. Although $10,000 is the most she can save in the first year, she expects her salary to increase each year so that she will be able to increase her savings by 5% per year. With this plan, if she earns 10% per year on her savings, how much will Ellen have in her account at age 65?

SOLUTION

PLAN

Her new savings plan is represented by the following timeline:

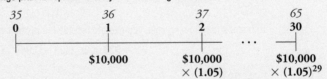

This example involves a 30-year growing annuity, with a growth rate of 5%, and an initial cash flow of $10,000. We can use Eq. 4.8 to solve for the present value of this growing annuity. Then we can use Eq. 4.1 to calculate the future value.

---

[4]Equation 4.8 does not work for $g = r$. But in that case, growth and discounting cancel out, and the present value is equivalent to receiving all the cash flows at date 1: $PV = C \times N/(1+r)$.

EXECUTE

The present value of Ellen's growing annuity is given by

$$PV = \$10,000 \times \frac{1}{0.10 - 0.05}\left(1 - \left(\frac{1.05}{1.10}\right)^{30}\right)$$

$$= \$10,000 \times 15.0463$$

$$= \$150,463 \text{ today}$$

Ellen's proposed savings plan is equivalent to having $150,463 in the bank *today*. To determine the amount she will have at age 65, we need to move this amount forward 30 years:

$$FV = \$150,463 \times 1.10^{30}$$

$$= \$2.625 \text{ million in 30 years}$$

EVALUATE

Ellen will have $2.625 million at age 65 using the new savings plan. This sum is almost $1 million more than she had without the additional annual increases in savings. Because she is increasing her savings amount each year and the interest on the cumulative increases continues to compound, her final savings is much greater.

CONCEPT CHECK

7. How can an infinitely growing stream of cash flows have a finite value?

8. What is an example of a growing perpetuity?

4.5 Solving for Variables Other Than Present Value or Future Value

So far, we have calculated the present value or future value of a stream of cash flows. Sometimes, however, we know the present value or future value, but do not know one of the variables that so far we have been given as an input. For example, when you take out a loan, you may know the amount you would like to borrow, but may not know the loan payments that will be required to repay it. Or, if you make a deposit into a bank account, you may want to calculate how long it will take before your balance reaches a certain level. In such situations, we use the present and/or future values as inputs, and solve for the variable we are interested in. We examine several special cases in this section.

Solving for the Cash Flows

Let's consider an example where we know the present value of an investment, but do not know the cash flows. The best example is a loan—you know how much you want to borrow (the present value) and you know the interest rate, but you do not know how much you need to repay each year. Suppose you are opening a business that requires an initial investment of $100,000. Your bank manager has agreed to lend you this money. The terms of the loan state that you will make equal annual payments for the next 10 years and will pay an interest rate of 8% with the first payment due one year from today. What is your annual payment?

From the bank's perspective, the timeline looks like this:

$$
\begin{array}{ccccccc}
0 & & 1 & & 2 & & 10 \\
\vert & & \vert & & \vert & \cdots & \vert \\
-\$100{,}000 & & +C & & +C & & +C
\end{array}
$$

The bank will give you $100,000 today in exchange for 10 equal payments over the next decade. You need to determine the size of the payment C that the bank will require. For the bank to be willing to lend you $100,000, the loan cash flows must have a present value of $100,000 when evaluated at the bank's interest rate of 8%. That is:

$$100{,}000 = PV(\text{10-year annuity of } C \text{ per year, evaluated at the loan rate})$$

Using the formula for the present value of an annuity (Eq. 4.5),

$$100{,}000 = C \times \frac{1}{0.08}\left(1 - \frac{1}{1.08^{10}}\right) = C \times 6.71$$

Solving this equation for C gives:

$$C = \frac{100{,}000}{6.71} = 14{,}903$$

You will be required to make 10 annual payments of $14,903 in exchange for $100,000 today.

We can also solve this problem with a financial calculator or Excel (from your standpoint the $100,000 is positive and the payments are negative):

	N	I/Y	PV	PMT	FV
Given:	10	8	100,000		0
Solve for:				−14,903	
Excel Formula: =PMT(RATE,NPER,PV,FV)=PMT(0.08,10,100000,0)					

In general, when solving for a loan payment, think of the amount borrowed (the loan principal) as the present value of the payments. If the payments of the loan are an annuity, we can solve for the payment of the loan by inverting the annuity formula. Writing the equation for the payments formally for a loan with principal P, requiring N periodic payments of C and interest rate r, we have:

Cash Flow in an Annuity (Loan Payment)

$$C = \frac{P}{\dfrac{1}{r}\left(1 - \dfrac{1}{(1+r)^N}\right)} \tag{4.9}$$

PROBLEM

Your firm plans to buy a warehouse for $100,000. The bank offers you a 30-year loan with equal annual payments and an interest rate of 8% per year. The bank requires that your firm pays 20% of the purchase price as a down payment, so you can borrow only $80,000. What is the annual loan payment?

SOLUTION

PLAN

We start with the timeline (from the bank's perspective):

Using Eq. 4.9, we can solve for the loan payment, C, given $N = 30$, $r = 0.08$, and $P = \$80,000$.

EXECUTE

Equation 4.9 gives the following payment (cash flow):

$$C = \frac{P}{\frac{1}{r}\left(1 - \frac{1}{(1+r)^N}\right)} = \frac{80{,}000}{\frac{1}{0.08}\left(1 - \frac{1}{(1.08)^{30}}\right)}$$

$$= \$7106.19$$

Using a financial calculator or Excel:

	N	I/Y	PV	PMT	FV
Given:	30	8	−80,000		0
Solve for:				7106.19	
Excel Formula: =PMT(RATE,NPER,PV,FV)=PMT(0.08,30,−80000,0)					

EVALUATE

Your firm will need to pay $7106.19 each year to repay the loan. The bank is willing to accept these payments because the PV of 30 annual payments of $7106.19 at 8% interest rate per year is exactly equal to the $80,000 it is giving you today.

We can use this same idea to solve for the cash flows when we know the future value rather than the present value. As an example, suppose you have just graduated from college and you decide to be prudent and start saving for a down payment on a house. You would like to have $60,000 saved in 10 years. If you can earn 7% per year on your savings, how much do you need to save each year to meet your goal?

The timeline for this example is:

That is, you plan to save some amount C per year, and then withdraw $60,000 from the bank in 10 years. Therefore, we need to find the annuity payment that has a future value of $60,000 in 10 years. Use the formula for the future value of an annuity from Eq. 4.6:

$$60{,}000 = FV(\text{annuity}) = C \times \frac{1}{0.07}(1.07^{10} - 1) = C \times 13.816$$

Therefore, $C = \dfrac{60{,}000}{13.816} = \$4343$. Thus, you need to save $4343 per year. If you do, then at a 7% interest rate your savings will grow to $60,000 in 10 years when you are ready to buy a house.

Now let's solve this problem using a financial calculator or Excel:

	N	I/Y	PV	PMT	FV
Given:	10	7	0		60,000
Solve for:				−4343	
Excel Formula: =PMT(RATE,NPER,PV,FV)=PMT(0.07,10,0,60000)					

Once again, we find that you need to save $4343 per year for 10 years to accumulate $60,000.

Rate of Return

In some situations, you know the cost of an investment opportunity and the expected cash flows from it, but you do not know the rate of return. The rate of return on the investment opportunity is the rate at which the present value of the benefits exactly offsets the cost.

For example, suppose you have an investment opportunity that requires a $1000 investment today and will have a $2000 payoff in six years. This would appear on a timeline as:

One way to analyze this investment is to ask the question: What interest rate, r, would you need so that the present value of what you get is exactly equal to the present value of what you give up?

$$1000 = \frac{2000}{(1+r)^6}$$

Rearranging this calculation gives the following:

$$1000 \times (1+r)^6 = 2000$$

That is, r is the interest rate you would need to earn on your $1000 to have a future value of $2000 in six years. We can solve for r as follows:

$$1 + r = \left(\frac{2000}{1000}\right)^{\frac{1}{6}} = 1.1225$$

Or, $r = 0.1225$. This rate is the rate of return of this investment opportunity. Making this investment is like earning 12.25% per year on your money for six years.

When there are just two cash flows, as in the preceding example, it is straightforward to compute the rate of return. Consider the general case in which you invest an amount P today, and receive FV in N years:

$$P \times (1 + r)^N = FV$$

$$1 + r = (FV/P)^{1/N}$$

That is, we take the total return of the investment over N years, FV/P, and convert it to an equivalent one-year rate by raising it to the power $1/N$.

Now let's consider a more sophisticated example. Suppose your firm needs to purchase a new forklift. The dealer gives you two options: (1) a price for the forklift if you pay cash and (2) the annual payments if you take out a loan from the dealer. To evaluate the loan that the dealer is offering, you will want to compare the rate on the loan with the rate that your bank is willing to offer you. Given the loan payment that the dealer quotes, how do you compute the interest rate charged by the dealer?

In this case, we need to compute the rate of return of the dealer's loan. Suppose the cash price of the forklift is $40,000, and the dealer offers financing with no down payment and four annual payments of $15,000. This loan has the following timeline:

From the timeline, it is clear that the loan is a four-year annuity with a payment of $15,000 per year and a present value of $40,000. Setting the present value of the cash flows equal to zero requires that the present value of the payments equals the purchase price:

$$40{,}000 = 15{,}000 \times \frac{1}{r}\left(1 - \frac{1}{(1+r)^4}\right)$$

The value of r that solves this equation is the interest rate charged on the loan. Unfortunately, in this case, there is no simple way to solve for the interest rate r.[5] The only way to solve this equation is to guess at values of r until you find the right one.

Start by guessing $r = 10\%$. In this case, the value of the annuity is:

$$15{,}000 \times \frac{1}{0.10}\left(1 - \frac{1}{(1.10)^4}\right) = 47{,}548$$

The present value of the payments is too large. To lower it, we need to use a higher interest rate. This time we guess 20%:

$$15{,}000 \times \frac{1}{0.20}\left(1 - \frac{1}{(1.20)^4}\right) = 38{,}831$$

Now the present value of the payments is too low, so we must pick a rate between 10% and 20%. We continue to guess until we find the right rate. Let's try 18.45%:

$$15{,}000 \times \frac{1}{0.1845}\left(1 - \frac{1}{(1.1845)^4}\right) = 40{,}000$$

The interest rate charged by the dealer is 18.45%.

An easier solution than guessing the rate of return and manually calculating values is to use a spreadsheet or calculator to automate the guessing process. When the cash flows are an annuity, as in this example, we can use a financial calculator or Excel to compute the rate of return. Both solve (with slightly varying notation—recall that I/Y is the discount rate and PMT is the cash flow or payment) the following equation:

$$0 = PV + PMT \times \frac{1}{I/Y}\left(1 - \frac{1}{(1+I/Y)^N}\right) + \frac{FV}{(1+I/Y)^N}$$

The equation ensures that the value of investing in the annuity is zero in that the present value of the costs and benefits exactly offset each other. When the unknown variable is the

---

[5]With five or more periods and general cash flows, there is *no* general formula to solve for r; trial and error (by hand or computer) is the *only* way to compute it.

interest rate, it will solve for the interest rate that sets the equation equal to zero. For this case, you could use a financial calculator or Excel, as follows:

	N	I/Y	PV	PMT	FV
Given:	4		40,000	−15,000	0
Solve for:		18.45			
	Excel Formula: =RATE(NPER,PMT,PV,FV)=RATE(4,−15000,40000,0)				

Both the financial calculator and Excel correctly compute a rate of return of 18.45%. Note that the calculator returns *I/Y* as 18.45, but it should be read as 18.45%, which is 0.1845, the number Excel returns.

PERSONAL FINANCE

EXAMPLE 4.9

Computing the
Rate of Return
with a Financial
Calculator

MyFinanceLab

PROBLEM

Let's return to the lottery prize in Example 4.4. How high of a rate of return do you need to earn by investing on your own in order to prefer the $15 million payout?

SOLUTION

PLAN

Recall that the lottery offers you the following deal: take either (a) 30 payments of $1 million per year starting immediately, or (b) a $15 million lump sum payment immediately. The first option is an annuity of 29 payments of $1 million plus an initial $1 million payment.

```
0           1           2                    29
|-----------|-----------|-----  ...  --------|
$1 million  $1 million  $1 million        $1 million
```

We need to solve for the rate of return that makes the two offers equivalent. Anything above that rate of return would make the present value of the annuity lower than the $15 million lump sum payment, and anything below that rate of return would make it greater than the $15 million payment.

EXECUTE

We set the present value of option (a) equal to option (b), which is already in present value since it is an immediate payment of $15 million:

$$\$15 \text{ million} = \$1 \text{ million} + \$1 \text{ million} \times \frac{1}{r}\left(1 - \frac{1}{(1+r)^{29}}\right)$$

$$\$14 \text{ million} = \$1 \text{ million} \times \frac{1}{r}\left(1 - \frac{1}{(1+r)^{29}}\right)$$

Using a financial calculator to solve for *r*:

	N	I/Y	PV	PMT	FV
Given:	29		−14,000,000	1,000,000	0
Solve for:		5.72			
	Excel Formula: =RATE(NPER,PMT,PV,FV)=RATE(29,1000000,−14000000,0)				

The rate of return equating the two options is 5.72%.

EVALUATE

5.72% is the rate of return that makes giving up the $15 million payment and taking the 30 installments of $1 million an even trade in terms of present value. If you could earn more than 5.72% investing on your own, then you could take the $15 million, invest it and generate 30 installments that are each more than $1 million. If you could not earn at least 5.72% on your investments, you would be unable to replicate the $1 million installments on your own and would be better off choosing the installment plan.

Solving for the Number of Periods

In addition to solving for cash flows or the interest rate, we can solve for the amount of time it will take a sum of money to grow to a known value. In this case, the interest rate, present value, and future value are all known. We need to compute how long it will take for the present value to grow to the future value.

Suppose we invest $10,000 in an account paying 10% interest, and we want to know how long it will take for the amount to grow to $20,000.
We want to determine N.

In terms of our formulas, we need to find N so that the future value of our investment equals $20,000:

$$FV = \$10{,}000 \times 1.10^N = \$20{,}000 \qquad (4.10)$$

One approach is to use trial and error to find N, as with the rate of return we calculated earlier. For example, with $N = 7$ years, $FV = \$19{,}487$, so it will take longer than 7 years. With $N = 8$ years, $FV = \$21{,}436$, so it will take between 7 and 8 years.

Alternatively, this problem can be solved on a financial calculator or Excel. In this case, we solve for N:

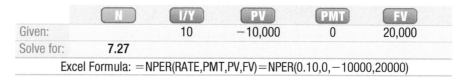

	N	I/Y	PV	PMT	FV
Given:		10	−10,000	0	20,000
Solve for:	7.27				
Excel Formula: =NPER(RATE,PMT,PV,FV)=NPER(0.10,0,−10000,20000)					

It will take about 7.3 years for our savings to grow to $20,000. The problem of solving for the number of periods can also be solved mathematically using logarithms.

PERSONAL FINANCE

EXAMPLE 4.10

Solving for the
Number of Periods
in a Savings Plan

MyFinanceLab

PROBLEM

Let's return to your savings for a down payment on a house. Imagine that some time has passed and you have $10,050 saved already, and you can now afford to save $5000 per year at the end of each year. Also, interest rates have increased so that you now earn 7.25% per year on your savings. How long will it take to reach your goal of $60,000?

SOLUTION

PLAN

The timeline for this problem is:

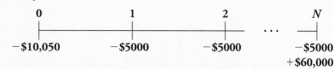

We need to find N so that the future value of your current savings plus the future value of your planned additional savings (which is an annuity) equals your desired amount. There are two contributors to the future value: the initial lump sum of $10,050 that will continue to earn interest, and the annuity contributions of $5000 per year that will earn interest as they are contributed. Thus, we need to find the future value of the lump sum plus the future value of the annuity.

(Continued)

EXECUTE

We can solve this problem using a financial calculator or Excel:

	N	I/Y	PV	PMT	FV
Given:		7.25	−10,050	−5000	60,000
Solve for:	7.00				
Excel Formula: =NPER(RATE,PMT,PV,FV)=NPER(0.0725,−5000,−10050,60000)					

There is also a mathematical solution. We can calculate the future value of the initial cash flow by using Eq. 4.1 and the future value of the annuity using Eq. 4.6:

$$10{,}050 \times 1.0725^N + 5000 \times \frac{1}{0.0725}(1.0725^N - 1) = 60{,}000$$

Rearranging the equation to solve for N,

$$1.0725^N = \frac{60{,}000 \times 0.0725 + 5000}{10{,}050 \times 0.0725 + 5000} = 1.632$$

we can then solve for N:

$$N = \frac{\ln(1.632)}{\ln(1.0725)} = 7 \text{ years}$$

EVALUATE

It will take seven years to save the down payment.

CONCEPT CHECK

9. What are examples of times you would need to solve for the cash flow in an annuity?

10. When you are solving for the interest rate, if you keep PV and FV constant, but extend the time period, will the interest rate be higher or lower?

4.6 Non-Annual Cash Flows

Until now, we have only considered cash flow streams that occur at annual intervals. Do the same tools apply if the cash flows occur at another interval, say monthly? The answer is yes: Everything we have learned about annual cash flow streams applies to monthly cash flow streams as long as:

1. The interest rate is specified as a monthly rate.
2. The number of periods is expressed in months.

For example, suppose you have a credit card that charges 2% interest per month. If you have a $1000 balance on the card today, and make no payments for six months, your future balance in one year's time will be

$$FV = C \times (1 + r)^n = \$1000 \times (1.02)^6 = \$1126.16$$

We apply the future value formula exactly as before, but with r equal to the *monthly* interest rate and n equal to the number of *months*.

The same logic applies to annuities, as shown in Example 4.11.

EXAMPLE 4.11

Evaluating an
Annuity with Monthly
Cash Flows

MyFinanceLab

PROBLEM

You are about to purchase a new car and have two payment options. You can pay $20,000 in cash immediately, or you can get a loan that requires you to pay $500 each month for the next 48 months (four years). If the monthly interest rate you earn on your cash is 0.5%, which option should you choose?

SOLUTION

Let's start by writing down the timeline of the loan payments:

```
              1          2           48
  |-----------|----------|--- ... ---|
  0          500        500         500
```

The timeline shows that the loan is a 48-period annuity. Using the annuity formula, the present value is

$$PV(\text{48-period annuity of \$500}) = \$500 \times \frac{1}{0.005}\left(1 - \frac{1}{1.005^{48}}\right)$$

$$= \$21,290$$

Alternatively, we may use the annuity spreadsheet to solve the problem:

	NPER	RATE	PV	PMT	FV
Given:	48	0.50%		500	0
Solve for:			(21,290)		
Excel Formula: =PV(0.005,48,500,0)					

EVALUATE

Thus, taking the loan is equivalent to paying $21,290 today, which is costlier than paying cash. You should pay cash for the car.

What should you do if you aren't given a monthly rate? In Chapter 5, we will discuss how interest rates are quoted and you will learn how to convert between annual and monthly (or quarterly) rates.

The Big Picture

We began this chapter with the goal of further developing the tools a financial manager needs to be able to apply the Valuation Principle by valuing the costs and benefits of a decision. Starting from Chapter 3's fundamental concept of the time value of money—a dollar today is worth more than a dollar tomorrow—we learned how to calculate the equivalent value of a stream of future cash flows today and today's cash flows in the future. We then learned some shortcuts for handling common sets of regular cash flows such as those found in perpetuities and loans. As we have seen, the discount rate is a critical input to any of our present value or future value calculations. Throughout this chapter, we have taken the discount rate as given.

What determines these discount rates? The Valuation Principle shows us that we must rely on market information to assess the value of cash flows across time. In Chapter 5, we will learn the drivers of market interest rates as well as how they are quoted. Understanding interest rate quoting conventions will also allow us to extend the tools we developed in this chapter to situations where the interest rate is compounded more frequently than once per year.

CONCEPT
CHECK

11. Do the present and future value formulas depend upon the cash flows occurring at annual intervals?

12. When cash flows occur at a non-annual interval, what interest rate must you use? What number of periods must you use?

MyFinanceLab

Here is what you should know after reading this chapter. MyFinanceLab will help you identify what you know, and where to go when you need to practice.

KEY POINTS AND EQUATIONS	KEY TERMS	ONLINE PRACTICE
4.1 Valuing a Stream of Cash Flows • The present value of a cash flow stream is: $$PV = C_0 + \frac{C_1}{(1+r)} + \frac{C_2}{(1+r)^2} + \cdots + \frac{C_N}{(1+r)^N} \quad (4.3)$$	stream of cash flows, p. 94	MyFinanceLab Study Plan 4.1
4.2 Perpetuities • A perpetuity is a stream of equal cash flows C paid every period, forever. The present value of a perpetuity is: $$PV(C \text{ in Perpetuity}) = \frac{C}{r} \quad (4.4)$$	consol, p. 98 perpetuity, p. 98	MyFinanceLab Study Plan 4.2
4.3 Annuities • An annuity is a stream of equal cash flows C paid every period for N periods. The present value of an annuity is: $$C \times \frac{1}{r}\left(1 - \frac{1}{(1+r)^N}\right) \quad (4.5)$$ • The future value of an annuity at the end of the annuity is: $$C \times \frac{1}{r}\left((1+r)^N - 1\right) \quad (4.6)$$	annuity, p. 101	MyFinanceLab Study Plan 4.3 Interactive Annuity Calculator Financial Calculator Tutorials: Calculating the Present Value of an Annuity and Solving for the Future Value of an Annuity
4.4 Growing Cash Flows • In a growing perpetuity, the cash flows grow at a constant rate g each period. The present value of a growing perpetuity is: $$\frac{C}{r-g} \quad (4.7)$$ • A growing annuity is like a growing perpetuity, but with an ending point. The present value of a growing annuity is: $$PV = C \times \frac{1}{r-g}\left(1 - \left(\frac{1+g}{1+r}\right)^N\right) \quad (4.8)$$	growing annuity, p. 108 growing perpetuity, p. 106	MyFinanceLab Study Plan 4.4
4.5 Solving for Variables Other Than Present Value or Future Value • The annuity and perpetuity formulas can be used to solve for the annuity payments when either the present value or the future value is known.		MyFinanceLab Study Plan 4.5

- The periodic payment on an N-period loan with principal P and interest rate r is:

$$C = \frac{P}{\frac{1}{r}\left(1 - \frac{1}{(1+r)^N}\right)} \qquad (4.9)$$

- The rate of return of an investment opportunity is the interest rate at which the PV of the benefits of the investment opportunity exactly offset the PV of the costs.
- The annuity formulas can be used to solve for the number of periods it takes to save a fixed amount of money.

4.6 Non-Annual Cash Flows

- Monthly cash flow streams (or any other period length) can be evaluated in exactly the same way as annual cash flow streams as long as the interest rate and number of periods are expressed in monthly terms.

MyFinanceLab Study
Plan 4.6

CRITICAL THINKING

1. What is the intuition behind the fact that the present value of a stream of cash flows is just the sum of the present values of each individual cash flow?

2. What must be true about a cash flow stream in order for us to be able to use the shortcut formulas?

3. What is the difference between an annuity and a perpetuity?

4. What are some examples of perpetuities?

5. How can a perpetuity have a finite value?

6. What are some examples of annuities?

7. What must be true about the growth rate in order for a growing perpetuity to have a finite value?

8. In what types of situations would it be useful to solve for the number of periods or the rate of return?

PROBLEMS

All problems are available in MyFinanceLab. The ▦ *icon indicates problems that are easier to solve using Excel and have data in an Excel format available in MyFinanceLab. An asterisk * indicates problems with a higher level of difficulty.*

Valuing a Stream of Cash Flows

1. a. What is the present value of the following set of cash flows, discounted at 10% per year?

Year	1	2	3	4	5
CF	10	20	30	40	50

b. What is the present value of the following set of cash flows, discounted at 10% per year?

Year	1	2	3	4	5
CF	50	40	30	20	10

c. Each set contains the same cash flows (10, 20, 30, 40, 50), so why is the present value different?

2. What is the present value of the following set of cash flows, discounted at 15% per year?

Year	1	2	3	4
CF	100	−100	200	−200

3. You want to borrow $10,000. You figure that you can make the following payments. If the interest rate on the loan is 8.5% per year, will your payments be enough to pay off the $10,000 loan?

Year	1	2	3	4
Payment	2000	3000	3500	3975

4. You have a balance of $5000 on your credit card, which charges an interest rate of 1.5% per month. Looking at your budget, you figure you can make the following payments. Will they be enough to pay off your credit card?

Month	1	2	3	4	5	6	7	8
Payment	500	550	600	650	700	750	800	850

5. You have just taken out a five-year loan from a bank to buy an engagement ring. The ring costs $5000. You plan to put down $1000 and borrow $4000. You will need to make annual payments of $1000 at the end of each year. Show the timeline of the loan from your perspective. How would the timeline differ if you created it from the bank's perspective?

6. You currently have a one-year-old loan outstanding on your car. You make monthly payments of $300. You have just made a payment. The loan has four years to go (i.e., it had an original term of five years). Show the timeline from your perspective. How would the timeline differ if you created it from the bank's perspective?

7. You plan to deposit $500 in a bank account now and $300 at the end of one year. If the account earns 3% interest per year, what will the balance be in the account right after you make the second deposit?

8. You have just received a windfall from an investment you made in a friend's business. She will be paying you $10,000 at the end of this year, $20,000 at the end of next year, and $30,000 at the end of the year after that (three years from today). The interest rate is 3.5% per year.
   a. What is the present value of your windfall?
   b. What is the future value of your windfall in three years (on the date of the last payment)?

9. Suppose you receive $100 at the end of each year for the next three years.
   a. If the interest rate is 8%, what is the present value of these cash flows?

b. What is the future value in three years of the present value you computed in (a)?

c. Suppose you deposit the cash flows in a bank account that pays 8% interest per year. What is the balance in the account at the end of each of the next three years (after your deposit is made)? How does the final bank balance compare with your answer in (b)?

10. You have a loan outstanding. It requires making three annual payments of $1000 each at the end of the next three years. Your bank has offered to allow you to skip making the next two payments in lieu of making one large payment at the end of the loan's term in three years. If the interest rate on the loan is 5%, what final payment will the bank require you to make so that it is indifferent to the two forms of payment?

11. Assume you can earn 9% per year on your investments.
    a. If you invest $100,000 for retirement at age 30, how much will you have 35 years later for retirement?
    b. If you wait until age 40 to invest the $100,000, how much will you have 25 years later for retirement?
    c. Why is the difference so large?

Perpetuities

12. You want to endow a scholarship that will pay $10,000 per year forever, starting one year from now. If the school's endowment discount rate is 7%, what amount must you donate to endow the scholarship?

13. How would your answer to Problem 12 change if you endow it now, but it makes the first award to a student 10 years from today?

14. The British government has a consol bond outstanding paying £100 per year forever. Assume the current interest rate is 4% per year.
    a. What is the value of the bond immediately after a payment is made?
    b. What is the value of the bond immediately before a payment is made?

15. You are offered the right to receive $1000 per year forever, starting in one year. If your discount rate is 5%, what is this offer worth to you?

16. You have $100,000 to donate to your college. You want to endow a perpetual scholarship that makes its first payment in 1 year. If the college's discount rate is 4%, how large will the annual scholarship payment be?

17. If you still donate the $100,000 from Problem 16 today, but ask the college to delay the scholarship payment so that the first scholarship payment is made 10 years from today, then how large will the annual payment be?

Annuities

18. What is the present value of $1000 paid at the end of each of the next 100 years if the interest rate is 7% per year?

19. Your grandmother has been putting $1000 into a savings account on every birthday since your first (that is, when you turned one). The account pays an interest rate of 3%. How much money will be in the account immediately after your grandmother makes the deposit on your 18th birthday?

20. Assume that your parents wanted to have $160,000 saved for college by your 18th birthday and they started saving on your first birthday. They saved the same amount each year on your birthday and earned 8% per year on their investments.
    a. How much would they have to save each year to reach their goal?

b. If they think you will take five years instead of four to graduate and decide to have $200,000 saved just in case, how much more would they have to save each year to reach their new goal?

*21. When you purchased your car, you took out a five-year annual-payment loan with an interest rate of 6% per year. The annual payment on the car is $5000. You have just made a payment and have now decided to pay off the loan by repaying the outstanding balance. What is the payoff amount for the following scenarios?

a. You have owned the car for one year (so there are four years left on the loan)?

b. You have owned the car for four years (so there is one year left on the loan)?

22. You figure that the total cost of college will be $100,000 per year 18 years from today. If your discount rate is 8% compounded annually, what is the present value today of four years of college costs starting 18 years from today?

23. Assume that Social Security promises you $40,000 per year starting when you retire 45 years from today (the first $40,000 will be paid 45 years from now). If your discount rate is 7%, compounded annually, and you plan to live for 15 years after retiring (so that you will receive a total of 16 payments including the first one), what is the value today of Social Security's promise? (*See* MyFinanceLab *for the data in Excel Format.*)

*24. When Alex Rodriguez moved to the Texas Rangers in 2001, he received a lot of attention for his "$252 million" contract (the total of the payments promised was $252 million). He later moved to the Yankees, but assume the following in order to determine the value of his contract when he signed it:

Rodriguez earns $16 million in the first year, $17 million in years 2 through 4, $19 million in years 5 and 6, $23 million in year 7, and $27 million in years 8 through 10. He also receives his $10 million signing bonus spread equally over the first 5 years ($2 million per year). His deferred payments begin in 2011. The deferred payment amounts total $33 million and are $5 million, then $4 million, then eight amounts of $3 million (ending in 2020). However, the actual payouts will be different. All of the deferred payments will earn 3% per year until they are paid. For example, the $5 million is deferred from 2001 to 2011, or 10 years, meaning that it will actually be $6.7196 million when paid. Assume that the $4 million payment deferred to 2012 is deferred from 2002 (each payment is deferred 10 years).

The contract is a 10-year contract, but each year has a deferred component so that cash flows are paid out over a total of 20 years. The contractual payments, signing bonus, and deferred components are given below. Note that, by contract, the deferred components are not paid in the year they are earned, but instead are paid (plus interest) 10 years later.

2001	2002	2003	2004	2005	2006	2007	2008	2009	2010
$16M	$17M	$17M	$17M	$19M	$19M	$23M	$27M	$27M	$27M
$2M	$2M	$2M	$2M	$2M					
Deferred									
$5M	$4M	$3M	$3M	$3M	$3M	$3M	$3M	$3M	$3M

Assume that an appropriate discount rate for A-Rod to apply to the contract payments is 7% per year.

a. Calculate the true promised payments under this contract, including the deferred payments with interest.

b. Draw a timeline of all of the payments.

c. Calculate the present value of the contract.

d. Compare the present value of the contract to the quoted value of $252 million. What explains the difference?

*25. You are trying to decide how much to save for retirement. Assume you plan to save $5000 per year with the first investment made one year from now. You think you can earn 10% per year on your investments and you plan to retire in 43 years, immediately after making your last $5000 investment.

   a. How much will you have in your retirement account on the day you retire?

   b. If, instead of investing $5000 per year, you wanted to make one lump-sum investment today for your retirement that will result in the same retirement saving, how much would that lump sum need to be?

   c. If you hope to live for 20 years in retirement, how much can you withdraw every year in retirement (starting one year after retirement) so that you will just exhaust your savings with the 20th withdrawal (assume your savings will continue to earn 10% in retirement)?

   d. If, instead, you decide to withdraw $300,000 per year in retirement (again with the first withdrawal one year after retiring), how many years will it take until you exhaust your savings? (Use trial-and-error, a financial calculator: solve for "N," or Excel: function NPER)

   e. Assuming the most you can afford to save is $1000 per year, but you want to retire with $1 million in your investment account, how high of a return do you need to earn on your investments? (Use trial-and-error, a financial calculator: solve for the interest rate, or Excel: function RATE)

Growing Cash Flows

26. A rich relative has bequeathed you a growing perpetuity. The first payment will occur in a year and will be $1000. Each year after that, you will receive a payment on the anniversary of the last payment that is 8% larger than the last payment. This pattern of payments will go on forever. Assume that the interest rate is 12% per year.

   a. What is today's value of the bequest?

   b. What is the value of the bequest immediately after the first payment is made?

*27. You are thinking of building a new machine that will save you $1000 in the first year. The machine will then begin to wear out so that the savings decline at a rate of 2% per year forever. What is the present value of the savings if the interest rate is 5% per year?

28. When Alfred Nobel died, he left the majority of his estate to fund five prizes, each to be awarded annually in perpetuity starting one year after he died (the sixth one, in economics, was added later).

   a. If he wanted the cash award of each of the five prizes to be $45,000 and his estate could earn 7% per year, how much would he need to fund his prizes?

   b. If he wanted the value of each prize to grow by 4% per year (perhaps to keep up with inflation), how much would he need to leave? Assume that the first amount was still $45,000.

   c. His heirs were surprised by his will and fought it. If they had been able to keep the amount of money you calculated in (b), and had invested it at 7% per year, how much would they have in 2014, 118 years after his death?

29. You work for a pharmaceutical company that has developed a new drug. The patent on the drug will last 17 years. You expect that the drug's profits will be $2 million in its first year and that this amount will grow at a rate of 5% per year for the next 17 years. Once the patent expires, other pharmaceutical companies will be able to produce the same drug and competition will likely drive profits to zero. What is the present value of the new drug if the interest rate is 10% per year?

30. A rich aunt has promised you $5000 one year from today. In addition, each year after that, she has promised you a payment (on the anniversary of the last payment) that is 3% larger than the last payment. She will continue to show this generosity for 20 years, giving a total of 20 payments. If the interest rate is 5%, what is her promise worth today?

Solving for Variables Other Than Present Value or Future Value

31. You are thinking about buying a savings bond. The bond costs $50 today and will mature in 10 years with a value of $100. What annual interest rate will the bond earn?

32. You have an investment account that started with $1000 10 years ago and which now has grown to $5000.
    a. What annual rate of return have you earned (you have made no additional contributions to the account)?
    b. If the savings bond earns 15% per year from now on, what will the account's value be 10 years from now?

33. You have an investment opportunity that requires an initial investment of $5000 today and will pay $6000 in one year. What is the rate of return of this opportunity?

34. You have decided to buy a perpetual bond. The bond makes one payment at the end of every year forever and has an interest rate of 5%. If the bond initially costs $1000, what is the payment every year?

35. You are thinking of purchasing a house. The house costs $350,000. You have $50,000 in cash that you can use as a down payment on the house, but you need to borrow the rest of the purchase price. The bank is offering a 30-year mortgage that requires annual payments and has an interest rate of 7% per year. What will your annual payment be if you sign this mortgage?

*36. You are thinking about buying a piece of art that costs $50,000. The art dealer is proposing the following deal: He will lend you the money, and you will repay the loan by making the same payment every two years for the next 20 years (i.e., a total of 10 payments). If the interest rate is 4% per year, how much will you have to pay every two years?

*37. You would like to buy the house and take the mortgage described in Problem 35. You can afford to pay only $23,500 per year. The bank agrees to allow you to pay this amount each year, yet still borrow $300,000. At the end of the mortgage (in 30 years), you must make a balloon payment; that is, you must repay the remaining balance on the mortgage. How much will this balloon payment be?

*38. You are saving for retirement. To live comfortably, you decide you will need to save $2 million by the time you are 65. Today is your 22nd birthday, and you decide, starting today and continuing on every birthday up to and including your 65th birthday, that you will put the same amount into a savings account. If the interest rate is 5%, how much must you set aside each year to ensure that you will have $2 million in the account on your 65th birthday?

39. You receive a $10,000 check from your grandparents for graduation. You decide to save it toward a down payment on a house. You invest it earning 10% per year and you think you will need to have $20,000 saved for the down payment. How long will it be before the $10,000 has grown to $20,000?

40. A local bank is running the following advertisement: "For just $1000 we will pay you $100 forever!" The fine print says that for a $1000 deposit, the bank will pay $100 every year in perpetuity, starting one year after the deposit is made. What interest rate is the bank advertising (what is the rate of return of this investment)?

*41. You are thinking of making an investment in a new factory. The factory will generate revenues of $1 million per year for as long as you maintain it. You expect that the maintenance costs will start at $50,000 per year and will increase 5% per year thereafter. Assume that all revenue and maintenance costs occur at the end of the year. You intend to run the factory as long as it continues to make a positive cash flow (as long as the cash generated by the plant exceeds the maintenance costs). The factory can be built and become operational immediately and the interest rate is 6% per year.

a. What is the present value of the revenues?

b. What is the present value of the maintenance costs?

c. If the plant costs $10 million to build, should you invest in the factory?

 *42. You have just turned 22 years old, received your bachelor's degree, and accepted your first job. Now you must decide how much money to put into your retirement plan. The plan works as follows: Every dollar in the plan earns 7% per year. You cannot make withdrawals until you retire on your 65th birthday. After that, you can make withdrawals as you see fit. You decide that you will plan to live to 100 and work until you turn 65. You estimate that to live comfortably in retirement, you will need $100,000 per year, starting at the end of the first year of retirement and ending on your 100th birthday. You will contribute the same amount to the plan at the end of every year that you work. How much do you need to contribute each year to fund your retirement?

Non-Annual Cash Flows

43. Suppose you currently have $5000 in your savings account, and your bank pays interest at a rate of 0.5% per month. If you make no further deposits or withdrawals, how much will you have in the account in five years?

44. Your firm spends $5000 every month on printing and mailing costs, sending statements to customers. If the interest rate is 0.5% per month, what is the present value of eliminating this cost by sending the statements electronically?

45. You are looking to buy a car and can afford to pay $200 per month. If the interest rate on a car loan is 0.75% per month for a 60-month loan, what is the most expensive car you can afford to buy?

46. You have just entered college and have decided to pay for your living expenses using a credit card that has no minimum monthly payment. You intend to charge $1000 per month on the card for the next 45 months. The card carries a monthly interest rate of 1%. How much money will you owe on the card 46 months from now, when you receive your first statement post-graduation?

47. You intend to endow a scholarship that pays $5000 every 6 months, starting 6 months from now. If the appropriate discount rate is 2% per 6-month period, how much money will you have to donate today to endow the scholarship?

48. You have just deposited $1000 in an unusual bank account that pays interest biannually (once every 2 years). If the 2-year interest rate is 8% (total interest over 2 years is 8%, not 8% per year), how much will you have in the account after 6 years?

DATA CASE

Assume that today is August 5, 2015. Natasha Kingery is 30 years old and has a Bachelor of Science degree in computer science. She is currently employed as a Tier 2 field service representative for a telephony corporation located in Seattle, Washington, and earns $38,000 a year that she anticipates will grow at 3% per year. Natasha hopes to retire at age 65 and has just begun to think about the future.

Natasha has $75,000 that she recently inherited from her aunt. She invested this money in 10-year Treasury bonds. She is considering whether she should further her education and would use her inheritance to pay for it.

She has investigated a couple of options and is asking for your help as a financial planning intern to determine the financial consequences associated with each option. Natasha has already been accepted to two programs and could start either one soon.

One alternative that Natasha is considering is attaining a certification in network design. This certification would automatically promote her to a Tier 3 field service representative in her company. The base salary for a Tier 3 representative is $10,000 more than the salary of a Tier 2 representative, and she anticipates that this salary differential will grow at a rate of 3% a year for as long as she remains employed. The certification program requires the completion of 20 Web-based courses and a score of 80% or better on the final exam. She has learned that the average amount of time necessary to finish the program is one year. The total cost of the program is $5000, due when she enrolls in the program. Because she will do all the work for the certification on her own time, Natasha does not expect to lose any income during the certification process.

Another option is going back to school for an MBA degree. With an MBA degree, Natasha expects to be promoted to a managerial position in her current firm. The managerial position pays $20,000 a year more than her current position. She expects that this salary differential will also grow at a rate of 3% per year for as long as she keeps working. The evening program, which will take three years to complete, costs $25,000 per year, due at the beginning of each of her three years in school. Because she will attend classes in the evening, Natasha doesn't expect to lose any income while she is earning her MBA if she chooses to undertake it.

1. Determine the interest rate Natasha is currently earning on her inheritance by going to Yahoo! Finance (http://finance.yahoo.com) and clicking the 10 Yr Bond link in the Market Summary section or enter ^TNX in the symbol lookup field. Then go to the Historical Prices link and enter the appropriate date, August 5, 2015, to obtain the closing yield or interest rate that she is earning. Use this interest rate as the discount rate for the remainder of this problem.

2. Create a timeline in Excel for Natasha's current situation, as well as the certification program and MBA degree options, using the following assumptions:
   a. Salaries for the year are paid only once, at the end of the year.
   b. The salary increase becomes effective immediately upon graduating from the MBA program or being certified. That is, because the increases become effective immediately but salaries are paid at the end of the year, the first salary increase will be paid exactly one year after graduation or certification.

3. Calculate the present value of the salary differential for completing the certification program. Subtract the cost of the program to get the value of undertaking the certification program.

4. Calculate the present value of the salary differential for completing the MBA degree. Calculate the present value of the cost of the MBA program. Based on your calculations, determine the value of undertaking the MBA.

5. Based on your answers to Questions 3 and 4, what advice would you give to Natasha? What if the two programs are mutually exclusive? If Natasha undertakes one of the programs, there is no further benefit to undertaking the other program. Would your advice change?

Specifying Decimal Places

Make sure you have plenty of decimal places displayed!

HP-10BII

TI BAII Plus Professional

Toggling Between the Beginning and End of a Period

You should always make sure that your calculator is in *end-of-period* mode.

HP-10BII

TI BAII Plus Professional

Set the Number of Periods per Year

To avoid a lot of confusion later, always set your periods per year (P/Y) to 1:

HP-10BII

TI BAII Plus Professional

General TVM Buttons

HP-10BII

TI BAII Plus Professional

Solving for the Future Value of an Annuity (Example 4.5)

Ellen is 35 years old, and she has decided it is time to plan seriously for her retirement. At the end of each year until she is 65, she will save $10,000 in a retirement account. If the account earns 10% per year, how much will Ellen have in her account at age 65? [*Answer*: $1,644,940]

HP-10BII

Press [Orange Shift] and then the [C] button to clear all previous entries.

Enter the Number of periods.

Enter the market annual interest rate.

Enter the Payment amount per period.

Indicate that there is no initial amount in the retirement account.

Solve for the Future Value.

TI-BAII Plus Professional

Press [2ND] and then the [FV] button to clear all previous entries.

Enter the Number of periods.

Enter the market annual interest rate.

Enter the payment amount per period.
Indicate that there is no initial amount in the retirement account.

Solve for the Future Value.

Solving for the Rate of Return

If you have an initial cash outflow of $2000 and one cash inflow per year for the following four years of $1000, $400, $400, and $800, what is the rate of return on the project per year (sometimes called the *Internal Rate of Return* or *IRR* on the calculators)? [*Answer*: 12.12%]

HP-10BII

Press [Orange Shift] and then the [C] button to clear all previous entries.

Enter the initial cash outflow.

Enter the first cash inflow.

Enter the second cash inflow.

Enter the number of consecutive periods the second cash inflow occurs.

Enter the fourth cash inflow.

Press [Orange Shift] and then the [CST] button to calculate the IRR/year.

TI-BAII Plus Professional

CF	Access Cash Flow Worksheet.
2ND CE|C	Press [2ND] and then the [CE/C] button to clear all previous entries.
2 0 0 0 +/− ENTER	Enter the initial cash outflow.
↓ 1 0 0 0 ENTER	Enter the first cash inflow.
↓	Leave the frequency of the initial cash inflow at 1 (Default Setting).
↓ 4 0 0 ENTER	Enter the second cash inflow.
↓ 2 ENTER	Enter the frequency of the second cash inflow as 2.
↓ 8 0 0 ENTER	Enter the fourth cash inflow.
↓	Leave the frequency of the fourth cash inflow at 1 (Default Setting).
IRR CPT	Solve for the IRR.

5

Interest Rates

LEARNING OBJECTIVES

- Understand the different ways interest rates are quoted

- Use quoted rates to calculate loan payments and balances

- Know how inflation, expectations, and risk combine to determine interest rates

- See the link between interest rates in the market and a firm's opportunity cost of capital

notation				
	APR	annual percentage rate	*m*	number of compounding periods per year
	APY	annual percentage yield	*n*	number of periods
	C	cash flow		
	C_n	cash flow that arrives in period n	*N*	date of the last cash flow in a stream of cash flows
	EAR	effective annual rate	*PV*	present value
	FV	future value	*r*	interest rate or discount rate
			r_n	interest rate or discount rate for an n-year term

In Chapters 3 and 4, we explored the mechanics of computing present values and future values given a market interest rate. Recall that an interest rate allows us to convert money at one point in time to another. But how do we determine that interest rate? In this chapter, we consider the factors that affect interest rates and discuss how to determine the appropriate discount rate for a set of cash flows. We begin by looking at the way interest is paid and interest rates are quoted, and we show how to calculate the effective interest paid in one year given different quoting conventions. We then consider some of the main determinants of interest rates—namely, inflation and economic growth. Because interest rates tend to change over time, investors will demand different interest rates for different investment horizons, based on their expectations and the risk involved in longer time horizons.

Interest Rate Quotes and Adjustments

If you spend some time looking through a newspaper, you will find literally dozens of interest rates discussed and advertised, from savings deposit rates to auto loan rates to interest rates being paid on the government's debt. Interest rates are clearly central to the functioning of any financial system. To understand interest rates, it's important to think of interest rates as a price—the price of using money. When you borrow money to buy a car, you are using the bank's money now to get the car and paying the money back over time. The interest rate on your loan is the price you pay to be able to convert your future loan payments into a car today. Similarly, when you deposit money into a savings account, you are letting the bank use your money until you withdraw it later. The interest the bank pays you on your deposit is the price it pays to use your money (for things like making car loans).

Just like any other price, interest rates are set by market forces, in particular the supply of and demand for funds. When the supply (savings) is high and the demand (borrowing) is low, interest rates are low, other things being equal. Additionally, as we discuss later in the chapter, interest rates are also influenced by expected inflation and risk.

In order to be able to study and use interest rates, we have to understand how they are quoted. In practice, interest is paid, and interest rates are quoted, in different ways. For example, in early-2016, Ally Bank offered savings accounts with a rate of 1.00% annually with interest paid on a daily basis, while other banks offered savings rates with interest paid on a quarterly or annual basis. Interest rates can also differ depending on the investment horizon. In April 2016, investors earned around 0.60% on one-year risk-free U.S. Treasury Bills, but could earn around 2.20% on 20-year Treasuries. Interest rates can also vary due to risk or tax consequences: The U.S. government is able to borrow at a lower interest rate than Johnson & Johnson, which in turn can borrow at a lower rate than American Airlines.

Because interest rates may be quoted for different time intervals, such as monthly, semi-annually, or annually, it is often necessary to adjust the interest rate to a time period that matches that of our cash flows. We explore these mechanics of interest rates in this section.

The Effective Annual Rate

effective annual rate (EAR) or annual percentage yield (APY) The total amount of interest that will be earned at the end of one year.

Interest rates are often reported as an **effective annual rate (EAR)** or **annual percentage yield (APY)**, which indicates the total amount of interest that will be earned at the end of one year.[1] We have used this method of quoting the interest rate thus far in this book, and in Chapters 3 and 4 we used the EAR as the discount rate r in our time value of money calculations. For example, with an EAR of 5%, a $100 investment grows to

$$\$100 \times (1+r) = \$100 \times (1.05) = \$105$$

in one year. After two years it will grow to:

$$\$100 \times (1+r)^2 = \$100 \times (1.05)^2 = \$110.25$$

Month:	0		1		2
Cash flow:	$100	× (1.05)	= $105	× (1.05)	= $110.25
	$100	×	(1.05)²	=	$110.25
	$100	×	(1.1025)	=	$110.25

---

[1] The effective annual rate is also referred to as the *effective annual yield* (EAY).

Adjusting the Discount Rate to Different Time Periods

The preceding example shows that earning an effective annual rate of 5% for two years is equivalent to earning 10.25% in total interest over the entire period:

$$\$100 \times (1.05)^2 = \$100 \times 1.1025 = \$110.25$$

In general, by raising the interest rate factor $(1+r)$ to the appropriate power, we can compute an equivalent interest rate for a longer time period.

We can use the same method to find the equivalent interest rate for periods shorter than one year. In this case, we raise the interest rate factor $(1+r)$ to the appropriate fractional power. For example, earning 5% interest in one year is equivalent to receiving

$$(1+r)^{0.5} = (1.05)^{0.5} = \$1.0247$$

for each \$1 invested every six months (0.5 years). That is, a 5% effective annual rate is equivalent to an interest rate of approximately 2.47% earned every six months. We can verify this result by computing the interest we would earn in one year by investing for two six-month periods at this rate:

$$(1+r)^2 = (1.0247)^2 = \$1.05$$

Month:	0	$\frac{1}{2}$	1

Cash flow:	\$1	× (1.0247)	= \$1.0247 × (1.0247)	= \$1.05
	\$1	×	$(1.0247)^2$	=	\$1.05
	\$1	×	(1.05)	=	\$1.05

In general, we can convert a discount rate of r for one period to an equivalent discount rate for n periods using the following formula:

$$\text{Equivalent } n\text{-period Discount Rate} = (1+r)^n - 1 \qquad (5.1)$$

In this formula, n can be larger than 1 (to compute a rate over more than one period) or smaller than 1 (to compute a rate over a fraction of a period).

When computing present or future values, you should adjust the discount rate to match the time period of the cash flows.

This adjustment is necessary to apply the perpetuity or annuity formulas to non-annual cash flows, as shown in Example 5.1.

PERSONAL FINANCE

EXAMPLE 5.1

Valuing Monthly Cash Flows

MyFinanceLab

PROBLEM

Suppose your bank account pays interest monthly with an effective annual rate of 6%. What amount of interest will you earn each month?

If you have no money in the bank today, how much will you need to save at the end of each month to accumulate \$100,000 in 10 years?

SOLUTION

PLAN

We can use Eq. 5.1 to convert the EAR to a monthly rate, answering the first question. The second question is a future value of an annuity question. It is asking how big a monthly annuity we would have to deposit in order to end up with \$100,000 in 10 years. However, in order to solve this problem, we need to write the timeline in terms of monthly periods because our cash flows (deposits) will be monthly:

(Continued)

That is, we can view the savings plan as a monthly annuity with $10 \times 12 = 120$ monthly payments. We have the future value of the annuity ($100,000), the length of time (120 months), and we will have the monthly interest rate from the answer to the first part of the question. We can then use the future value of an annuity formula (Eq. 4.6) to solve for the monthly deposit.

EXECUTE

From Eq. 5.1, a 6% EAR is equivalent to earning $(1.06)^{1/12} - 1 = 0.4868\%$ per month. The exponent in this equation is $1/12$ because the period is $1/12$th of a year (a month).

To determine the amount to save each month to reach the goal of $100,000 in 120 months, we must determine the amount C of the monthly payment that will have a future value of $100,000 in 120 months, given an interest rate of 0.4868% per month. Now that we have all of the inputs in terms of months (monthly payment, monthly interest rate, and total number of months), we use the future value of annuity formula from Chapter 4 to solve this problem:

$$FV\,(\,annuity\,) = C \times \frac{1}{r}[\,(\,1 + r\,)^{\,n} - 1\,]$$

We solve for the payment C using the equivalent monthly interest rate $r = 0.4868\%$, and $n = 120$ months:

$$C = \frac{FV\,(\,Annuity\,)}{\frac{1}{r}[\,(1 + r)^{\,n} - 1\,]} = \frac{\$100,000}{\frac{1}{0.004868}[\,(\,1.004868\,)^{\,120} - 1\,]} = \$615.47 \text{ per month}$$

We can also compute this result using a financial calculator or spreadsheet:

	N	**I/Y**	**PV**	**PMT**	**FV**
Given:	120	0.4868	0		100,000
Solve for:				−615.47	
Excel Formula: = PMT(RATE,NPER,PV,FV)=PMT(0.004868,120,0,100000)					

EVALUATE

Thus, if we save $615.47 per month and we earn interest monthly at an effective annual rate of 6%, we will have $100,000 in 10 years. Notice that the timing in the annuity formula must be consistent for all of the inputs. In this case, we had a monthly deposit, so we needed to convert our interest rate to a monthly interest rate and then use total number of months (120) instead of years.

Annual Percentage Rates

annual percentage rate (APR) Indicates the amount of interest earned in one year without the effect of compounding.

The most common way to quote interest rates is in terms of an **annual percentage rate (APR)**, which indicates the amount of simple interest earned in one year, that is, the amount of interest earned *without* the effect of compounding. Because it does not include the effect of compounding, the APR quote is typically less than the actual amount of interest that you will earn. To compute the actual amount that you will earn in one year, you must first convert the APR to an effective annual rate.

For example, suppose Granite Bank advertises savings accounts with an interest rate of "6% APR with monthly compounding." When it quotes a rate this way, Granite Bank really means that you will earn 6%/12 = 0.5% every month. That is, an APR with monthly compounding is actually a way of quoting a *monthly* interest rate, rather than an annual interest rate. In this case, the actual rate being quoted is 0.5% *per month*, and by convention,

COMMON MISTAKE

Using the EAR in the Annuity Formula

At this point, many students make the mistake of trying to use the EAR in the annuity formula. The interest rate in the annuity formula must match the frequency of the cash flows. That's why in Example 5.1, we first converted the EAR into a monthly rate and then used the annuity formula to compute the monthly loan payments. The common mistake in this case would be to use the EAR in the annuity formula to obtain annual cash flows, and then divide those cash flows by 12 to obtain the monthly payments.

This process will produce the wrong answer. To see why, consider the timing of the first deposit in Example 5.1. With a monthly

rate and monthly payments, the annuity formula assumes that the first payment will be made one month from now. It then assumes that you will be making 11 more monthly deposits before the end of the first year. Each of those deposits will start earning interest as soon as you make it. In contrast, if you use an EAR and calculate an annual cash flow, the formula assumes that you will make your first deposit one *year* from now, so that you will forgo a whole year of interest before you start earning anything. Thus, you can see that the EAR approach misses the fact that you are making deposits earlier and more often than annually, so you are adding to your interest-earning principal more frequently than once per year.

the bank states it as an APR by multiplying by 12 months. Because the interest compounds each month, you will actually have

$$\$1 \times (1.005)^{12} = \$1.061678$$

at the end of one year, for an effective annual rate of 6.1678%. The 6.1678% that you earn on your deposit is higher than the quoted 6% APR due to compounding: In later months, you earn interest on the interest paid in earlier months. To summarize, an actual rate of 0.5% *per month* can be stated in either of the following ways:

- 6% APR, compounded monthly
- EAR of 6.1678%, which is the actual rate earned *per year*

It is important to remember that because the APR does not reflect the true amount you will earn over one year, *the APR itself cannot be used as a discount rate*. Instead, the APR is a way of quoting the actual interest earned each compounding period:

$$\text{Interest Rate per Compounding Period} = \frac{APR}{m}$$

$$(m = \text{number of compounding periods per year}) \qquad (5.2)$$

Once we have computed the interest earned per compounding period from Eq. 5.2, we can compute the equivalent interest rate for any other time interval using Eq. 5.1. Thus, the effective annual rate corresponding to an APR is given by the following conversion formula:

Converting an APR to an EAR

$$1 + EAR = \left(1 + \frac{APR}{m}\right)^m$$

$$(m = \text{number of compounding periods per year}) \qquad (5.3)$$

Table 5.1 shows the effective annual rates that correspond to an APR of 6% with different compounding intervals. The EAR increases with the frequency of compounding because of the ability to earn interest on interest sooner. Investments can compound even more frequently than daily. In principle, the compounding interval could be hourly or every second. As a practical matter, compounding more frequently than daily has a negligible impact on the effective annual rate and is rarely observed.

When working with APRs, we must first convert the APR to a discount rate per compounding interval using Eq. 5.2, or to an EAR using Eq. 5.3, before evaluating the present or future value of a set of cash flows.

TABLE 5.1

Effective Annual Rates for a 6% APR with Different Compounding Periods

Compounding Interval	Effective Annual Rate
Annual	$\left(1 + \dfrac{0.06}{1}\right)^1 - 1 = 6\%$
Semiannual	$\left(1 + \dfrac{0.06}{2}\right)^2 - 1 = 6.09\%$
Monthly	$\left(1 + \dfrac{0.06}{12}\right)^{12} - 1 = 6.1678\%$
Daily	$\left(1 + \dfrac{0.06}{365}\right)^{365} - 1 = 6.1831\%$

EXAMPLE 5.2

Converting the APR to a Discount Rate

MyFinanceLab

PROBLEM

Your firm is purchasing a new telephone system that will last for four years. You can purchase the system for an up-front cost of $150,000, or you can lease the system from the manufacturer for $4000 paid at the end of each month. The lease price is offered for a 48-month lease with no early termination—you cannot end the lease early. Your firm can borrow at an interest rate of 6% APR with monthly compounding. Should you purchase the system outright or pay $4000 per month?

SOLUTION

PLAN

The cost of leasing the system is a 48-month annuity of $4000 per month:

Month:	0	1	2	48
Payment:		$4000	$4000	... $4000

We can compute the present value of the lease cash flows using the annuity formula, but first we need to compute the discount rate that corresponds to a period length of one month. To do so, we convert the borrowing cost of 6% APR with monthly compounding to a monthly discount rate using Eq. 5.2. Once we have a monthly rate, we can use the present value of annuity formula Eq. 4.5 to compute the present value of the monthly payments and compare it to the cost of buying the system.

EXECUTE

As Eq. 5.2 shows, the 6% APR with monthly compounding really means 6%/12 = 0.5% every month. The 12 comes from the fact that there are 12 monthly compounding periods per year. Now that we have the true rate corresponding to the stated APR, we can use that discount rate in the annuity formula Eq. 4.5 to compute the present value of the monthly payments:

$$PV = 4000 \times \frac{1}{0.005}\left(1 - \frac{1}{1.005^{48}}\right) = \$170,321.27$$

Using a financial calculator or spreadsheet:

	N	I/Y	PV	PMT	FV
Given:	48	0.5		−4000	0
Solve for:			170,321.27		

Excel Formula: =PV(RATE,NPER,PMT,FV)=PV(0.005,48,−4000,0)

EVALUATE

Thus, paying $4000 per month for 48 months is equivalent to paying a present value of $170,321.27 today. This cost is $170,321.27 − $150,000 = $20,321.27 higher than the cost of purchasing the system, so it is better to pay $150,000 for the system rather than lease it. One way to interpret this result is as follows: At a 6% APR with monthly compounding, by promising to repay $4000 per month your firm can borrow $170,321 today. With this loan it could purchase the phone system and have an additional $20,321 to use for other purposes.

1. What is the difference between an EAR and an APR quote?
2. Why can't the APR be used as a discount rate?

5.2 Application: Discount Rates and Loans

Now that we have explained how to compute the discount rate from an interest rate quote, let's apply the concept to solve two common financial problems: calculating a loan payment and calculating the remaining balance on a loan.

Computing Loan Payments

amortizing loan A loan on which the borrower makes monthly payments that include interest on the loan plus some part of the loan balance.

Many loans, such as mortgages and car loans, have monthly payments and are quoted in terms of an APR with monthly compounding. These types of loans are **amortizing loans**, which means that each month you pay interest on the loan plus some part of the loan balance. Each monthly payment is the same, and the loan is fully repaid with the final payment. Typical terms for a new car loan might be "6.75% APR for 60 months." When the compounding interval for the APR is not stated explicitly, it is equal to the interval between the payments, or one month in this case. Thus, this quote means that the loan will be repaid with 60 equal monthly payments, computed using a 6.75% APR with monthly compounding. It sometimes helps to look at the loan from the bank's point of view: The bank will give you $30,000 in cash today to use to buy the car. In return, you will give the bank 60 equal payments each month for 60 months, starting one month from now. In order for the bank to be willing to accept this exchange, it must be true that the present value of what you will give the bank, discounted at the loan's interest rate, is equal to the amount of cash the bank is giving you now. Consider the timeline for a $30,000 car loan with these terms:

Month: 0   1   2   ...   60

Cash flow: $30,000 $-C$ $-C$ $-C$

The payment, C, is set so that the present value of the cash flows, evaluated using the loan interest rate, equals the original principal amount of $30,000. In this case, the 6.75% APR with monthly compounding corresponds to a one-month discount rate of 6.75%/12 = 0.5625%. It is important that the discount rate matches the frequency of the cash flows—here we have a monthly discount rate and a monthly loan payment, so we can proceed. Because the loan payments are an annuity, we can use Eq. 4.9 to find C:

$$C = \frac{P}{\frac{1}{r}\left(1 - \frac{1}{(1+r)^N}\right)} = \frac{30{,}000}{\frac{1}{0.005625}\left(1 - \frac{1}{(1+0.005625)^{60}}\right)} = \$590.50$$

Alternatively, we can solve for the payment C using a financial calculator or spreadsheet:

	N	I/Y	PV	PMT	FV
Given:	60	0.5625	30,000		0
Solve for:				−590.50	
Excel Formula: =PMT(RATE,NPER,PV,FV)=PMT(0.005625,60,30000,0)					

Your loan payment each month includes interest and repayment of part of the principal, reducing the amount you still owe. Because the loan balance (the amount you still owe) is decreasing each month, the interest that accrues on that balance is decreasing. As a result, even though your payment stays the same over the entire 60-month life of the loan, the part of that payment needed to cover interest each month is constantly decreasing and the part left over to reduce the principal further is constantly increasing. We illustrate this effect in Panel (a) of Figure 5.1, where we show the proportion of each

FIGURE 5.1

Amortizing Loan

Panel (a) shows how the interest (red) and principal portions (blue) of the monthly payment on the $30,000 car loan change over the life of the loan. Panel (b) illustrates the effect on the outstanding balance (principal) of the loan. Note that as the balance decreases, the amount of the payment needed to cover interest on that balance decreases, allowing more of the payment to be used to reduce the principal.

Panel (a)

Panel (b)

Teaser Rates and Subprime Loans

Some loans, such as adjustable rate mortgages (ARMs), have interest rates that are not constant over the life of the loan. When the interest rate on such a loan changes, the loan payments are recalculated based on the loan's current outstanding balance, the new interest rate, and the remaining life of the loan.

Adjustable rate mortgages were the most common type of so-called "subprime" loans made to homebuyers with poor credit histories. These loans often featured low initial rates, aptly named teaser rates. After a short period (often 2 to 5 years) the interest rate would jump to a higher rate, implying that the monthly payment would also jump. For example, a $500,000 30-year mortgage with a teaser rate of 4.8% would have monthly payments of $2623.33 initially. If, after 2 years, the rate increased to 7.2%, the new monthly interest rate would be 7.2%/12 = 0.6% per month. With the higher rate, the monthly payment would jump to $3355.62!

While the loan might have been affordable at the initial teaser rate, many subprime borrowers could not afford the higher payments that were required after the loan rate adjusted. Prior to 2007, while interest rates remained low and home prices were high (and increasing), such borrowers were able to avoid default simply by refinancing their loans into new loans that also featured low initial teaser rates. In this way, they were able to keep their payments low. But as mortgage rates increased and housing prices began to decline in 2007, this strategy for keeping their loan payments low was no longer possible. In many cases, the outstanding loan balance exceeded the market value of the home, making lenders unwilling to refinance the loans. Stuck with a loan at a now unaffordable interest rate, many homeowners defaulted, and the rate of foreclosure on subprime loans skyrocketed.

To prevent future lenders from using teaser rates to get borrowers into loans they might not ultimately be able to afford, the Dodd-Frank Act requires lenders to verify that borrowers have sufficient income to repay their loans even after the teaser rate expires.

monthly loan payment that covers interest (red) and the portion left over to reduce the principal (blue). As you can see, $168.75 of your first $590.50 payment is needed just to cover interest accrued over the first month ($30,000 \times 0.005625 = \$168.75$). However, this amount steadily decreases so that by the end of the loan, nearly all of your payment is going toward principal.

Panel (b) of Figure 5.1 shows the effect of your payments on the loan balance. When you make your first payment of $590.50, $168.75 covers interest on the loan, leaving $421.75 to reduce the principal to $30,000 − $421.75 = $29,578.25. The next month, you owe interest only on the $29,578.25 loan balance, which is $166.38, leaving more of your $590.50 payment to reduce the principal further. This effect continues so that each month more of your payment is available to reduce the principal, causing the principal to decrease rapidly toward the end of the loan as you are taking bigger and bigger chunks out of the balance.

Computing the Outstanding Loan Balance

As Figure 5.1 shows, the outstanding balance on an amortizing loan is different each month. The amount you owe at any point can be calculated as the present value of your future obligations on the loan. So, the outstanding balance, also called the *outstanding principal,* is equal to the present value of the remaining future loan payments, again evaluated using the loan interest rate. We calculate the outstanding loan balance by determining the present value of the remaining loan payments using the loan rate as the discount rate.

EXAMPLE 5.3

Computing the
Outstanding Loan
Balance

MyFinanceLab

PROBLEM

Let's say that you are now three years into your $30,000 car loan from the previous section and you decide to sell the car. When you sell the car, you will need to pay whatever the remaining balance is on your car loan. After 36 months of payments, how much do you still owe on your car loan?

SOLUTION

PLAN

We have already determined that the monthly payments on the loan are $590.50. The remaining balance on the loan is the present value of the remaining two years, or 24 months, of payments. Thus, we can just use the annuity formula with the monthly rate of 0.5625%, a monthly payment of $590.50, and 24 months remaining.

EXECUTE

$$\text{Balance with 24 months remaining} = \$590.50 \times \frac{1}{0.005625}\left(1 - \frac{1}{1.005625^{24}}\right) = \$13{,}222.32$$

Thus, after three years, you owe $13,222.32 on the loan.
Using a financial calculator or spreadsheet:

	N	I/Y	PV	PMT	FV
Given:	24	0.5625		−590.50	0
Solve for:			13,222.32		

Excel Formula: =PV(RATE,NPER,PMT,FV)=PV(0.005625,24,−590.50,0)

You could also compute this as the FV of the original loan amount after deducting payments:

	N	I/Y	PV	PMT	FV
Given:	36	0.5625	30,000	−590.50	
Solve for:					13,222.56

Excel Formula: =FV(RATE,NPER,PMT,PV)=FV(0.005625,36,−590.50,30000)

The 24 cent difference is due to rounding on the payment amount.

EVALUATE

At any point in time, including when you first take out the loan, you can calculate the balance of the loan as the present value of your remaining payments. Recall that when the bank gave you the $30,000 in the first place, it was willing to take 60 monthly payments of $590.50 in return only because the present value of those payments was equivalent to the cash it was giving you. Any time that you want to end the loan, the bank will charge you a lump sum equal to the present value of what it would receive if you continued making your payments as planned. As the second approach shows, the amount you owe can also be thought of as the future value of the original amount borrowed after deducting payments made along the way.

**CONCEPT
CHECK**

3. How is the principal repaid in an amortizing loan?

4. Why does the part of your loan payment covering interest change over time?

5.3 The Determinants of Interest Rates

Now that we understand how interest rates are quoted and used in loans, we turn to a broader question: How are interest rates determined? Fundamentally, interest rates are determined by market forces based on the relative supply and demand of funds. This supply and demand is in turn determined by the willingness of individuals, banks, and firms to borrow, save, and lend. Changes in interest rates affect consumer decisions, such as how much you can borrow for a car loan or mortgage. Because they change the present value of future cash flows, changes in interest rates also have a broad impact on capital budgeting decisions within the firm. In this section, we look at some of the factors that may influence interest rates, such as inflation, current economic activity, and expectations of future growth.

Inflation and Real Versus Nominal Rates

Inflation measures how the purchasing power of a given amount of currency declines due to increasing prices. How many times have you heard the expression, "A dollar just doesn't buy what it used to"? We've all witnessed the steady upward climb of prices—for example, your morning coffee probably costs a little more today than it did five years ago. Inflation affects how we evaluate the interest rates being quoted by banks and other financial institutions. Those interest rates, and the ones we have used for discounting cash flows in this book, are **nominal interest rates**, which indicate the rate at which your money will grow if invested for a certain period. Of course, if prices in the economy are also increasing due to inflation, the nominal interest rate does not represent the true increase in purchasing power that will result from investing.

nominal interest rates Interest rates quoted by banks and other financial institutions that indicate the rate at which money will grow if invested for a certain period of time.

For example, let's say that a cup of coffee costs $1 this year. If you have $100, you could buy 100 coffees. Instead, if you put that $100 in a bank account earning 5.06% per year, you will have $105.06 at the end of the year. But how much better off will you really be? That depends on how much prices have increased over the same year. If inflation was 3% over the year, then that cup of coffee would cost 3% more, or $1.03 at the end of the year. Thus, you could take your $105.06 and buy $105.06/$1.03 = 102 coffees, so you're really only 2% better off.

real interest rate The rate of growth of purchasing power, after adjusting for inflation.

That 2% is your **real interest rate**: the rate of growth of your purchasing power, after adjusting for inflation. Just as in the example, we can calculate the rate of growth of purchasing power as follows:

$$\text{Growth in Purchasing Power} = 1 + \text{Real Rate} = \frac{1 + \text{Nominal Rate}}{1 + \text{Inflation Rate}}$$

$$= \frac{\text{Growth of Money}}{\text{Growth of Prices}} \quad (5.4)$$

We can rearrange Eq. 5.4 to find the following formula for the real interest rate, together with a convenient approximation for the real interest rate when inflation rates are low:

The Real Interest Rate

$$\text{Real Rate} = \frac{\text{Nominal Rate} - \text{Inflation Rate}}{1 + \text{Inflation Rate}} \approx \text{Nominal Rate} - \text{Inflation Rate} \quad (5.5)$$

That is, the real interest rate is approximately equal to the nominal interest rate less the rate of inflation.[2]

---

[2]The real interest rate should not be used as a discount rate for future cash flows. It can be used as a discount rate only if the cash flows are not the expected cash flows that will be paid, but are the equivalent cash flows before adjusting them for growth due to inflation (in that case, we say the cash flows are in *real terms*). This approach is error prone, however, so throughout this book we will always forecast cash flows including any growth due to inflation, and discount using nominal interest rates.

EXAMPLE 5.4

Calculating the Real
Interest Rate

MyFinanceLab

PROBLEM

At the start of 2008, one-year U.S. government bond rates were about 3.3%, while the inflation rate that year was 0.1%. At the start of 2011, one-year interest rates were about 0.3%, and the inflation rate that year was about 3.0%. What were the real interest rates in 2008 and in 2011?

SOLUTION

Using Eq. 5.5, the real interest rate in 2008 was $(3.3\% - 0.1\%) / (1.001) = 3.20\%$. In 2011, the real interest rate was $(0.3\% - 3.0\%) / (1.03) = -2.62\%$.

EVALUATE

Note that the real interest rate was negative in 2011, indicating that interest rates were insufficient to keep up with inflation: Investors in U.S. government bonds were able to buy less at the end of the year than they could have purchased at the start of the year. On the other hand, there was hardly any inflation.

Figure 5.2 shows the history of nominal interest rates and inflation rates in the United States since 1955. Note that the nominal interest rate tends to move with inflation. Intuitively, individuals' willingness to save will depend on the growth in purchasing power they can expect (given by the real interest rate). Thus, when the inflation rate is high, a higher nominal interest rate is needed to induce individuals to save. This was evident in the late 1970s and early 1980s when inflation reached double-digits in the United States, and nominal rates increased in response.

Investment and Interest Rate Policy

Interest rates affect not only individuals' propensity to save, but also firms' incentive to raise capital and invest. Consider an opportunity that requires an up-front investment of

FIGURE 5.2

U.S. Interest Rates
and Inflation Rates,
1962–2016

The graph shows U.S. nominal interest rates (in blue) and inflation rates (in red) from 1962–2016. Note that interest rates tend to be high when inflation is high. The interest rates we graph here are one-year Treasury rates, and the inflation rates are the increase in the U.S. Bureau of Labor Statistics' consumer price index over the coming year, with both series computed on a monthly basis. The difference between them thus reflects the approximate real interest rate earned by holding Treasuries.

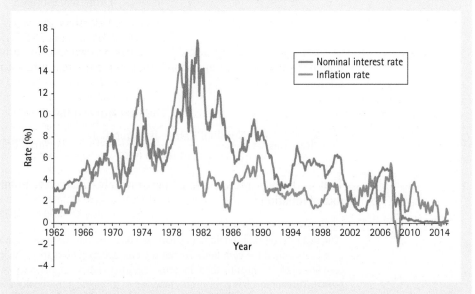

Source: St. Louis Federal Reserve Economic Data (FRED).

$10 million and generates a cash flow of $3 million per year for four years. If the interest rate is 5%, this investment's benefits have a PV of:

$$PV = \frac{3}{1.05} + \frac{3}{1.05^2} + \frac{3}{1.05^3} + \frac{3}{1.05^4} = \$10.638 \text{ million}$$

If the interest rate is 9%, the PV falls to

$$PV = \frac{3}{1.09} + \frac{3}{1.09^2} + \frac{3}{1.09^3} + \frac{3}{1.09^4} = \$9.719 \text{ million}$$

and the investment is no longer profitable given its $10 million cost. The reason, of course, is that we are discounting the positive cash flows at a higher rate, which reduces their present value. The cost of $10 million occurs today, however, so its present value is independent of the discount rate.

More generally, when the costs of an investment precede the benefits, an increase in the interest rate will make the investment less attractive. All else being equal, higher interest rates will therefore tend to shrink the set of good investments available to firms. The Federal Reserve in the United States and central banks in other countries attempt to use this relationship between interest rates and investment incentives when trying to guide the economy. They will often lower interest rates in an attempt to stimulate investment if the economy is slowing, and they will raise interest rates to reduce investment if the economy is "overheating" and inflation is on the rise.

Monetary Policy, Deflation, and the 2008 Financial Crisis. When the 2008 financial crisis struck the economy, the U.S. Federal Reserve responded quickly to mitigate its impact on the broader economy by cutting its short-term interest rate target to 0% by year's end. But while this use of monetary policy is generally quite effective, because consumer prices were falling in late 2008, the inflation rate was negative, and so even with a 0% nominal interest rate the real interest rate remained positive initially. The consequence of this deflation, and the risk that it might continue, meant that the Federal Reserve was "out of

 How Is Inflation Actually Calculated?

Inflation is calculated as the rate of change in the *Consumer Price Index* (CPI). The CPI measures what it costs each month to purchase a standard set of goods that the average consumer would buy. How controversial can price data be?

To gather the price information, data collectors visit stores and gather 80,000 retail price quotes and 5000 housing rent quotes. The data is sent daily to Washington, DC, where analysts at the Bureau of Labor Statistics seek to determine if part of a price change captures a change in quality or inflation. Because this adjustment can be subjective, herein lies the controversy in the CPI calculation. The *Wall Street Journal*, covering the controversy, reported the following examples:

• A 57-inch television in which the price dropped from $2238.99 to $1909.97. Going over the checklist, the data gatherer in the field discovered the old version had a built-in high-definition tuner. The new one did not. The analyst estimated that the tuner was valued at $513.69. This turned what appeared to be a 14.7% price decrease into a 10.7% increase.

• A 27-inch television where the price appeared to stay the same, but an analyst determined that the price had declined. The latest model had a flat screen, something that consumers value more than the curved screen in the old model. The newer TV also had a 10-watt stereo, compared with the weaker 6-watt stereo in the older model.

Critics argue that this quality adjustment most often ends up making a price increase look smaller or even turning it into a decline. Thus, they conclude that the government underestimates the true rate of inflation. Supporters argue that these adjustments are necessary because paying more for a better product is not equivalent to paying more for the same product. This debate is important because many union contracts, for example, have wages linked to inflation, and investors need good inflation data to determine what interest rate to demand.

WSJ Source: Aeppel, T., "New and Improved: An Inflation Debate Brews Over Intangibles at the Mall—Critics Say U.S. Plays Down CPI Through Adjustments For Quality, Not Just Price—Value of a TV's Flat Screen," 9 May 2005, A1.

ammunition" with regard to its usual weapon against an economic slowdown—it could not lower rates further. This problem was one of the reasons the United States and other governments began to consider other measures, such as increased government spending and investment, to stimulate their economies. Former Federal Reserve Governor Kevin Warsh further discusses monetary policy responses to the economic crisis in both the United States and Europe in the interview box on page 146.

Why couldn't the Federal Reserve go further and make nominal interest rates negative? Since individuals can always hold cash and earn at least a zero return, the nominal interest rate can never be *significantly* negative. But because storing cash is costly, and because investors viewed many banks as unsafe, short-term U.S. Treasury interest rates were actually slightly negative (down to –0.05%) at several points throughout this period! Perhaps more notable is the fact that in 2016, several central banks, including the European Central Bank and the Bank of Japan set negative deposit rates to encourage banks to lend in order to boost economic growth. As we stated above, negative rates are hard to sustain and in fact, in response to the Bank of Japan announcement, there was a run on safes by Japanese savers! So, while we correctly think of zero as the appropriate floor for interest rates (you would not choose to pay to give someone the use of your money), the global financial crisis and its aftermath have produced several examples of special cases of negative rates being driven by depositor risk-aversion, costly substitutes, and the ability of monetary authorities to impose such rates on their member banks. (See Chapter 6 for further discussion.)

The Yield Curve and Discount Rates

The interest rates that banks offer on investments or charge on loans depend on the horizon, or *term*, of the investment or loan. For example, suppose you are willing to put your

FIGURE 5.3

Term Structure of Risk-Free U.S. Interest Rates, November 2006, 2007, and 2008

The figure shows the interest rate available from investing in risk-free U.S. Treasury securities with different investment terms. In each case, the interest rates differ depending on the horizon. For example, in 2008, the interest rate on a 10-year loan (3.41%) was more than three times the rate on a 1-year loan (0.91%).

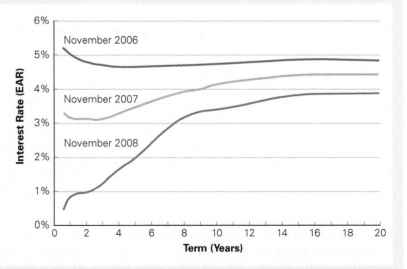

Term	Date		
(years)	Nov-06	Nov-07	Nov-08
0.5	5.23%	3.32%	0.47%
1	4.99%	3.16%	0.91%
2	4.80%	3.16%	0.98%
3	4.72%	3.12%	1.26%
4	4.63%	3.34%	1.69%
5	4.64%	3.48%	2.01%
6	4.65%	3.63%	2.49%
7	4.66%	3.79%	2.90%
8	4.69%	3.96%	3.21%
9	4.70%	4.00%	3.38%
10	4.73%	4.18%	3.41%
15	4.89%	4.44%	3.86%
20	4.87%	4.45%	3.87%

(Data from U.S. Treasury securities.)

money in a CD (certificate of deposit)[3] that matures in two years (meaning that you cannot get the money back before then without a penalty). The bank will offer you a higher rate of interest for this CD than if you put your money in a statement savings account, where you can withdraw your funds at any time. The relationship between the investment term and the interest rate is called the **term structure** of interest rates. We can plot this relationship on a graph called the **yield curve**. Figure 5.3 shows the term structure and corresponding yield curve of U.S. interest rates that were available to investors in November 2006, 2007, and 2008. In each case, note that the interest rate depends on the horizon, and that the difference between short-term and long-term interest rates was especially pronounced in 2008. The rates plotted are interest rates for U.S. Treasury securities, which are considered to be free of any risk of default (the U.S. government will not default on its loans). Thus, each of these rates is a **risk-free interest rate**, which is the interest rate at which money can be borrowed or lent without risk over a given period.

> **term structure** The relationship between the investment term and the interest rate.
>
> **yield curve** A plot of bond yields as a function of the bonds' maturity date.
>
> **risk-free interest rate** The interest rate at which money can be borrowed or lent without risk over a given period.

We can use the term structure to compute the present and future values of a risk-free cash flow over different investment horizons. For example, $100 invested for one year at the one-year interest rate in November 2008 would grow to a future value of

$$\$100 \times 1.0091 = \$100.91$$

at the end of one year, and $100 invested for 10 years at the 10-year interest rate in November 2008 would grow to:[4]

$$\$100 \times (1.0341)^{10} = \$139.84$$

We can apply the same logic when computing the present value of cash flows with different maturities. A risk-free cash flow received in two years should be discounted at the two-year interest rate, and a cash flow received in 10 years should be discounted at the 10-year interest rate. In general, a risk-free cash flow of C_n received in n years has the present value

$$PV = \frac{C_n}{(1 + r_n)^n} \tag{5.6}$$

where r_n is the risk-free interest rate for an n-year term. In other words, when computing a present value we must match the term of the cash flow and term of the discount rate.

Combining Eq. 5.6 for cash flows in different years leads to the general formula for the present value of a cash flow stream:

Present Value of a Cash Flow Stream Using a Term Structure of Discount Rates

$$PV = \frac{C_1}{1 + r_1} + \frac{C_2}{(1 + r_2)^2} + \cdots + \frac{C_N}{(1 + r_N)^N} \tag{5.7}$$

Note the difference between Eq. 5.7 and Eq. 4.3. Here, we use a different discount rate for each cash flow, based on the rate from the yield curve with the same term. When interest rates are very similar across maturities, we say that the yield curve is flat, because it is close to a flat line. When the yield curve is relatively flat, as it was in November 2006, the distinction of using different rates for each cash flow is relatively minor and is often ignored by discounting using a single "average" interest rate r. But when short-term and long-term interest rates vary widely, as they did in November 2008, Eq. 5.7 should be used.

---

[3]A certificate of deposit is a short- or medium-term debt instrument offered by banks. You deposit money in the bank for a stated period of time and normally receive a fixed rate of interest. The rate is higher than it would be on a savings account because you cannot withdraw your money early without paying a penalty.
[4]We could also invest for 10 years by investing at the one-year interest rate for 10 years in a row. However, because we do not know what future interest rates will be, our ultimate payoff would not be risk free.

Warning: All of our shortcuts for computing present values (annuity and perpetuity formulas, and financial calculators) are based on discounting all of the cash flows *at the same rate*. They *cannot* be used in situations in which cash flows need to be discounted at different rates.

INTERVIEW WITH

KEVIN M. WARSH

Kevin M. Warsh, *a lecturer at Stanford's Graduate School of Business and a distinguished visiting fellow at the Hoover Institution*, was a Federal Reserve governor from 2006 to 2011, serving as chief liaison to the financial markets.

QUESTION: *What are the main policy instruments used by central banks to control the economy?*

ANSWER: The Federal Reserve (Fed) deploys several policy tools to achieve its goals of price stability, maximum sustainable employment, and financial stability. Lowering the federal funds short-term interest rate, the primary policy instrument, stimulates the economy. Raising the federal funds rate generally slows the economy. Buying and selling short-term U.S. Treasury securities through *open market operations* is standard practice. Prior to the 2007–2009 financial crisis, the Fed's balance sheet ranged from $700–$900 billion. But when the Fed was unable to lower interest rates further because rates were so close to zero already, it resorted to large-scale, longer-term open market operations to increase liquidity in the financial system in the hopes of stimulating the economy further, thus growing its balance sheet significantly. With *open mouth operations*, the Fed's announcements of its intent to buy or sell assets indicates its desired degree of future policy accommodation, often prompting markets to react by adjusting interest rates immediately. The Fed's Lender-of-Last-Resort authority allows it to lend money against good collateral to troubled institutions under certain conditions.

QUESTION: *What factors limit the effectiveness of Fed policy?*

ANSWER: Monetary policy does not act in isolation. Fiscal (taxing and spending), trade, and regulatory policies have huge consequence on the state of economic and financial conditions. In the short term, monetary policy can help buy time for an economy to improve, but it cannot cure structural failings of an economy in isolation or compensate for the country's growing indebtedness.

QUESTION: *What tools did the Fed create to address the 2007–2009 financial crisis?*

ANSWER: During the darkest days of the crisis, markets did not operate effectively, prices for securities did not clear, and banks and other financial institutions lacked clarity and confidence in the financial wherewithal of each other. One effective, innovative tool, the *Term Auction Facility (TAF)*, stimulated the economy by providing cheap and readily available term funding to banks, large and small, on the front lines of the economy, thus encouraging them to extend credit to businesses and consumers. After reducing the policy rate to near zero to help revive the economy, the Fed instituted two *Quantitative Easing (QE)* programs—special purchases of government and agency securities—to increase money supply, promote lending, and according to some proponents, increase prices of riskier assets.

The Fed also addressed the global financial crisis by establishing temporary *central bank liquidity swap lines* with the European Central Bank and other major central banks. Using this facility, a foreign central bank is able to obtain dollar funding for its customers by swapping euros for dollars or another currency and agreeing to reverse the swap at a later date. The Fed does not take exchange rate risk, but it is subject to the credit risk of its central bank counterparty.

QUESTION: *What tools is the European Central Bank (ECB) using to address the sovereign debt crisis? How does its approach compare to the Fed's approach to the 2007–2009 financial crisis?*

ANSWER: As a novel economic federation, the ECB finds itself in a more difficult position than the Fed. The underlying economies and competitiveness are markedly different across the Eurozone—in Germany versus Greece, for example. From 2007 until mid-2010, many European financiers and policymakers believed that global financial crisis was largely American-made, with some strains exported to the continent. By mid-2010, however, they recognized that it was indeed a global crisis. The ECB is formally charged with a single mandate of ensuring price stability, rather than the broader mandate of the Fed. Still, its actions ultimately mirrored many of those undertaken by the Fed: lowering the effective policy rate to record lows, providing direct liquidity to the Eurozone's financial institutions to avoid a potential run on the banking system, and instituting the Security Market Purchase program (buying sovereign credit of some of its distressed countries).

EXAMPLE 5.5

Using the Term Structure to Compute Present Values

MyFinanceLab

PROBLEM

Compute the present value of a risk-free five-year annuity of $1000 per year, given the yield curve for November 2008 in Figure 5.3.

SOLUTION

PLAN

The timeline of the cash flows of the annuity is:

We can use the table next to the yield curve to identify the interest rate corresponding to each length of time: 1, 2, 3, 4, and 5 years. With the cash flows and those interest rates, we can compute the PV.

EXECUTE

From Figure 5.3, we see that the interest rates are: 0.91%, 0.98%, 1.26%, 1.69%, and 2.01%, for terms of 1, 2, 3, 4, and 5 years, respectively.

To compute the present value, we discount each cash flow by the corresponding interest rate:

$$PV = \frac{1000}{1.0091} + \frac{1000}{1.0098^2} + \frac{1000}{1.0126^3} + \frac{1000}{1.0169^4} + \frac{1000}{1.0201^5} = \$4775$$

EVALUATE

The yield curve tells us the market interest rate per year for each different maturity. In order to correctly calculate the PV of cash flows from five different maturities, we need to use the five different interest rates corresponding to those maturities. Note that we cannot use the annuity formula here because the discount rates differ for each cash flow.

COMMON MISTAKE

Using the Annuity Formula When Discount Rates Vary

When computing the present value of an annuity, a common mistake is to use the annuity formula with a single interest rate even though interest rates vary with the investment horizon. For example, we *cannot* compute the present value of the five-year annuity in Example 5.5 using the five-year interest rate from November 2008:

$$PV \neq \$1000 \times \frac{1}{0.0201}\left(1 - \frac{1}{1.0201^5}\right) = \$4712$$

If we want to find the single interest rate that we could use to value the annuity, we must first compute the present value of the annuity using Eq. 5.7 and then solve for its rate of return. For the annuity in Example 5.5, we use a financial calculator or spreadsheet to find its rate of return of 1.55%. The rate of return of the annuity is always between the highest and lowest discount rates used to calculate its present value, as is the case in this example.

	N	I/Y	PV	PMT	FV
Given:	5		−4775	1000	0
Solve for:		1.55			
Excel Formula:	=RATE(NPER,PMT,PV,FV)=RATE(5,1000,−4775,0)				

The Yield Curve and the Economy

As Figure 5.4 illustrates, the yield curve changes over time. Sometimes, short-term rates are close to long-term rates, and at other times they may be very different. What accounts for the changing shape of the yield curve?

FIGURE 5.4

Yield Curve Shapes

The figure shows three different yield curve shapes. The blue line represents a "normal" yield curve. Most of the time the yield curve has this shape—moderately upward sloping. The red line depicts a steep yield curve—note the larger than normal difference between short-term rates (2%) and long-term rates (7%), making the yield curve look steeper than normal. This example of a steep yield curve is from October 1991. Finally, the green line depicts an inverted yield curve, so called because it slopes downward instead of upward. This happens when short-term rates are higher than long-term rates as they were in January 1981. We discuss why the shape of the yield curve changes over time in the rest of this section.

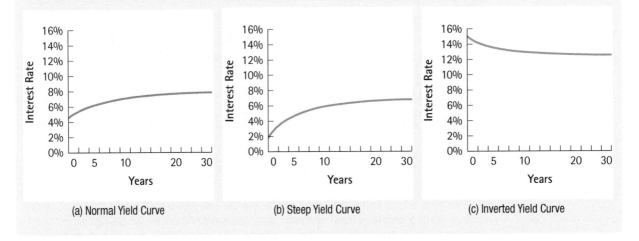

(a) Normal Yield Curve   (b) Steep Yield Curve   (c) Inverted Yield Curve

Interest Rate Determination. The Federal Reserve determines very short-term interest rates through its influence on the **federal funds rate**, which is the rate at which banks can borrow cash reserves on an overnight basis. All other interest rates on the yield curve are set in the market and are adjusted until the supply of lending matches the demand for borrowing at each loan term. As we shall see, expectations of future interest rate changes have a major effect on investors' willingness to lend or borrow for longer terms and, therefore, on the shape of the yield curve.

federal funds rate The overnight loan rate charged by banks with excess reserves at a Federal Reserve bank (called *federal funds*) to banks that need additional funds to meet reserve requirements.

Suppose short-term interest rates are equal to long-term interest rates. If interest rates are expected to rise in the future, investors would not want to make long-term investments. Instead, they could do better by investing on a short-term basis and then reinvesting after interest rates rise. Thus, if interest rates are expected to rise, long-term interest rates will tend to be higher than short-term rates to attract investors.

Similarly, if interest rates are expected to fall in the future, then borrowers would not wish to borrow at long-term rates that are equal to short-term rates. They would do better by borrowing on a short-term basis, and then taking out a new loan after rates fall. So, if interest rates are expected to fall, long-term rates will tend to be lower than short-term rates to attract borrowers.

Yield Curve Shape. These arguments indicate that the shape of the yield curve will be strongly influenced by interest rate expectations. A sharply increasing (*steep*) yield curve, with long-term rates much higher than short-term rates, generally indicates that interest rates are expected to rise in the future. A decreasing (*inverted*) yield curve, with long-term rates lower than short-term rates, generally signals an expected decline in future interest rates. Because interest rates tend to drop in response to a slowdown in the economy, an inverted yield curve is often interpreted as a negative forecast for economic growth. Indeed, as Figure 5.5 illustrates, each of the last seven recessions in the United States was preceded by a period in which the yield curve was inverted (note the red shaded areas before the gray

FIGURE 5.5

Short-Term Versus Long-Term U.S. Interest Rates and Recessions

One-year and 10-year U.S. Treasury rates are plotted, with the spread between them shaded in green if the shape of the yield curve is increasing (the one-year rate is below the 10-year rate) and in red if the yield curve is inverted (the one-year rate exceeds the 10-year rate). Gray bars show the dates of U.S. recessions as determined by the National Bureau of Economic Research. Note that inverted yield curves tend to precede recessions as determined by the National Bureau of Economic Research. In recessions, interest rates tend to fall, with short-term rates dropping further. As a result, the yield curve tends to be steep coming out of a recession.

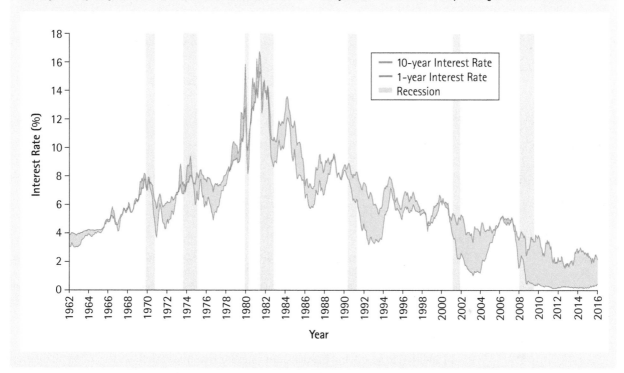

bars indicating a recession). Conversely, the yield curve tends to be steep (shaded green) as the economy comes out of a recession and interest rates are expected to rise.

The normal shape of the yield curve is moderately upward sloping. This would be the case if investors almost always believed that interest rates were going to rise in the future. But that is unlikely, so there have to be other forces at work to cause long-term interest rates normally to be higher than short-term rates. The most commonly cited reason is that long-term loans are riskier than short-term loans. If you make a 30-year loan today and lock in the interest rate, the present value of the payments you receive on the loan is very sensitive to even small changes in market interest rates. This sensitivity is due to the effect of compounding a change in interest rates over a 30-year period. To see this effect, consider Example 5.6.

EXAMPLE 5.6

Long-Term Versus Short-Term Loans

MyFinanceLab

PROBLEM

You work for a bank that has just made two loans. In one, you lent $909.09 today in return for $1000 in one year. In the other, you lent $909.09 today in return for $15,863.08 in 30 years. The difference between the loan amount and repayment amount is based on an interest rate of 10% per year. Imagine that immediately after you make the loans, news about economic growth is announced that increases inflation expectations, so that the market interest rate for loans like these jumps to 11%. Loans make up a major part of a bank's assets, so you are naturally concerned about the value of these loans. What is the effect of the interest rate change on the value to the bank of the promised repayment of these loans?

(Continued)

SOLUTION

PLAN

Each of these loans has only one repayment cash flow at the end of the loan. They differ only by the time to repayment:

The effect on the value of the future repayment to the bank today is just the PV of the loan repayment, calculated at the new market interest rate.

EXECUTE

For the one-year loan:

$$PV = \frac{\$1000}{(1.11)^1} = \$900.90$$

For the 30-year loan:

$$PV = \frac{\$15,863.08}{(1.11)^{30}} = \$692.94$$

EVALUATE

The value of the one-year loan decreased by $909.09 − $900.90 = $8.19, or 0.9%, but the value of the 30-year loan decreased by $909.09 − $692.94 = $216.15, or almost 24%! The small change in market interest rates, compounded over a longer period, resulted in a much larger change in the present value of the loan repayment. You can see why investors and banks view longer-term loans as being riskier than short-term loans.

In addition to specifying the discount rates for risk-free cash flows that occur at different horizons, it is also a potential leading indicator of future economic growth. Due to these qualities, the yield curve provides extremely important information for a business manager.

CONCEPT CHECK
5. What is the difference between a nominal and real interest rate?

6. How are interest rates and the level of investment made by businesses related?

5.4 The Opportunity Cost of Capital

opportunity cost of capital or cost of capital The best available expected return offered in the market on an investment of comparable risk and term to the cash flow being discounted; the return the investor forgoes on an alternative investment of equivalent risk and term when the investor takes on a new investment.

As we have seen in this chapter, the interest rates we observe in the market will vary based on quoting conventions, the term of the investment, and risk. In this chapter, we have developed the tools to account for these differences and gained insights into how interest rates are determined. This knowledge will provide the foundation for our study of bonds in Chapter 6.

In Chapter 3, we argued that the Valuation Principle tells us to use the "market interest rate" to compute present values and evaluate an investment opportunity. But with so many interest rates to choose from, the term "market interest rate" is inherently ambiguous. Therefore, going forward in the book, we will base the discount rate that we use to evaluate cash flows on the investor's **opportunity cost of capital** (or more simply, the **cost of capital**), which is *the best available expected return offered in the market on an investment of comparable risk and term to the cash flow being discounted.*

Interest Rates, Discount Rates, and the Cost of Capital

By now, you may have noticed that we are using three terms to refer to rates of return. While many people use these terms interchangeably, they are distinct. Throughout this book, we will use "interest rate" to mean a quoted rate in the market. A "discount rate" is the appropriate rate for discounting a given cash flow, *matched to the frequency of the cash flow*. Finally, we use "cost of capital" to indicate the rate of return on an investment of similar risk.

In order to understand the definition of opportunity cost of capital, it helps to think of yourself as a financial manager competing with financial managers at other firms to attract investors' funds (capital). In order to attract investors to invest in your firm or creditors to lend to your firm, you have to be able to offer them an expected return at least as good as what they could get elsewhere in the market for the same risk and length of investment. Now it is easier to see where the term (opportunity) cost of capital comes from—investors in your firm are giving up the opportunity to invest their funds elsewhere. This is an opportunity cost to them and to overcome it you must offer them a return equal to or better than their opportunity cost of capital. Even if you already have the funds internally in the firm to invest, the logic still applies. You could either return the funds to your shareholders to invest elsewhere, or reinvest them in a new project; however, you should only reinvest them if doing so provides a better return than the shareholders' other opportunities.

The opportunity cost of capital is the return the investor forgoes when the investor takes on a new investment. For a risk-free project, it will typically correspond to the interest rate on U.S. Treasury securities with a similar term. But the cost of capital is a much more general concept that can be applied to risky investments as well.

EXAMPLE 5.7
The Opportunity Cost of Capital

MyFinanceLab

PROBLEM

Suppose a friend offers to borrow $100 from you today and in return pay you $110 one year from today. Looking in the market for other options for investing the $100, you find your best alternative option that you view as equally risky as lending it to your friend. That option has an expected return of 8%. What should you do?

SOLUTION

PLAN

Your decision depends on what the opportunity cost is of lending your money to your friend. If you lend her the $100, then you cannot invest it in the alternative with an 8% expected return. Thus, by making the loan, you are giving up the opportunity to invest for an 8% expected return. You can make your decision by using your 8% opportunity cost of capital to value the $110 in one year.

EXECUTE

The value of the $110 in one year is its present value, discounted at 8%:

$$PV = \frac{\$110}{(1.08)^1} = \$101.85$$

The $100 loan is worth $101.85 to you today, so you make the loan.

EVALUATE

The Valuation Principle tells us that we can determine the value of an investment by using market prices to value the benefits net of the costs. As this example shows, market prices determine what our best alternative opportunities are, so that we can decide whether an investment is worth the cost.

Chapter 3 introduced the Valuation Principle as a unifying theme in finance. In this and the preceding chapters, we have developed the fundamental tools a financial manager needs to value cash flows at different points in time. In this last section, we reiterated the importance of using market information to determine the opportunity cost of capital, which is your discount rate in valuation calculations. In Chapter 6, we will study bonds and how they are priced, which provides us with an immediate application of the knowledge we have built so far.

COMMON MISTAKE

States Dig a $3 Trillion Hole by Discounting at the Wrong Rate

Almost all states in the United States offer their employees a defined benefit pension plan guaranteeing a retirement income based on the duration of their employment with the state and their final salary. These promised payments are the plan's liabilities—and because the payouts are guaranteed, they are comparable to a risk-free bond. To meet these liabilities, states put aside funds and invest them in risky assets like stocks and corporate bonds.

Unfortunately, states make a critical, but common, mistake when determining their funding requirements: They compute the present value of the liabilities using an arbitrary discount rate (typically 8%) that is unrelated to the riskiness of the plan's liabilities.

Because of their guaranteed nature, the risk-free rate, which is currently well below 8%, is the correct discount rate for plan liabilities.[5] This error has led states to grossly underestimate the value of their liabilities—and underfunded pension plans impose a potential future obligation on taxpayers. How large is this obligation? Professors Robert Novy-Marx and Joshua Rauh[6] found that total state pension underfunding in 2008 amounted to at least $3 *trillion*. They also estimated that there is less than a 5% probability that, over the next 15 years, states will be able to meet their pension obligations without turning to taxpayers. Worse still, states are most likely to need the money in market downturns, precisely when taxpayers are least able to pay.

CONCEPT CHECK
7. What is the opportunity cost of capital?
8. Can you ignore the cost of capital if you already have the funds inside the firm?

MyFinanceLab

Here is what you should know after reading this chapter. MyFinanceLab will help you identify what you know, and where to go when you need to practice.

KEY POINTS AND EQUATIONS	KEY TERMS	ONLINE PRACTICE
5.1 Interest Rate Quotes and Adjustments • Just like any other price, interest rates are set by market forces, in particular the supply and demand of funds. • The effective annual rate (EAR) (or annual percentage yield—APY) indicates the actual amount of interest earned in one year. The EAR can be used as a discount rate for annual cash flows. • Given an EAR r, the equivalent discount rate for an n-year time interval, where n may be more than one year or less than or equal to one year (a fraction), is: $$\text{Equivalent } n\text{-period Discount Rate} = (1+r)^n - 1 \qquad (5.1)$$ • An annual percentage rate (APR) is a common way of quoting interest rates. The actual interest rate per period is the APR/number of compounding periods per year. APRs cannot be used as discount rates.	annual percentage rate (APR), p. 134 annual percentage yield (APY), 132 effective annual rate (EAR), p. 132 simple interest, p. 134	MyFinanceLab Study Plan 5.1

---

[5]States often justify the 8% rate as the return they expect to earn on their investments. But the risks of their investments and of their liabilities are not comparable (for example, the return on stocks is not guaranteed), so this argument is fundamentally flawed.

[6]R. Novy-Marx and J. Rau, The Liabilities and Risks of State-Sponsored Pension Plans, *Journal of Economic Perspectives* (Fall 2009) Vol. 23, No. 4.

- We need to know the compounding interval of an APR to determine the EAR:

$$1 + EAR = \left(1 + \frac{APR}{m}\right)^m \qquad (5.3)$$

m = number of compounding periods per year.
- For a given APR, the EAR increases with the compounding frequency.

5.2 Application: Discount Rates and Loans • Loan rates are typically stated as APRs. The outstanding balance of a loan is equal to the present value of the loan cash flows, when evaluated using the actual interest rate per payment interval based on the loan rate. • In each loan payment on an amortizing loan, you pay interest on the loan plus some part of the loan balance.	amortizing loan, p. 137	MyFinanceLab Study Plan 5.2

5.3 The Determinants of Interest Rates
• Quoted interest rates are nominal interest rates, which indicate the rate of growth of the money invested. The real interest rate indicates the rate of growth of one's purchasing power after adjusting for inflation.
	federal funds rate,
	  p. 148
	nominal interest
	  rates, p. 141
	real interest rate,
	  p. 141
	risk-free interest rate,
	  p. 145
	term structure,
	  p. 145
	yield curve, p. 145
		MyFinanceLab
		Study Plan 5.3
		
		Interactive Yield
		Curve

- Given a nominal interest rate and an inflation rate, the real interest rate is:

$$\text{Real Rate} = \frac{\text{Nominal Rate} - \text{Inflation Rate}}{1 + \text{Inflation Rate}}$$

$$\approx \text{Nominal} - \text{Inflation Rate} \qquad (5.5)$$

- Nominal interest rates tend to be high when inflation is high and low when inflation is low.
- Higher interest rates tend to reduce the attractiveness of typical investment projects. The U.S. Federal Reserve raises interest rates to moderate investment and combat inflation and lowers interest rates to stimulate investment and economic growth.
- Interest rates differ with the investment horizon according to the term structure of interest rates. The graph plotting interest rates as a function of the horizon is called the yield curve.
- Cash flows should be discounted using the discount rate that is appropriate for their horizon. Thus, the PV of a cash flow stream is:

$$PV = \frac{C_1}{1 + r_1} + \frac{C_2}{(1 + r_2)^2} + \cdots + \frac{C_N}{(1 + r_N)^N} \qquad (5.7)$$

- Annuity and perpetuity formulas cannot be applied when discount rates vary with the horizon.

- The shape of the yield curve tends to vary with investors' expectations of future economic growth and interest rates. It tends to be inverted prior to recessions and to be steep coming out of a recession. Because investors view long-term loans as riskier, long-term rates are generally higher than short-term rates.

5.4 The Opportunity Cost of Capital • An investor's opportunity cost of capital (or simply, the cost of capital) is the best available expected return offered in the market on an investment of comparable risk and term to the cash flow being discounted.	(opportunity) cost of capital, p. 150	MyFinanceLab Study Plan 5.4

CRITICAL THINKING

1. Explain how an interest rate is just a price.

2. Why is the EAR for 6% APR, with semiannual compounding, higher than 6%?

3. Why is it so important to match the frequency of the interest rate to the frequency of the cash flows?

4. Why aren't the payments for a 15-year mortgage twice the payments for a 30-year mortgage at the same rate?

5. What mistake do you make when you discount real cash flows with nominal discount rates?

6. How do changes in inflation expectations impact interest rates?

7. Can the nominal interest rate available to an investor be negative? (*Hint*: Consider the interest rate earned from saving cash "under the mattress.") Can the real interest rate be negative?

8. In the early 1980s, inflation was in the double-digits and the yield curve sloped sharply downward. What did the yield curve say about investors' expectations about future inflation rates?

9. What do we mean when we refer to the "opportunity cost" of capital?

PROBLEMS

All problems are available in MyFinanceLab. *The* [×] *icon indicates problems that are easier to solve using Excel and have data in an Excel format available in* MyFinanceLab. *An asterisk * indicates problems with a higher level of difficulty.*

Interest Rate Quotes and Adjustments

1. You are considering a car loan with a stated APR of 6% based on monthly compounding. What is the effective annual rate of this loan?

2. Your bank is offering you an account that will pay 20% interest in total for a two-year deposit. Determine the equivalent discount rate for a period length of
   a. six months.
   b. one year.
   c. one month.

3. You are looking to buy a car and you have been offered a loan with an APR of 6%, compounded monthly.
   a. What is the true monthly rate of interest?
   b. What is the EAR?

4. You are considering two ways of financing a spring break vacation. You could put it on your credit card, at 15% APR, compounded monthly, or borrow the money from your parents, who want an 8% interest payment every six months. Which is the lower rate?

5. An online bank is offering to pay 0.25% interest per month on deposits. Your local bank offers to pay 0.75% interest quarterly (every 3 months). Which is the higher interest rate?

6. Which do you prefer: a bank account that pays 5% per year (EAR) for three years or
   a. an account that pays 2.5% every six months for three years?
   b. an account that pays 7.5% every 18 months for three years?
   c. an account that pays 0.5% per month for three years?

*7. You have been offered a job with an unusual bonus structure. As long as you stay with the firm, you will get an extra $70,000 every seven years, starting seven years from now. What is the present value of this incentive if you plan to work for the company for 42 years and the interest rate is 6% (EAR)?

8. You have found three investment choices for a one-year deposit: 10% APR compounded monthly, 10% APR compounded annually, and 9% APR compounded daily. Compute the EAR for each investment choice. (Assume that there are 365 days in the year.)

9. Your bank account pays interest with an EAR of 5%. What is the APR quote for this account based on semiannual compounding? What is the APR with monthly compounding?

10. Suppose the interest rate is 8% APR with monthly compounding. What is the present value of an annuity that pays $100 every six months for five years?

11. A payday loan is structured to obscure the true interest rate you are paying. For example, in Washington, you pay a $30 "fee" for a two-week $200 payday loan (when you repay the loan, you pay $230). What is the effective annual interest rate for this loan?

12. You have been accepted into college. The college guarantees that your tuition will not increase for the four years you attend. The first $10,000 tuition payment is due in six months. After that, the same payment is due every six months until you have made a total of eight payments. The college offers a bank account that allows you to withdraw money every six months and has a fixed APR of 4% (semiannual) guaranteed to remain the same over the next four years. How much money must you deposit today if you intend to make no further deposits and would like to make all the tuition payments from this account, leaving the account empty when the last payment is made?

Application: Discount Rates and Loans

13. You make monthly payments on your car loan. It has a quoted APR of 5% (monthly compounding). What percentage of the outstanding principal do you pay in interest each month?

14. Suppose Capital One is advertising a 60-month, 5.99% APR motorcycle loan. If you need to borrow $8000 to purchase your dream Harley-Davidson, what will your monthly payment be?

15. Assume you graduate from college with $30,000 in student loans. If your interest rate is fixed at 4.66% APR with monthly compounding and you will repay the loans over a 10-year period, what will be your monthly payment?

16. Ironwood Bank is offering a 30-year mortgage with an APR of 6.00% based on monthly compounding. If you plan to borrow $160,000, what will be your monthly payment?

17. You have just taken out a $20,000 car loan with a 6% APR, compounded monthly. The loan is for five years. When you make your first payment in one month, how much of the payment will go toward the principal of the loan and how much will go toward interest?

*18. Consider the loan from the previous question: a 60-month, $20,000 car loan with a 6% APR, compounded monthly. Assume that right after you make your 50th payment, the balance on the loan is $3,762.32. How much of your next payment goes toward principal and how much goes toward interest? Compare this with your answer in the last question—what is happening?

*19. You are buying a house and the mortgage company offers to let you pay a "point" (1% of the total amount of the loan) to reduce your APR from 6.5% to 6.25% on your $400,000, 30-year mortgage with monthly payments. If you plan to be in the house for at least five years, should you do it?

20. You have decided to refinance your mortgage. You plan to borrow whatever is outstanding on your current mortgage. The current monthly payment is $2356 and you have made every payment on time. The original term of the mortgage was 30 years, and the mortgage is exactly four years and eight months old. You have just made your monthly payment. The mortgage interest rate is 6.375% (APR). How much do you owe on the mortgage today?

*21. You have just sold your house for $1,000,000 in cash. Your mortgage was originally a 30-year mortgage with monthly payments and an initial balance of $800,000. The mortgage is currently exactly 18½ years old, and you have just made a payment. If the interest rate on the mortgage is 5.25% (APR), how much cash will you have from the sale once you pay off the mortgage?

22. You have just purchased a car and taken out a $50,000 loan. The loan has a five-year term with monthly payments and an APR of 6%.
    a. How much will you pay in interest, and how much will you pay in principal, during the first month, second month, and first year? (*Hint*: Compute the loan balance after one month, two months, and one year.)
    b. How much will you pay in interest, and how much will you pay in principal, during the fourth year (i.e., between three and four years from now)?

23. You are thinking about leasing a car. The purchase price of the car is $30,000. The residual value (the amount you could pay to keep the car at the end of the lease) is $15,000 at the end of 36 months. Assume the first lease payment is due one month after you get the car. The interest rate implicit in the lease is 6% APR, compounded monthly. What will your lease payments be for a 36-month lease?

*24. You have some extra cash this month and you are considering putting it toward your car loan. Your interest rate is 7%, your loan payments are $600 per month, and you have 36 months left on your loan. If you pay an additional $1000 with your next regular $600 payment (due in one month), how much will it reduce the amount of time left to pay off your loan?

*25. You have an outstanding student loan with required payments of $500 per month for the next four years. The interest rate on the loan is 9% APR (monthly). You are considering making an extra payment of $100 today (i.e., you will pay an extra $100 that you are not required to pay). If you are required to continue to make payments of $500 per month until the loan is paid off, what is the amount of your final payment? What rate of return (expressed as an APR with monthly compounding) have you earned on the $100?

*26. Consider again the setting of Problem 25. Now that you realize your best investment is to prepay your student loan, you decide to prepay as much as you can each month.

Looking at your budget, you can afford to pay an extra $250 per month in addition to your required monthly payments of $500, or $750 in total each month. How long will it take you to pay off the loan?

 *27. Oppenheimer Bank is offering a 30-year mortgage with an APR of 5.25% based on monthly compounding. With this mortgage your monthly payments would be $2,000 per month. In addition, Oppenheimer Bank offers you the following deal: Instead of making the monthly payment of $2,000 every month, you can make half the payment every two weeks (so that you will make 52/2 = 26 payments per year). With this plan, how long will it take to pay off the mortgage if the EAR of the loan is unchanged?

 *28. Your friend tells you he has a very simple trick for taking one-third off the time it takes to repay your mortgage: Use your Christmas bonus to make an extra payment on January 1 of each year (that is, pay your monthly payment due on that day twice). Assume that the mortgage has an original term of 30 years and an APR of 12%.
   a. If you take out your mortgage on January 1, so that your first payment is due on February 1, and you make your first extra payment at the end of the first year, in what year will you finish repaying your mortgage?
   b. If you take out your mortgage on July 1 (so the first payment is August 1) and make the extra payment each January, in how many months will you pay off your mortgage?
   c. How will the amount of time it takes to pay off the loan given this strategy vary with the interest rate on the loan?

 29. The mortgage on your house is five years old. It required monthly payments of $1402, had an original term of 30 years, and had an interest rate of 10% (APR). In the intervening five years, interest rates have fallen and so you have decided to refinance—that is, you will roll over the outstanding balance into a new mortgage. The new mortgage has a 30-year term, requires monthly payments, and has an interest rate of $6\,5/8$% (APR).
   a. What monthly repayments will be required with the new loan?
   b. If you still want to pay off the mortgage in 25 years, what monthly payment should you make after you refinance?
   c. Suppose you are willing to continue making monthly payments of $1402. How long will it take you to pay off the mortgage after refinancing?
   d. Suppose you are willing to continue making monthly payments of $1402, and want to pay off the mortgage in 25 years. How much additional cash can you borrow today as part of the refinancing?

 30. You have credit card debt of $25,000 that has an APR (monthly compounding) of 15%. Each month you pay the minimum monthly payment. You are required to pay only the outstanding interest. You have received an offer in the mail for an otherwise identical credit card with an APR of 12%. After considering all your alternatives, you decide to switch cards, roll over the outstanding balance on the old card into the new card, and borrow additional money as well. How much can you borrow today on the new card without changing the minimum monthly payment you will be required to pay?

 31. Your firm has taken out a $500,000 loan with 9% APR (compounded monthly) for some commercial property. As is common in commercial real estate, the loan is a five-year loan based on a 15-year amortization. This means that your loan payments will be calculated as if you will take 15 years to pay off the loan, but you actually must do so in five years. To do this, you will make 59 equal payments based on the 15-year amortization schedule and then make a final 60th payment to pay the remaining balance.
   a. What will your monthly payments be?
   b. What will your final payment be?

*32. Five years ago you took out a 5/1 adjustable rate mortgage and the five-year fixed rate period has just expired. The loan was originally for $300,000 with 360 payments at 4.2% APR, compounded monthly.

a. Now that you have made 60 payments, what is the remaining balance on the loan?

b. If the interest rate increases by 1%, to 5.2% APR, compounded monthly, what will your new payments be?

The Determinants of Interest Rates

33. In 1975, interest rates were 7.85% and the rate of inflation was 12.3% in the United States. What was the real interest rate in 1975? How would the purchasing power of your savings have changed over the year?

34. If the rate of inflation is 5%, what nominal interest rate is necessary for you to earn a 3% real interest rate on your investment?

35. Assume the inflation rate is 3% APR, compounded annually. Would you rather earn a nominal return of 5% APR, compounded semiannually, or a real return of 2% APR, compounded quarterly?

36. Assume inflation is 0.2% per month. Would you rather earn a nominal return of 0.75% per month, or a real return of 6.5% APR, compounded annually?

37. You are pleased to see that you have been given a 5% raise this year. However, you read on the *Wall Street Journal* Web site that inflation over the past year has been 2%. How much better off are you in terms of real purchasing power?

38. What is the shape of the yield curve given in the following term structure? What expectations are investors likely to have about future interest rates?

Term (in years)	1	2	3	5	7	10	20
Rate (EAR, %)	1.99	2.41	2.74	3.32	3.76	4.13	4.93

39. See the Treasury Yield Curve from June 2013 below. At the time, some were concerned about whether the Federal Reserve's stimulus activities would lead to high inflation. Based on the Yield Curve, can you tell whether the bond market was concerned about inflation? Explain.

Term (in years)	1	2	3	5	7	10	30
Rate (EAR, %)	0.13	0.32	0.53	1.12	1.62	2.21	3.36

The Opportunity Cost of Capital

40. You are thinking about investing $5000 in your friend's landscaping business. Even though you know the investment is risky and you can't be sure, you expect your investment to be worth $5750 next year. You notice that the rate for one-year Treasury bills is 1%. However, you feel that other investments of equal risk to your friend's landscape business offer a 10% expected return for the year. What should you do?

41. You have invested in a business that proudly reports that it is profitable. Your investment of $5000 has produced a profit of $300. The managers think that if you leave your $5000 invested with them, they should be able to generate $300 per year in profits for you in perpetuity. Evaluating other investment opportunities, you note that other long-term investments of similar risk offer an expected return of 8%. Should you remain invested in this firm?

6

Bonds

LEARNING OBJECTIVES

- Understand bond terminology

- Compute the price and yield to maturity of a zero-coupon bond

- Compute the price and yield to maturity of a coupon bond

- Analyze why bond prices change over time

- Know how credit risk affects the expected return from holding a corporate bond

notation					
	CPN	coupon payment on a bond	y	yield to maturity
	FV	face value of a bond	YTM	yield to maturity
	n	number of periods	YTM_n	yield to maturity on a zero-coupon bond with n periods to maturity
	P	initial price of a bond		
	PV	present value		

In this chapter, we introduce bonds and apply our tools for valuing cash flows to them. Bonds are simply loans. When an investor buys a bond from an issuer, the investor is lending money to the bond issuer. Who are the issuers of bonds? Federal and local governments issue bonds to finance long-term projects, and many companies issue bonds as part of their debt financing.

Understanding bonds and their pricing is useful for several reasons. First, we can use the prices of risk-free government bonds to determine the risk-free interest rates that produce the yield curves discussed in Chapter 5. As we saw there, the yield curve provides important information for valuing risk-free cash flows and assessing expectations of inflation and economic growth. Second, firms often issue bonds to fund their own investments. The return investors receive on those bonds is one factor that determines a firm's cost of capital. Finally, bonds provide an opportunity to begin our study of how securities are priced in a competitive market. The bond markets are very large and very liquid; there are more than $39 *trillion* of bonds outstanding in the U.S. markets alone.[1] Further, the ideas we develop in this chapter will be helpful when we turn to the topic of valuing stocks in Chapter 7.

Pricing bonds gives us an opportunity to apply what we've learned in the last three chapters about valuing cash flows using competitive market prices. As we explained in Chapter 3, the Valuation Principle implies that the price of a security in a competitive market should be the present value of the cash flows an investor will receive from owning it. Thus, we begin the chapter by evaluating the promised cash flows for different types of bonds. If a bond is risk-free, so that the promised cash flows will be paid with certainty, we can use the Law of One Price to directly relate the return of a bond and its price. We then discuss how and why bond prices change over time. Once we have a firm understanding of the pricing of bonds in the absence of risk, we add the risk of default, where cash flows are not known with certainty. The risk of default and its implications are important considerations for a financial manager who is considering issuing corporate bonds. (In Chapter 15, we will discuss the details of issuing debt financing and cover some additional corporate bond features.)

6.1 Bond Terminology

bond certificate States the terms of a bond as well as the amounts and dates of all payments to be made.

maturity date The final repayment date of a bond.

term The time remaining until the final repayment date of a bond.

face value, par value, principal amount The notional amount of a bond used to compute its interest payments. The face value of the bond is generally due at the bond's maturity.

coupons The promised interest payments of a bond, paid periodically until the maturity date of the bond.

coupon rate Determines the amount of each coupon payment of a bond. The coupon rate, expressed as an APR, is set by the issuer and stated on the bond certificate.

Recall from Chapter 1 that a bond is a security sold by governments and corporations to raise money from investors today in exchange for a promised future payment. The terms of the bond are described as part of the **bond certificate**, which indicates the amounts and dates of all payments to be made. A bond certificate is shown in Figure 6.1. Payments on the bond are made until a final repayment date called the **maturity date** of the bond. The time remaining until the repayment date is known as the **term** of the bond.

Bonds typically make two types of payments to their holders. The principal or **face value** (also known as **par value** or **principal amount**) of a bond is the notional amount we use to compute the interest payments. Typically, the face value is repaid at maturity. It is generally denominated in standard increments such as $1000. A bond with a $1000 face value, for example, is often referred to as a "$1000 bond."

In addition to the face value, some bonds also promise additional payments called **coupons**. The bond certificate typically specifies that the coupons will be paid periodically (for example, semiannually) until the maturity date of the bond. As you can see from Figure 6.1, historically, on a payment date, the holder of the bond would clip off the next coupon for the next payment and present it for payment. It follows that the interest payments on the bond are called *coupon payments*. Today, the majority of bonds are registered electronically but the term remains.

The amount of each coupon payment is determined by the **coupon rate** of the bond. This coupon rate is set by the issuer and stated on the bond certificate. By convention, the coupon rate is expressed as an APR, so the amount of each coupon payment, *CPN*, is:

Coupon Payment

$$CPN = \frac{\text{Coupon Rate} \times \text{Face Value}}{\text{Number of Coupon Payments per Year}} \qquad (6.1)$$

For example, a "$1000 bond with a 10% coupon rate and semiannual payments" will pay coupon payments of $(10\% \times \$1000)/2 = \$50$ every six months.

Table 6.1 summarizes the bond terminology we have presented thus far.

---

[1]Outstanding U.S. Bond Market Debt, www.sifma.org. December 2009.

FIGURE 6.1

A Bearer Bond
and Its Unclipped
Coupons Issued by
the Elmira and
Williamsport Railroad
Company for $500

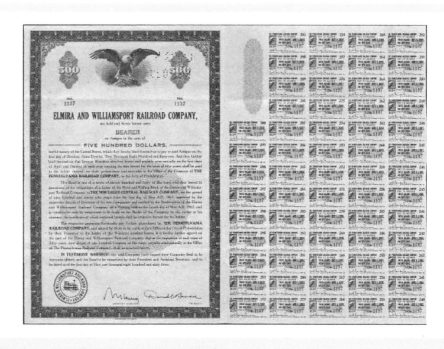

Source: Courtesy Heritage Auctions, Inc. © 1999–2006.

TABLE 6.1

Review of Bond
Terminology

Bond Certificate	States the terms of a bond as well as the amounts and dates of all payments to be made.
Coupons	The promised interest payments of a bond. Usually paid semiannually, but the frequency is specified in the bond certificate. They are determined by the coupon rate, which is stated on the bond certificate. The amount paid is equal to: $$\frac{\text{Coupon Rate} \times \text{Face Value}}{\text{Number of Coupon Payments per Year}}$$
Maturity Date	Final repayment date of the bond. Payments continue until this date.
Principal or Face Value	The notional amount used to compute the interest payment. It is usually repaid on the maturity date. Also called *par value*.
Term	The time remaining until the repayment date.

CONCEPT CHECK

1. What types of cash flows does a bond buyer receive?

2. How are the periodic coupon payments on a bond determined?

6.2   Zero-Coupon Bonds

zero-coupon bond A
bond that makes only one
payment at maturity.

Treasury bills Zero-
coupon bonds, issued by
the U.S. government, with a
maturity of up to one year.

Not all bonds have coupon payments. Bonds without coupons are called **zero-coupon bonds.** As these are the simplest type of bond, we shall analyze them first. The only cash payment an investor in a zero-coupon bond receives is the face value of the bond on the maturity date. **Treasury bills,** which are U.S. government bonds with a maturity of up to one year, are zero-coupon bonds. The general name for risk-free zero coupon bonds is "STRIPS," which is an abbreviation of Separately Tradable Registered Interest and Principal Securities.

Zero-Coupon Bond Cash Flows

There are only two cash flows if we purchase and hold a zero-coupon bond. First, we pay the bond's current market price at the time we make the purchase. Then, at the maturity date, we receive the bond's face value. For example, suppose that a one-year, risk-free, zero-coupon bond with a $100,000 face value has an initial price of $96,618.36. If you purchased this bond and held it to maturity, you would have the following cash flows:

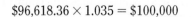

Note that although the bond pays no "interest" directly, as an investor you are compensated for the time value of your money by purchasing the bond at a discount to its face value. Recall from Chapter 3 that the present value of a future cash flow is less than the cash flow itself. As a result, prior to its maturity date, the price of a zero-coupon bond is always less than its face value. That is, zero-coupon bonds always trade at a **discount** (a price lower than the face value), so they are also called **pure discount bonds**.

discount A price at which bonds trade that is less than their face value.

pure discount bonds Zero-coupon bonds.

Yield to Maturity of a Zero-Coupon Bond

Now that we understand the cash flows associated with a zero-coupon bond, we can calculate the rate of return of buying a bond and holding it until maturity. Recall from Chapter 4 that we can always find the rate of return of an investment opportunity as the discount rate that equates the present value of the investment to its costs. With a zero-coupon bond, the price is the cost of the bond. So, the rate of return on the zero-coupon bond is the discount rate that makes the present value of the future cash flow received (that is, the bond principal) equal to the cost of the bond. We can extend this concept to a coupon bond: the rate of return is the discount rate at which the present value of all future cash flows from the bond equals the price of the bond. The rate of return of an investment in a bond is given a special name, the **yield to maturity (YTM)** or just the *yield*:

yield to maturity (YTM) The rate of return of an investment in a bond that is held to its maturity date, or the discount rate that sets the present value of the promised bond payments equal to the current market price of the bond.

> *The yield to maturity of a bond is the discount rate that sets the present value of the promised bond payments equal to the current market price of the bond.*

Intuitively, the yield to maturity for a zero-coupon bond is the return you will earn as an investor by buying the bond at its current market price, holding the bond to maturity, and receiving the promised face value payment.

Let's determine the yield to maturity of the one-year zero-coupon bond discussed earlier. According to the definition, the yield to maturity of the one-year bond solves the following equation:

$$96,618.36 = \frac{100,000}{1 + YTM_1}$$

In this case:

$$1 + YTM_1 = \frac{100,000}{96,618.36} = 1.035$$

That is, the yield to maturity for this bond is 3.5%. Because the bond is risk free, investing in this bond and holding it to maturity is like earning 3.5% interest on your initial investment:

$$\$96,618.36 \times 1.035 = \$100,000$$

Negative Bond Yields

On December 9, 2008, in the midst of one of the worst financial crises in history, the unthinkable happened: For the first time since the Great Depression, U.S. Treasury Bills traded at a negative yield. That is, these risk-free pure discount bonds traded at premium. As Bloomberg.com reported: "If you invested $1 million in three-month bills at today's negative discount rate of 0.01%, for a price of 100.002556, at maturity you would receive the par value for a loss of $25.56."

A negative yield on a Treasury bill implies that investors have an arbitrage opportunity: By selling the bill, and holding the proceeds in cash, they would have a risk-free profit of $25.56. Why did investors not rush to take advantage of the arbitrage opportunity and thereby eliminate it?

Well, first, the negative yields did not last very long, suggesting that, in fact, investors did rush to take advantage of this opportunity. But second, after closer consideration, the opportunity might not have been a sure risk-free arbitrage. When selling a Treasury security, the investor must choose where to invest, or at least hold, the proceeds. In normal times, investors would be happy to deposit the proceeds with a bank, and consider this deposit to be risk free. But these were not normal times—many investors had great concerns about the financial stability of banks and other financial intermediaries. Perhaps investors shied away from this "arbitrage" opportunity because they

were worried that the cash they would receive could not be held safely anywhere (even putting it "under the mattress" has a risk of theft!). Thus, we can view the $25.56 as the price investors were willing to pay to have the U.S. Treasury hold their money safely for them at a time when no other investments seemed truly safe.

This phenomenon repeated itself in Europe starting in mid-2012. In this case, negative yields emerged due to a concern about the both the safety of European banks as well as the stability of the euro as a currency. As investors in Greece or other countries began to worry their economies might depart from the euro, they were willing to hold German and Swiss government bonds even at negative yields as a way to protect themselves against the Eurozone unraveling. By mid-2015, almost 25% of European government bonds had negative yields, with some Swiss bonds having yields close to −1%!

These persistent and significantly negative yields are challenging to explain. Most of the holders of these bonds are institutions and pension funds who are restricted to hold very safe assets. And while they could hold currency instead, obtaining, storing, and securing large quantities of cash would also be very costly. (Indeed, Swiss banks have reportedly refused large currency withdrawals by hedge funds attempting to exploit the arbitrage opportunity.) Bonds are also much easier to trade, and use as collateral, than giant vaults of cash. Together, the safety and convenience of these bonds must be worth the nearly 1% per year these investors are willing to sacrifice.

We can use a similar method to find the yield to maturity for any maturity zero-coupon bond:

Yield to Maturity of an *n*-Year Zero-Coupon Bond

$$1 + YTM_n = \left(\frac{\text{Face Value}}{\text{Price}} \right)^{1/n} \tag{6.2}$$

The yield to maturity (YTM_n) in Eq. 6.2 is the per-period rate of return for holding the bond from today until maturity on date n.

EXAMPLE 6.1
Yields for Different Maturities

MyFinanceLab

PROBLEM

Suppose the following zero-coupon bonds are trading at the prices shown below per $100 face value. Determine the corresponding yield to maturity for each bond.

Maturity	1 year	2 years	3 years	4 years
Price	$96.62	$92.45	$87.63	$83.06

SOLUTION

PLAN

We can use Eq. 6.2 to solve for the YTM of the bonds. The table gives the prices and number of years to maturity and the face value is $100 per bond.

EXECUTE

Using Eq. 6.2, we have

$$YTM_1 = (100/96.62)^{1/1} - 1 = 3.50\%$$
$$YTM_2 = (100/92.45)^{1/2} - 1 = 4.00\%$$

(Continued)

$$YTM_3 = (100/87.63)^{1/3} - 1 = 4.50\%$$

$$YTM_4 = (100/83.06)^{1/4} - 1 = 4.75\%$$

EVALUATE

Solving for the YTM of a zero-coupon bond is the same process we used to solve for the rate of return in Chapter 4. Indeed, the YTM is the rate of return of buying the bond.

Risk-Free Interest Rates

Above, we calculated the yield to maturity of the one-year risk-free bond as 3.5%. But recall that the Valuation Principle's Law of One Price implies that all one-year risk-free investments must earn this same return of 3.5%. That is, 3.5% must be *the* competitive-market risk-free interest rate.

More generally, in Chapter 5, we discussed the competitive market interest rate r_n available from today until date n for risk-free cash flows. Recall that we used this interest rate as the cost of capital for a risk-free cash flow that occurs on date n. A default-free zero-coupon bond that matures on date n provides a risk-free return over the same period. So the Law of One Price guarantees that the risk-free interest rate equals the yield to maturity on such a bond. Consequently, we will often refer to the yield to maturity of the appropriate maturity, zero-coupon risk-free bond as *the* risk-free interest rate. Some financial professionals also use the term **spot interest rates** to refer to these default-free, zero-coupon yields because these rates are offered "on the spot" at that point in time.

In Chapter 5, we introduced the yield curve, which plots the risk-free interest rate for different maturities. These risk-free interest rates correspond to the yields of risk-free zero-coupon bonds. Thus, the yield curve we introduced in Chapter 5 is also referred to as the **zero-coupon yield curve**. Figure 6.2 illustrates the yield curve consistent with the zero-coupon bond prices in Example 6.1.

spot interest rates Default-free, zero-coupon yields.

zero-coupon yield curve A plot of the yield of risk-free zero-coupon bonds (STRIPS) as a function of the bond's maturity date.

FIGURE 6.2

Zero-Coupon Yield Curve Consistent with the Bond Prices in Example 6.1

Recall from Chapter 5 that a yield curve simply plots the yield to maturity of investments of different maturities. In this figure, we show the yield curve that would be produced by plotting the yield to maturities determined by the bond prices in Example 6.1. Note that as in this figure, the longer maturities generally have higher yields.

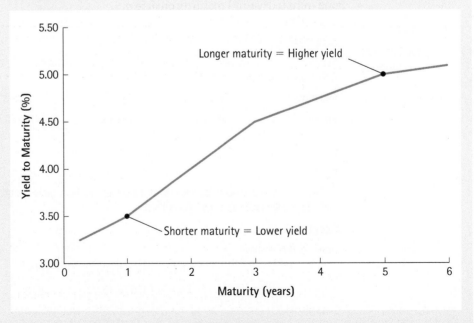

In Example 6.1, we used the bond's price to compute its yield to maturity. But from the definition of the yield to maturity, we can also use a bond's yield to compute its price. In the case of a zero-coupon bond, the price is simply equal to the present value of the bond's face value, discounted at the bond's yield to maturity.

EXAMPLE 6.2

Computing the Price of a Zero-Coupon Bond

MyFinanceLab

PROBLEM

Given the yield curve shown in Figure 6.2, what is the price of a five-year risk-free zero-coupon bond with a face value of $100?

SOLUTION

PLAN

We can compute the bond's price as the present value of its face amount, where the discount rate is the bond's yield to maturity. From the yield curve, the yield to maturity for five-year risk-free zero-coupon bonds is 5.0%.

EXECUTE

$$P = 100/(1.05)^5 = 78.35$$

EVALUATE

We can compute the price of a zero-coupon bond simply by computing the present value of the face amount using the bond's yield to maturity. Note that the price of the five-year zero-coupon bond is even lower than the price of the other zero-coupon bonds in Example 6.1, because the face amount is the same but we must wait longer to receive it.

CONCEPT CHECK

3. Why would you want to know the yield to maturity of a bond?

4. What is the relationship between a bond's price and its yield to maturity?

6.3 Coupon Bonds

coupon bonds Bonds that pay regular coupon interest payments up to maturity, when the face value is also paid.

Similar to zero-coupon bonds, **coupon bonds** pay investors their face value at maturity. In addition, these bonds make regular coupon interest payments. As Table 6.2 indicates, two types of U.S. Treasury coupon securities are currently traded in financial markets: **Treasury notes**, which have original maturities from one to ten years, and **Treasury bonds**, which have original maturities of more than ten years. The original maturity is the term of the bond at the time it was originally issued.

Treasury notes A type of U.S. Treasury coupon security, currently traded in financial markets, with original maturities from one to ten years.

Treasury bonds A type of U.S. Treasury coupon security, currently traded in financial markets, with original maturities of more than ten years.

TABLE 6.2

Existing U.S. Treasury Securities

Treasury Security	Type	Original Maturity
Bills	Discount	4, 13, 26, and 52 weeks
Notes	Coupon	2, 3, 5, and 10 year
Bonds	Coupon	20 and 30 year

Coupon Bond Cash Flows

While an investor's return on a zero-coupon bond comes from buying it at a discount to its principal value, the return on a coupon bond comes from two sources: (1) any difference between the purchase price and the principal value, and (2) its periodic coupon payments. Before we can compute the yield to maturity of a coupon bond, we need to know all of its cash flows, including the coupon interest payments and when they are paid. In Example 6.3, we take a bond description and translate it into the bond's cash flows.

PROBLEM

Assume that it is May 15, 2010, and the U.S. Treasury has just issued securities with a May 2015 maturity, $1000 par value, and a 2.2% coupon rate with semiannual coupons. Since the original maturity is only five years, these would be called "notes" as opposed to "bonds." The first coupon payment will be paid on November 15, 2010. What cash flows will you receive if you hold this note until maturity?

SOLUTION

PLAN

The description of the note should be sufficient to determine all of its cash flows. The phrase "May 2015 maturity, $1000 par value" tells us that this is a note with a face value of $1000 and five years to maturity. The phrase "2.2% coupon rate with semiannual coupons" tells us that the note pays a total of 2.2% of its face value each year in two equal semiannual installments. Finally, we know that the first coupon is paid on November 15, 2010.

EXECUTE

The face value of this note is $1000. Because this note pays coupons semiannually, using Eq. 6.1 you can compute that you will receive a coupon payment every six months of $CPN = (2.2\% \times \$1000)/2 = \$11$. Here is the timeline based on a six-month period and there are a total of 10 cash flows:

May 2010	Nov. 2010	May 2011	Nov. 2011	May 2015
	$11	$11	$11	$11 + $1000

Note that the last payment occurs five years (10 six-month periods) from now and is composed of both a coupon payment of $11 and the face value payment of $1000.

EVALUATE

Since a note is just a package of cash flows, we need to know those cash flows in order to value the note. That's why the description of the note contains all of the information we would need to construct its cash flow timeline.

 The U.S. Treasury Market

In most years, the U.S. Federal Government spends more than it takes in through taxes and other revenue sources. To finance this deficit, the U.S. Department of the Treasury issues debt instruments, commonly known as "Treasuries." The market for Treasury securities is huge and extremely liquid. At the end of 2015, the total amount of public debt outstanding was over $18.15 *trillion*. Treasury securities are held by institutional investors such as insurance companies, pension funds and bond mutual funds, individual investors, and even other governmental agencies (such as the Federal Reserve) as shown in the pie chart below. The figures are in *billions* of dollars (7489 billion is 7.489 trillion).

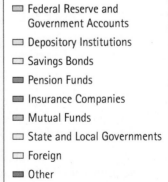

Source: Treasury Bulletin Ownership of Federal Securities, https://www.fiscal.treasury.gov/fsreports/rpt/treasBulletin/treasBulletin_home.htm, September 2015.

Yield to Maturity of a Coupon Bond

Once we have determined the coupon bond's cash flows, given its market price we can determine its yield to maturity. Recall that the yield to maturity for a bond is the rate of return of investing in the bond and holding it to maturity. This investment has the cash flows shown in the timeline below:

The yield to maturity of the bond is the *single* discount rate that equates the present value of the bond's remaining cash flows to its current price. For zero-coupon bonds, there were only two cash flows. But coupon bonds have many cash flows, complicating the yield to maturity calculation. From the timeline, we see that the coupon payments represent an annuity, so the yield to maturity is the interest rate y that solves the following equation:

Yield to Maturity of a Coupon Bond

$$P = CPN \times \overbrace{\frac{1}{y}\left(1 - \frac{1}{(1+y)^N}\right)}^{\text{Annuity Factor using the YTM } (y)} + \frac{FV}{(1+y)^N} \qquad (6.3)$$

Present Value of all of the periodic coupon payments $\qquad$ Present Value of the Face Value repayment using the YTM (y)

Unfortunately, unlike zero-coupon bonds, there is no simple formula to solve for the yield to maturity directly. Instead, we need to use either trial and error or, more commonly, a financial calculator or a spreadsheet (both of which we demonstrate in Example 6.4).

When we calculate a bond's yield to maturity by solving Eq. 6.3, the yield we compute will be a rate *per coupon interval*. However, yields are typically quoted as APRs, so we multiply by the number of coupons per year, thereby converting the answer into an APR quote with the same compounding interval as the coupon rate.

EXAMPLE 6.4

Computing the Yield to Maturity of a Coupon Bond

MyFinanceLab

PROBLEM

Consider the five-year, $1000 bond with a 2.2% coupon rate and semiannual coupons described in Example 6.3. If this bond is currently trading for a price of $963.11, what is the bond's yield to maturity?

SOLUTION

PLAN

We worked out the bond's cash flows in Example 6.3. From the cash flow timeline, we can see that the bond consists of an annuity of 10 payments of $11, paid every six months, and one lump-sum payment of $1000 in five years (in 10 six-month periods). We can use Eq. 6.3 to solve for the yield to maturity. However, we must use six-month intervals consistently throughout the equation.

EXECUTE

Because the bond has 10 remaining coupon payments, we compute its yield y by solving Eq. 6.3 for this bond:

$$963.11 = 11 \times \frac{1}{y}\left(1 - \frac{1}{(1+y)^{10}}\right) + \frac{1000}{(1+y)^{10}}$$

(Continued)

We can solve it by trial and error, a financial calculator, or a spreadsheet. To use a financial calculator, we enter the price we pay as a negative number for the PV (it is a cash outflow), the coupon payments as the PMT, and the bond's par value as its FV. Finally, we enter the number of coupon payments remaining (10) as N.

	N	I/Y	PV	PMT	FV
Given:	10		−963.11	11	1000
Solve for:		1.50			

Excel Formula: =RATE(NPER,PMT,PV,FV)=RATE(10,11,−963.11,1000)

Therefore, $y = 1.5\%$. Because the bond pays coupons semiannually, this yield is for a six-month period. We convert it to an APR by multiplying by the number of coupon payments per year. Thus, the bond has a yield to maturity equal to a 3% APR with semiannual compounding.

EVALUATE

As the equation shows, the yield to maturity is the discount rate that equates the present value of the bond's cash flows with its price. Note that the YTM is higher than the coupon rate and the price is lower than the par value. We will discuss why in the next section.

We can also use Eq. 6.3 to compute a bond's price based on its yield to maturity. We simply discount the cash flows using the yield, as in Example 6.5.

EXAMPLE 6.5

Computing a Bond Price from Its Yield to Maturity

MyFinanceLab

PROBLEM

Consider again the five-year, $1000 bond with a 2.2% coupon rate and semiannual coupons in Example 6.4. Suppose interest rates drop and the bond's yield to maturity decreases to 2% (expressed as an APR with semiannual compounding). What price is the bond trading for now? And what is the effective annual yield on this bond?

SOLUTION

PLAN

Given the yield, we can compute the price using Eq. 6.3. First, note that a 2% APR is equivalent to a semiannual rate of 1%. Also, recall that the cash flows of this bond are an annuity of 10 payments of $11, paid every six months, and one lump-sum cash flow of $1000 (the face value), paid in five years (10 six-month periods). In Chapter 5, we learned how to compute an effective annual rate from an APR using Eq. 5.3. We do the same here to compute the effective annual yield from the bond's yield to maturity expressed as an APR.

EXECUTE

Using Eq. 6.3 and the six-month yield of 1%, the bond price must be:

$$P = 11 \times \frac{1}{0.01}\left(1 - \frac{1}{1.01^{10}}\right) + \frac{1000}{1.01^{10}} = \$1009.47$$

We can also use a financial calculator or spreadsheet:

	N	I/Y	PV	PMT	FV
Given:	10	1		11	1000
Solve for:			−1009.47		

Excel Formula: =PV(RATE,NPER,PMT,FV)=PV(.01,10,11,1000)

The effective annual yield corresponding to 1% every six months is:

$$(1 + .01)^2 - 1 = .0201, \text{ or } 2.01\%$$

EVALUATE

The bond's price has risen to $1009.47, lowering the return from investing in it from 1.5% to 1% per six-month period. Interest rates have dropped, so the lower return brings the bond's yield into line with the lower competitive rates being offered for similar risk and maturity elsewhere in the market.

Finding Bond Prices on the Web

Unlike the NYSE where many stocks are traded, there is no particular physical location where bonds are traded. Instead, they are traded electronically. Recently, the Financial Industry Regulatory Authority (FINRA) has made an effort to make bond prices more widely available. Their Web site, http://finra-markets.morningstar.com/BondCenter/Default.jsp, allows anyone to search for the most recent trades and quotes for bonds. Here, we show a screenshot from the Web site displaying the pricing information for one of Procter and Gamble's (PG) bonds.

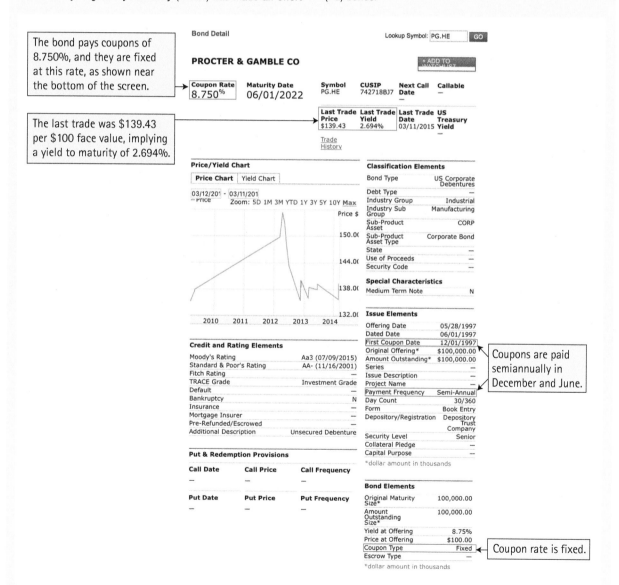

The bond pays coupons of 8.750%, and they are fixed at this rate, as shown near the bottom of the screen.

The last trade was $139.43 per $100 face value, implying a yield to maturity of 2.694%.

Coupons are paid semiannually in December and June.

Coupon rate is fixed.

Coupon Bond Price Quotes

Because we can convert any price into a yield, and vice versa, prices and yields are often used interchangeably. For example, the bond in Example 6.5 could be quoted as having a yield of 2% or a price of $1009.47 per $1000 face value. Indeed, bond traders generally quote bond yields rather than bond prices. One advantage of quoting the yield to maturity rather than the price is that the yield is independent of the face value of the bond. When prices are quoted in the bond market, they are conventionally quoted per $100 face value. Thus, the bond in Example 6.5 would be quoted as having a price of $100.947 (per $100 face value), which would imply an actual price of $1009.47 given the $1000 face value of the bond.

CONCEPT CHECK

5. What cash flows does a company pay to investors holding its coupon bonds?

6. What do we need in order to value a coupon bond?

6.4 Why Bond Prices Change

As we mentioned earlier, zero-coupon bonds always trade for a discount—that is, prior to maturity, their price is less than their face value. But as shown in Examples 6.4 and 6.5, coupon bonds may trade at a discount, or at a **premium** (a price greater than their face value). In this section, we identify when a bond will trade at a discount or premium, as well as how the bond's price will change due to the passage of time and fluctuations in interest rates.

premium A price at which coupon bonds trade that is greater than their face value.

Most issuers of coupon bonds choose a coupon rate so that the bonds will *initially* trade at, or very close to, **par** (that is, at the bond's face value). For example, the U.S. Treasury sets the coupon rates on its notes and bonds in this way. After the issue date, the market price of a bond generally changes over time for two reasons. First, as time passes, the bond gets closer to its maturity date. Holding fixed the bond's yield to maturity, the present value of the bond's remaining cash flows changes as the time to maturity decreases. Second, at any point in time, changes in market interest rates affect the bond's yield to maturity and its price (the present value of the remaining cash flows). We explore these two effects in the remainder of this section.

par A price at which coupon bonds trade that is equal to their face value.

Interest Rate Changes and Bond Prices

If a bond sells at par (at its face value), the only return investors will earn is from the coupons that the bond pays. Therefore, the bond's coupon rate will exactly equal its yield to maturity. As interest rates in the economy fluctuate, the yields that investors demand to invest in bonds will also change. Imagine that your company issues a bond when market interest rates imply a YTM of 8%, setting the coupon rate to be 8%. Suppose interest rates then rise so that new bonds have a YTM of 9%. These new bonds would have a coupon rate of 9% and sell for $1000. So, for $1000, the investor would get $90 per year until the bond matured. Your existing bond was issued when rates were lower such that its coupon is fixed at 8%, so it offers payments of $80 per year until maturity. Because its cash flows are lower, the 8% bond must have a lower price than the 9% bond.[2] Thus, the price of the 8% bond will fall until the investor is indifferent between buying the 8% bond and buying the 9% bond. Figure 6.3 illustrates the relationship between the bond's price and its yield to maturity.

---

[2]Otherwise, if the 8% bond had the same or higher price, there would be an arbitrage opportunity: One could sell the 8% bond and buy the 9% bond, receiving cash today and higher coupons going forward.

In our example, the price of the 8% bond will drop to below face value ($1000), so it will be trading at a discount (also called trading *below par*). If the bond trades at a discount, an investor who buys the bond will earn a return both from receiving the coupons *and* from receiving a face value that exceeds the price paid for the bond. As a result, if a bond trades at a discount, its yield to maturity will exceed its coupon rate.

A bond that pays a coupon can also trade at a premium to its face value (trading *above par*). Imagine what would have happened in our example if interest rates had gone down to 7% instead of up to 9%. Then, the holder of the existing 8% bond would not part with it for $1000. Instead, its price would have to rise until the yield to maturity from buying it at that price would be 7%. In this case, an investor's return from the coupons is diminished by receiving a face value less than the price paid for the bond. *Thus, a bond trades at a premium whenever its yield to maturity is less than its coupon rate.*[3]

FIGURE 6.3

A Bond's Price Versus Its Yield to Maturity

At a price of $1000, the 8% semiannual coupon bond offers an 8% YTM. In order for the 8% coupon bond to offer a competitive yield to maturity, its price must fall until its yield to maturity rises to the 9% yield being offered by otherwise similar bonds. In the example depicted here, for a bond with five years left to maturity, its price must fall to $960.44 before investors will be indifferent between buying it and the 9% coupon bond priced at $1000. The curve depicts this bond's price at yields to maturity between 6% and 10%.

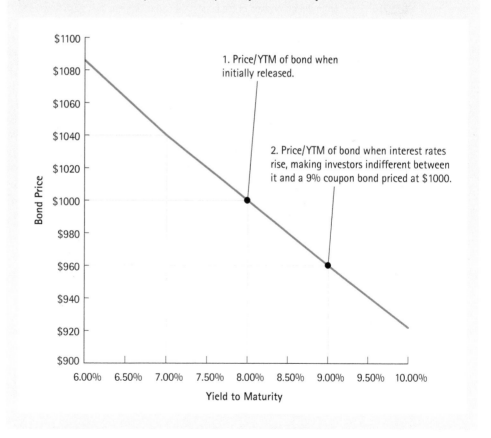

[3]The terms "discount" and "premium" are simply descriptive and are not meant to imply that you should try to buy bonds at a discount and avoid buying bonds at a premium. In a competitive market, the Law of One Price ensures that all similar bonds are priced to earn the same return. When you buy a bond, the price exactly equals the present value of the bond's cash flows, so that you earn a fair return, but not an abnormally good (or bad) return.

This example illustrates a general phenomenon. A higher yield to maturity means that investors demand a higher return for investing. They apply a higher discount rate to the bond's remaining cash flows, reducing their present value and hence the bond's price. The reverse holds when interest rates fall. Investors then demand a lower yield to maturity, reducing the discount rate applied to the bond's cash flows and raising the price. Therefore, *as interest rates and bond yields rise, bond prices will fall, and vice versa, so that interest rates and bond prices always move in the opposite direction.*

Table 6.3 summarizes the relationship between interest rates and bond prices.

EXAMPLE 6.6

Determining the Discount or Premium of a Coupon Bond

MyFinanceLab

PROBLEM

Consider three 30-year bonds with annual coupon payments. One bond has a 10% coupon rate, one has a 5% coupon rate, and one has a 3% coupon rate. If the yield to maturity of each bond is 5%, what is the price of each bond per $100 face value? Which bond trades at a premium, which trades at a discount, and which trades at par?

SOLUTION

PLAN

From the description of the bonds, we can determine their cash flows. Each bond has 30 years to maturity and pays its coupons annually. Therefore, each bond has an annuity of coupon payments, paid annually for 30 years, and then the face value paid as a lump sum in 30 years. They are all priced so that their yield to maturity is 5%, meaning that 5% is the discount rate that equates the present value of the cash flows to the price of the bond. Therefore, we can use Eq. 6.3 to compute the price of each bond as the PV of its cash flows, discounted at 5%.

EXECUTE

For the 10% coupon bond, the annuity cash flows are $10 per year (10% of each $100 face value). Similarly, the annuity cash flows for the 5% and 3% bonds are $5 and $3 per year. We use a $100 face value for all of the bonds.

Using Eq. 6.3 and these cash flows, the bond prices are:

$$P(10\% \text{ coupon}) = 10 \times \frac{1}{0.05}\left(1 - \frac{1}{1.05^{30}}\right) + \frac{100}{1.05^{30}} = \$176.86 \text{ (trades at a premium)}$$

$$P(5\% \text{ coupon}) = 5 \times \frac{1}{0.05}\left(1 - \frac{1}{1.05^{30}}\right) + \frac{100}{1.05^{30}} = \$100.00 \text{ (trades at par)}$$

$$P(3\% \text{ coupon}) = 3 \times \frac{1}{0.05}\left(1 - \frac{1}{1.05^{30}}\right) + \frac{100}{1.05^{30}} = \$69.26 \text{ (trades at a discount)}$$

EVALUATE

The prices reveal that when the coupon rate of the bond is higher than its yield to maturity, it trades at a premium. When its coupon rate equals its yield to maturity, it trades at par. When its coupon rate is lower than its yield to maturity, it trades at a discount.

TABLE 6.3

Bond Prices Immediately After a Coupon Payment

When the bond price is . . .	greater than the face value	equal to the face value	less than the face value
We say the bond trades . . .	"above par" or "at a premium"	"at par"	"below par" or "at a discount"
This occurs when . . .	Coupon Rate > Yield to Maturity	Coupon Rate = Yield to Maturity	Coupon Rate < Yield to Maturity

Time and Bond Prices

Let's consider the effect of time on the price of a bond. As the next payment from a bond grows nearer, the price of the bond increases to reflect the increasing present value of that cash flow. Take a bond paying semiannual coupons of $50 and imagine tracking the price of the bond starting on the day after the last coupon payment was made. The price would slowly rise over the following six months as the next $50 coupon payment grows closer and closer. It will peak right before the coupon payment is made, when buying the bond still entitles you to receive the $50 payment immediately. If you buy the bond right after the coupon payment is made, you do not have the right to receive that $50 coupon. The price you are willing to pay for the bond will therefore be $50 less than it was right before the coupon was paid. This pattern—the price slowly rising as a coupon payment nears and then dropping abruptly after the payment is made—continues for the life of the bond. Figure 6.4 illustrates this phenomenon.

FIGURE 6.4

The Effect of Time on Bond Prices

The graph illustrates the effects of the passage of time on bond prices when the yield remains constant, in this case 5%. The price of a zero-coupon bond rises smoothly. The prices of the coupon bonds are indicated by the zigzag lines. Notice that the prices rise between coupon payments, but tumble on the coupon date, reflecting the amount of the coupon payment. For each coupon bond, the gray line shows the trend of the bond price just after each coupon is paid.

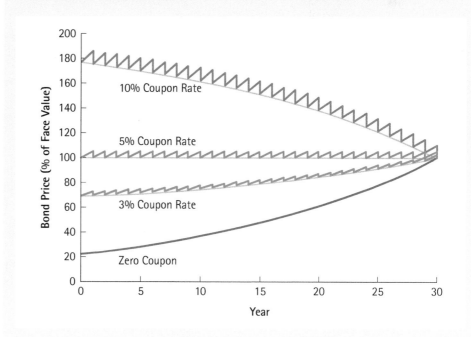

EXAMPLE 6.7

The Effect of Time on the Price of a Bond

MyFinanceLab

PROBLEM

Suppose you purchase a 30-year, zero-coupon bond with a yield to maturity of 5%. For a face value of $100, the bond will initially trade for:

$$P\,(\,30\text{ years to maturity}\,) = \frac{100}{1.05^{30}} = \$23.14$$

If the bond's yield to maturity remains at 5%, what will its price be five years later? If you purchased the bond at $23.14 and sold it five years later, what would the rate of return of your investment be?

(Continued)

SOLUTION

PLAN

If the bond was originally a 30-year bond and five years have passed, then it has 25 years left to maturity. If the yield to maturity does not change, then you can compute the price of the bond with 25 years left exactly as we did for 30 years, but using 25 years of discounting instead of 30.

Once you have the price in five years, you can compute the rate of return of your investment just as we did in Chapter 4. The FV is the price in five years, the PV is the initial price ($23.14), and the number of years is five.

EXECUTE

$$P\left(25 \text{ years to maturity}\right) = \frac{100}{1.05^{25}} = \$29.53$$

If you purchased the bond for $23.14 and then sold it after five years for $29.53, the rate of return of your investment would be

$$\left(\frac{29.53}{23.14}\right)^{1/5} - 1 = 5.0\%$$

That is, your return is the same as the yield to maturity of the bond.

EVALUATE

Note that the bond price is higher, and hence the discount from its face value is smaller, when there is less time to maturity. The discount shrinks because the yield has not changed, but there is less time until the face value will be received. This example illustrates a more general property for bonds: *If a bond's yield to maturity does not change, then the rate of return of an investment in the bond equals its yield to maturity even if you sell the bond early.*

Interest Rate Risk and Bond Prices

While the effect of time on bond prices is predictable, unpredictable changes in interest rates will also affect bond prices. Further, bonds with different characteristics will respond differently to changes in interest rates—some bonds will react more strongly than others. We showed in Chapter 5 that investors view long-term loans to be riskier than short-term loans. Because bonds are just loans, the same is true of short- versus long-term bonds.

The example illustrates how bonds of different maturity will have different sensitivities to interest rate changes. However, even bonds with the same maturity will differ in

EXAMPLE 6.8
The Interest Rate
Sensitivity of Bonds

MyFinanceLab

PROBLEM

Consider a 10-year coupon bond and a 30-year coupon bond, both with 10% annual coupons. By what percentage will the price of each bond change if its yield to maturity increases from 5% to 6%?

SOLUTION

PLAN

We need to compute the price of each bond for each yield to maturity and then calculate the percentage change in the prices. For both bonds, the cash flows are $10 per year for $100 in face value and then the $100 face value repaid at maturity. The only difference is the maturity: 10 years and 30 years. With those cash flows, we can use Eq. 6.3 to compute the prices.

EXECUTE

YTM	10-Year, 10% Annual Coupon Bond	30-Year, 10% Annual Coupon Bond
5%	$10 \times \dfrac{1}{0.05}\left(1 - \dfrac{1}{1.05^{10}}\right) + \dfrac{100}{1.05^{10}} = \$138.61$	$10 \times \dfrac{1}{0.05}\left(1 - \dfrac{1}{1.05^{30}}\right) + \dfrac{100}{1.05^{30}} = \$176.86$
6%	$10 \times \dfrac{1}{0.06}\left(1 - \dfrac{1}{1.06^{10}}\right) + \dfrac{100}{1.06^{10}} = \$129.44$	$10 \times \dfrac{1}{0.06}\left(1 - \dfrac{1}{1.06^{30}}\right) + \dfrac{100}{1.06^{30}} = \$155.06$

The price of the 10-year bond changes by $(129.44 - 138.61)/138.61 = -6.6\%$ if its yield to maturity increases from 5% to 6%.

For the 30-year bond, the price change is $(155.06 - 176.86)/176.86 = -12.3\%$.

EVALUATE

The 30-year bond is almost twice as sensitive to a change in the yield than is the 10-year bond. In fact, if we graph the price and yields of the two bonds, we can see that the line for the 30-year bond, shown in blue, is steeper throughout than the green line for the 10-year bond, reflecting its heightened sensitivity to interest rate changes.

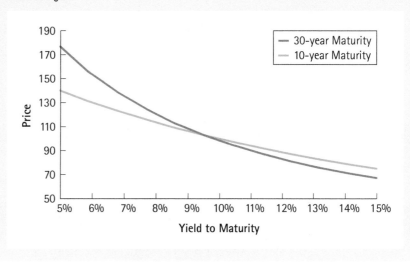

interest rate sensitivity if their coupon rates are different. Bonds with higher coupon rates—because they pay higher cash flows up-front—are less sensitive to interest rate changes than otherwise identical bonds with lower coupon rates.[4] Table 6.4 summarizes this conclusion.

TABLE 6.4

Bond Prices and Interest Rates

Bond Characteristic	Effect on Interest Rate Risk
Longer term to maturity	Increase
Higher coupon payments	Decrease

---

[4]The *duration* of a bond measures its sensitivity to interest rate changes. A full discussion of the concept of duration is beyond the scope of this book.

EXAMPLE 6.9

Coupons
and Interest Rate
Sensitivity

MyFinanceLab

PROBLEM

Consider two bonds, each of which pays semiannual coupons and has five years left until maturity. One has a coupon rate of 5% and the other has a coupon rate of 10%, but both currently have a yield to maturity of 8%. By what percentage will the price of each bond change if its yield to maturity decreases from 8% to 7%?

SOLUTION

PLAN

As in Example 6.8, we need to compute the price of each bond at 8% and 7% yield to maturities and then compute the percentage change in price. Each bond has 10 semiannual coupon payments remaining along with the repayment of par value at maturity. The cash flows per $100 of face value for the first bond are $2.50 every six months and then $100 at maturity. The cash flows per $100 of face value for the second bond are $5 every six months and then $100 at maturity. Since the cash flows are semiannual, the yield to maturity is quoted as a semiannually compounded APR, so we convert the yields to match the frequency of the cash flows by dividing by two. With semiannual rates of 4% and 3.5%, we can use Eq. 6.3 to compute the prices.

EXECUTE

YTM	Five-Year, 5% Coupon Bond	Five-Year, 10% Coupon Bond
8%	$2.50 \times \dfrac{1}{0.04}\left(1 - \dfrac{1}{1.04^{10}}\right) + \dfrac{100}{1.04^{10}} = \$87.83$	$5 \times \dfrac{1}{0.04}\left(1 - \dfrac{1}{1.04^{10}}\right) + \dfrac{100}{1.04^{10}} = \$108.11$
7%	$2.50 \times \dfrac{1}{0.035}\left(1 - \dfrac{1}{1.035^{10}}\right) + \dfrac{100}{1.035^{10}} = \$91.68$	$5 \times \dfrac{1}{0.035}\left(1 - \dfrac{1}{1.035^{10}}\right) + \dfrac{100}{1.035^{10}} = \$112.47$

The 5% coupon bond's price changed from $87.83 to $91.68, or 4.4%, but the 10% coupon bond's price changed from $108.11 to $112.47, or 4.0%. You can calculate the price change very quickly with a financial calculator or spreadsheet. For example, take the 5% coupon bond at 8% YTM (4% per 6 months):

	N	I/Y	PV	PMT	FV
Given:	10	4		2.50	100
Solve for:			−87.83		
Excel Formula: =PV(RATE,NPER,PMT,FV)=PV(.04,10,2.5,100)					

With all of the basic bond information entered, you can simply change the I/Y by entering 3.5 and pressing I/Y and then solve for PV again. So, with just a few keystrokes, you will have the new price of $91.68.

EVALUATE

The bond with the smaller coupon payments is more sensitive to changes in interest rates. Because its coupons are smaller relative to its par value, a larger fraction of its cash flows are received later. As we learned in Example 6.8, later cash flows are affected more greatly by changes in interest rates, so compared to the 10% coupon bond, the effect of the interest change is greater for the cash flows of the 5% coupon bond.

Clean and Dirty Prices for Coupon Bonds

As Figure 6.4 illustrates, coupon bond prices fluctuate around the time of each coupon payment in a sawtooth pattern: The value of the coupon bond rises as the next coupon payment gets closer and then drops after it has been paid. This fluctuation occurs even if there is no change in the bond's yield to maturity.

Bond traders are more concerned about changes in the bond's price that arise due to changes in the bond's yield, rather than these predictable patterns around coupon payments. As a result, they often do not quote the price of a bond in terms of its actual cash price, which is also called the **dirty price** or **invoice price** of the bond. Instead, bonds are often quoted in terms of a **clean price**, which is the bond's cash price less an adjustment for accrued interest, the amount of the next coupon payment that has already accrued:

$$\text{Clean Price} = \text{Cash (Dirty) Price} - \text{Accrued Interest}$$

$$\text{Accrued Interest} = \text{Coupon Amount} \times \left(\frac{\text{Days Since Last Coupon Payment}}{\text{Days in Current Coupon Period}} \right)$$

Note that immediately before a coupon payment is made, the accrued interest will equal the full amount of the coupon. Immediately after the coupon payment is made, the accrued interest will be zero. Thus, accrued interest will rise and fall in a sawtooth pattern as each coupon payment passes.

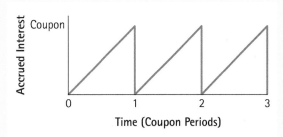

If we subtract accrued interest from the bond's cash price and compute the clean price, the sawtooth pattern is eliminated.

dirty price or invoice price A bond's actual cash price.

clean price A bond's cash price less an adjustment for accrued interest, the amount of the next coupon payment that has already accrued.

Bond Prices in Practice

In actuality, bond prices are subject to the effects of both the passage of time and changes in interest rates. Bond prices converge to the bond's face value due to the time effect, but simultaneously move up and down due to unpredictable changes in bond yields. Figure 6.5 illustrates this behavior by demonstrating how the price of the 30-year, zero-coupon bond might change over its life. Note that the bond price tends to converge to the face value as the bond approaches the maturity date, but also moves higher when its yield falls and lower when its yield rises.

As the fluctuating price in Figure 6.5 demonstrates, prior to maturity the bond is exposed to interest rate risk. If an investor chooses to sell and the bond's yield to maturity has decreased, then the investor will receive a high price and earn a high return. If the yield to maturity has increased, the bond price is low at the time of sale and the investor will earn a low return.

CONCEPT CHECK

7. Why do interest rates and bond prices move in opposite directions?

8. If a bond's yield to maturity does not change, how does its cash price change between coupon payments?

FIGURE 6.5

Yield to Maturity
and Bond Price
Fluctuations
over Time

The graphs illustrate changes in price and yield for a 30-year zero-coupon bond over its life. Panel (a) illustrates the changes in the bond's yield to maturity (YTM) over its life. In Panel (b), the actual bond price is shown in blue. Because the YTM does not remain constant over the bond's life, the bond's price fluctuates as it converges to the face value over time. Also shown is the price if the YTM remained fixed at 4%, 5%, or 6%. Panel (a) shows that the bond's YTM mostly remained between 4% and 6%. The broken lines in Panel (b) show the price of the bond if its YTM had remained constant at those levels. Note that in all cases, the bond's price must eventually converge to $100 on its maturity date.

Panel (a) The Bond's Yield to Maturity over Time

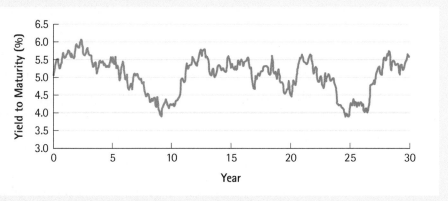

Panel (b) The Bond's Price over Time (Price = $100 on Maturity Date)

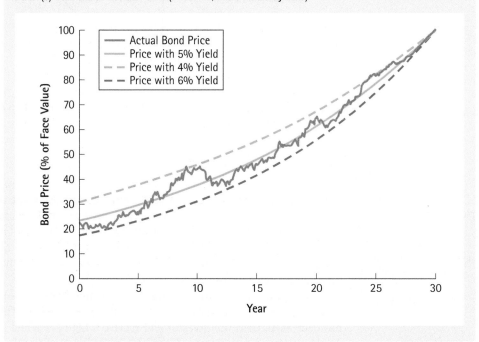

6.5 Corporate Bonds

In the previous sections, we developed the basics of bond pricing in the context of U.S. Treasury bonds, which have no risk of default. In this section, our focus is on **corporate bonds**, which are bonds issued by corporations. We will examine the role of default risk in the price and yield to maturity of corporate bonds. As we will see, corporations with higher default risk will need to pay higher coupons to attract buyers to their bonds.

corporate bonds Bonds
issued by corporations.

TABLE 6.5

Interest Rates on
Five-Year Bonds for
Various Borrowers,
December 2015

Borrower	Interest Rate	Credit Spread
U.S. Government (Treasury Notes)	1.70%	
Johnson & Johnson	1.86%	0.16%
McDonalds Corp.	2.84%	1.14%
Baidu, Inc.	3.16%	1.46%
Xerox Corp.	4.03%	2.33%
Gap, Inc.	4.85%	3.15%

Credit Risk

Table 6.5 lists the interest rates paid by a number of different borrowers at the end of 2015 for a five-year bond. Why do these interest rates vary so widely? The lowest interest rate is the 1.70% rate paid on U.S. Treasury notes. United States Treasury securities are widely regarded to be risk-free because there is virtually no chance the government will fail to pay the interest and default on these bonds. Thus, as we noted in Section 6.2, when we refer to the "risk-free interest rate," we mean the rate on U.S. Treasuries.

The remaining bonds are all corporate bonds. With corporate bonds, the bond issuer may default—that is, it might not pay back the full amount promised in the bond prospectus. For example, a company with financial difficulties may be unable to fully repay the loan. This risk of default, which is known as the **credit risk** of the bond, means that the bond's cash flows are not known with certainty. To compensate for the risk that the firm may default, investors demand a higher interest rate than the rate on U.S. Treasuries.[5] The difference between the interest rate of the loan and the Treasury rate will depend on investors' assessment of the likelihood that the firm will default. For example, investors place a higher probability of default on Gap than on Johnson & Johnson, forcing Gap to pay a larger credit spread, which is reflected in a higher interest rate.

credit risk The risk of default by the issuer of any bond that is not default free; it is an indication that the bond's cash flows are not known with certainty.

Are Treasuries Really Default-Free Securities?

Most investors treat U.S. Treasury securities as risk free, meaning that they believe there is no chance of default (a convention we follow in this book). But are Treasuries really risk free? The answer depends on what you mean by "risk free."

No one can be certain that the U.S. government will never default on its bonds—but most people believe the probability of such an event is very small. More importantly, the default probability is smaller than for any other bond. So saying that the yield on a U.S. Treasury security is risk free really means that the Treasury security is the lowest-risk investment denominated in U.S. dollars in the world.

That said, there have been occasions in the past where Treasury holders did not receive exactly what they were promised: In 1790,

Treasury Secretary Alexander Hamilton lowered the interest rate on outstanding debt and in 1933 President Franklin Roo-sevelt suspended bondholders' right to be paid in gold rather than currency.

A new risk emerged in mid-2011 when a series of large budget deficits brought the United States up against the debt ceiling, a constraint imposed by Congress limiting the overall amount of debt the government can incur. An act of Congress was required by August 2011 for the Treasury to meet its obligations and avoid a default. In response to the political uncertainty about whether Congress would raise the ceiling in time, Standard & Poor's downgraded its rating of U.S. Government bonds. Congress ultimately raised the debt ceiling and no default occurred. Given persistent budget deficits, however, similar debt ceiling debates recurred in 2013 and 2015. These incidents serve as a recurring reminder that perhaps no investment is truly "risk free."

---

[5]Because trading in corporate bonds is much less liquid than trading in Treasuries, part of the increased interest rate is to compensate investors for this lack of liquidity.

LISA BLACK

Lisa Black is Managing Director at Teachers Insurance and Annuity Association, a major financial services company. A Chartered Financial Analyst, she oversees a variety of fixed income funds, including money market, intermediate bond, high-yield, emerging market debt, and inflation-linked bond funds.

QUESTION: *When people think about the financial markets, many of them picture the equity markets. How big and how active are the bond markets compared to the equity markets?*

ANSWER: The dollar volume of bonds traded daily is about 10 times that of equity markets. For example, a single $15 billion issue of 10-year Treasury bonds will sell in one day. The market value of the Barclays Capital U.S. Universal Bond Index of dollar-denominated debt as of June 30, 2009, was $13.8 trillion, with the U.S. Aggregate Index (investment-grade debt) accounting for almost 90%. It includes Treasuries, agencies, corporate bonds, and mortgage-backed securities. Other major sectors of the Universal Index include corporate high-yield bonds, Eurodollar bonds, emerging markets, and private placements.

QUESTION: *How do the bond markets operate?*

ANSWER: Firms and governments turn to bond markets when they need to borrow money to fund new construction projects, finance acquisitions, and for general corporate purposes. On the other side, institutions like TIAA-CREF, endowments, and foundations have funds to invest. Wall Street investment bankers serve as intermediaries, matching up borrowers with creditors in terms of maturity needs and risk appetite. Because we provide annuities for college professors, for example, we invest money for longer periods of time than an insurance company that needs funds to pay claims. In the institutional world, bond funds typically trade in blocks of bonds ranging from $5 million to $50 million at a time.

QUESTION: *What drives changes in the values of Treasury bonds?*

ANSWER: The simple answer is that when interest rates rise, bond prices fall. The key is to dig below that reality to see *why* interest rates rise and fall. A major factor is investors' expectations for inflation and economic growth. Interest rates generally rise when the expectation is that growth will accelerate, because inflation won't be far behind. During the 2008–2009 recession, interest rates dropped as the Federal Reserve injected liquidity into the system. There was also a flight to quality after the bankruptcy of Lehman Brothers. The value of The Reserve Fund fell drastically as its holdings of about $785 million of Lehman's short-term debt securities became all but worthless. Worried retail and institutional investors sold their money market funds and purchased U.S. Treasury bills and notes to protect their principal. With increased demand, interest rates on risk-free Treasury securities fell sharply. At one point, T-bills even had a negative yield.

QUESTION: *What impact did the 2008–2009 financial crisis have on the bond market? What changes do you anticipate going forward as a result?*

ANSWER: While the effects of the crisis on equity markets have been widely discussed, the effects on the bond market have been just as profound. Particularly noteworthy is the role governments and central bankers have played—and likely will continue to play—to stabilize financial institutions deemed too big or important to fail. The Fed introduced an unprecedented number of stimulus programs to unfreeze credit markets, including programs to guarantee money funds. The challenge will be how and when the various support programs and financial infusions will end and/or be paid back. In addition, the rating agencies' role and ratings methodologies will likely be subject to greater scrutiny, both from regulators and investors.

In the corporate sector, many borrowers—the automotive industries, for example—could not raise debt financing during the crisis. Credit spreads widened dramatically as investors shunned even AAA- and AA-rated credits. Major institutional investors sat on the sidelines for several months, and the corporate bond new-issue market was essentially nonexistent. Not until the federal government announced programs to increase liquidity did institutional investors reenter the market, first buying only the highest credit-quality instruments, such as first mortgage bonds issued by utilities and government-guaranteed mortgage-backed securities. Investors then began to move down the credit-quality chain, selectively focusing on issuers that could weather an economic downturn.

Corporate Bond Yields

How does the credit risk of default affect bond prices and yields? The cash flows promised by the bond are the most that bondholders can hope to receive. Due to credit risk, the cash flows that a purchaser of a corporate bond actually *expects* to receive may be less than that amount. For example, GM struggled financially in 2006 and 2007, substantially increasing the chance that they would default on their bonds, and GM subsequently did in 2009. Realizing this risk, investors in GM bonds incorporated an increased probability that the bond payments would not be made as promised and prices of the bonds fell. Because the yield to maturity of GM's bonds is computed by comparing the price to the *promised* cash flows, the yield to maturity *increased* as the probability of being paid as promised decreased. This example highlights the following general truths:

1. Investors pay less for bonds with credit risk than they would for an otherwise identical default-free bond.

2. Because the yield to maturity for a bond is calculated using the promised cash flows instead of the *expected* cash flows, the yield of bonds with credit risk will be higher than that of otherwise identical default-free bonds.

These two points lead us to an important conclusion: *the yield to maturity of a defaultable bond is not equal to the expected return of investing in the bond.* The promised cash flows used to determine the yield to maturity are always higher than the expected cash flows investors use to calculate the expected return. As a result, the yield to maturity will always be higher than the expected return of investing in the bond. *Moreover, a higher yield to maturity does not necessarily imply that a bond's expected return is higher.*

Bond Ratings

investment-grade bonds Bonds in the top four categories of creditworthiness with a low risk of default.

The probability of default is clearly important to the price you are willing to pay for a corporate bond. How do you assess a firm's likelihood of default? Several companies rate the creditworthiness of bonds and make this information available to investors. By consulting these ratings, investors can assess the creditworthiness of a particular bond issue. The ratings therefore encourage widespread investor participation and relatively liquid markets. The two best-known bond-rating companies are Standard & Poor's and Moody's. Table 6.6 summarizes the rating classes each company uses. Bonds with the highest rating (Aaa or AAA) are judged to be least likely to default.

speculative bonds, junk bonds, or high-yield bonds Bonds in one of the bottom five categories of creditworthiness (below investment grade) that have a high risk of default.

Bonds in the top four categories are often referred to as **investment-grade bonds** because of their low default risk. Bonds in the bottom five categories are often called **speculative bonds**, **junk bonds**, **or high-yield bonds** because their likelihood of default is high and so they promise higher yields. The rating depends on the risk of bankruptcy as well as the bondholders' ability to lay claim to the firm's assets in the event of such a bankruptcy. Thus, debt issues with a low-priority claim in bankruptcy will have a lower rating than issues from the same company that have a high priority in bankruptcy or that are backed by a specific asset such as a building or a plant.

Corporate Yield Curves

default spread or credit spread The difference between the risk-free interest rate on U.S. Treasury notes and the interest rates on all other loans. The magnitude of the credit spread will depend on investors' assessment of the likelihood that a particular firm will default.

Just as we can construct a yield curve from risk-free Treasury securities, we can plot a similar yield curve for corporate bonds. Figure 6.6 shows the average yields of U.S. corporate coupon bonds with three different Standard & Poor's bond ratings: two curves are for investment-grade bonds (AAA and BBB) and one is for junk bonds (B). Figure 6.6 also includes the U.S. (coupon-paying) Treasury yield curve. We refer to the difference between the yields of the corporate bonds and the Treasury yields as the **default spread** or **credit spread**. This difference can be seen in Figure 6.6 as the distance between the bottom blue line for Treasuries and each of the red, green, and purple lines as default probability increases. Credit spreads fluctuate as perceptions regarding the probability of default change. Note that the credit spread is high for bonds with low ratings and therefore a greater likelihood of default.

TABLE 6.6

Bond Ratings and the Number of U.S. Public Firms with Those Ratings in March 2016

Moody's	Standard & Poor's	Number of Public Firms	Description (Moody's)
Investment Grade Debt			
Aaa	AAA	3*	Judged to be of the best quality. They carry the smallest degree of investment risk and are generally referred to as "gilt edged."
Aa	AA	29	Judged to be of high quality by all standards. Together with the Aaa group, they constitute what are generally known as high-grade bonds.
A	A	221	Possess many favorable investment attributes and are considered as upper-medium-grade obligations. Factors giving security to principal and interest are considered adequate at present, but may not remain that way.
Baa	BBB	515	Are considered as medium-grade obligations (i.e., they are neither highly protected nor poorly secured).
Speculative Bonds ("Junk Bonds")			
Ba	BB	363	Judged to have speculative elements; their future cannot be considered as well assured.
B	B	255	Generally lack characteristics of the desirable investment. Assurance of interest and principal payments over any long period may be small.
Caa	CCC	41	Are of poor standing. Such issues may be in default or there may be present elements of danger with respect to principal or interest.
Ca	CC	5	Are speculative to a high degree. Such issues are often in default or have other marked shortcomings.
C	C, D	10	Lowest-rated class of bonds, and issues so rated can be regarded as having extremely poor prospects of ever attaining any real investment standing.

*The three AAA-rated companies were Microsoft, Johnson & Johnson, and ExxonMobil. However, ExxonMobil was downgraded at the end of April, 2016.
Source: www.moodys.com and S&P Compustat.

FIGURE 6.6

Corporate Yield Curves for Various Ratings, May 2016

This figure shows the yield curve for U.S. Treasury securities (in yellow) and yield curves for corporate securities with ratings AA (in blue), and BBB (in green). Note how the yield to maturity is higher for the corporate bonds, which have a higher probability of default than the U.S. Treasury securities.

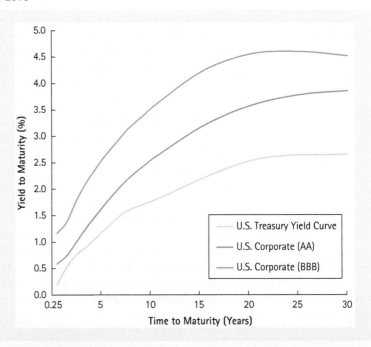

Source: Bloomberg.

EXAMPLE 6.10

Credit Spreads and
Bond Prices

MyFinanceLab

PROBLEM

Your firm has a credit rating of AA. You notice that the credit spread for 10-year maturity AA debt is 90 basis points (0.90%). Your firm's 10-year debt has a coupon rate of 5%. You see that new 10-year Treasury notes are being issued at par with a coupon rate of 4.5%. What should be the price of your outstanding 10-year bonds?

SOLUTION

PLAN

If the credit spread is 90 basis points, then the yield to maturity (YTM) on your debt should be the YTM on similar Treasuries plus 0.9%. The fact that new 10-year Treasuries are being issued at par with coupons of 4.5% means that with a coupon rate of 4.5%, these notes are selling for $100 per $100 face value. Thus, their YTM is 4.5% and your debt's YTM should be 4.5% + 0.9% = 5.4%. The cash flows on your bonds are $5 per year for every $100 face value, paid as $2.50 every six months. The six-month rate corresponding to a 5.4% yield is 5.4%/2 = 2.7%. Armed with this information, you can use Eq. 6.3 to compute the price of your bonds.

EXECUTE

$$2.50 \times \frac{1}{0.027}\left(1 - \frac{1}{1.027^{20}}\right) + \frac{100}{1.027^{20}} = \$96.94$$

EVALUATE

Your bonds offer a higher coupon (5% vs. 4.5%) than Treasuries of the same maturity, but sell for a lower price ($96.94 vs. $100). The reason is the credit spread. Your firm's higher probability of default leads investors to demand a higher YTM on your debt. To provide a higher YTM, the purchase price for the debt must be lower. If your debt paid 5.4% coupons, it would sell at $100, the same as the Treasuries. But to get that price, you would have to offer coupons that are 90 basis points higher than those on the Treasuries—exactly enough to offset the credit spread.

 The Credit Crisis and Bond Yields

The financial crisis that engulfed the world's economies in 2008 originated as a credit crisis that first emerged in August 2007. At that time, problems in the mortgage market had led to the bankruptcy of several large mortgage lenders. The default of these firms, and the downgrading of many of the bonds backed by mortgages these firms had made, caused many investors to reassess the risk of other bonds in their portfolios. As perceptions of risk increased, and investors attempted to move into safer U.S. Treasury securities, the prices of corporate bonds fell and so their credit spreads rose relative to Treasuries, as shown in Figure 6.7. Panel (a) shows the yield spreads for long-term corporate bonds, where we can see that spreads of even the highest-rated Aaa bonds increased dramatically, from a typical level of 0.5% to over 2% by the fall of 2008. Panel (b) shows a similar pattern for the rate banks had to pay on short-term loans compared to the yields of short-term Treasury bills. This increase in borrowing costs made it more costly for firms to raise the capital needed for new investment, slowing economic growth. The decline in these spreads in early 2009 was viewed by many as an important first step in mitigating the ongoing impact of the financial crisis on the rest of the economy.

As we indicated at the beginning of this chapter, the bond market, while less well-known than the stock markets, is large and important. Because debt is a substantial part of the financing of most corporations, a financial manager needs to understand bonds and how investors price the company's bonds. In this chapter, we have introduced the major types of bonds, how bonds repay investors, and how they are priced. In Chapter 15, we will discuss the bond markets further, including the process a firm goes through to issue debt.

FIGURE 6.7

Yield Spreads and the
Financial Crisis

Panel (a) shows the yield spread between long-term (30-year) U.S. corporate and Treasury bonds. Panel (b) shows the yield spread of short-term loans to major international banks (called LIBOR) and U.S. Treasury bills (also referred to as the *Treasury-Eurodollar* or *"TED" spread*). Note the dramatic increase in these spreads beginning in August 2007 and again in September 2008, before beginning to decline in late 2008 and early 2009. While spreads returned to pre-crisis levels by mid-2011, note the increase in spreads in 2012 in response to the European debt crisis. Spreads began rising again in 2015, partly in response to a surge in corporate borrowing, as well as declining demand from banks facing tighter regulation of their trading activities.

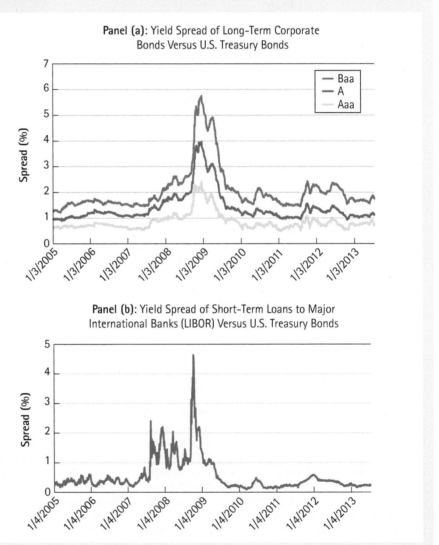

Panel (a): Yield Spread of Long-Term Corporate
Bonds Versus U.S. Treasury Bonds

Panel (b): Yield Spread of Short-Term Loans to Major
International Banks (LIBOR) Versus U.S. Treasury Bonds

Source: Bloomberg.com.

**CONCEPT
CHECK**

9. What is a junk bond?

10. How will the yield to maturity of a bond vary with the bond's risk of default?

MyFinanceLab

Here is what you should know after reading this chapter. MyFinanceLab will help you identify what you know, and where to go when you need to practice.

KEY POINTS AND EQUATIONS	KEY TERMS	ONLINE PRACTICE
6.1 Bond Terminology • Bonds pay both coupon and principal or face value payments to investors. By convention, the coupon rate of a bond is expressed as an APR, so the amount of each coupon payment, *CPN*, is: $$CPN = \frac{\text{Coupon Rate} \times \text{Face Value}}{\text{Number of Coupon Payments per Year}} \quad (6.1)$$	bond certificate, p. 160 coupon rate, p. 160 coupons, p. 160 face value, p. 160 maturity date, p. 160 par value, p. 160 principal amount, p. 160 term, p. 160	MyFinanceLab Study Plan 6.1
6.2 Zero-Coupon Bonds • Zero-coupon bonds make no coupon payments, so investors receive only the bond's face value. • The rate of return of a bond is called its yield to maturity (or yield). The yield to maturity of a bond is the discount rate that sets the present value of the promised bond payments equal to the current market price of the bond. • The yield to maturity for a zero-coupon bond is given by: $$1 + YTM_n = \left(\frac{\text{Face Value}}{\text{Price}}\right)^{1/n} \quad (6.2)$$ • The risk-free interest rate for an investment until date *n* equals the yield to maturity of a risk-free zero-coupon bond that matures on date *n*. A plot of these rates against maturity is called the zero-coupon yield curve.	discount, p. 162 pure discount bond, p. 162 spot interest rates, p. 164 Treasury bills, p. 161 yield to maturity (YTM), p. 162 zero-coupon bond, p. 161 zero-coupon yield curve, p. 164	MyFinanceLab Study Plan 6.2 Financial Calculator Tutorial: Solving for the Yield to Maturity of a Bond
6.3 Coupon Bonds • The yield to maturity for a coupon bond is the discount rate, y, that equates the present value of the bond's future cash flows with its price: $$P = CPN \times \frac{1}{y}\left(1 - \frac{1}{(1+y)^N}\right) + \frac{FV}{(1+y)^N} \quad (6.3)$$	coupon bonds, p. 165 Treasury bonds, p. 165 Treasury notes, p. 165	MyFinanceLab Study Plan 6.3 Financial Calculator Tutorial: Bond Valuation with Interest Compounded Semiannually

6.4 Why Bond Prices Change

- A bond will trade at a premium if its coupon rate exceeds its yield to maturity. It will trade at a discount if its coupon rate is less than its yield to maturity. If a bond's coupon rate equals its yield to maturity, it trades at par.
- As a bond approaches maturity, the price of the bond approaches its face value.
- Bond prices change as interest rates change. When interest rates rise, bond prices fall, and vice versa.
- Long-term zero-coupon bonds are more sensitive to changes in interest rates than are short-term zero-coupon bonds.
- Bonds with low coupon rates are more sensitive to changes in interest rates than are similar maturity bonds with high coupon rates.

clean price, p. 177
dirty price, p. 177
invoice price, p. 177
par, p. 170
premium, p. 170

MyFinanceLab
Study Plan 6.4

Interactive
Interest Rate
Sensitivity
Analysis

6.5 Corporate Bonds

- When a bond issuer does not make a bond payment in full, the issuer has defaulted.
- The risk that default can occur is called default or credit risk. United States Treasury securities are free of default risk.
- The expected return of a corporate bond, which is the firm's debt cost of capital, equals the risk-free rate of interest plus a risk premium. The expected return is less than the bond's yield to maturity because the yield to maturity of a bond is calculated using the promised cash flows, not the expected cash flows.
- Bond ratings summarize the creditworthiness of bonds for investors.
- The difference between yields on Treasury securities and yields on corporate bonds is called the credit spread or default spread. The credit spread compensates investors for the difference between promised and expected cash flows and for the risk of default.

corporate bonds, p. 178
credit risk, p. 179
default (credit) spread,
  p. 181
high-yield bonds,
  p. 181
investment-grade
  bonds, p. 181
junk bonds, p. 181
speculative bonds,
  p. 181

MyFinanceLab
Study Plan 6.5

CRITICAL THINKING

1. How is a bond like a loan?

2. How does an investor receive a return from buying a bond?

3. How is yield to maturity related to the concept of rate of return?

4. Does a bond's yield to maturity determine its price or does the price determine the yield to maturity?

5. Explain why the yield of a bond that trades at a discount exceeds the bond's coupon rate.

6. Explain the relationship between interest rates and bond prices.

7. Why are longer-term bonds more sensitive to changes in interest rates than shorter-term bonds?

8. Explain why the expected return of a corporate bond does not equal its yield to maturity.

PROBLEMS

All problems are available in MyFinanceLab*. The* *icon indicates problems that are easier to solve using Excel and have data in an Excel format available in* MyFinanceLab.

Bond Terminology

1. Consider a 10-year bond with a face value of $1000 that has a coupon rate of 5.5%, with semiannual payments.
   a. What is the coupon payment for this bond?
   b. Draw the cash flows for the bond on a timeline.

2. Assume that a bond will make payments every six months as shown on the following timeline (using six-month periods):

   a. What is the maturity of the bond (in years)?
   b. What is the coupon rate (in percent)?
   c. What is the face value?

3. Your company wants to raise $10 million by issuing 20-year zero-coupon bonds. If the yield to maturity on the bonds will be 6% (annually compounded APR), what total principal amount of bonds must you issue?

Zero-Coupon Bonds

4. The following table summarizes prices of various default-free zero-coupon bonds (expressed as a percentage of face value):

Maturity (years)	1	2	3	4	5
Price (per $100 face value)	$95.51	$91.05	$86.38	$81.65	$76.51

   a. Compute the yield to maturity for each bond.
   b. Plot the zero-coupon yield curve (for the first five years).
   c. Is the yield curve upward sloping, downward sloping, or flat?

Use the following information for Problems 5–7. The current zero-coupon yield curve for risk-free bonds is as follows:

Maturity (years)	1	2	3	4	5
YTM	5.00%	5.50%	5.75%	5.95%	6.05%

5. What is the price per $100 face value of a two-year, zero-coupon, risk-free bond?

6. What is the price per $100 face value of a four-year, zero-coupon, risk-free bond?

7. What is the risk-free interest rate for a five-year maturity?

8. In the Global Financial Crisis box in Section 6.2, Bloomberg.com reported that the three-month Treasury bill sold for $100.002556 per $100 face value. What is the yield to maturity of this bond, expressed as an EAR?

Coupon Bonds

9. For each of the following pairs of Treasury securities (each with $1000 par value), identify which will have the higher price:
   a. A three-year zero-coupon bond or a five-year zero coupon bond?
   b. A three-year zero-coupon bond or a three-year 4% coupon bond?
   c. A two-year 5% coupon bond or a two-year 6% coupon bond?

10. The yield to maturity of a $1000 bond with a 7% coupon rate, semiannual coupons, and two years to maturity is 7.6% APR, compounded semiannually. What must its price be?

11. Assume the current Treasury yield curve shows that the spot rates for six months, one year, and 1½ years are 1%, 1.1%, and 1.3%, all quoted as semiannually compounded APRs. What is the price of a $1000 par, 4% coupon bond maturing in 1½ years (the next coupon is exactly six months from now)?

12. Suppose a 10-year, $1000 bond with an 8% coupon rate and semiannual coupons is trading for $1034.74.
   a. What is the bond's yield to maturity (expressed as an APR with semiannual compounding)?
   b. If the bond's yield to maturity changes to 9% APR, what will the bond's price be?

13. Suppose a five-year, $1000 bond with annual coupons has a price of $900 and a yield to maturity of 6%. What is the bond's coupon rate?

14. Assume that the six-month Treasury spot rate is 1.6% APR, and the one-year rate is 2% APR, both compounded semiannually. What is the price of a one-year $1000 par Treasury bond with 2% coupons?

Why Bond Prices Change

15. The prices of several bonds with face values of $1000 are summarized in the following table:

Bond	A	B	C	D
Price	$972.50	$1040.75	$1150.00	$1000.00

For each bond, state whether it trades at a discount, at par, or at a premium.

16. You have purchased a 10% coupon bond for $1040. What will happen to the bond's price if market interest rates rise?

17. Suppose a seven-year, $1000 bond with an 8% coupon rate and semiannual coupons is trading with a yield to maturity of 6.75%.
   a. Is this bond currently trading at a discount, at par, or at a premium? Explain.
   b. If the yield to maturity of the bond rises to 7.00% (APR with semiannual compounding), what price will the bond trade for?

Suppose that General Motors Acceptance Corporation issued a bond with 10 years until maturity, a face value of $1000, and a coupon rate of 7% (annual payments). The yield to maturity on this bond when it was issued was 6%. Use this information to solve Problems 18–20.

18. What was the price of this bond when it was issued?

19. Assuming the yield to maturity remains constant, what is the price of the bond immediately before it makes its first coupon payment?

20. Assuming the yield to maturity remains constant, what is the price of the bond immediately after it makes its first coupon payment?

21. Your company currently has $1000 par, 6% coupon bonds with 10 years to maturity and a price of $1078. If you want to issue new 10-year coupon bonds at par, what coupon rate do you need to set? Assume that for both bonds, the next coupon payment is due in exactly six months.

22. Suppose you purchase a 10-year bond with 6% annual coupons. You hold the bond for four years, and sell it immediately after receiving the fourth coupon. If the bond's yield to maturity was 5% when you purchased and sold the bond, what cash flows will you pay and receive from your investment in the bond per $100 face value?

Consider the following bonds for Problems 23 and 24:

Bond	Coupon Rate (annual payments)	Maturity (years)
A	0%	15
B	0%	10
C	4%	15
D	8%	10

23. What is the percentage change in the price of each bond if its yield to maturity falls from 6% to 5%?

24. Which of the bonds A–D is most sensitive to a 1% drop in interest rates from 6% to 5% and why? Which bond is least sensitive? Provide an intuition explanation for your answer.

25. Suppose you purchase a 30-year, zero-coupon bond with a yield to maturity of 6%. You hold the bond for five years before selling it.
    a. If the bond's yield to maturity is 6% when you sell it, what is the annualized rate of return of your investment?
    b. If the bond's yield to maturity is 7% when you sell it, what is the annualized rate of return of your investment?
    c. If the bond's yield to maturity is 5% when you sell it, what is the annualized rate of return of your investment?
    d. Even if a bond has no chance of default, is your investment risk free if you plan to sell it before it matures? Explain.

Corporate Bonds

26. The following table summarizes the yields to maturity on several one-year, zero-coupon securities:

Security	Yield (%)
Treasury	3.1
AAA corporate	3.2
BBB corporate	4.2
B corporate	4.9

    a. What is the price (expressed as a percentage of the face value) of a one-year, zero-coupon corporate bond with an AAA rating?

    b. What is the credit spread on AAA-rated corporate bonds?

    c. What is the credit spread on B-rated corporate bonds?

    d. How does the credit spread change with the bond rating? Why?

27. Andrew Industries is contemplating issuing a 30-year bond with a coupon rate of 7% (annual coupon payments) and a face value of $1000. Andrew believes it can get a rating of A from Standard & Poor's. However, due to recent financial difficulties at the company, Standard & Poor's is warning that it may downgrade Andrew Industries bonds to BBB. Yields on A-rated, long-term bonds are currently 6.5%, and yields on BBB-rated bonds are 6.9%.

    a. What is the price of the bond if Andrew Industries maintains the A rating for the bond issue?

    b. What will the price of the bond be if it is downgraded?

28. Your firm has a credit rating of A. You notice that the credit spread for five-year maturity A debt is 85 basis points (0.85%). Your firm's five-year debt has a coupon rate of 6%. You see that new five-year Treasury notes are being issued at par with a coupon rate of 2.0%. What should the price of your outstanding five-year bonds be per $100 of face value?

29. HMK Enterprises would like to raise $10 million to invest in capital expenditures. The company plans to issue five-year bonds with a face value of $1000 and a coupon rate of 6.5% (annual payments). The following table summarizes the yield to maturity for five-year (annual-pay) coupon corporate bonds of various ratings:

Rating	AAA	AA	A	BBB	BB
YTM	6.20%	6.30%	6.50%	6.90%	7.50%

    a. Assuming the bonds will be rated AA, what will the price of the bonds be?

    b. How much of the total principal amount of these bonds must HMK issue to raise $10 million today, assuming the bonds are AA rated? (Because HMK cannot issue a fraction of a bond, assume that all fractions are rounded to the nearest whole number.)

    c. What must the rating of the bonds be for them to sell at par?

    d. Suppose that when the bonds are issued, the price of each bond is $959.54. What is the likely rating of the bonds? Are they junk bonds?

30. A BBB-rated corporate bond has a yield to maturity of 8.2%. A U.S. Treasury security has a yield to maturity of 6.5%. These yields are quoted as APRs with semiannual compounding. Both bonds pay semiannual coupons at a rate of 7% and have five years to maturity.

    a. What is the price (expressed as a percentage of the face value) of the Treasury bond?

    b. What is the price (expressed as a percentage of the face value) of the BBB-rated corporate bond?

    c. What is the credit spread on the BBB bonds?

DATA CASE

You are an intern with Ford Motor Company in its corporate finance division. The firm is planning to issue $50 million of 12% annual coupon bonds with a 10-year maturity. The firm anticipates an increase in its bond rating. Your boss wants you to determine the gain in the proceeds of the new issue if it is rated above the firm's current bond rating. To prepare this information, you will have to determine Ford's current debt rating and the yield curve for its particular rating.

1. Begin by finding the current U.S. Treasury yield curve. At the Treasury Web site (www.treas.gov), search using the term "yield curve" and select "US Treasury—Daily Treasury Yield Curve." *Beware*: There will likely be two links with the same title. Look at the description below the link and select the one that does NOT say "Real Yield . . ." You want the nominal rates. Copy the table into Excel.

2. Find the current yield spreads for the various bond ratings. Unfortunately, the current spreads are available only for a fee, so you will use old ones. Go to BondsOnline (www.bondsonline.com) and click "Today's Market." Next, click "US Corporate Bond Spreads." Copy this table to the same Excel file as the Treasury yields.

3. Find the current bond rating for Ford Motor Co. Go to Standard & Poor's Web site. Select your country. Look for the "Find a Rating" box under "Ratings" and enter Ford Motor Co. and select Ford Motor Co. from the list it returns. At this point you will have to register (it's free) or enter the username and password provided by your instructor. Use the issuer credit rating for "local long term."

4. Return to Excel and create a timeline with the cash flows and discount rates you will need to value the new bond issue.
   a. To create the required spot rates for Ford's issue, add the appropriate spread to the Treasury yield of the same maturity.
   b. The yield curve and spread rates you have found do not cover every year that you will need for the new bonds. Specifically, you do not have yields or spreads for four-, six-, eight-, and nine-year maturities. Fill these in by linearly interpolating the given yields and spreads. For example, the four-year spot rate and spread will be the average of the three- and five-year rates. The six-year rate and spread will be the average of the five- and seven-year rates. For years eight and nine you will have to spread the difference between years seven and ten across the two years.
   c. To compute the spot rates for Ford's current debt rating, add the yield spread to the Treasury rate for each maturity. However, note that the spread is in basis points, which are 1/100th of a percentage point.
   d. Compute the cash flows that would be paid to bondholders each year and add them to the timeline.

5. Use the spot rates to calculate the present value of each cash flow paid to the bondholders.

6. Compute the issue price of the bond and its initial yield to maturity.

7. Repeat steps 4–6 based on the assumption that Ford is able to raise its bond rating by one full-step (for example, BBB to A). Compute the new yield based on the higher rating and the new bond price that would result.

8. Compute the additional cash proceeds that could be raised from the issue if the rating were improved.

**Chapter 6
APPENDIX A**

Solving for the Yield to Maturity of a Bond Using a Financial Calculator

You are looking to purchase a three-year, $1000 par, 10% annual coupon bond. Payments begin one year from now. The price of the bond is $1074.51 per $1000 par value. What is the yield to maturity of the bond? [answer: 7.15%]

HP-10BII

[Orange Shift] [C]	Press [Orange Shift] and then the [C] button to clear all previous entries.
3 N	Enter the number of periods.
1 0 0 PMT	Enter the payment amount per period.
1 0 0 0 FV	Enter the par value of the bond you will receive in year 3.
1 0 7 4 . 5 1 +/− PV	Enter present value or price of the bond you solved for earlier.
I/YR	Solves for the yield to maturity.

TI-BAII Plus Professional

2ND FV	Press [2ND] and then the [FV] button to clear all previous entries.
3 N	Enter the number of periods.
1 0 0 PMT	Enter the payment amount per period.
1 0 0 0 FV	Enter the par value of the bond you will receive in year 3.
1 0 7 4 . 5 1 +/− PV	Enter present value or price of the bond you solved for earlier.
CPT I/Y	Solves for the yield to maturity.

Chapter 6 APPENDIX B

The Yield Curve and the Law of One Price

Thus far, we have focused on the relationship between the price of an individual bond and its yield to maturity. In this section, we explore the relationship between the prices and yields of different bonds. In Chapter 3, we saw how market forces keep the same asset from having two prices at the same time—we call this the Valuation Principle's *Law of One Price*. Using the Law of One Price, we show that given the spot interest rates, which are the yields of default-free zero-coupon bonds, we can determine the price and yield of any other default-free bond. As a result, the yield curve provides sufficient information to evaluate all such bonds.

Valuing a Coupon Bond with Zero-Coupon Prices

We begin with the observation that it is possible to replicate the cash flows of a coupon bond using zero-coupon bonds. Therefore, we can use the Law of One Price to compute the price of a coupon bond from the prices of zero-coupon bonds. For example, we can replicate a three-year, $1000 bond that pays 10% annual coupons using three zero-coupon bonds as follows:

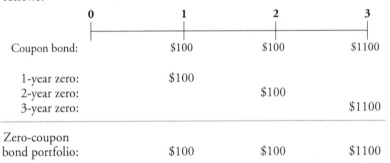

We match each coupon payment to a zero-coupon bond with a face value equal to the coupon payment and a term equal to the time remaining to the coupon date. Similarly, we match the final bond payment (final coupon plus return of face value) in three years to a three-year zero-coupon bond with a corresponding face value of $1100. Because the coupon bond cash flows are identical to the cash flows of the portfolio of zero-coupon bonds, the Law of One Price states that the price of the portfolio of zero-coupon bonds must be the same as the price of the coupon bond.

To illustrate, assume that current zero-coupon bond yields and prices are as shown in Table 6.7 (they are the same as in Example 6.1).

We can calculate the cost of the zero-coupon bond portfolio that replicates the three-year coupon bond as follows:

Zero-Coupon Bond	Face Value Required	Cost
1 Year	100	96.62
2 Years	100	92.45
3 Years	1100	$11 \times 87.63 = 963.93$
		Total Cost: $1153.00

TABLE 6.7

Yields and Prices (per
$100 Face Value) for
Zero-Coupon Bonds

Maturity	1 Year	2 Years	3 Years	4 Years
YTM	3.50%	4.00%	4.50%	4.75%
Price	$96.62	$92.45	$87.63	$83.06

By the Law of One Price, the three-year coupon bond must trade for a price of $1153. If the price of the coupon bond were higher, you could earn an arbitrage profit by selling the coupon bond and buying the zero-coupon bond portfolio. If the price of the coupon bond were lower, you could earn an arbitrage profit by buying the coupon bond and selling the zero-coupon bonds.

Valuing a Coupon Bond Using Zero-Coupon Yields

To this point, we have used the zero-coupon bond *prices* to derive the price of the coupon bond. Alternatively, we can use the zero-coupon bond *yields*. Recall that the yield to maturity of a zero-coupon bond is the competitive market interest rate for a risk-free investment with a term equal to the term of the zero-coupon bond. Since the cash flows of the bond are its coupon payments and face value repayment, the price of a coupon bond must equal the present value of its coupon payments and face value discounted at the competitive market interest rates (see Eq. 5.7 in Chapter 5):

Price of a Coupon Bond

$$P = PV(\text{Bond Cash Flows})$$
$$= \frac{CPN}{1 + YTM_1} + \frac{CPN}{(1 + YTM_2)^2} + \cdots + \frac{CPN + FV}{(1 + YTM_n)^n} \tag{6.4}$$

where CPN is the bond coupon payment, YTM_n is the yield to maturity of a *zero-coupon* bond that matures at the same time as the nth coupon payment, and FV is the face value of the bond. For the three-year, $1000 bond with 10% annual coupons considered earlier, we can use Eq. 6.4 to calculate its price using the zero-coupon yields in Table 6.7:

$$P = \frac{100}{1.035} + \frac{100}{1.04^2} + \frac{100 + 1000}{1.045^3} = \$1153$$

This price is identical to the price we computed earlier by replicating the bond. Thus, we can determine the no-arbitrage price of a coupon bond by discounting its cash flows using the zero-coupon yields. In other words, the information in the zero-coupon yield curve is sufficient to price all other risk-free bonds.

Coupon Bond Yields

Given the yields for zero-coupon bonds, we can use Eq. 6.4 to price a coupon bond. In Section 6.3, we saw how to compute the yield to maturity of a coupon bond from its price. Combining these results, we can determine the relationship between the yields of zero-coupon bonds and coupon-paying bonds.

Consider again the three-year, $1000 bond with 10% annual coupons. Given the zero-coupon yields in Table 6.7, we calculate a price for this bond of $1153. From Eq. 6.3, the yield to maturity of this bond is the rate y that satisfies:

$$P = 1153 = \frac{100}{(1 + y)} + \frac{100}{(1 + y)^2} + \frac{100 + 1000}{(1 + y)^3}$$

We can solve for the yield by using a financial calculator or spreadsheet:

	N	I/Y	PV	PMT	FV
Given:	3		−1153	100	1000
Solve for:		4.44			
		Excel Formula: =RATE(NPER,PMT,PV,FV)=RATE(3,100,−1153,1000)				

Therefore, the yield to maturity of the bond is 4.44%. We can check this result directly as follows:

$$P = \frac{100}{1.0444} + \frac{100}{1.0444^2} + \frac{100 + 1000}{1.0444^3} = \$1153$$

Because the coupon bond provides cash flows at different points in time, the yield to maturity of a coupon bond is a weighted average of the yields of the zero-coupon bonds of equal and shorter maturities. The weights depend (in a complex way) on the magnitude of the cash flows each period. In this example, the zero-coupon bonds yields were 3.5%, 4.0%, and 4.5%. For this coupon bond, most of the value in the present value calculation comes from the present value of the third cash flow because it includes the principal, so the yield is closest to the three-year zero-coupon yield of 4.5%.

<table>
<tr><td>

EXAMPLE 6.11

Yields on Bonds with the Same Maturity

MyFinanceLab

</td><td>

PROBLEM
Given the following zero-coupon yields, compare the yield to maturity for a three-year zero-coupon bond, a three-year coupon bond with 4% annual coupons, and a three-year coupon bond with 10% annual coupons. All of these bonds are default free.

Maturity	1 Year	2 Years	3 Years	4 Years
Zero-Coupon YTM	3.50%	4.00%	4.50%	4.75%

SOLUTION

PLAN
From the information provided, the yield to maturity of the three-year zero-coupon bond is 4.50%. Also, because the yields match those in Table 6.7, we already calculated the yield to maturity for the 10% coupon bond as 4.44%. To compute the yield for the 4% coupon bond, we first need to calculate its price, which we can do using Eq. 6.4. Since the coupons are 4%, paid annually, they are $40 per year for three years. The $1000 face value will be repaid at that time. Once we have the price, we can use Eq. 6.3 to compute the yield to maturity.

EXECUTE
Using Eq. 6.4, we have:

$$P = \frac{40}{1.035} + \frac{40}{1.04^2} + \frac{40 + 1000}{1.045^3} = \$986.98$$

The price of the bond with a 4% coupon is $986.98. From Eq. 6.4:

$$\$986.98 = \frac{40}{(1 + y)} + \frac{40}{(1 + y)^2} + \frac{40 + 1000}{(1 + y)^3}$$

We can calculate the yield to maturity using a financial calculator or spreadsheet:

	N	I/Y	PV	PMT	FV
Given:	3		−986.98	40	1000
Solve for:		4.47			
		Excel Formula: =RATE(NPER,PMT,PV,FV)=RATE(3,40,−986.98,1000)				

</td></tr>
</table>

(Continued)

To summarize, for the three-year bonds considered:

Coupon Rate	0%	4%	10%
YTM	4.50%	4.47%	4.44%

EVALUATE

Note that even though the bonds all have the same maturity, they have different yields. In fact, holding constant the maturity, the yield decreases as the coupon rate increases. We discuss why below.

Example 6.11 shows that coupon bonds with the same maturity can have different yields depending on their coupon rates. The yield to maturity of a coupon bond is a weighted average of the yields on the zero-coupon bonds. As the coupon increases, earlier cash flows become relatively more important than later cash flows in the calculation of the present value. The shape of the yield curve keys us in on trends with the yield to maturity:

1. If the yield curve is upward sloping (as it is for the yields in Example 6.11), the resulting yield to maturity decreases with the coupon rate of the bond.
2. When the zero-coupon yield curve is downward sloping, the yield to maturity will increase with the coupon rate.
3. With a flat yield curve, all zero-coupon and coupon-paying bonds will have the same yield, independent of their maturities and coupon rates.

Treasury Yield Curves

As we have shown in this section, we can use the zero-coupon yield curve to determine the price and yield to maturity of other risk-free bonds. The plot of the yields of coupon bonds of different maturities is called the *coupon-paying yield curve*. When U.S. bond traders refer to "the yield curve," they are often referring to the coupon-paying Treasury yield curve. As we showed in Example 6.11, two coupon-paying bonds with the same maturity may have different yields. By convention, practitioners always plot the yield of the most recently issued bonds, termed the *on-the-run bonds*. Using similar methods to those employed in this section, we can apply the Law of One Price to determine the zero-coupon bond yields using the coupon-paying yield curve. Thus, either type of yield curve provides enough information to value all other risk-free bonds.

7

Stock Valuation

LEARNING OBJECTIVES

- Understand the tradeoff between dividends and growth in stock valuation

- Appreciate the limitations of valuing a stock based on expected dividends

- Value a stock as the present value of the company's total payout

- Describe the basics of common stock, preferred stock, and stock quotes

- Compare how trades are executed on the NYSE and NASDAQ

- Value a stock as the present value of its expected future dividends

notation

Div_t	dividends paid in year t	P_t	stock price at the end of year t
EPS_t	earnings per share on date t	PV	present value
g	expected dividend growth rate	r_E	equity cost of capital
N	terminal date or forecast horizon		

At 5:00 P.M. on March 21, 2013, footwear and apparel maker Nike, Inc., announced that its quarterly earnings would be higher than expected and that orders for the following year would be strong as well. The next day, Nike's stock price increased by 11% on the New York Stock Exchange to $59.53, with more than 19 million shares being traded—more than four times its average daily volume.

How might an investor decide whether to buy or sell a stock such as Nike at this price? Why would the stock suddenly be worth 11% more after the announcement of this news? What actions can Nike's managers take to further increase the stock price?

To answer these questions, we turn to the Valuation Principle. The Valuation Principle indicates that the price of a security should equal the present value of the expected cash flows an investor will receive from owning it. In this chapter, we apply this idea to stocks. Thus, to value a stock, we need to know the expected cash flows an investor will receive and the appropriate cost of capital with which to discount those cash flows. Both these quantities can be challenging to estimate, and we will develop many of the details needed to do so throughout the remainder of this text.

We begin our study of stock valuation by contrasting the different types of stocks, interpreting a stock quote, and explaining how specialists execute stock trades. We then turn to our first model of stock valuation, the *dividend-discount model*, which considers the dividends and capital gains received by investors who hold the stock for different periods.

7.1   Stock Basics

As discussed in Chapter 1, the ownership of a corporation is divided into shares of stock. A public corporation has many owners and its shares trade on a stock market that provides liquidity for a company's shares and determines the market price for those shares. In this section, we explain what a stock market quote is and introduce the two types of stocks, *common* and *preferred*.

Stock Market Reporting: Stock Quotes

common stock A share of ownership in the corporation, which confers rights to any common dividends as well as rights to vote on election of directors, mergers, and other major events.

ticker symbol A unique abbreviation assigned to a publicly traded company.

Figure 7.1 shows a stock quote with basic information about Nike's stock from Google Finance (www.google.com/finance) for June 25, 2013.[1] Nike's stock is **common stock**, which means a share of ownership in the corporation gives its owner rights to any common dividends as well as rights to vote on the election of directors, mergers, and other major events. The Web page notes that the company is a public corporation (its shares are widely held and traded in a market) and that its shares trade on the NYSE (New York Stock Exchange) under the *ticker symbol* NKE. A **ticker symbol** is a unique abbreviation assigned to a publicly traded company used when its trades are reported on the ticker (a real-time electronic display of trading activity). Traditionally, shares on the NYSE have ticker symbols consisting of three or fewer characters, while shares on the NASDAQ generally have four or more characters in their ticker symbols. However, for recent listings, such as Facebook, which goes by FB on the NASDAQ and Twitter (TWTR on the NYSE), this convention no longer applies.

During the period mid-February through late June 2013, Nike paid two quarterly dividends to its common shareholders, on February 28, and May 30. The dividends are marked by a "D" and the amount of the dividend. In this case, the dividend was 21 cents per share. Thus, if you owned 1000 shares of NKE, you would have received $0.21 \times 1000 = $210 when Nike paid each dividend. The chart also clearly shows the jump in the price of NKE shares in March 2013 that we discussed in the chapter introduction.

Finally, the Web page displays some basic information about the performance of NKE stock. Notice the price of the last trade of NKE shares in the market ($60.39), the price that shares started at when the market opened that day ($60.42), the range of low to high prices reached during trading that day ($59.95 to $60.99), and the volume of trading for the day (5.45 million shares). The total value of all the equity of NKE is its market capitalization, equal to the price per share multiplied by the number of shares outstanding: on June 25, 2013, it was $60.39 \times 893.61 million = $53.97 billion. Over the preceding 52 weeks, NKE achieved a high price of $66.07 and a low price of $42.55 and had an average daily volume of shares traded of 3.54 million shares. Also, note some basic information about the company: the price-earnings ratio (P/E) and earnings per share (EPS), both of which we discussed in Chapter 2. The Web page also notes that NKE's *beta* is 0.88.[2]

---

[1] There are many places on the Internet to get free stock information, such as Google Finance (http://www.google.com/finance), MSN Money (http://www.msn.com/money), the *Wall Street Journal*'s Web site (www.wsj.com), and the exchange sites www.nyse.com and www.nasdaq.com.

[2] *Beta* is a measure of risk that we will discuss in Chapter 12.

FIGURE 7.1

Stock Price Quote
for Nike (NKE)

This screenshot from Google Finance shows the basic stock price information and price history charting for the common stock of Nike. The historical price chart covers the period mid-February through late June 2013. The price of $60.39 is for June 25, 2013.

Source: www.google.com/finance?q=nke.

In preceding chapters, we have learned how financial managers make decisions that affect the value of their company. Although the current price of NKE is $60.39, the stock's price has varied over time, reflecting the expected effects of new decisions and the results of past decisions.

Common Stock

We now examine the rights of common stockholders, including their voice in the running of the corporation. All rights accruing to the shareholders are in proportion to the number of shares they hold.

straight voting Voting for directors where shareholders must vote for each director separately, with each shareholder having as many votes as shares held.

Shareholder Voting. To illustrate the shareholder voting process, consider an election of 10 directors at a company with only two shareholders: Donna and Jonathan. Donna has 600 shares and Jonathan has 400, but they have very different views of how the company should be run. If the company has **straight voting**, each shareholder has as many votes for each director as shares held. That is, for each director, Donna will have 600 votes and

cumulative voting Voting for directors where each shareholder is allocated votes equal to the number of open spots multiplied by his or her number of shares.

classes Different types of common stock for the same company, often carrying different voting rights.

annual meeting Meeting held once per year where shareholders vote on directors and other proposals as well as ask managers questions.

proxy A written authorization for someone else to vote your shares.

proxy contest When two or more groups are competing to collect proxies to prevail in a matter up for shareholder vote (such as election of directors).

preferred stock Stock with preference over common shares in payment of dividends and in liquidation.

cumulative preferred stock Preferred stock where all missed preferred dividends must be paid before any common dividends can be paid.

non-cumulative preferred stock Preferred stock where missed dividends do not accumulate. Only the current dividend is owed before common dividends can be paid.

Jonathan 400, so Jonathan will lose every vote and have no representation on the board. If the company has **cumulative voting**, each shareholder's total vote allocation for all directors is equal to the number of open spots multiplied by his or her number of shares. With 10 directors up for election, Jonathan is allocated a total of 10×400 votes (4000 votes) and Donna is allocated 10×600 votes (6000 votes) to use across the 10 director spots. Jonathan could allocate all his votes to four directors, ensuring that he has four directors representing his views on the board. Donna would do the same for six directors, ensuring her representation. With cumulative voting, even shareholders with minority blocks (less than 50%) have a chance at representation on the board.

This example is based on the concept of one share, one vote. Some companies have different types of common stock, called **classes**, which carry different voting rights. This is typical in companies that are family run, or where the founder is still active. For example, Nike has Class A and Class B stock. Phil Knight, Nike's founder, owns almost all the Class A stock, which carries the rights to elect 9 of the company's 12 directors. Alphabet Inc. (Google) has Class A, Class B, and Class C stock. Class A stock has been sold to the public, while Google's founders and managers hold all the Class B stock, each share of which carries 10 times the voting power of a share of Class A stock. Class C stock, which was split from Class A stock in April 2014, has no voting rights.

Shareholder Rights. Each year, companies hold an **annual meeting** at which managers and directors answer questions from shareholders, and shareholders vote on the election of directors and other proposals. All shareholders have the right to attend the annual meeting and cast their votes directly. In practice, though, most either allow the board to vote for them or direct that their shares be voted for them via **proxy**, or explicit instructions on how they should be voted. Typically, matters at the annual meeting are uncontested, but occasionally a dissident shareholder group will propose an alternative slate of directors or oppose a management proposal. In that case, each side will actively solicit the proxies of all the shareholders so they may win the vote in a **proxy contest**.

As an ownership claim, common stock carries the right to share in the profits of the corporation through dividend payments. Recall from Chapter 1 that dividends are periodic payments, usually in the form of cash, that firms make to shareholders as a partial return on their investment in the corporation. The board of directors decides the timing and amount of each dividend. Shareholders are paid dividends in proportion to the number of shares they own. If the company is liquidated through bankruptcy and there are assets left over after satisfying the claims of the creditors, shareholders divide the remaining assets proportionally based on each shareholder's number of shares.

Preferred Stock

Some companies have an additional issue of stock called **preferred stock**, which has preference over common shares in the distribution of dividends or cash during liquidation. While the directors can, at their discretion, choose not to pay the preferred shareholders a dividend, they cannot pay a dividend to common stockholders unless they pay the promised dividend to preferred shareholders first. For example, Nike has preferred shares that pay a $0.10 dividend per share each year. The firm must pay this dividend before common shareholders can receive a dividend.

Cumulative Versus Non-Cumulative Preferred Stock. There are two types of preferred stock: *cumulative* and *non-cumulative*. With **cumulative preferred stock**, any unpaid dividends are carried forward. For example, if DuPont fails to pay its preferred dividend for several years, its obligation to its cumulative preferred shareholders accumulates, and it cannot pay any dividends to common shareholders until it has paid all the unpaid preferred dividends. With **non-cumulative preferred stock**, missed dividends do not accumulate, and the firm can pay current dividend payments first to preferred and then to common stock shareholders. Almost all preferred stock is cumulative. Some preferred stock also gives preferred shareholders the right to elect one or more directors to the board if the firm is substantially in arrears on preferred dividends.

Preferred Stock: Equity or Debt? You may be wondering how to think about preferred stock—is it equity or is it debt? Economically, it is like a perpetual bond because it has a promised cash flow to holders and there are consequences if those cash flows are not paid. However, unlike debtholders, preferred shareholders cannot force the firm into bankruptcy. Preferred shareholders stand in line in front of common shareholders for annual dividends, but behind regular bondholders, because interest is paid before dividends. If the firm is bankrupt, the same priority is followed in settling claims: bondholders, preferred shareholders, and then common shareholders. Finally, as long as the firm is meeting its preferred dividend obligations, the preferred shareholders have none of the control rights of owners, such as voting on directors or other important matters. However, despite all these similarities to debt, preferred shares are, for all tax and legal purposes, treated as equity.

CONCEPT CHECK

1. What is a share of stock and what are dividends?

2. What are some key differences between preferred and common stock?

7.2 The Mechanics of Stock Trades

Suppose you decide to invest in Nike (NKE), and so you place a market order to buy 100 shares of its stock. A *market order* means you do not specify a price, rather you want the order to execute immediately at the most favorable price available. If instead you wanted to specify a maximum price you were willing to pay, and you were willing to wait until the shares were available at that price, you would place a *limit order*.

What actually happens when you place this market order to buy Nike stock? In market parlance, 100 shares is a "round lot" and would be considered a small order. Small orders such as this would typically be transmitted electronically to the stock exchange via a system called the *Super Display Book System* (which replaced the old SuperDOT system in 2009). Upon reaching the exchange, it would go directly to the workstation of the specialist who oversees trading in Nike stock. Recall from Chapter 1 that a specialist holds a trading license at the NYSE and acts as a market maker for a particular stock, maintaining orderly trading and stepping in to provide liquidity when needed. The small order would automatically execute against the specialist's inventory in a few *milliseconds*.

If you were making a very large or complex trade, the process would involve people. At a physical stock market such as the NYSE, your trade would still be transmitted electronically to the exchange, but it would be sent to the wireless handheld terminal of a *floor broker*. A **floor broker** holds a trading license at the NYSE and works to get the best execution possible for investors. In this case, the floor broker would find the best way to execute the trade, which may be electronically, or may mean going to the physical location where the NKE's designated market maker is. The floor broker would take note of the bid and ask and then negotiate with any selling brokers to buy 15,000 shares at as low a price as possible. Depending on how many shares are offered for sale at the best (lowest) ask price, the trade may need to execute above the ask price in order to clear the full order. So, depending on the size of your order and the current market conditions, an order on the NYSE may be executed very quickly through electronic algorithms or through traditional interaction between floor brokers.

floor broker A person at the NYSE with a trading license who represents orders on the floor, balancing speed and price to get the best execution.

If you were buying a stock on an electronic exchange such as NASDAQ, the trade would proceed slightly differently. Recall from Chapter 1 that NASDAQ is a computer network with no physical location. Also, each stock listed on NASDAQ has multiple dealers posting bid and ask quotes and trading at those prices for their own accounts and for customer accounts. The NASDAQ Market Center integrates these bids and asks with the limit orders of all market participants. If you place an order through your broker or online brokerage account to buy 100 shares of Facebook (FB), the order will be transmitted electronically to the NASDAQ Market Center where it automatically executes against the best (lowest) ask quote for Facebook. If you are trying to buy a very large block of shares, then you can proceed the same way, transmitting your order and having it execute against the limit order book. Depending on the depth of the limit order book (the number of shares for sale close to the best ask price), you may prefer to split your order into smaller trades over a longer period, or even use a dark pool.

But how do you decide whether to buy or sell a stock in the first place? You must estimate the value of the stock and compare it to the current market price. In the rest of this chapter, we discuss one traditional approach to valuing a stock, the *dividend-discount model*.[3]

CONCEPT CHECK

3. What is the role of a floor broker at the NYSE?

4. What is the role of a dealer at the NASDAQ?

7.3 The Dividend-Discount Model

The Valuation Principle implies that to value any security, we must determine the expected cash flows that an investor will receive from owning it. We begin our analysis of stock valuation by considering the cash flows for an investor with a one-year investment horizon. We will show how the stock's price and the investor's return from the investment are related. We then consider the perspective of investors with a long investment horizon. Finally, we will reach our goal of establishing the first stock valuation method: the *dividend-discount model*.

A One-Year Investor

There are two potential sources of cash flows from owning a stock:

1. The firm might pay out cash to its shareholders in the form of a dividend.
2. The investor might generate cash by selling the shares at some future date.

The total amount received in dividends and from selling the stock will depend on the investor's investment horizon. Let's begin by considering the perspective of a one-year investor.

When an investor buys a stock, she will pay the current market price for a share, P_0. While she continues to hold the stock, she will be entitled to any dividends the stock pays. Let Div_1 be the total dividends the investor expects to be paid per share during the year. At the end of the year, the investor will sell her share at the new market price. Let P_1 be the price the investor expects to sell her share at at the end of the year. Assuming for simplicity that all dividends are paid at the end of the year, we have the following timeline for this investment:

$$
\begin{array}{cc}
0 & 1 \\
\hline
-P_0 & Div_1 + P_1
\end{array}
$$

[3]In Chapter 10, we return to the question of stock valuation with a discussion of additional approaches. As you will see, when estimating the value of a stock, it is best to try several different approaches to increase the confidence in your estimate.

Of course, the future dividend payment and stock price in this timeline are not known with certainty. Rather, these values are based on the investor's expectations at the time the stock is purchased. Given these expectations, the investor will be willing to pay a price today up to the point at which the benefits equal the cost—that is, up to the point at which the current price equals the present value of the expected future dividend and sale price.

Because these cash flows are risky, we cannot discount them using the risk-free interest rate, but instead must use the cost of capital for the firm's equity. We have previously defined the cost of capital of any investment to be the expected return that investors could earn on their best alternative investment with similar risk and maturity. Thus, we must discount the equity cash flows based on the **equity cost of capital**, r_E, for the stock, which is the expected return of other investments available in the market with equivalent risk to the firm's shares. Doing so leads to the following equation for the stock price:

$$P_0 = \frac{Div_1 + P_1}{1 + r_E} \tag{7.1}$$

equity cost of capital The expected rate of return available in the market on other investments that have equivalent risk to the risk associated with the firm's shares.

If the current stock price were less than this amount, the cost would be less than the PV of the benefits, so investors would rush in and buy it, driving up the stock's price. If the stock price exceeded this amount, selling would be attractive and the stock price would quickly fall.

Dividend Yields, Capital Gains, and Total Returns

A critical part of Eq. 7.1 for determining the stock price is the firm's equity cost of capital, r_E. At the beginning of this section, we pointed out that an investor's return from holding a stock comes from dividends and cash generated from selling the stock. We can rewrite Eq. 7.1 to show these two return components. If we multiply by $(1 + r_E)$, divide by P_0, and subtract 1 from both sides, we have

Total Return

$$r_E = \frac{Div_1 + P_1}{P_0} - 1 = \underbrace{\frac{Div_1}{P_0}}_{\text{Dividend Yield}} + \underbrace{\frac{P_1 - P_0}{P_0}}_{\text{Capital Gain Rate}} \tag{7.2}$$

dividend yield The expected annual dividend of a stock divided by its current price; the percentage return an investor expects to earn from the dividend paid by the stock.

The first term on the right side of Eq. 7.2 is the stock's **dividend yield**, which is the expected annual dividend of the stock divided by its current price. The dividend yield is the percentage return the investor expects to earn from the dividend paid by the stock. The second term on the right side of Eq. 7.2 reflects the **capital gain** the investor will earn on the stock, which is the difference between the expected sale price and the original purchase price for the stock, $P_1 - P_0$. We divide the capital gain by the current stock price to express the capital gain as a percentage return, called the **capital gain rate**.

capital gain The amount by which the selling price of an asset exceeds its initial purchase price.

The sum of the dividend yield and the capital gain rate is called the **total return** of the stock. The total return is the expected return the investor will earn for a one-year investment in the stock. Equation 7.2 states that the stock's total return should equal the equity cost of capital. In other words, *the expected total return of the stock should equal the expected return of other investments available in the market with equivalent risk.*

capital gain rate An expression of capital gain as a percentage of the initial price of the asset.

This result is exactly what we would expect: The firm must pay its shareholders a return commensurate with the return they can earn elsewhere while taking the same risk. If the stock offered a higher return than other securities with the same risk, investors would sell those other investments and buy the stock instead. This activity would then drive up the stock's current price, lowering its dividend yield and capital gain rate until Eq. 7.2 holds true. If the stock offered a lower expected return, investors would sell the stock and drive down its price until Eq. 7.2 was again satisfied.

total return The sum of a stock's dividend yield and its capital gain rate.

EXAMPLE 7.1

Stock Prices
and Returns

MyFinanceLab

PROBLEM

Suppose you expect Longs Drug Stores to pay an annual dividend of $0.56 per share in the coming year and to trade for $45.50 per share at the end of the year. If investments with equivalent risk to Longs' stock have an expected return of 6.80%, what is the most you would pay today for Longs' stock? What dividend yield and capital gain rate would you expect at this price?

SOLUTION

PLAN

We can use Eq. 7.1 to solve for the beginning price we would pay now (P_0) given our expectations about dividends ($Div_1 = \$0.56$) and future price ($P_1 = \$45.50$) and the return we need to expect to earn to be willing to invest ($r_E = 0.068$). We can then use Eq. 7.2 to calculate the dividend yield and capital gain rate.

EXECUTE

Using Eq. 7.1, we have

$$P_0 = \frac{Div_1 + P_1}{1 + r_E} = \frac{\$0.56 + \$45.50}{1.0680} = \$43.13$$

Referring to Eq. 7.2, we see that at this price, Longs' dividend yield is $Div_1/P_0 = 0.56/43.13 = 1.30\%$. The expected capital gain is $\$45.50 - \$43.13 = \$2.37$ per share, for a capital gain rate of $2.37/43.13 = 5.50\%$.

EVALUATE

At a price of $43.13, Longs' expected total return is $1.30\% + 5.50\% = 6.80\%$, which is equal to its equity cost of capital (the return being paid by investments with equivalent risk to Longs'). This amount is the most we would be willing to pay for Longs' stock. If we paid more, our expected return would be less than 6.8% and we would rather invest elsewhere.

A Multiyear Investor

We now extend the intuition we developed for the one-year investor's return to a multiyear investor. Equation 7.1 depends upon the expected stock price in one year, P_1. But suppose we planned to hold the stock for two years. Then we would receive dividends in both year 1 and year 2 before selling the stock, as shown in the following timeline:

```
0              1              2
|--------------|--------------|
-P_0          Div_1        Div_2 + P_2
```

Setting the stock price equal to the present value of the future cash flows in this case implies:[4]

$$P_0 = \frac{Div_1}{1 + r_E} + \frac{Div_2 + P_2}{(1 + r_E)^2} \tag{7.3}$$

Equations 7.1 and 7.3 are different: As a two-year investor we care about the dividend and stock price in year 2, but these terms do not appear in Eq. 7.1. Does this difference imply that a two-year investor will value the stock differently than a one-year investor?

---

[4]In using the same equity cost of capital for both periods, we are assuming that the equity cost of capital does not depend on the term of the cash flows; that is, r_E is not different for year 2 (or any other year). Otherwise, we would need to adjust for the term structure of the equity cost of capital (as we did with the yield curve for risk-free cash flows in Chapter 5). This step would complicate the analysis but would not change its results.

The answer to this question is no. A one-year investor does not care about the dividend and stock price in year 2 directly. She will care about them indirectly, however, because they will affect the price for which she can sell the stock at the end of year 1. For example, suppose the investor sells the stock to another one-year investor with the same expectations. The new investor will expect to receive the dividend and stock price at the end of year 2, so he will be willing to pay

$$P_1 = \frac{Div_2 + P_2}{1 + r_E}$$

for the stock. Substituting this expression for P_1 into Eq. 7.1, we get the same result as in Eq. 7.3:

$$P_0 = \frac{Div_1 + P_1}{1 + r_E} = \frac{Div_1}{1 + r_E} + \frac{1}{1 + r_E}\overbrace{\left(\frac{Div_2 + P_2}{1 + r_E}\right)}^{P_1}$$

$$= \frac{Div_1}{1 + r_E} + \frac{Div_2 + P_2}{(1 + r_E)^2}$$

Thus, the formula for the stock price for a two-year investor is the same as that for a sequence of two one-year investors.

Dividend-Discount Model Equation

dividend-discount model A model that values shares of a firm according to the present value of the future dividends the firm will pay.

We can continue this process for any number of years by replacing the final stock price with the value that the next holder of the stock would be willing to pay. Doing so leads to the general **dividend-discount model** for the stock price, where the horizon N is arbitrary:

Dividend-Discount Model

$$P_0 = \frac{Div_1}{1 + r_E} + \frac{Div_2}{(1 + r_E)^2} + \cdots + \frac{Div_N}{(1 + r_E)^N} + \frac{P_N}{(1 + r_E)^N} \qquad (7.4)$$

Equation 7.4 applies to a single N-year investor, who will collect dividends for N years and then sell the stock, or to a series of investors who hold the stock for shorter periods and then resell it. Note that Eq. 7.4 holds for *any* horizon N. As a consequence, all investors (with the same expectations) will attach the same value to the stock, independent of their investment horizons. How long they intend to hold the stock and whether they collect their return in the form of dividends or capital gains is irrelevant. For the special case in which the firm eventually pays dividends and is never acquired or liquidated, it is possible to hold the shares forever. In this scenario, rather than having a stopping point where we sell the shares, we rewrite Eq. 7.4 to show that the dividends go on into the future:

$$P_0 = \frac{Div_1}{1 + r_E} + \frac{Div_2}{(1 + r_E)^2} + \frac{Div_3}{(1 + r_E)^3} + \cdots \qquad (7.5)$$

That is, *the price of the stock is equal to the present value of all of the expected future dividends it will pay.*

CONCEPT CHECK

5. How do you calculate the total return of a stock?

6. What discount rate do you use to discount the future cash flows of a stock?

Estimating Dividends in the Dividend-Discount Model

Equation 7.5 expresses the value of a stock in terms of the expected future dividends the firm will pay. Of course, estimating these dividends—especially for the distant future—is difficult. A commonly used approximation is to assume that in the long run, dividends will grow at a constant rate. In this section, we consider the implications of this assumption for stock prices and explore the tradeoff between dividends and growth.

Constant Dividend Growth

The simplest forecast for the firm's future dividends states that they will grow at a constant rate, g, forever. That case yields the following timeline for the cash flows for an investor who buys the stock today and holds it:

Because the expected dividends are a constant growth perpetuity, we can use Eq. 4.7 to calculate their present value. We then obtain the following simple formula for the stock price:[5]

constant dividend growth model A model for valuing a stock by viewing its dividends as a constant growth perpetuity.

Constant Dividend Growth Model

$$P_0 = \frac{Div_1}{r_E - g} \tag{7.6}$$

According to the **constant dividend growth model**, the value of the firm depends on the dividend level next year, divided by the equity cost of capital adjusted by the growth rate.

EXAMPLE 7.2

Valuing a Firm with Constant Dividend Growth

MyFinanceLab

PROBLEM

Consolidated Edison, Inc. (Con Ed) is a regulated utility company that services the New York City area. Suppose Con Ed plans to pay $2.30 per share in dividends in the coming year. If its equity cost of capital is 7% and dividends are expected to grow by 2% per year in the future, estimate the value of Con Ed's stock.

SOLUTION

PLAN

Because the dividends are expected to grow perpetually at a constant rate, we can use Eq. 7.6 to value Con Ed. The next dividend (Div_1) is expected to be $2.30, the growth rate ($g$) is 2%, and the equity cost of capital (r_E) is 7%.

EXECUTE

$$P_0 = \frac{Div_1}{r_E - g} = \frac{\$2.30}{0.07 - 0.02} = \$46.00$$

EVALUATE

You would be willing to pay 20 times this year's dividend of $2.30 to own Con Ed stock because you are buying a claim to this year's dividend *and* to an infinite growing series of future dividends.

---

[5]As discussed in Chapter 4, this formula requires that $g < r_E$. Otherwise, the present value of the growing perpetuity is infinite. The implication here is that it is impossible for a stock's dividends to grow at a rate $g > r_E$ *forever*. If the growth rate does exceed r_E, the situation must be temporary, and the constant growth model cannot be applied in such a case.

For another interpretation of Eq. 7.6, note that we can rearrange it as follows:

$$r_E = \frac{Div_1}{P_0} + g \tag{7.7}$$

Comparing Eq. 7.7 with Eq. 7.2, we see that g equals the expected capital gain rate. In other words, with constant expected dividend growth, the expected growth rate of the share price matches the growth rate of the dividends.

Dividends Versus Investment and Growth

In Eq. 7.6, the firm's share price increases with the current dividend level, Div_1, and the expected growth rate, g. To maximize its share price, a firm would like to increase both these quantities. Often, however, the firm faces a tradeoff: Increasing growth may require investment, and money spent on investment cannot be used to pay dividends. The constant dividend growth model provides insight into this tradeoff.

A Simple Model of Growth. What determines the rate of growth of a firm's dividends? If we define a firm's **dividend payout rate** as the fraction of its earnings that the firm pays as dividends each year, then we can write the firm's dividend per share at date t as follows:

dividend payout rate The fraction of a firm's earnings that the firm pays out as dividends each year.

$$Div_t = \underbrace{\frac{\text{Earnings}_t}{\text{Shares Outstanding}_t}}_{EPS_t} \times \text{Dividend Payout Rate}_t \tag{7.8}$$

That is, the dividend each year is equal to the firm's earnings per share (EPS) multiplied by its dividend payout rate. The firm can, therefore, increase its dividend in three ways:

1. It can increase its earnings (net income).
2. It can increase its dividend payout rate.
3. It can decrease its number of shares outstanding.

Suppose for now that the firm does not issue new shares (or buy back its existing shares), so that the number of shares outstanding remains fixed. We can then explore the tradeoff between options 1 and 2.

A firm can do one of two things with its earnings: It can pay them out to investors, or it can retain and reinvest them. By investing cash today, a firm can increase its future dividends. For simplicity, let's assume that absent reinvesting its retained earnings, the firm does not grow, so the current level of earnings generated by the firm remains constant. If all increases in future earnings result exclusively from new investment made with retained earnings, then

$$\text{Change in Earnings} = \text{New Investment} \times \text{Return on New Investment} \tag{7.9}$$

retention rate The fraction of a firm's current earnings that the firm retains.

New investment equals the firm's earnings multiplied by its **retention rate**, or the fraction of current earnings that the firm retains:

$$\text{New Investment} = \text{Earnings} \times \text{Retention Rate} \tag{7.10}$$

Substituting Eq. 7.10 into Eq. 7.9 and dividing by earnings gives an expression for the growth rate of earnings:

$$\text{Earnings Growth Rate} = \frac{\text{Change in Earnings}}{\text{Earnings}}$$

$$= \text{Retention Rate} \times \text{Return on New Investment} \tag{7.11}$$

If the firm chooses to keep its dividend payout rate constant, then the growth in its dividends will equal the growth in its earnings:

$$g = \text{Retention Rate} \times \text{Return on New Investment} \tag{7.12}$$

Profitable Growth. Equation 7.12 shows that a firm can increase its growth rate by retaining more of its earnings. But if the firm retains more earnings, and as a result pays out a smaller fraction of those earnings as dividends, then according to Eq. 7.8 the firm may have to cut its dividend in the short run. If a firm wants to increase its share price, should it cut its dividend and invest more, or should it cut its investments and increase its dividend? Not surprisingly, the answer to this question will depend on the profitability of the firm's investments. Let's consider an example.

EXAMPLE 7.3

Cutting Dividends
for Profitable Growth

MyFinanceLab

PROBLEM

Crane Sporting Goods expects to have earnings per share of $6 in the coming year. Rather than reinvest these earnings and grow, the firm plans to pay out all of its earnings as a dividend. With these expectations of no growth, Crane's current share price is $60.

Suppose Crane could cut its dividend payout rate to 75% for the foreseeable future and use the retained earnings to open new stores. The return on its investment in these stores is expected to be 12%. If we assume that the risk of these new investments is the same as the risk of its existing investments, then the firm's equity cost of capital is unchanged. What effect would this new policy have on Crane's stock price?

SOLUTION

PLAN

To figure out the effect of this policy on Crane's stock price, we need to know several things. First, we need to compute its equity cost of capital. Next, we must determine Crane's dividend and growth rate under the new policy.

Because we know that Crane currently has a growth rate of 0 ($g = 0$), a dividend of $6, and a price of $60, we can use Eq. 7.7 to estimate r_E. Next, the new dividend will simply be 75% of the old dividend of $6. Finally, given a retention rate of 25% and a return on new investment of 12%, we can use Eq. 7.12 to compute the new growth rate (g). Finally, armed with the new dividend, Crane's equity cost of capital, and its new growth rate, we can use Eq. 7.6 to compute the price of Crane's shares if it institutes the new policy.

EXECUTE

Using Eq. 7.7 to estimate r_E, we have

$$r_E = \frac{Div_1}{P_0} + g = \frac{\$6}{\$60} + 0\% = 0.10 + 0$$

In other words, to justify Crane's stock price under its current policy, the expected return of other stocks in the market with equivalent risk must be 10%.

Next, we consider the consequences of the new policy. If Crane reduces its dividend payout rate to 75%, then from Eq. 7.8 its dividend this coming year will fall to $Div_1 = EPS_1 \times 75\% = \$6 \times 75\% = \$4.50$.

At the same time, because the firm will now retain 25% of its earnings to invest in new stores, from Eq. 7.12 its growth rate will increase to

$$g = \text{Retention Rate} \times \text{Return on New Investment} = 0.25 \times 0.12 = 0.03 = 3\%$$

Assuming Crane can continue to grow at this rate, we can compute its share price under the new policy using the constant dividend growth model of Eq. 7.6:

$$P_0 = \frac{Div_1}{r_E - g} = \frac{\$4.50}{0.10 - 0.03} = \$64.29$$

EVALUATE

Crane's share price should rise from $60 to $64.29 if the company cuts its dividend in order to increase its investment and growth. By using its earnings to invest in projects that offer a rate of return (12%) greater than its equity cost of capital (10%), Crane has created value for its shareholders.

In Example 7.3, cutting the firm's dividend in favor of growth raised the firm's stock price. This is not always the case, however, as Example 7.4 demonstrates.

EXAMPLE 7.4

Unprofitable Growth

MyFinanceLab

PROBLEM

Suppose Crane Sporting Goods decides to cut its dividend payout rate to 75% to invest in new stores, as in Example 7.3. But now suppose that the return on these new investments is 8%, rather than 12%. Given its expected earnings per share this year of $6 and its equity cost of capital of 10% (we again assume that the risk of the new investments is the same as its existing investments), what will happen to Crane's current share price in this case?

SOLUTION

PLAN

We will follow the steps in Example 7.3, except that in this case, we assume a return on new investments of 8% when computing the new growth rate (g) instead of 12% as in Example 7.3.

EXECUTE

Just as in Example 7.3, Crane's dividend will fall to $6 \times 0.75 = \$4.50$. Its growth rate under the new policy, given the lower return on new investment, will now be $g = 0.25 \times 0.08 = 0.02 = 2\%$. The new share price is therefore

$$P_0 = \frac{Div_1}{r_E - g} = \frac{\$4.50}{0.10 - 0.02} = \$56.25$$

EVALUATE

Even though Crane will grow under the new policy, the return on its new investments is too low. The company's share price will fall if it cuts its dividend to make new investments with a return of only 8%. By reinvesting its earnings at a rate (8%) that is lower than its equity cost of capital (10%), Crane has reduced shareholder value.

Comparing Example 7.3 with Example 7.4, we see that the effect of cutting the firm's dividend to grow crucially depends on the value of the new investments the firm plans to make. In Example 7.3, the return on new investment of 12% exceeds the firm's equity cost of capital of 10%, so the investment is a good one. In Example 7.4, however, the return on new investment is only 8%, so the new investment's return is below the firm's cost of capital. In that case, the new investment is not worthwhile even though it will lead to earnings growth. In this example, we can check that cutting the firm's dividend to increase investment will create value and raise the stock price if, and only if, the new investments generate a return greater than their cost of capital. In Chapter 8, we will consider more generally how to identify projects that create value and thus increase the stock price.

Changing Growth Rates

Successful young firms often have very high initial earnings growth rates. During this period of high growth, firms often retain 100% of their earnings to exploit profitable investment opportunities. As they mature, their growth slows to rates more typical of established companies. At that point, their earnings exceed their investment needs and they begin to pay dividends.

We cannot use the constant dividend growth model to value the stock of such a firm for two reasons:

1. These firms often pay *no* dividends when they are young.

2. Their growth rate continues to change over time until they mature.

However, we can use the general form of the dividend-discount model to value such a firm by applying the constant growth model to calculate the future share price of the stock P_N once the firm matures and its expected growth rate stabilizes:

Specifically, if the firm is expected to grow at a long-term rate g after year $N + 1$, then from the constant dividend growth model:

$$P_N = \frac{Div_{N+1}}{r_E - g} \tag{7.13}$$

We can then use this estimate of P_N as a final cash flow in the dividend-discount model. Intuitively, we value the stock as the present value of the dividends we will receive plus the present value of the price we expect to be able to sell the stock for in the future. For example, consider a company with expected dividends of $2.00, $2.50, and $3.00 in each of the next three years. After that point, its dividends are expected to grow at a constant rate of 5%. If its equity cost of capital is 12%, we can find the current price. Using Eq. 7.13, we can compute the price in year 3:

$$P_N = \frac{Div_{N+1}}{r_E - g} = \left(\frac{\$3.00\,(1.05)}{0.12 - 0.05} \right) = 45.00$$

Now, using Eq. 7.4, we calculate the current price as the PV of the first 3 years' dividends and then the price at the end of year 3:

$$P_0 = \frac{\$2.00}{1.12} + \frac{\$2.50}{(1.12)^2} + \frac{\$3.00}{(1.12)^3} + \frac{\$45.00}{(1.12)^3} = \$37.94$$

This example also reinforces an important point: The constant dividend growth model (Eq. 7.13) is just a special case of the general dividend-discount formula (Eq. 7.4). We can always value all the stream of dividends using Eq. 7.4. However, if we assume constant growth, we can apply the growing perpetuity shortcut to all or part of the dividend stream, depending on whether the constant growth starts now or at some point in the future.

COMMON MISTAKE

Forgetting to "Grow" This Year's Dividend

The most common mistake in handling growing dividends is to use the current period's dividend in the numerator of the growing perpetuity formula. In the example just discussed in the text above, the dividends reached $3 in year 3, and then grew by 5% per year thereafter. A common mistake is to calculate the growing stream of dividends as

$$\frac{3.00}{0.12 - 0.05},$$

forgetting that next year's dividend (the numerator) has already grown by 5%! As we show in the example, the correct calculation is

$$\frac{3.00 \times (1.05)}{0.12 - 0.05} = \$45.$$

Also, remember to avoid the common mistake from Chapter 4: The growing perpetuity formula gives the value in year N for dividends starting in year $N + 1$. In the example above, the formula gives the value in year 3 of the growing dividend stream starting in year 4. That is why we discount the $45 back only three years.

EXAMPLE 7.5

Valuing a Firm
with Two Different
Growth Rates

MyFinanceLab

PROBLEM

Small Fry, Inc., has just invented a potato chip that looks and tastes like a french fry. Given the phenomenal market response to this product, Small Fry is reinvesting all of its earnings to expand its operations. Earnings were $2 per share this past year and are expected to grow at a rate of 20% per year until the end of year 4. At that point, other companies are likely to bring out competing products. Analysts project that at the end of year 4, Small Fry will cut its investment and begin paying 60% of its earnings as dividends. Its growth will also slow to a long-run rate of 4%. If Small Fry's equity cost of capital is 8%, what is the value of a share today?

SOLUTION

PLAN

We can use Small Fry's projected earnings growth rate and payout rate to forecast its future earnings and dividends. After year 4, Small Fry's dividends will grow at a constant 4%, so we can use the constant dividend growth model (Eq. 7.13) to value all dividends after that point. Finally, we can pull everything together with the dividend-discount model (Eq. 7.4).

EXECUTE

The following spreadsheet projects Small Fry's earnings and dividends:

Year	0	1	2	3	4	5	6
Earnings							
1 EPS Growth Rate (versus prior year)		20%	20%	20%	20%	4%	4%
2 EPS	$2.00	$2.40	$2.88	$3.46	$4.15	$4.31	$4.49
Dividends							
3 Dividend Payout Rate		0%	0%	0%	60%	60%	60%
4 Div	$ —	$ —	$ —	$2.49	$2.59	$2.69	

Starting from $2.00 in year 0, EPS grows by 20% per year until year 4, after which growth slows to 4%. Small Fry's dividend payout rate is zero until year 4, when competition reduces its investment opportunities and its payout rate rises to 60%. Multiplying EPS by the dividend payout ratio, we project Small Fry's future dividends in line 4.

After year 4, Small Fry's dividends will grow at the constant expected long-run rate of 4% per year. Thus, we can use the constant dividend growth model to project Small Fry's share price at the end of year 3. Given its equity cost of capital of 8%,

$$P_3 = \frac{Div_4}{r_E - g} = \frac{\$2.49}{0.08 - 0.04} = \$62.25$$

We then apply the dividend-discount model (Eq. 7.4) with this terminal value:

$$P_0 = \frac{Div_1}{1 + r_E} + \frac{Div_2}{(1 + r_E)^2} + \frac{Div_3}{(1 + r_E)^3} + \frac{P_3}{(1 + r_E)^3} = \frac{\$62.25}{(1.08)^3} = \$49.42$$

EVALUATE

The dividend-discount model is flexible enough to handle any forecasted pattern of dividends. Here, the dividends were zero for several years and then settled into a constant growth rate, allowing us to use the constant dividend growth model as a shortcut.

TABLE 7.1

The Dividend-Discount Model

General formula	$P_0 = \dfrac{Div_1}{1 + r_E} + \dfrac{Div_2}{(1 + r_E)^2} + \cdots + \dfrac{Div_N}{(1 + r_E)^N} + \dfrac{P_N}{(1 + r_E)^N}$
If dividend growth is constant	$P_0 = \dfrac{Div_1}{r_E - g}$
If early growth is variable followed by constant growth	$P_0 = \dfrac{Div_1}{1 + r_E} + \dfrac{Div_2}{(1 + r_E)^2} + \cdots + \dfrac{Div_N}{(1 + r_E)^N} + \left(\dfrac{1}{(1 + r_E)^N}\right)\left(\dfrac{Div_{N+1}}{r_E - g}\right)$

Table 7.1 summarizes the dividend-discount model, including how to apply the shortcut for constant growth.

Value Drivers and the Dividend-Discount Model

Now that we have fully developed the dividend-discount model, it is worth assessing how well it does capturing the intuitive drivers of stock value. When we think about how valuable a company is, we usually focus on how profitable it is now and how that profitability will grow or decline in the future, along with the risk of investing in the company. Where are these measures captured in the dividend-discount model? Profitability determines the company's ability to pay dividends, so, implicitly in the forecasted dividend stream, we are forecasting the company's profitability. As for the risk, that is captured in the equity cost of capital we use to discount those forecasted dividends. Riskier investments require higher expected returns, which enter the dividend-discount model as higher equity cost of capital.

CONCEPT CHECK

7. What are three ways that a firm can increase the amount of its future dividends per share?

8. Under what circumstances can a firm increase its share price by cutting its dividend and investing more?

7.5   Limitations of the Dividend-Discount Model

The dividend-discount model has two fundamental limitations that we will now address: its reliance on dividend forecasts and lack of applicability to non-dividend-paying stocks.

Uncertain Dividend Forecasts

The dividend-discount model values a stock based on a forecast of the future dividends paid to shareholders. But unlike a Treasury bond, whose cash flows are known with virtual certainty, a firm's future dividends carry a tremendous amount of uncertainty.

Let's reconsider the example of Nike (NKE). In 2013, NKE paid annual dividends of $0.84 (by paying four quarterly dividends of $0.21 each). If we assume an equity cost of capital of 10% and expected dividend growth of 8.5%, the constant dividend growth model implies a share price for NKE of

$$P_0 = \frac{Div_1}{r_E - g} = \frac{\$0.84\,(1 + 0.085)}{0.10 - 0.085} = \$60.76$$

which is quite close to the $60.39 share price that the stock had at the time. With a 9% dividend growth rate, however, this estimate would rise to more than $91 per share; with a 6% dividend growth rate, the estimate falls to less than $23 per share. As we see in Figure 7.2, even small changes in the assumed dividend growth rate can lead to large changes in the estimated stock price.

FIGURE 7.2

Implied NKE Stock
Prices for Different
Expected Growth
Rates

The figure shows what the price of Nike would be in 2013 for different dividend growth expectations. Stock prices are based on the constant dividend growth model. We assume a dividend in 2013 of $0.84 and an equity cost of capital of 10%. The expected dividend growth rate varies from 0% to 9%. Note how even a small change in the expected growth rate produces a large change in the stock price, especially at higher growth rates.

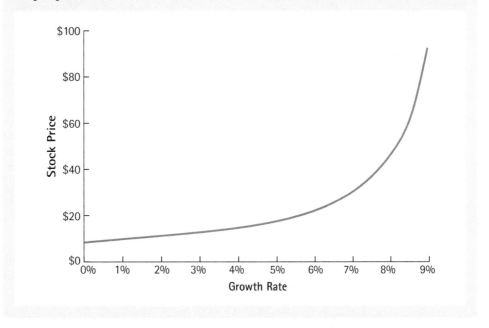

Furthermore, it is difficult to know which estimate of the dividend growth rate is more reasonable. NKE more than doubled its dividend between 2005 and 2010, but its earnings growth then moderated. Consequently, that rate of increase was not sustainable and its dividend increased by about 40% from 2010 to 2013. However, continued strong growth allowed Nike to increase dividends by over 50% from 2013 to the end of 2015 and the stock price increased to nearly $130 per share. From Eq. 7.8, forecasting dividends requires forecasting the firm's earnings, dividend payout rate, and future share count. Future earnings, however, will depend on interest expenses (which, in turn, depend on how much the firm borrows), and the firm's share count and dividend payout rate will depend on whether NKE uses a portion of its earnings to repurchase shares. Because borrowing and repurchase decisions are at management's discretion, they are more difficult to forecast reliably than other fundamental aspects of the firm's cash flows.[6]

Non-Dividend-Paying Stocks

Many companies do not pay dividends—Facebook, Amazon.com, and Google are just a few examples. How then do we value those stocks? In the next section, we discuss a small modification to the dividend-discount model to capture total payouts to shareholders, whether the payouts are dividends or not. In Chapter 10, we will discuss other valuation approaches that do not rely on payouts. Those approaches will be more meaningful once we have covered how financial managers create value within the firm through decisions about which projects to approve. So, in Chapters 8 and 9, we will cover investment decision rules and project evaluation.

**CONCEPT
CHECK**

9. What are the main limitations of the dividend-discount model?

10. What pieces of information are needed to forecast dividends?

---

[6]We discuss management's decision to borrow funds or repurchase shares in Part 6 of the text.

7.6   Share Repurchases and the Total Payout Model

share repurchase A transaction in which a firm uses cash to buy back its own stock.

In our discussion of the dividend-discount model, we implicitly assumed that any cash paid out by the firm to shareholders takes the form of a dividend. In recent years, an increasing number of firms have replaced dividend payouts with *share repurchases*. In a **share repurchase**, the firm uses excess cash to buy back its own stock. Share repurchases have two consequences for the dividend-discount model. First, the more cash the firm uses to repurchase shares, the less cash it has available to pay dividends. Second, by repurchasing shares, the firm decreases its share count, which increases its earnings and dividends on a per-share basis.

In the dividend-discount model, we valued a share from the perspective of a single shareholder, discounting the dividends the shareholder will receive:

$$P_0 = PV(\text{Future Dividends per Share}) \qquad (7.14)$$

total payout model A method that values shares of a firm by discounting the firm's total payouts to equity holders (that is, all the cash distributed as dividends and stock repurchases) and then dividing by the current number of shares outstanding.

An alternative method that may be more reliable when a firm repurchases shares is the **total payout model**, which values *all* of the firm's equity, rather than a single share. To use this model, we discount the total payouts that the firm makes to shareholders, which is the total amount spent on both dividends *and* share repurchases (net of new share issuance).[7] This gives the total value of the firm's equity. We then divide by the current number of shares outstanding to determine the share price:

Total Payout Model

$$P_0 = \frac{PV(\text{Future Total Dividends and Net Repurchases})}{\text{Shares Outstanding}_0} \qquad (7.15)$$

We can apply the same simplifications to the total payout method that we obtained by assuming constant growth in Section 7.3. The only change is that *we discount total dividends and share repurchases and use the growth rate of earnings (rather than earnings per share) when forecasting the growth of the firm's total payouts*. When the firm uses share repurchases, this method can be more reliable and easier to apply than the dividend-discount model.

EXAMPLE 7.6
Valuation with Share Repurchases

MyFinanceLab

PROBLEM

Titan Industries has 217 million shares outstanding and expects earnings at the end of this year of $860 million. Titan plans to pay out 50% of its earnings in total, paying 30% as a dividend and using 20% to repurchase shares. If Titan's earnings are expected to grow by 7.5% per year and these payout rates remain constant, determine Titan's share price assuming an equity cost of capital of 10%.

SOLUTION

PLAN

Based on the equity cost of capital of 10% and an expected earnings growth rate of 7.5%, we can compute the present value of Titan's future payouts as a constant growth perpetuity. The only input missing here is Titan's total payouts this year, which we can calculate as 50% of its earnings. The present value of all of Titan's future payouts is the value of its total equity. To obtain the price of a share, we divide the total value by the number of shares outstanding (217 million).

EXECUTE

Titan will have total payouts this year of 50% × $860 million = $430 million. Using the constant growth perpetuity formula, we have

---

[7]You can think of the total payouts as the amount you would receive if you owned 100% of the firm's shares: You would receive all the dividends, plus the proceeds from selling shares back to the firm in the share repurchase.

$$PV(\text{Future Total Dividends and Repurchases}) = \frac{\$430 \text{ million}}{0.10 - 0.075} = \$17.2 \text{ billion}$$

This present value represents the total value of Titan's equity (i.e., its market capitalization). To compute the share price, we divide by the current number of shares outstanding:

$$P_0 = \frac{\$17.2 \text{ billion}}{217 \text{ million shares}} = \$79.26 \text{ per share}$$

EVALUATE

Using the total payout method, we did not need to know the firm's split between dividends and share repurchases. To compare this method with the dividend-discount model, note that Titan will pay a dividend of $30\% \times (\$860 \text{ million}/217 \text{ million shares}) = \$1.19$ per share, for a dividend yield of $1.19/79.26 = 1.50\%$. From Eq. 7.7, we can solve for Titan's expected growth rates of EPS, dividend, and share price:

$$g = r_E - \frac{Div_1}{P_0} = .10 - \frac{1.19}{79.26} = 0.085 = 8.5\%.$$

This growth rate exceeds the 7.50% growth rate of earnings because Titan's share count will decline over time owing to its share repurchases.[8]

CONCEPT CHECK

11. How does the total payout model address part of the dividend-discount model's limitations?

12. How does the growth rate used in the total payout model differ from the growth rate used in the dividend-discount model?

7.7 Putting It All Together

We now return to the questions posed at the beginning of the chapter. First, how would an investor decide whether to buy or sell Nike stock? She would value the stock using her own expectations. We showed one set of expectations about dividend growth that would be consistent with the price. If her expectations were substantially different, she might conclude that the stock was over- or under-priced at $60.39 in 2013. Based on that conclusion, she would sell or buy the stock, and time would reveal whether her expectations were better than the market's.

Second, how could Nike stock suddenly be worth 11% more after Nike's announcement in March of 2013? As investors digested the news in Nike's announcement and updated their expectations, they would have determined that the previous day's closing price was too low based on the new information about future earnings growth. Buying pressure would then drive the stock price up until the buys and sells came into balance.

Third, what should Nike's managers do to raise the stock price further? The only way to raise the stock price is to make value-increasing decisions. We turn to this task in the next section of the book. As shown in Chapters 8 and 9, through capital budgeting analysis, managers can identify projects that add value to the company. By increasing the value of the company through good investment decisions, Nike's managers can increase the stock price. Chapter 10 returns to the question of stock valuation and extends the techniques developed here to incorporate the lessons of the next two chapters on project selection.

---

[8]We can check that an 8.5% EPS growth rate is consistent with 7.5% earnings growth and Titan's repurchase plans as follows: Given an expected share price of $79.26 \times 1.085 = \$86.00$ next year, Titan will repurchase $20\% \times \$860$ million $\div (\$86.00$ per share$) = 2$ million shares next year. With the decline in the number of shares from 217 million to 215 million, EPS grows by a factor of $1.075 \times (217/215) = 1.085$ or by 8.5%.

MyFinanceLab

Here is what you should know after reading this chapter. MyFinanceLab will help you identify what you know, and where to go when you need to practice.

KEY POINTS AND EQUATIONS	KEY TERMS	ONLINE PRACTICE
7.1 Stock Basics • Ownership in a corporation is divided into shares of stock. These shares carry rights to share in the profits of the firm through future dividend payments. • The shares also come with rights to vote to elect directors and decide on other important matters. • Some firms issue preferred stock, which has preference over common stock in the payment of dividends and in liquidation, but typically carries no voting rights.	annual meeting, p. 200 classes, p. 200 common stock, p. 198 cumulative preferred stock, p. 200 cumulative voting, p. 200 non-cumulative preferred stock, p. 200 preferred stock, p. 200 proxy, p. 200 proxy contest, p. 200 straight voting, p. 199 ticker symbol, p. 198	MyFinanceLab Study Plan 7.1
7.2 The Mechanics of Stock Trades • The NYSE has a physical trading location, but many small trades execute electronically. • NASDAQ is a computer network without a specific trading location. Many trades execute automatically, while larger trades must be negotiated with one or more of the stock's dealers.	floor broker, p. 201	MyFinanceLab Study Plan 7.2
7.3 The Dividend-Discount Model • The Valuation Principle states that the value of a stock is equal to the present value of the dividends and future sale price the investor will receive. Because these cash flows are risky, they must be discounted at the equity cost of capital, which is the expected return of other securities available in the market with equivalent risk to the firm's equity. The total return of a stock is equal to the dividend yield plus the capital gain rate. The expected total return of a stock should equal its equity cost of capital:	capital gain, p. 203 capital gain rate, p. 203 dividend-discount model, p. 205 dividend yield, p. 203 equity cost of capital, p. 203 total return, p. 203	MyFinanceLab Study Plan 7.3 Using Excel: Building a Dividend-Discount Model

$$r_E = \frac{Div_1 + P_1}{P_0} - 1 = \underbrace{\frac{Div_1}{P_0}}_{\text{Dividend Yield}} + \underbrace{\frac{P_1 - P_0}{P_0}}_{\text{Capital Gain Rate}} \quad (7.2)$$

• When investors have the same beliefs, the dividend-discount model states that, for any horizon N, the stock price satisfies the following equation:

$$P_0 = \frac{Div_1}{1 + r_E} + \frac{Div_2}{(1 + r_E)^2} + \cdots + \frac{Div_N}{(1 + r_E)^N} + \frac{P_N}{(1 + r_E)^N}$$

$$(7.4)$$

• If the stock eventually pays dividends and is never acquired, the dividend-discount model implies that the stock price equals the present value of all future dividends.

7.4 Estimating Dividends in the Dividend-Discount Model

- The constant dividend growth model assumes that dividends grow at a constant expected rate, g. In that case, g is also the expected capital gain rate, and

$$P_0 = \frac{Div_1}{r_E - g} \qquad (7.6)$$

- Future dividends depend on earnings, shares outstanding, and the dividend payout rate:

$$Div_t = \underbrace{\frac{Earnings_t}{Shares\ Outstanding_t}}_{EPS_t} \times Dividend\ Payout\ Rate_t \quad (7.8)$$

- If all increases in future earnings result exclusively from new investments made with retained earnings, then earnings growth can be found as:

$$Earnings\ Growth\ Rate = \frac{Change\ in\ Earnings}{Earnings} \qquad (7.11)$$

$$= Retention\ Rate \times Return\ on\ New\ Investment$$

(where Retention Rate $= 1 -$ Payout Rate)

- If the dividend payout rate and the number of shares outstanding is constant, and if earnings change only as a result of new investment from retained earnings, then the growth rate of the firm's earnings, dividends, and share price is calculated as follows:

$$g = Retention\ Rate \times Return\ on\ New\ Investment \quad (7.12)$$

- Cutting the firm's dividend to increase investment will raise the stock price if, and only if, the new investments generate a return greater than their cost of capital.
- If the firm has a long-term growth rate of g after the period $N + 1$, then we can apply the dividend-discount model and use the constant dividend growth formula to estimate the terminal stock value P_N.

constant dividend
growth model,
p. 206
dividend payout rate,
p. 207
retention rate, p. 207

MyFinanceLab
Study Plan 7.4

7.5 Limitations of the Dividend-Discount Model

- The dividend-discount model is sensitive to the dividend growth rate, which is difficult to estimate accurately.
- The dividend-discount model is not practical for valuing the majority of stocks not paying dividends. In Chapter 10, we discuss alternative approaches.

MyFinanceLab
Study Plan 7.5

7.6 Share Repurchases and the Total Payout Model

- If the firm undertakes share repurchases, it is more reliable to use the total payout model to value the firm. In this model, the value of equity equals the present value of future total dividends and repurchases. To determine the stock price, we divide the equity value by the initial number of shares outstanding of the firm:

$$P_0 = \frac{PV\left(Future\ Total\ Dividends\ and\ Repurchases\right)}{Shares\ Outstanding_0} \quad (7.15)$$

- The growth rate of the firm's total payout is governed by the growth rate of earnings, not earnings per share.

share repurchase,
p. 214
total payout model,
p. 214

MyFinanceLab
Study Plan 7.6

CRITICAL THINKING

1. What rights come with a share of stock?

2. Which two components make up the total return to an investor in a share of stock?

3. What does the dividend-discount model say about valuing shares of stock?

4. What is the relationship between the return from reinvesting cash flows and the change in the price of the stock?

5. How can the dividend-discount model be used with changing growth rates in future dividends?

6. What are some of the drawbacks of the dividend-discount model?

7. What are share repurchases, and how can they be incorporated into the valuation of a stock?

PROBLEMS

All problems are available in MyFinanceLab. *An asterisk * indicates problems with a higher level of difficulty.*

Stock Basics

1. If you own 15,000 shares of stock of Nike and it pays a dividend of $0.21 per share, then what is the total dividend you will receive?

2. You own 20% of the stock of a company that has 10 directors on its board. How much representation can you get on the board if the company has cumulative voting? How much representation can you ensure if the company has straight voting?

3. Anzio, Inc., has two classes of shares. Class B has 10 times the voting rights as Class A. If you own 10% of the class A shares and 20% of the Class B shares, what percentage of the total voting rights do you hold?

The Dividend-Discount Model

4. Assume Evco, Inc., has a current stock price of $50 and will pay a $2 dividend in one year; its equity cost of capital is 15%. What price must you expect Evco stock to sell for immediately after the firm pays the dividend in one year to justify its current price?

5. You just purchased a share of SPCC for $100. You expect to receive a dividend of $5 in one year. If you expect the price after the dividend is paid to be $110, what total return will you have earned over the year? What was your dividend yield? Your capital gain rate?

6. Assume Coleco pays an annual dividend of $1.50 and has a share price of $37.50. It announces that its annual dividend will increase to $1.75. If its dividend yield is to stay the same, what should its new share price be?

7. Anle Corporation has a current stock price of $20 and is expected to pay a dividend of $1 in one year. Its expected stock price right after paying that dividend is $22.
   a. What is Anle's equity cost of capital?
   b. How much of Anle's equity cost of capital is expected to be satisfied by dividend yield and how much by capital gain?

8. Achi Corp. has preferred stock with an annual dividend of $3. If the required return on Achi's preferred stock is 8%, what is its price? (*Hint*: For a preferred stock, the dividend growth rate is zero.)

9. Ovit, Inc., has preferred stock with a price of $20 and a dividend of $1.50 per year. What is its dividend yield?

10. Suppose Acap Corporation will pay a dividend of $2.80 per share at the end of this year and a dividend of $3 per share next year. You expect Acap's stock price to be $52 in two years. Assume that Acap's equity cost of capital is 10%.
    a. What price would you be willing to pay for a share of Acap stock today, if you planned to hold the stock for two years?
    b. Suppose instead you plan to hold the stock for one year. For what price would you expect to be able to sell a share of Acap stock in one year?
    c. Given your answer to (b), what price would you be willing to pay for a share of Acap stock today, if you planned to hold the stock for one year? How does this price compare to your answer in (a)?

11. Krell Industries has a share price of $22.00 today. If Krell is expected to pay a dividend of $0.88 this year and its stock price is expected to grow to $23.54 at the end of the year, what is Krell's dividend yield and equity cost of capital?

Estimating Dividends in the Dividend-Discount Model

12. NoGrowth Corporation currently pays a dividend of $0.50 per quarter, and it will continue to pay this dividend forever. What is the price per share of NoGrowth stock if the firm's equity cost of capital is 15%?

13. Summit Systems will pay a dividend of $1.50 this year. If you expect Summit's dividend to grow by 6% per year, what is its price per share if the firm's equity cost of capital is 11%?

14. Dorpac Corporation has a dividend yield of 1.5%. Its equity cost of capital is 8%, and its dividends are expected to grow at a constant rate.
    a. What is the expected growth rate of Dorpac's dividends?
    b. What is the expected growth rate of Dorpac's share price?

15. Laurel Enterprises expects earnings next year of $4 per share and has a 40% retention rate, which it plans to keep constant. Its equity cost of capital is 10%, which is also its expected return on new investment. Its earnings are expected to grow forever at a rate of 4% per year. If its next dividend is due in one year, what do you estimate the firm's current stock price to be?

*16. DFB, Inc., expects earnings at the end of this year of $5 per share, and it plans to pay a $3 dividend to shareholders (assume that is one year from now). DFB will retain $2 per share of its earnings to reinvest in new projects that have an expected return of 15% per year. Suppose DFB will maintain the same dividend payout rate, retention rate, and return on new investments in the future and will not change its number of outstanding shares.
    a. What growth rate of earnings would you forecast for DFB?
    b. If DFB's equity cost of capital is 12%, what price would you estimate for DFB stock today?
    c. Suppose instead that DFB paid a dividend of $4 per share at the end of this year and retained only $1 per share in earnings. That is, it chose to pay a higher dividend instead of reinvesting in as many new projects. If DFB maintains this higher payout rate in the future, what stock price would you estimate for the firm now? Should DFB raise its dividend?

17. Cooperton Mining just announced it will cut its dividend from $4 to $2.50 per share and use the extra funds to expand. Prior to the announcement, Cooperton's dividends

were expected to grow at a 3% rate, and its share price was $50. With the planned expansion, Cooperton's dividends are expected to grow at a 5% rate. What share price would you expect after the announcement? (Assume that the new expansion does not change Cooperton's risk.) Is the expansion a good investment?

18. Assume Gillette Corporation will pay an annual dividend of $0.65 one year from now. Analysts expect this dividend to grow at 12% per year thereafter until the fifth year. After then, growth will level off at 2% per year. According to the dividend-discount model, what is the value of a share of Gillette stock if the firm's equity cost of capital is 8%?

19. CX Enterprises has the following expected dividends: $1 in one year, $1.15 in two years, and $1.25 in three years. After that, its dividends are expected to grow at 4% per year forever (so that year 4's dividend will be 4% more than $1.25 and so on). If CX's equity cost of capital is 12%, what is the current price of its stock?

20. Assume Highline Company has just paid an annual dividend of $0.96. Analysts are predicting an 11% per year growth rate in earnings over the next five years. After then, Highline's earnings are expected to grow at the current industry average of 5.2% per year. If Highline's equity cost of capital is 8.5% per year and its dividend payout ratio remains constant, for what price does the dividend-discount model predict Highline stock should sell?

*21. Halliford Corporation expects to have earnings this coming year of $3 per share. Halliford plans to retain all of its earnings for the next two years. Then, for the subsequent two years, the firm will retain 50% of its earnings. It will retain 20% of its earnings from that point onward. Each year, retained earnings will be invested in new projects with an expected return of 25% per year. Any earnings that are not retained will be paid out as dividends. Assume Halliford's share count remains constant and all earnings growth comes from the investment of retained earnings. If Halliford's equity cost of capital is 10%, what price would you estimate for Halliford stock?

Share Repurchases and the Total Payout Model

22. Shatin Intl. has 10 million shares, an equity cost of capital of 13% and is expected to pay a total dividend of $20 million each year forever. It announces that it will increase its payout to shareholders. Instead of increasing its dividend, it will keep it constant and will start repurchasing $10 million of stock each year as well. How much will its stock price increase?

23. Zoom Enterprises expects that one year from now it will pay a total dividend of $5 million and repurchase $5 million worth of shares. It plans to spend $10 million on dividends and repurchases every year after that forever, although it may not always be an even split between dividends and repurchases. If Zoom's equity cost of capital is 13% and it has 5 million shares outstanding, what is its share price today?

24. Tolo Co. plans the following repurchases: $10 million in one year, nothing in two years, and $20 million in three years. After that, it will stop repurchasing and will issue dividends totaling $25 million in four years. The total paid in dividends is expected to increase by 3% per year thereafter. If Tolo has 2 million shares outstanding and an equity cost of capital of 11%, what is its price per share today?

25. AFW Industries has 200 million shares outstanding and expects earnings at the end of this year of $700 million. AFW plans to pay out 60% of its earnings in total, paying 40% as a dividend and using 20% to repurchase shares. If AFW's earnings are expected to grow by 8% per year and these payout rates remain constant, determine AFW's share price assuming an equity cost of capital of 12%.

26. Suppose Compco Systems pays no dividends but spent $5 billion on share repurchases last year. If Compco's equity cost of capital is 12%, and if the amount spent on repurchases is expected to grow by 8% per year, estimate Compco's market capitalization. If Compco has 6 billion shares outstanding, to what stock price does this correspond?

*27. Maynard Steel plans to pay a dividend of $3 this year. The company has an expected earnings growth rate of 4% per year and an equity cost of capital of 10%.
   a. Assuming that Maynard's dividend payout rate and expected growth rate remain constant, and that the firm does not issue or repurchase shares, estimate Maynard's share price.
   b. Suppose Maynard decides to pay a dividend of $1 this year and to use the remaining $2 per share to repurchase shares. If Maynard's total payout rate remains constant, estimate Maynard's share price.
   c. If Maynard maintains the dividend and total payout rate given in (b), at what rates are Maynard's dividends and earnings per share expected to grow?

2 Integrative Case

This case draws on material from Chapters 3–7.

Adam Rust looked at his mechanic and sighed. The mechanic had just pronounced a death sentence on his road-weary car. The car had served him well—at a cost of $500 it had lasted through four years of college with minimal repairs. Now, he desperately needs wheels. He has just graduated, and has a good job at a decent starting salary. He hopes to purchase his first new car. The car dealer seems very optimistic about his ability to afford the car payments, another first for him.

The car Adam is considering is $35,000. The dealer has given him three payment options:

1. *Zero percent financing.* Make a $4000 down payment from his savings and finance the remainder with a 0% APR loan for 48 months. Adam has more than enough cash for the down payment, thanks to generous graduation gifts.

2. *Rebate with no money down.* Receive a $4000 rebate, which he would use for the down payment (and leave his savings intact), and finance the rest with a standard 48-month loan, with an 8% APR. He likes this option, as he could think of many other uses for the $4000.

3. *Pay cash.* Get the $4000 rebate and pay the rest with cash. While Adam doesn't have $35,000, he wants to evaluate this option. His parents always paid cash when they bought a family car; Adam wonders if this really was a good idea.

Adam's fellow graduate, Jenna Hawthorne, was lucky. Her parents gave her a car for graduation. Okay, it was a little Hyundai, and definitely not her dream car, but it was serviceable, and Jenna didn't have to worry about buying a new car. In fact, Jenna has been trying to decide how much of her new salary she could save. Adam knows that with a hefty car payment, saving for retirement would be very low on his priority list. Jenna believes she could easily set aside $3000 of her $45,000 salary. She is considering putting her savings in a stock fund. She just turned 22 and has a long way to go until retirement at age 65, and she considers this risk level reasonable. The fund she is looking at has earned an average of 9% over the past 15 years and could be expected to continue earning this amount, on average. While she has no current retirement savings, five years ago Jenna's grandparents gave her a new 30-year U.S. Treasury bond with a $10,000 face value.

Jenna wants to know her retirement income if she both (1) sells her Treasury bond at its current market value and invests the proceeds in the stock fund and (2) saves an additional $3000 at the end of each year in the stock fund from now until she turns 65. Once she retires, Jenna wants those savings to last for 25 years until she is 90.

Both Adam and Jenna need to determine their best options.

Case Questions

1. What are the cash flows associated with each of Adam's three car financing options?

2. Suppose that, similar to his parents, Adam had plenty of cash in the bank so that he could easily afford to pay cash for the car without running into debt now or in the foreseeable future. If his cash earns interest at a 5.4% APR (based on monthly compounding) at the bank, what would be his best purchase option for the car?

3. In fact, Adam doesn't have sufficient cash to cover all his debts including his (substantial) student loans. The loans have a 10% APR, and any money spent on the car could not be used to pay down the loans. What is the best option for Adam now? (*Hint*: Note that having an extra $1 today saves Adam roughly $1.10 next year because he can pay down the student loans. So, 10% is Adam's time value of money in this case.)

4. Suppose instead Adam has a lot of credit card debt, with an 18% APR, and he doubts he will pay off this debt completely before he pays off the car. What is Adam's best option now?

5. Suppose Jenna's Treasury bond has a coupon interest rate of 6.5%, paid semi-annually, while current Treasury bonds with the same maturity date have a yield to maturity of 5.4435% (expressed as an APR with semiannual compounding). If she has just received the bond's 10th coupon, for how much can Jenna sell her treasury bond?

6. Suppose Jenna sells the bond, reinvests the proceeds, and then saves as she planned. If, indeed, Jenna earns a 9% annual return on her savings, how much could she withdraw each year in retirement? (Assume she begins withdrawing the money from the account in equal amounts at the end of each year once her retirement begins.)

7. Jenna expects her salary to grow regularly. While there are no guarantees, she believes an increase of 4% a year is reasonable. She plans to save $3000 the first year, and then increase the amount she saves by 4% each year as her salary grows. Unfortunately, prices will also grow due to inflation. Suppose Jenna assumes there will be 3% inflation every year. In retirement, she will need to increase her withdrawals each year to keep up with inflation. In this case, how much can she withdraw at the end of the first year of her retirement? What amount does this correspond to in today's dollars? (*Hint*: Build a spreadsheet in which you track the amount in her retirement account each year.)

8. Should Jenna sell her Treasury bond and invest the proceeds in the stock fund? Give at least one reason for and against this plan.

9. At the last minute, Jenna considers investing in Coca-Cola stock at a price of $55.55 per share instead. The stock just paid an annual dividend of $1.76 and she expects the dividend to grow at 4% annually. If the next dividend is due in one year, what expected return is Coca-Cola stock offering?

8

Investment Decision Rules

LEARNING OBJECTIVES

- Calculate Net Present Value

- Use the NPV rule to make investment decisions

- Understand alternative decision rules and their drawbacks

- Choose between mutually exclusive alternatives

- Evaluate projects with different lives

- Rank projects when a company's resources are limited so that it cannot take all positive-NPV projects

notation

CF_n	cash flow that arrives at date n	
g	growth rate	
IRR	internal rate of return	
$MIRR$	modified internal rate of return	

NPV	net present value
PV	present value
r	discount rate

Managers are constantly faced with major investment decisions. In 2007, Apple decided to introduce its first mobile phone. In 2013, Microsoft tried to jumpstart its own phone business with a $7 billion acquisition of Nokia's phone unit. Amazon.com entered the mobile phone business in 2014 and exited it in 2015. That same year, Tesla started offering a mid-market sedan for pre-sale, priced at less than half of its popular premium S-series. Amazon.com decided to start flying its own cargo planes, leasing 20 Boeing 767 freighters in 2016. How did Apple, Microsoft, Amazon, and Tesla managers decide to commit substantial capital to these initiatives? In this chapter, we focus on the decision-making tools managers use to evaluate investment decisions. Examples of these decisions include new products, equipment purchases, and marketing campaigns.

We begin by introducing the *net present value (NPV) rule*. Although the NPV investment rule maximizes the value of the firm, some firms nevertheless use other techniques to evaluate investments and decide which projects to pursue. As a result, it is important to understand those techniques, so we will explain some commonly used alternative techniques—namely, the *payback rule* and the *internal rate of return (IRR) rule*. In each case, we define the decision rule and compare decisions based on this rule to decisions based on the NPV rule. We also illustrate the circumstances in which each of the alternative rules is likely to lead to bad investment decisions.

After establishing these rules in the context of a single, stand-alone project, we broaden our perspective to include evaluating multiple opportunities to select the best one. We conclude with a look at project selection when the firm faces limits on capital or managers' time.

8.1 The NPV Decision Rule

In the previous chapters, we learned how to convert between cash today and cash in the future using the discount rate. As long as we convert costs and benefits to the same point in time, we can use the Valuation Principle to make a decision. In practice, most corporations prefer to measure values in terms of their present value—that is, in terms of cash today. In this section, we apply the Valuation Principle to derive the concept of the *net present value* or *NPV*, which we can use to define the "golden rule" of financial decision making, the *NPV rule*.

Net Present Value

net present value (NPV) The difference between the present value of a project's or investment's benefits and the present value of its costs.

When the value of a cost or benefit is computed in terms of cash today, we refer to it as the present value (PV). Similarly, we define the **net present value (NPV)** of a project or investment as the difference between the present value of its benefits and the present value of its costs:

Net Present Value
$$NPV = PV(\text{Benefits}) - PV(\text{Costs}) \tag{8.1}$$

Let's consider a simple example. Suppose your firm is offered the following investment opportunity: In exchange for $500 today, you will receive $550 in one year. If the interest rate is 8% per year, then:

$$PV(\text{Benefit}) = (\$550 \text{ in one year}) \div (\$1.08 \text{ in one year}/\$1 \text{ today})$$
$$= \$509.26 \text{ today}$$

This PV is the amount you would need to put in the bank today to generate $550 in one year ($509.26 \times 1.08 = \$550$). In other words, *the present value is the amount you need to invest at the current interest rate to recreate the cash flow*. We can think of this as the cash cost today of generating the cash flow ourselves.

Once the costs and benefits are in present value terms, we can compare them by computing the investment's NPV:

$$NPV = \$509.26 - \$500 = \$9.26 \text{ today}$$

The NPV is positive, so the benefits outweigh the costs, which means the firm should undertake this investment opportunity.

But what if you don't have the $500 needed to cover the initial cost of the project? Does the project still have the same value? Because we computed the value using competitive market prices, it should not depend on your tastes or the amount of cash you have in the bank. If you don't have the $500, suppose you borrow $509.26 from the bank at the 8% interest rate and then take the project. What are your cash flows in this case?

Today: $509.26 (loan) − $500 (invested in the project) = $9.26

In one year: $550 (from project) − $509.26 × 1.08 (loan balance) = $0

This transaction leaves you with exactly $9.26 extra cash in your pocket today and no future net obligations. So taking the project is similar to having an extra $9.26 in cash upfront. Thus, the NPV expresses the value of an investment decision as an amount of cash received today. *As long as the NPV is positive, the decision increases the value of the firm and is a good decision regardless of your current cash needs or preferences regarding when to spend the money.*

EXAMPLE 8.1

The NPV Is Equivalent to Cash Today

MyFinanceLab

PROBLEM

After saving $1500 by waiting tables, you are about to buy a 50-inch TV. You notice that the store is offering a "one year same as cash" deal. You can take the TV home today and pay nothing until one year from now, when you will owe the store the $1500 purchase price. If your savings account earns 5% per year, what is the NPV of this offer? Show that its NPV represents cash in your pocket.

SOLUTION

PLAN

You are getting something worth $1500 today (the TV) and in exchange will need to pay $1500 in one year. Think of it as getting back the $1500 you thought you would have to spend today to get the TV. We treat it as a positive cash flow.
Cash flows:

Today	In one year
+$1500	−$1500

The discount rate for calculating the present value of the payment in one year is your interest rate of 5%. You need to compare the present value of the cost ($1500 in one year) to the benefit today (a $1500 TV).

EXECUTE

$$NPV = +1500 - \frac{1500}{(1.05)} = 1500 - 1428.57 = \$71.43$$

You could take $1428.57 of the $1500 you had saved for the TV and put it in your savings account. With interest, in one year it would grow to $1428.57 \times (1.05) = $1500, enough to pay the store. The extra $71.43 is money in your pocket to spend as you like (or put toward the speaker system for your new media room).

EVALUATE

By taking the delayed payment offer, we have extra net cash flows of $71.43 today. If we put $1428.57 in the bank, it will be just enough to offset our $1500 obligation in the future. Therefore, this offer is equivalent to receiving $71.43 today, without any future net obligations.

The NPV Decision Rule

As shown in Example 8.1, the Valuation Principle implies that we should undertake projects with a positive NPV because undertaking those projects increases wealth. That is, good projects are those for which the present value of the benefits exceeds the present value of the costs. As a result, the value of the firm increases and investors are wealthier. Projects with negative NPVs have costs that exceed their benefits. Accepting them is equivalent to losing money today.

NPV decision rule When choosing among investment alternatives, take the alternative with the highest NPV. Choosing this alternative is equivalent to receiving its NPV in cash today.

We capture this logic in the **NPV Decision Rule**:

When making an investment decision, take the alternative with the highest NPV. Choosing this alternative is equivalent to receiving its NPV in cash today.

Because NPV is expressed in terms of cash today, using the NPV decision rule is a simple way to apply the Valuation Principle. Decisions that increase wealth are superior to those that decrease wealth. We don't need to know anything about the investor's preferences to reach this conclusion. As long as we have correctly captured all the cash flows of a project and applied the appropriate discount rate, we can determine whether the project makes us wealthier. Being wealthier increases our options and makes us better off, whatever our preferences are.

A common way companies apply the NPV rule in financial practices is when deciding whether to accept or reject a project. Because rejecting the project generally has $NPV = 0$ (there are no new costs or benefits from not doing the project), the NPV decision rule implies that we should

- Accept positive-NPV projects; accepting them is equivalent to receiving their NPV in cash today, and
- Reject negative-NPV projects; accepting them would reduce the value of the firm, whereas rejecting them has no cost ($NPV = 0$).

If the NPV is exactly zero, then you will neither gain nor lose by accepting the project instead of rejecting it, which also has an NPV of zero. It is not a bad project because it does not reduce the firm's value, but it does not add value to the firm either.

CONCEPT CHECK
1. What is the NPV decision rule? How is it related to the Valuation Principle?
2. Why doesn't the NPV decision rule depend on the investor's preferences?

8.2 Using the NPV Rule

We continue our discussion of investment decision rules by considering a take-it-or-leave-it decision about a single, stand-alone project. By undertaking this project, the firm does not constrain its ability to take other projects. In the case of a stand-alone project, the alternatives we are considering are to accept or reject a project. The NPV rule then implies that we should compare the project's NPV to zero (the NPV of rejecting the project and doing nothing). Thus, we should accept the project if its NPV is positive.[1]

Organizing the Cash Flows and Computing the NPV

Researchers at Fredrick's Feed and Farm have made a breakthrough. They believe they can produce a new, environmentally friendly fertilizer at a substantial cost saving over the company's existing line of fertilizer. The fertilizer will require a new plant that can be built immediately at a cost of $81.6 million. Financial managers estimate that the benefits of the new fertilizer will be $28 million per year, starting at the end of the first year and lasting for four years, as shown by the following timeline:

Year:	0	1	2	3	4
Cash flow (in millions):	−$81.60	+$28	+$28	+$28	+$28

Thus, the cash flows are an immediate $81.6 million outflow followed by an annuity inflow of $28 million per year for four years. Therefore, given a discount rate r, the NPV of this project is:

---

[1]Some prefer to state the rule that the project should be accepted if its NPV is non-negative. Since the firm should be indifferent at an NPV of exactly zero (you will neither gain nor lose by accepting the project instead of rejecting it), we prefer to state it this way. A zero NPV project is not a bad project because it does not reduce the firm's value, but it does not add value to the firm either.

$$NPV = -81.6 + \frac{28}{1+r} + \frac{28}{(1+r)^2} + \frac{28}{(1+r)^3} + \frac{28}{(1+r)^4} \qquad (8.2)$$

We can also use the annuity formula from Chapter 4 to write the NPV as:

$$NPV = -81.6 + \frac{28}{r}\left(1 - \frac{1}{(1+r)^4}\right) \qquad (8.3)$$

To apply the NPV rule, we need to know the cost of capital. The financial managers responsible for this project estimate a cost of capital of 10% per year. If we replace r in Eq. 8.2 or 8.3 with the project's cost of capital of 10%, we get an NPV of $7.2 million, which is positive. Recall that a net present value tells us the present value of the benefits (positive cash flows) net of the costs (negative cash flows) of the project. By putting everything into present values, it puts all the costs and benefits on an equal footing for comparison. In this case, the benefits outweigh the costs by $7.2 million in present value. The NPV investment rule indicates that by making the investment, Fredrick's will increase the value of the firm today by $7.2 million, so Fredrick's should undertake this project.

The NPV Profile

NPV profile A graph of a project's NPV over a range of discount rates.

The NPV of the project depends on its appropriate cost of capital. Often, there may be some uncertainty regarding the project's cost of capital. In that case, it is helpful to compute an **NPV profile**, which graphs the project's NPV over a range of discount rates. It is easiest to prepare the NPV profile using a spreadsheet such as Excel. We simply repeat our calculation of the NPV above using a range of different discount rates instead of only 10%. Figure 8.1 presents the NPV profile for Fredrick's project by plotting the NPV as a function of the discount rate, r.[2]

FIGURE 8.1

NPV of Fredrick's New Project

The graph in Panel (b) shows the NPV as a function of the discount rate based on the data in Panel (a). The NPV is positive, represented by the green-shaded area, only for discount rates that are less than 14%, the *internal rate of return (IRR)*. Given the cost of capital of 10%, the project has a positive NPV of $7.2 million. The red-shaded area indicates discount rates above the 14% IRR with negative NPVs.

Panel (a)

Discount Rate	NPV ($ millions)
0%	$30.4
2%	$25.0
4%	$20.0
6%	$15.4
8%	$11.1
10%	$7.2
12%	$3.4
14%	$0.0
16%	−$3.3
18%	−$6.3
20%	−$9.1
22%	−$11.8
24%	−$14.3

Panel (b)

---

[2]In the online appendix to this chapter, we show you how to create an NPV profile in Excel. You can find this in the chapter resources section of MyFinanceLab.

internal rate of return (IRR) The interest rate that sets the net present value of the cash flows equal to zero.

Notice that the NPV is positive only for discount rates that are less than 14% (the green shaded area in Figure 8.1). Referring to the graph and the accompanying data table, we see that at 14% the NPV is zero. The discount rate that sets the net present value of the cash flows equal to zero is an investment's **internal rate of return (IRR)**. Thus, by constructing the NPV profile, we have determined that Fredrick's project has an IRR of 14%. We can also compute the IRR without graphing the NPV by using a financial calculator or a spreadsheet's IRR function (see the appendix to Chapter 4. The calculator instructions for solving for the rate of return can be used to solve for the IRR).

	N	I/Y	PV	PMT	FV
Given:	4		−81.6	28	0
Solve for:		14			
Excel Formula: =RATE(NPER,PMT,PV,FV)=RATE(4,28,−81.6,0)					

Measuring Sensitivity with IRR

In our Fredrick's example, the firm's managers provided the cost of capital. If you are unsure of your cost of capital estimate, it is important to determine how sensitive your analysis is to errors in this estimate. The IRR can provide this information. For Fredrick's, if the cost of capital estimate is more than the 14% IRR, the NPV will be negative (see the red shaded area in Figure 8.1). Therefore, as long as our estimate of the cost of capital of 10% is within 4% of the true cost of capital, our decision to accept the project is correct. In general, the difference between the cost of capital and the IRR tells us the amount of estimation error in the cost of capital estimate that can exist without altering the original decision.

Alternative Rules Versus the NPV Rule

The NPV rule indicates that Fredrick's should undertake the investment in fertilizer technology. As we evaluate alternative rules for project selection in the subsequent sections, keep in mind that sometimes other investment rules may give the same answer as the NPV rule, but at other times they may disagree. When the rules conflict, always base your decision on the NPV rule, which is the most accurate and reliable decision rule.

CONCEPT CHECK

3. Explain the NPV rule for stand-alone projects.

4. How can you interpret the difference between the cost of capital and the IRR?

8.3 Alternative Decision Rules

Even though the NPV rule is the most accurate and reliable rule, in practice a wide variety of rules are applied, often in tandem with the NPV rule. In a 2001 study, John Graham and Campbell Harvey[3] found that 75% of the firms they surveyed used the NPV rule for making investment decisions. This result is substantially different from that found in a similar study in 1977 by L. J. Gitman and J. R. Forrester,[4] who found that only 10% of firms used

---

[3]John Graham and Campbell Harvey, "The Theory and Practice of Corporate Finance: Evidence from the Field," *Journal of Financial Economics* 60 (2001): 187–243.

[4]L. J. Gitman and J. R. Forrester, Jr., "A Survey of Capital Budgeting Techniques Used by Major U.S. Firms," *Financial Management* 6 (1977): 66–71.

Here we discuss how to use Microsoft Excel to solve for NPV and IRR. We also identify some pitfalls to avoid when using Excel.

NPV Function: Leaving Out Date 0

Excel's NPV function has the format *NPV (rate, value1, value2, . . .)*, where "rate" is the interest rate per period used to discount the cash flows, and "value1", "value2", etc., are the cash flows (or ranges of cash flows). The NPV function computes the present value of the cash flows *assuming the first cash flow occurs at date 1*. Therefore, if a project's first cash flow occurs at date 0, we cannot use the NPV function by itself to compute the NPV. We can use the NPV function to compute the present value of the cash flows from date 1 onward, and then we must add the date 0 cash flow to that result to calculate the NPV. The screenshot below shows the difference. The first NPV calculation (outlined in blue) is correct: we used the NPV function for all of the cash flows occurring at time 1 and later and then added on the first cash flow occurring at time 0 since it is already in present value. The second calculation (outlined in green) is incorrect: we used the NPV function for all of the cash flows, but the function assumed that the first cash flow occurs in period 1 instead of immediately.

NPV Function: Ignoring Blank Cells

Another pitfall with the NPV function is that cash flows that are left blank are treated differently from cash flows that are equal to zero. If the cash flow is left blank, *both the cash flow and the period are ignored.* For example, the second set of cash flows below is equivalent to the first—we have simply left the cash flow for date 2 blank instead of entering a "0." However, the NPV function ignores the blank cell at date 2 and assumes the cash flow is 10 at date 1 and 110 at date 2, which is clearly not what is intended and produces an incorrect answer (outlined in red).

Because of these idiosyncrasies, we avoid using Excel's NPV function. It is more reliable to compute the present value of each cash flow separately in Excel, and then sum them to determine the NPV.

IRR FUNCTION

Excel's IRR function has the format *IRR (values, guess)*, where "values" is the range containing the cash flows, and "guess" is an optional starting guess where Excel begins its search for an IRR. Two things to note about the IRR function:

1. The values given to the IRR function should include all of the cash flows of the project, including the one at date 0. In this sense, the IRR and NPV functions in Excel are inconsistent.

2. Like the NPV function, the IRR ignores the period associated with any blank cells.

The bar graph shows the most popular decision rules used by CFOs in Professors Graham and Harvey's 2001 survey. Many CFOs used more than one method, but no other methods were mentioned by more than half of CFOs.

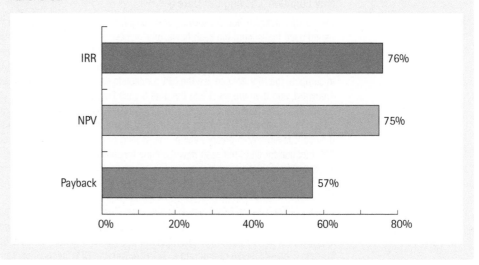

the NPV rule. Business students in recent years have been listening to their finance professors! Even so, Graham and Harvey's study indicates that one-fourth of U.S. corporations do not use the NPV rule. Exactly why other capital budgeting techniques are used in practice is not always clear. Figure 8.2 summarizes the top three decision rules given in the survey. Because you may encounter these techniques in the business world, you should know what they are, how they are used, and how they compare to NPV. In this section, we examine alternative decision rules for single, stand-alone projects within the firm. The focus here is on *the payback rule* and *the IRR rule*.

The Payback Rule

payback investment rule Only projects that pay back their initial investment within a prespecified period are undertaken.

The simplest investment rule is the **payback investment rule**, which states that you should only accept a project if its cash flows pay back its initial investment within a prespecified period. The rule is based on the notion that an opportunity that pays back its initial investment quickly is a good idea. To apply the payback rule,

1. Calculate the amount of time it takes to pay back the initial investment, called the **payback period**.

payback period The amount of time until the cash flows from a project offset the initial investment. The time it takes to pay back the initial investment.

2. Accept the project if the payback period is less than a prespecified length of time—usually a few years.

3. Reject the project if the payback period is greater than that prespecified length of time.

For example, a firm might adopt any project with a payback period of less than two years.

PROBLEM
Assume Fredrick's requires all projects to have a payback period of two years or less. Would the firm undertake the fertilizer project under this rule?

SOLUTION

PLAN

In order to implement the payback rule, we need to know whether the sum of the inflows from the project will exceed the initial investment before the end of two years. The project has inflows of $28 million per year and an initial investment of $81.6 million.

EXECUTE

The sum of the cash flows for years 1 and 2 is $28 \times 2 = \$56$ million, which will not cover the initial investment of $81.6 million. In fact, it will not be until year 3 that the cash inflows exceed the initial investment ($28 \times 3 = \$84$ million). Because the payback period for this project exceeds two years, Fredrick's will reject the project.

EVALUATE

While simple to compute, the payback rule requires us to use an arbitrary cutoff period in summing the cash flows. Furthermore, note that the payback rule does not discount future cash flows. Instead, it simply sums the cash flows and compares them to a cash outflow in the present. In this case, Fredrick's would have rejected a project that would have increased the value of the firm.

Relying on the payback rule analysis in Example 8.2, Fredrick's will reject the project. However, as we saw earlier, with a cost of capital of 10%, the NPV is $7.2 million. Following the payback rule would be a mistake because Fredrick's will pass up a project worth $7.2 million.

The payback rule is not as reliable as the NPV rule because it (1) ignores the time value of money, (2) ignores cash flows after the payback period, and (3) lacks a decision criterion grounded in economics (what is the right number of years to require for a payback period?). Some companies have addressed the first failing by computing the payback period using discounted cash flows, called the **discounted payback rule**. However, this does not solve the fundamental problem because the other two failings remain. Despite these failings, Graham and Harvey found that about 57% of the firms they surveyed reported using the payback rule as part of the decision-making process.

Why do some companies consider the payback rule? The answer probably relates to its simplicity. This rule is typically used for small investment decisions—for example, whether to purchase a new copy machine or to service the old one. In such cases, the cost of making an incorrect decision might not be large enough to justify the time required to calculate the NPV. The appeal of the payback rule is that it favors short-term projects. Some firms are unwilling to commit capital to long-term investments. Also, if the required payback period is short (one to two years), then most projects that satisfy the payback rule will have a positive NPV.

discounted payback rule Only accept projects where the sum of the discounted cash flows within the payback period is greater than or equal to the initial investment.

The Internal Rate of Return Rule

internal rate of return (IRR) investment rule A decision rule that accepts any investment opportunity where the IRR exceeds the opportunity cost of capital and otherwise rejects the opportunity.

Similar to NPV, the **internal rate of return (IRR) investment rule** is based on the concept that if the return on the investment opportunity you are considering is greater than the return on other alternatives in the market with equivalent risk and maturity (i.e., the project's cost of capital), you should undertake the investment opportunity. We state the rule formally as follows:

IRR investment rule: Take any investment opportunity whose IRR exceeds the opportunity cost of capital. Turn down any opportunity whose IRR is less than the opportunity cost of capital.

The IRR investment rule will give the correct answer (that is, the same answer as the NPV rule) in many—but not all—situations. For instance, it gives the correct answer for Fredrick's fertilizer opportunity. From Figure 8.1, whenever the cost of capital is in the green area below the IRR (14%), the project has a positive NPV and you should undertake the investment. Table 8.1 summarizes our analysis of Fredrick's new project. The NPV and IRR rules agree, but using the payback rule with a required payback period of two years or less would cause Fredrick's to reject the project.

TABLE 8.1

Summary of NPV, IRR, and Payback for Fredrick's New Project

NPV at 10%	$7.2 million	Accept ($7.2 million > 0)
Payback Period	3 years	Reject (3 years > 2 year required payback)
IRR	14%	Accept (14% > 10% cost of capital)

In general, the IRR rule works for a stand-alone project if all of the project's negative cash flows precede its positive cash flows. But in other cases, the IRR rule may disagree with the NPV rule and thus be incorrect. Let's examine several situations in which the IRR fails.

Delayed Investments. Star basketball player Evan Cole is graduating from college with a degree in finance and preparing for the NBA draft. Several companies have already approached him with endorsement contracts. Two competing sports drink companies are pursuing him. QuenchIt offers him a single up-front payment of $1 million to exclusively endorse their sports drink for three years. PowerUp offers $500,000 per year, payable at the end of each of the next three years, to endorse their product exclusively. Which offer is better? One direct way to compare the two contracts is to realize that signing with QuenchIt causes Evan to forgo the PowerUp contract, or $500,000 per year. Considering the risk of his alternative income sources and available investment opportunities, Evan estimates his opportunity cost of capital to be 10%. The timeline of Evan's investment opportunity is:

0	1	2	3
$1,000,000	−$500,000	−$500,000	−$500,000

The NPV of Evan's investment opportunity is:

$$NPV = 1,000,000 - \frac{500,000}{1+r} - \frac{500,000}{(1+r)^2} - \frac{500,000}{(1+r)^3}$$

By setting the NPV equal to zero and solving for r, we find the IRR. We can use either a financial calculator or a spreadsheet to find the IRR:

	N	I/Y	PV	PMT	FV
Given:	3		1,000,000	−500,000	0
Solve for:		23.38			

Excel Formula: =RATE(NPER,PMT,PV,FV)=RATE(3,−500000,1000000,0)

The 23.38% IRR is larger than the 10% opportunity cost of capital. According to the IRR rule, Evan should sign the deal. But what does the NPV rule say?

$$NPV = 1,000,000 - \frac{500,000}{1.1} - \frac{500,000}{1.1^2} - \frac{500,000}{1.1^3} = -\$243,426$$

At a 10% discount rate, the NPV is negative, so signing the deal would reduce Evan's wealth. He should not sign the endorsement deal with QuenchIt, and should sign with PowerUp instead.

To resolve this conflict, we can prepare an NPV profile for the QuenchIt contract. Figure 8.3 plots the NPV of the investment opportunity for a range of discount rates. It shows that, no matter what the cost of capital is, the IRR rule and the NPV rule will give exactly opposite recommendations. That is, the NPV is positive only when the opportunity cost of capital is *above* 23.38% (the IRR). Evan should accept the investment only when the opportunity cost of capital is greater than the IRR, the opposite of what the IRR rule recommends.

Figure 8.3 also illustrates the problem with using the IRR rule in this case. For most investment opportunities, expenses occur initially and cash is received later. In this case, Evan receives cash *upfront* from QuenchIt but the forgone cash flows from PowerUp occurred later. It is as if Evan borrowed money, and when you borrow money you prefer as *low* a rate as possible. Evan's optimal rule is to borrow money as long as the rate at which he borrows is *less* than the cost of capital.

Even though the IRR rule fails to give the correct answer in this case, the IRR itself still provides useful information *in conjunction* with the NPV rule. As mentioned earlier, the IRR provides information on how sensitive the investment decision is to uncertainty in the cost of capital estimate. In this case, the difference between the cost of capital and the IRR is large—10% versus 23.38%. Evan would have to have underestimated the cost of capital by 13.38% to make the NPV positive.

Multiple IRRs. Evan has informed QuenchIt that it needs to sweeten the deal before he will accept it. In response, the company has agreed to make an additional payment of $600,000 in 10 years as deferred compensation for the long-term increase in sales that

FIGURE 8.3

NPV of Evan Cole's $1 Million QuenchIt Deal

When all the benefits of an investment occur at time zero and before the costs, the NPV is an *increasing* function of the discount rate. The NPV is positive in the green-shaded areas and negative in the red-shaded areas. Notice that the NPV is positive when the cost of capital is above 23.38%, the IRR, so the NPV and IRR rules conflict.

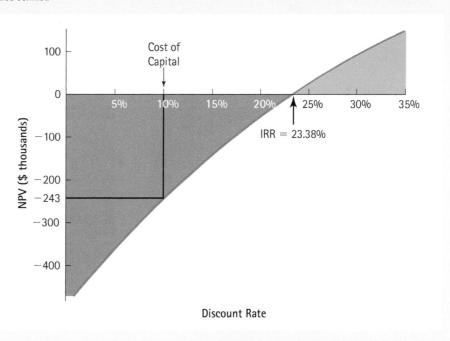

even a short-term endorsement by Evan would bring. Should he accept or reject the new offer?

We begin with the new timeline:

The NPV of Evan's new investment opportunity is:

$$NPV = 1,000,000 - \frac{500,000}{1+r} - \frac{500,000}{(1+r)^2} - \frac{500,000}{(1+r)^3} + \frac{600,000}{(1+r)^{10}}$$

We can find the IRR for this investment opportunity by creating an NPV profile and noting where it crosses zero. Figure 8.4 plots the NPV of the opportunity at different discount rates. In this case, there are *two* IRRs—that is, there are two values of r that set the NPV equal to zero. You can verify this fact by substituting IRRs of 5.79% and 13.80% for r into the equation. Because there is more than one IRR, we cannot apply the IRR rule. It is also worth noting that you should take special care when using a spreadsheet or financial calculator to determine the IRR. Both solve for the IRR through trial and error because you cannot calculate the IRR directly. In cases where there is more than one IRR, the spreadsheet or calculator will simply produce the first one that it finds, with no indication that there could be others! Some financial calculators will return an error message if there are multiple IRRs. Thus, it always pays to create the NPV profile.

For guidance, let's turn to the NPV rule. If the cost of capital were *either* below 5.79% or above 13.80%, Evan should undertake the opportunity. But given his cost of capital of 10%, he should still turn it down. Notice that even though the IRR rule fails in this case,

FIGURE 8.4

NPV of Evan's Sports Drink Deal with Additional Deferred Payments

The graph in Panel (b) shows the NPV of Evan's deal with additional deferred payment based on the data in Panel (a). In this case, there are two IRRs, invalidating the IRR rule. If the opportunity cost of capital is *either* below 5.79% or above 13.80%, Evan should accept the deal because the NPV is then positive, as indicated by the green-shaded areas. At any point between the two IRRs, the NPV is negative (see the red-shaded area).

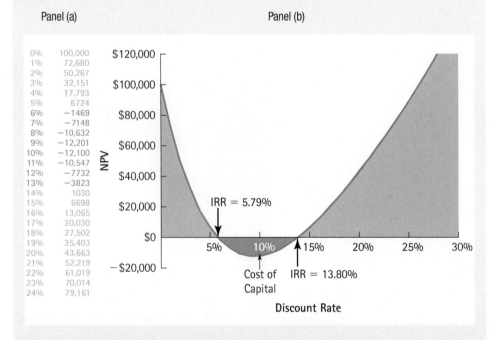

the two IRRs are still useful as bounds on the cost of capital estimate. If the cost of capital estimate is wrong, and it is actually smaller than 5.79% or larger than 13.80%, the decision not to pursue the project will change because it will have a positive NPV.

There is no easy fix for the IRR rule when there are multiple IRRs. Although the NPV is negative between the IRRs in this example, the reverse is also possible (see Figure 8.5). In that case, the project would have a positive NPV for discount rates between the IRRs rather than for discount rates lower or higher than the IRRs. Furthermore, there are situations in which more than two IRRs exist.[5] In such situations, our only choice is to rely on the NPV rule.

modified internal rate of return (MIRR) The discount rate that sets the NPV of modified cash flows of a project equal to zero. Cash flows are modified so there is only one negative cash flow (and one sign change) to ensure that only one IRR exists.

Modified Internal Rate of Return

The fact that there can be multiple IRRs for the cash flows from a project is a clear disadvantage for the IRR. To overcome this, some have proposed various ways of modifying the cash flows before computing the IRR. All these modifications have the common feature that they group the cash flows so that there is only one negative cash flow, occurring at either the beginning or the end. In that case, there is only one sign change for the cash flows as a whole and hence only one IRR. This new IRR, computed as the discount rate that sets the NPV of the modified cash flows of the project equal to zero, is called the **modified internal rate of return (MIRR)**.

FIGURE 8.5

NPV Profile for a Project with Multiple IRRs

The graph shows the NPV profile for a multiple-IRR project with cash flows of −$1000, $2500, and −$1540 in years 0, 1, and 2, respectively. As the NPV profile shows, the project has two IRRs: 10% and 40%.

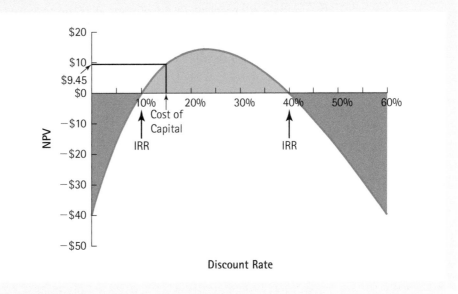

[5]In general, there can be as many IRRs as the number of times the project's cash flows change sign over time.

Why Do Rules Other Than the NPV Rule Persist?

Professors Graham and Harvey found that a sizable minority of firms (25%) in their study do not use the NPV rule at all. In addition, about 50% of firms surveyed used the payback rule. Furthermore, it appears that most firms use *both* the NPV rule and the IRR rule. Why do firms use rules other than NPV if they can lead to erroneous decisions?

One possible explanation for this phenomenon is that Graham and Harvey's survey results might be misleading. CFOs who were using the IRR as a sensitivity measure in conjunction with the NPV rule might have checked both the IRR box and the NPV box on the survey. The question they were asked was, "How frequently does your firm use the following techniques when deciding which projects or acquisitions to pursue?" By computing the IRR and using it in conjunction with the NPV rule to estimate the sensitivity of their results, they might have felt they were using *both* techniques.

Nevertheless, a significant minority of managers surveyed replied that they used only the IRR rule, so this explanation cannot be the whole story.

One common reason that managers give for using the IRR rule exclusively is that you do not need to know the opportunity cost of capital to calculate the IRR. On a superficial level, this is true: The IRR does not depend on the cost of capital. You may not need to know the cost of capital to *calculate* the IRR, but you certainly need to know the cost of capital when you *apply* the IRR rule. Consequently, the opportunity cost is as important to the IRR rule as it is to the NPV rule.

Nonetheless, part of the appeal of the IRR rule is that the IRR seems to sum up the attractiveness of an investment without requiring an assumption about the cost of capital. However, a more useful summary is the project's NPV profile, showing the NPV as a function of the discount rate. The NPV profile also does not require knowing the cost of capital, but it has the distinct advantage of being much more informative and reliable.

MIRR Technique. Let's clarify this with an example. You are considering a project that has the following three cash flows:

The NPV profile for this project, shown in Figure 8.5, identifies the two IRRs for this project as 10% and 40%.

Assume that your discount rate for this project is 15%. As Figure 8.5 shows, the NPV of the project at 15% is $9.45. We could modify the cash flows of the project to eliminate the multiple IRR problem. By discounting all of the negative cash flows to the present and compounding all of the positive cash flows to the end of the project, we have only two cash flows, yielding a single IRR. What discount rate and compounding rate should we use? One natural choice is our cost of capital for this project, which is 15%.

Figure 8.6 presents the NPV profile for our modified cash flows. As Figure 8.6 shows, there is now only a single IRR, at 15.25%. Because our cost of capital is 15%, we would properly accept the project using the IRR rule. Also note that the advantage of using 15% as our discount and compounding rates when modifying the cash flows is that the NPV of the modified cash flows at 15% is the same as the NPV of the true cash flows at 15%. Figure 8.6 also makes an important point: We are no longer evaluating the true cash flows of the project. Instead, we have modified them to force them to produce a single IRR. The NPV profile of the true cash flows of the project is given earlier in Figure 8.5 and is clearly different from the one produced by the modified cash flows in Figure 8.6.

FIGURE 8.6

NPV Profile of Modified
Cash Flows for the
Multiple-IRR Project
from Figure 8.5

The graph presents the NPV profile for the modified project cash flows of −2164.46 in year 0 and 2875 in year 2. The modified cash flows have only one IRR: 15.25%. Given the 15% cost of capital, the IRR rule confirms that we should accept the project.

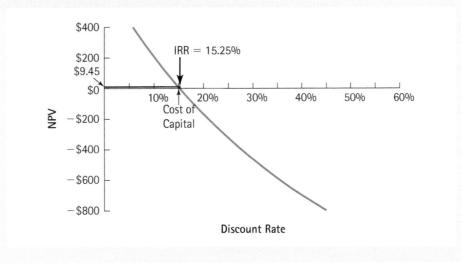

There is no set way to modify project cash flows to produce an MIRR. Two other approaches that each solve the multiple IRR problem are:

1. Discount all the negative cash flows to time 0 and leave the positive cash flows alone.

2. Leave the initial cash flow alone and compound all the remaining cash flows to the final period of the project. In this approach, you are implicitly reinvesting all the cash flows from the project at your compound rate until the project is complete.

Again, in either case, if you use the project's cost of capital as your discount and compounding rate, you will not alter the NPV of the project at that discount rate. Furthermore, a decision to accept or reject the project based on the modified IRR will be the same as the one based on the NPV decision rule.

MIRR: A Final Word. There is considerable debate about whether MIRR is actually better than IRR. Most of the argument centers on whether it is advisable to modify the cash flows of the project. The IRR is truly an internal rate of return based solely on the actual cash flows of the project. However, the IRR implicitly assumes that all cash flows generated by the project are reinvested at the project's IRR rather than at the firm's cost of capital until the project ends. For a project with a high IRR, this may be an unrealistic assumption. Furthermore, there may be more than one IRR, which complicates its use. The MIRR avoids these problems, but is based on a set of cash flows modified through the use of a chosen discount and compounding rate. Thus, it is not really an internal rate of return and is no longer based solely on the actual cash flows of the project. Finally, MIRR still does not solve some of the other problems associated with using IRR when choosing among projects.

CONCEPT
CHECK

5. How do you apply the payback rule?

6. Under what conditions will the IRR rule lead to the same decision as the NPV rule?

8.4 Choosing Among Projects

Thus far, we have considered only decisions where the choice is either to accept or to reject a single, stand-alone project. Sometimes, however, a firm must choose just one project from among several possible projects. For example, a manager may be evaluating alternative package designs for a new product. The manager must choose only one of the designs. When choosing any one project excludes us from taking the other projects, we are facing **mutually exclusive projects**.

mutually exclusive projects Projects that compete with one another; by accepting one, you exclude the others.

When projects, such as the package designs, are mutually exclusive, it is not enough to determine which projects have positive NPVs. With mutually exclusive projects, the manager's goal is to rank the projects and choose the best one. In this situation, the NPV rule provides a straightforward answer: *Pick the project with the highest NPV.*

EXAMPLE 8.3

NPV and Mutually Exclusive Projects

MyFinanceLab

PROBLEM

You own a small piece of commercial land near a university. You are considering what to do with it. You have been approached with an offer to buy it for $220,000. You are also considering three alternative uses yourself: a bar, a coffee shop, and an apparel store. You assume that you would operate your choice indefinitely, eventually leaving the business to your children. You have collected the following information about the uses. What should you do?

	Initial Investment	Cash Flow in the First Year (CF_1)	Growth Rate (g)	Cost of Capital (r)
Bar	$400,000	$60,000	3.5%	12%
Coffee Shop	$200,000	$40,000	3%	10%
Apparel Store	$500,000	$75,000	3%	13%

SOLUTION

PLAN

Since you can develop only one project (you only have one piece of land), these are mutually exclusive projects. In order to decide which project is most valuable, you need to rank them by NPV. Each of these projects (except for selling the land) has cash flows that can be valued as a growing perpetuity, so from Chapter 4, the present value of the inflows is $CF_1/(r-g)$. The NPV of each investment will be:

$$\frac{CF_1}{r-g} - \text{Initial Investment}$$

EXECUTE

The NPVs are:

$$\text{Bar: } \frac{\$60,000}{0.12 - 0.035} - \$400,000 = \$305,882$$

$$\text{Coffee Shop: } \frac{\$40,000}{0.10 - 0.03} - \$200,000 = \$371,429$$

$$\text{Apparel Store: } \frac{\$75,000}{0.13 - 0.03} - \$500,000 = \$250,000$$

So, the ranking is

Alternative	NPV
Coffee Shop	$371,429
Bar	$305,882
Apparel Store	$250,000
Sell the Land	$220,000

You should choose the coffee shop.

EVALUATE

All the alternatives have positive NPVs, but you can take only one of them, so you should choose the one that creates the most value. Even though the coffee shop has the lowest cash flows, its lower start-up cost coupled with its lower cost of capital (it is less risky) make it the best choice.

Because the IRR is a measure of the expected return of investing in the project, you might be tempted to extend the IRR investment rule to the case of mutually exclusive projects by picking the project with the highest IRR. Unfortunately, picking one project over another simply because it has a larger IRR can lead to mistakes. Problems arise when the mutually exclusive investments have differences in scale (require different initial investments) and when they have different cash flow patterns. We discuss each of these situations in turn.

Differences in Scale

Would you prefer a 200% return on $1 or a 10% return on $1 million? The former return certainly sounds impressive and gives you great bragging rights, but at the end of the day you make only $2. The latter opportunity may sound much more mundane, but you make $100,000. This comparison illustrates an important shortcoming of IRR: Because it is a return, you cannot tell how much value has actually been created without knowing the basis for the return—a 10% IRR can have very different value implications for an initial investment of $1 million versus an initial investment of $100 million.

If a project has a positive NPV, then if we can double its size, its NPV will double: By the Valuation Principle, doubling the cash flows of an investment opportunity must make it worth twice as much. However, the IRR rule does not have this property—it is unaffected by the scale of the investment opportunity because the IRR measures the average return of the investment. Thus, the IRR rule cannot be used to compare projects of different scales. Let's illustrate this concept in the context of an example.

Identical Scale. We begin by considering two mutually exclusive projects with the same scale. Maria is evaluating two investment opportunities. If she goes into business with her boyfriend, she would need to invest $10,000 and the business would generate incremental cash flows of $6000 per year for three years. Alternatively, she could start a courier/delivery service using two high-end drones. The drone setup will cost $10,000 and will generate $5000 per year for three years. The opportunity cost of capital for both opportunities is 12% and both will require all her time, so Maria must choose between them. How valuable is each opportunity, and which one should she choose?

Let's consider both the NPV and IRR of each project. The timeline for the investment with Maria's boyfriend is:

The NPV of the investment opportunity when $r = 0.12$ is:

$$NPV = -10,000 + \frac{6000}{1.12} + \frac{6000}{1.12^2} + \frac{6000}{1.12^3} = \$4411$$

We can determine the IRR of this investment by using a financial calculator or spreadsheet:

	N	**I/Y**	**PV**	**PMT**	**FV**
Given:	3		−10,000	6000	0
Solve for:		36.3			
	Excel Formula: =RATE(NPER,PMT,PV,FV)=RATE(3,6000,−10000,0)				

Thus, the IRR for Maria's investment in her boyfriend's business is 36.3%. The timeline for her investment in the drone delivery business is:

0	1	2	3
−10,000	+5000	+5000	+5000

The NPV of the investment opportunity when $r = 0.12$ is:

$$NPV = -10{,}000 + \frac{5000}{1.12} + \frac{5000}{1.12^2} + \frac{5000}{1.12^3} = \$2009$$

The \$2009 NPV of the delivery business is lower than the \$4411 NPV for her boyfriend's business, so Maria should join her boyfriend in business. Luckily, it appears that Maria does not need to choose between her money and her relationship!

We could also compare IRRs. For the delivery business, we would find that the IRR is 23.4%. The delivery business has a lower IRR than the investment in her boyfriend's business. As Figure 8.7 shows, in this case the project with the higher IRR has the higher NPV.

Change in Scale. What happens if we change the scale of one of the projects? Maria's finance professor points out that, given the potential for automation, she could manage

FIGURE 8.7

NPV of Maria's Investment Opportunities with the Two-Drone Delivery Service

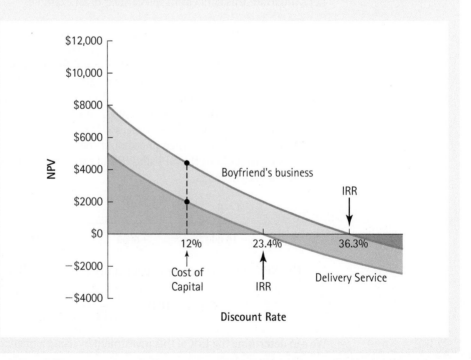

The NPV of her boyfriend's business is always larger than the NPV of the delivery service. The same is true for the IRR; the IRR of her boyfriend's business is 36.3%, while the IRR for the delivery service is 23.4%.

five times as many drones in her courier and delivery business. Her setup cost would now be $50,000 and her annual cash flows would be $25,000. What should Maria do now?

Note that the IRR is unaffected by the scale. Because we are scaling all the cash flows

	N	I/Y	PV	PMT	FV
Given:	3		−50,000	25,000	0
Solve for:		23.4			

Excel Formula: =RATE(NPER,PMT,PV,FV)=RATE(3,25000,−50000,0)

up by a factor of 5, a 10-drone delivery service has exactly the same IRR as a 2-drone service, so her boyfriend's business still has a higher IRR than the delivery service:

However, the NPV of the delivery service does grow by the scale—it is five times larger:

$$NPV = -50,000 + \frac{25,000}{1.12} + \frac{25,000}{1.12^2} + \frac{25,000}{1.12^3} = \$10,046$$

Now Maria should invest in the 10-drone delivery service. As Figure 8.8 shows, the NPV of the 10-drone delivery service exceeds the NPV of going into business with her boyfriend whenever the cost of capital is less than 20%. In this case, even though the IRR of going into business with her boyfriend exceeds the IRR of the delivery service, picking the investment opportunity with the higher IRR does not result in taking the opportunity with the higher NPV.

Percentage Return Versus Dollar Impact on Value. This result might seem counterintuitive and you can imagine Maria having a difficult time explaining to her boyfriend why

FIGURE 8.8

NPV of Maria's Investment Opportunities with the Ten-Drone Delivery Service

As in Figure 8.7, the IRR of her boyfriend's business is 36.3%, while the IRR for the delivery service is 23.4%. But in this case, the NPV of her boyfriend's business is larger than the NPV of the 10-drone delivery service only for discount rates over 20%.

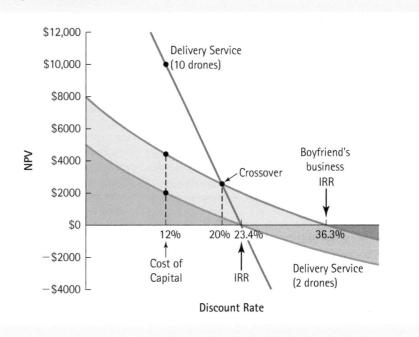

she is choosing a lower return over going into business with him. Why would anyone turn down an investment opportunity with a 36.3% return (IRR) in favor of one with only a 23.4% return? The answer is that the latter opportunity, the delivery service, makes more money. Recall the comparison at the beginning of this section: a 200% return on $1 versus a 10% return on $1 million. We agreed that ranking the returns was not the same as ranking the value created. The IRR is a measure of the average return, which can be valuable information. When you are comparing mutually exclusive projects of different scale, however, you need to know the dollar impact on value—the NPV.

INTERVIEW WITH DICK GRANNIS

Dick Grannis is Senior Vice President and Treasurer of QUALCOMM Incorporated, a world leader in digital wireless communications technology and semiconductors, headquartered in San Diego. He joined the company in 1991 and oversees the company's $10 billion cash investment portfolio. He works primarily on investment banking, capital structure, and international finance.

QUESTION: *QUALCOMM has a wide variety of products in different business lines. How does your capital budgeting process for new products work?*

ANSWER: QUALCOMM evaluates new projects (such as new products, equipment, technologies, research and development, acquisitions, and strategic investments) by using traditional financial measurements including DCF models, IRR levels, peak funding requirements, the time needed to reach cumulative positive cash flows, and the short-term impact of the investment on our reported net earnings. For strategic investments, we consider the possible value of financial, competitive, technology and/or market value enhancements to our core businesses—even if those benefits cannot be quantified. Overall, we make capital budgeting decisions based on a combination of objective analyses and our own business judgment.

We do not engage in capital budgeting and analysis if the project represents an immediate and necessary requirement for our business operations. One example is new software or production equipment to start a project that has already received approval.

We are also mindful of the opportunity costs of allocating our internal engineering resources on one project vs. another project. We view this as a constantly challenging but worthwhile exercise, because we have many attractive opportunities but limited resources to pursue them.

QUESTION: *How often does QUALCOMM evaluate its hurdle rates and what factors does it consider in setting them? How do you allocate capital across areas and regions and assess the risk of non-U.S. investments?*

ANSWER: QUALCOMM encourages its financial planners to utilize hurdle (or discount) rates that vary according to the risk of the particular project. We expect a rate of return commensurate with the project's risk. Our finance staff considers a wide range of discount rates and chooses one that fits the project's expected risk profile and time horizon. The range can be from 6.00% to 8.00% for relatively safe investments in the domestic market to 50% or more for equity investments in foreign markets that may be illiquid and difficult to predict. We re-evaluate our hurdle rates at least every year.

We analyze key factors including: (i) market adoption risk (whether or not customers will buy the new product or service at the price and volume we expect), (ii) technology development risk (whether or not we can develop and patent the new product or service as expected), (iii) execution risk (whether we can launch the new product or service cost effectively and on time), and (iv) dedicated asset risk (the amount of resources that must be consumed to complete the work).

QUESTION: *How are projects categorized and how are the hurdle rates for new projects determined? What would happen if QUALCOMM simply evaluated all new projects against the same hurdle rate?*

ANSWER: We primarily categorize projects by risk level, but we also categorize projects by the expected time horizon. We consider short-term and long-term projects to balance our needs and achieve our objectives. For example, immediate projects and opportunities may demand a great amount of attention, but we also stay focused on long-term projects because they often create greater long-term value for stockholders.

If we were to evaluate all new projects against the same hurdle rate, then our business planners would, by default, consistently choose to invest in the highest risk projects because those projects would appear to have the greatest expected returns in DCF models or IRR analyses. That approach would probably not work well for very long.

EXAMPLE 8.4

Computing the
Crossover Point

MyFinanceLab

PROBLEM

Solve for the crossover point for Maria from Figure 8.8.

SOLUTION

PLAN

The *crossover point* is the discount rate that makes the NPV of the two alternatives equal. We can find the discount rate by setting the equations for the NPV of each project equal to each other and solving for the discount rate. In general, we can always compute the effect of choosing the delivery service over her boyfriend's business as the difference of the NPVs. At the crossover point the difference is 0.

EXECUTE

Setting the difference equal to 0:

$$NPV = -50,000 + \frac{25,000}{1+r} + \frac{25,000}{(1+r)^2} + \frac{25,000}{(1+r)^3}$$

$$-\left(-10,000 + \frac{6000}{(1+r)} + \frac{6000}{(1+r)^2} + \frac{6000}{(1+r)^3}\right) = 0$$

combining terms, we have

$$-40,000 + \frac{19,000}{(1+r)} + \frac{19,000}{(1+r)^2} + \frac{19,000}{(1+r)^3} = 0$$

As you can see, solving for the crossover point is just like solving for the IRR, so we will need to use a financial calculator or spreadsheet:

	N	I/Y	PV	PMT	FV
Given:	3		−40,000	19,000	0
Solve for:		20.04			
	Excel Formula: =RATE(NPER,PMT,PV,FV)=RATE(3,19000,−40000,0)				

We find that the crossover occurs at a discount rate of 20.04%.

EVALUATE

Just as the NPV of a project tells us the value impact of taking the project, so the difference of the NPVs of two alternatives tells us the *incremental* impact of choosing one project over another. The crossover point is the discount rate at which we would be indifferent between the two projects because the incremental value of choosing one over the other would be zero.

Timing of the Cash Flows

Even when projects have the same scale, the IRR may lead you to rank them incorrectly due to differences in the timing of the cash flows. The reason for this is that the IRR is expressed as a return, but the dollar value of earning a given return—and therefore the NPV—depends on how long the return is earned. Consider a high-IRR project with cash flows paid back quickly. It may have a lower NPV than a project with a lower IRR whose cash flows are paid back over a longer period. This sensitivity to timing is another reason why you cannot use the IRR to choose between mutually exclusive investments. To see this in the context of an example, let's return to Maria's delivery business.

Maria believes that after starting the delivery business, she may be able to sell her stake in the business at the end of the first year for $40,000 (she will stay on and manage the business after she sells). Thus, counting her first-year profit of $25,000, she would earn a total of $65,000 after one year. In that case, the timeline is:

FIGURE 8.9

NPV with and without Selling

The IRR from selling after one year (30%) is larger than the IRR without selling (23.4%). However, the NPV from selling after one year exceeds the NPV without selling only for discount rates that are in excess of 16.3% (see the yellow-shaded area versus the blue-shaded area). Thus, given a cost of capital of 12%, it is better not to sell the delivery service after one year, despite the higher IRR.

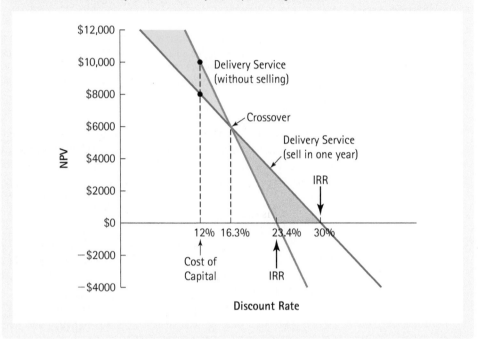

Figure 8.9 plots the NPV profile for the delivery service with and without selling it after one year. If Maria sells, the NPV profile crosses the *x*-axis at 30%, which is its IRR. The IRR for the delivery service if she does not sell is still 23.4%. Therefore, if Maria picks the alternative with the higher IRR, she will sell. However, since the height of each line indicates the NPV of that decision, we can see that his NPV given a 12% cost of capital is higher if she chooses not to sell. (In fact, the NPV is higher as long as the cost of capital is less than 16.3%.) The intuition is as follows: While the 30% IRR from selling is high, this return is only earned in the first year. While the 23.4% IRR from not selling is not as high, it is still attractive relative to the cost of capital, and it is earned over a longer period. Again, only by comparing the NPV can we determine which option is truly more valuable.

The Bottom Line on IRR. As these examples make clear, picking the investment opportunity with the largest IRR can lead to mistakes. In general, it is dangerous to use the IRR in cases where you are choosing between projects, or anytime when your decision to accept or reject one project would affect your decision on another project. In such a situation, always rely on NPV.

CONCEPT CHECK

7. What is the most reliable way to choose between mutually exclusive projects?

8. For mutually exclusive projects, explain why picking one project over another because it has a larger IRR can lead to mistakes.

8.5   Evaluating Projects with Different Lives

Often, a company will need to choose between two solutions to the same problem. A complication arises when those solutions last for different periods of time. For example, a firm could be considering two vendors for its internal network servers. Each vendor offers the same level of service, but they use different equipment. Vendor A offers a more expensive server with lower per-year operating costs that it guarantees for three years. Vendor B offers a less expensive server with higher per-year operating costs that it guarantees for two years. The costs are shown in Table 8.2 along with the present value of the costs of each option, discounted at the 10% cost of capital for this project.

TABLE 8.2

Cash Flows ($ thousands) for Network Server Options

Year	PV at 10%	0	1	2	3
A	−12.49	−10	−1	−1	−1
B	−10.47	−7	−2	−2	

Note that all of the cash flows are negative, and so is the present value. This is a choice of an internal server, where the project must be taken and the benefits are diffuse (the company could not function effectively without an internal network). Thus, we are trying to minimize the cost of providing this service for the company. Table 8.2 shows that option A is more expensive on a present value basis (−$12,487 versus −$10,471). However, the comparison is not that simple: Option A lasts for three years while option B lasts for two. The decision comes down to whether it is worth paying $2000 more for option A to get the extra year. One method that is used to evaluate alternatives such as these that have different lives is to compute the **equivalent annual annuity (EAA)** for each project, which is the level annual cash flow with the same present value as the cash flows of the project. The intuition is that we can think of the cost of each solution as the constant annual cost that gives us the same present value of the lumpy cash flows of buying and operating the server. On a timeline, equivalent annual annuity cash flows would appear as follows:

equivalent annual annuity (EAA) The level annual cash flow that has the same present value as the cash flows of a project. Used to evaluate alternative projects with different lives.

When you have a level cash flow at a constant interval, you are dealing with an annuity and that is exactly how to approach this problem. We know the present value (−$12.49) the number of years (3), and the discount rate (10%). We need to solve for the cash flow, of an equivalent annuity. Recall from Chapter 4 that the formula (Eq. 4.9) for solving for the cash flow in an annuity is:

$$\text{Cash Flow} = \frac{\text{Present Value}}{\frac{1}{r}\left(1 - \frac{1}{(1+r)^N}\right)} = \frac{-12.49}{\frac{1}{0.10}\left(1 - \frac{1}{(1.10)^3}\right)} = -5.02$$

So, buying and operating server A is equivalent to spending $5020 per year to have a network server. We can repeat the calculation for server B, but for a two-year annuity because server B has only a two-year life (the change in exponent is highlighted):

$$\text{Cash Flow} = \frac{\text{Present Value}}{\frac{1}{r}\left(1 - \frac{1}{(1+r)^N}\right)} = \frac{-10.47}{\frac{1}{0.10}\left(1 - \frac{1}{(1.10)^2}\right)} = -6.03$$

Therefore, we can reinterpret the cost of each alternative as shown in Table 8.3:

Now we are ready to choose between the two servers. Server A is equivalent to spending $5020 per year and server B is equivalent to spending $6030 per year to have a network server. Seen in this light, server A appears to be the less expensive solution.

TABLE 8.3

Cash Flows ($ thousands) for Network Server Options, Expressed as Equivalent Annual Annuities

Year	PV at 10%	0	1	2	3
A	−12.49	0	−5.02	−5.02	−5.02
B	−10.47	0	−6.03	−6.03	

EXAMPLE 8.5

Computing an Equivalent Annual Annuity

MyFinanceLab

PROBLEM

You are about to sign the contract for server A from Table 8.2 when a third vendor approaches you with another option that lasts for four years. The cash flows for server C are given below. Should you choose the new option or stick with server A?

	0	1	2	3	4
Server C ($ thousands)	−14	−1.2	−1.2	−1.2	−1.2

SOLUTION

PLAN

In order to compare this new option to server A, we need to put server C on an equal footing by computing its annual cost. We can do this by:

1. Computing its NPV at the 10% discount rate we used above.
2. Computing the equivalent four-year annuity with the same present value.

EXECUTE

$$PV = -14 - 1.2\left(\frac{1}{0.10}\right)\left[1 - \frac{1}{(1.10)^4}\right] = -17.80$$

$$\text{Cash Flow} = \frac{PV}{\frac{1}{r}\left[1 - \frac{1}{(1+r)^N}\right]} = \frac{-17.80}{\frac{1}{0.10}\left[1 - \frac{1}{(1.10)^4}\right]} = -5.62$$

Server C's annual cost of $5620 is greater than the annual cost of server A ($5020), so we should still choose server A.

EVALUATE

In this case, the additional cost associated with purchasing and maintaining server C is not worth the extra year we get from choosing it. By putting all of these costs into an equivalent annuity, the EAA tool allows us to see that.

Important Considerations When Using the Equivalent Annual Annuity

Although server A appears to be the lowest-cost alternative, there are several factors to consider before making our decision.

Required Life. We computed the equivalent annual cost of server A assuming we would use it for three years. But suppose it is likely that we will not need the server in the third year. Then we would be paying for something that we would not use. In that case, it may be cheaper to purchase server B, which provides coverage for the years we will need it at a lower total cost.[6]

---

[6]In this scenario, we should also consider any salvage value that server A might have if we sold it after two years.

Replacement Cost. When we compare servers A and B based on their equivalent annual cost, we are assuming that the cost of servers will not change over time. But suppose we believe a dramatic change in technology will reduce the cost of servers by the third year to an annual cost of $2000 per year. Then server B has the advantage that we can upgrade to the new technology sooner. The cost of three years of service from either server in this case can be represented as follows:

Year	PV at 10%	0	1	2	3
A	−12.49	0	−5.02	−5.02	−5.02
B	−11.97	0	−6.03	−6.03	−2.00

Therefore, when cost or performance is expected to change significantly over time, it may be cheaper to purchase server B despite its higher equivalent annual cost because it gives us the option to switch to the new technology sooner.

CONCEPT CHECK

9. Explain why choosing the option with the highest NPV is not always correct when the options have different lives.

10. What issues should you keep in mind when choosing among projects with different lives?

8.6 Choosing Among Projects When Resources Are Limited

In the previous sections, we compared projects that had *identical* resource needs. For example, in Maria's case, we assumed that both the delivery service and her boyfriend's business demanded all of her time. In this section, we develop an approach for situations where the choices have differing resource needs.

Evaluating Projects with Different Resource Requirements

In some situations, different investment opportunities demand different amounts of a particular resource. If there is a fixed supply of the resource so that you cannot undertake all possible opportunities, simply picking the highest NPV opportunity might not lead to the best decision.

We usually assume that you will be able to finance all positive NPV projects that you have. In reality, managers work within the constraint of a budget that restricts the amount of capital they may invest in a given period. Such a constraint would force a manager to choose among positive NPV projects to maximize the total NPV while staying within her budget. For example, assume you are considering the three projects in Table 8.4, and that you have a budget of $200 million. Table 8.4 shows the NPV of each project and the initial investment that each project requires. Project A has the highest NPV but it uses up the entire budget. Projects B and C can *both* be undertaken (together they use the entire budget), and their combined NPV exceeds the NPV of project A; thus, you should initiate them both. Together, their NPV is $145 million compared to $100 million for project A alone.

TABLE 8.4

Possible Projects for $200 Million Budget

Project	NPV ($ millions)	Initial Investment ($ millions)	NPV/Initial Investment
A	100	200	0.500
B	75	120	0.625
C	70	80	0.875

Profitability Index. Note that in the last column of Table 8.4 we included the ratio of the project's NPV to its initial investment. We can interpret this as telling us that for every dollar invested in project A, we will generate 50 cents in value (over and above the dollar investment).[7] Both projects B and C generate higher NPVs per dollar invested than project A, consistent with the fact that given our budget of $200 million, the two of them together created a higher NPV than project A alone.

In this simple example, identifying the optimal combination of projects to undertake is straightforward. In actual situations replete with many projects and resources, finding the optimal combination can be difficult. Practitioners often use the **profitability index (PI)** to help identify the optimal combination of projects to undertake in such situations:

profitability index (PI) Measures the NPV per unit of resource consumed.

Profitability Index

$$\text{Profitability Index} = \frac{\text{Value Created}}{\text{Resource Consumed}} = \frac{NPV}{\text{Resource Consumed}} \tag{8.4}$$

The profitability index measures the "bang for your buck"—that is, the value created in terms of NPV per unit of resource consumed. After computing the profitability index, we can rank projects based on it. Starting with the project with the highest index, we move down the ranking, taking all projects until the resource is consumed. In Table 8.4, the ratio in the last column is the profitability index. Note how the profitability index rule would correctly select projects B and C.

PROBLEM

Your division at NetIt, a large networking company, has put together a project proposal to develop a new home networking router. The expected NPV of the project is $17.7 million, and the project will require 50 software engineers. NetIt has 190 engineers available, and is unable to hire additional qualified engineers in the short run. Therefore, the router project must compete with the following other projects for these engineers:

Project	NPV ($ millions)	Engineering Headcount (EHC)
Router	17.7	50
Project A	22.7	47
Project B	8.1	44
Project C	14.0	40
Project D	11.5	61
Project E	20.6	58
Project F	12.9	32
Total	107.5	332

How should NetIt prioritize these projects?

SOLUTION

PLAN

The goal is to maximize the total NPV that we can create with 190 engineers (at most). We can use Eq. 8.4 to determine the profitability index for each project. In this case, since engineers are our limited resource, we will use Engineering Headcount in the denominator. Once we have the profitability index for each project, we can sort them based on the index.

---

[7]Sometimes, practitioners add 1 to this ratio such that the interpretation would be that every dollar invested returned $1.50. Leaving off the additional 1 allows the ratio to be applied to resources other than budgets as we show in Example 8.6.

EXECUTE

Project	NPV ($ millions)	Engineering Headcount (EHC)	Profitability Index (NPV per EHC)	Cumulative EHC Required
Project A	22.7	47	0.483	47
Project F	12.9	32	0.403	79 (47 + 32)
Project E	20.6	58	0.355	137 (79 + 58)
Router	17.7	50	0.354	187 (137 + 50)
Project C	14.0	40	0.350	
Project D	11.5	61	0.189	
Project B	8.1	44	0.184	

As shown in the table above, we assigned the resource to the projects in descending order according to the profitability index. The final column shows the cumulative use of the resource as each project is taken on until the resource is used up. To maximize NPV within the constraint of 190 engineers, NetIt should choose the first four projects on the list.

EVALUATE

By ranking projects in terms of their NPV per engineer, we find the most value we can create, given our 190 engineers. There is no other combination of projects that will create more value without using more engineers than we have. This ranking also shows us exactly what the engineering constraint costs us—this resource constraint forces NetIt to forgo three otherwise valuable projects (C, D, and B) with a total NPV of $33.6 million.

Shortcomings of the Profitability Index. Although the profitability index is simple to compute and use, in some situations it does not give an accurate answer. For example, suppose in Example 8.6 that NetIt has an additional small project with an NPV of only $100,000 that requires three engineers. The profitability index in this case is $0.1/3 = 0.03$, so this project would appear at the bottom of the ranking. However, notice that three of the 190 employees are not being used after the first four projects are selected. As a result, it would make sense to take on this project even though it would be ranked last because it would exactly use up our constraint.

In general, because the profitability index already includes the cost of capital (in computing the NPV), it would be better if the firm could raise additional funding to relieve the constraint. If the constraint is something else (such as engineers or physical capacity), there may be no way to relieve the constraint quickly enough to avoid having to choose among projects. Nonetheless, because all of the projects being ranked are value-increasing positive NPV projects, it is still better to focus on relieving the constraint.

A more serious problem occurs when multiple resource constraints apply. In this case, the profitability index can break down completely. The only surefire way to find the best combination of projects is to search through all of them. Although this process may sound exceedingly time-consuming, there are more advanced techniques that can tackle this specific kind of problem.[8] By using these techniques on a computer, the solution can usually be obtained almost instantaneously.

CONCEPT CHECK

11. Explain why picking the project with the highest NPV might not be optimal when you evaluate projects with different resource requirements.

12. What does the profitability index tell you?

---

[8]Specifically, there are techniques called *integer and linear programming* that can be used to find the combination with the highest NPV when there are multiple constraints that must be satisfied. These methods are available, for example, in many spreadsheet programs.

Putting It All Together

In Table 8.5, we summarize the decision rules outlined in this chapter. As a financial manager, you are likely to run into many different types of investment decision rules in your career. In fact, in the interview in this chapter, the Treasurer of QUALCOMM mentions five

TABLE 8.5

Summary of
Decision Rules

NPV	
Definition	• The difference between the present value of an investment's benefits and the present value of its costs
Rule	• Take any investment opportunity where the NPV is positive; turn down any opportunity where it is negative
Advantages	• Corresponds directly to the impact of the project on the firm's value • Direct application of the Valuation Principle
Disadvantages	• Relies on an accurate estimate of the discount rate • Can be time-consuming to compute
IRR	
Definition	• The interest rate that sets the net present value of the cash flows equal to zero; the average return of the investment
Rule	• Take any investment opportunity where its IRR exceeds the opportunity cost of capital; turn down any opportunity where its IRR is less than the opportunity cost of capital
Advantages	• Related to the NPV rule and usually yields the same (correct) decision
Disadvantages	• Hard to compute • Multiple IRRs lead to ambiguity • Cannot be used to choose among projects • Can be misleading if inflows come before outflows
Payback Period	
Definition	• The amount of time it takes to pay back the initial investment
Rule	• Accept the project if the payback period is less than a prespecified length of time—usually a few years; otherwise, turn it down
Advantages	• Simple to compute • Favors liquidity
Disadvantages	• No guidance as to correct payback cutoff • Ignores cash flows after the cutoff completely • Not necessarily consistent with maximizing shareholder wealth
Profitability Index	
Definition	• NPV/Resource Consumed
Rule	• Rank projects according to their PI based on the constrained resource and move down the list accepting value-creating projects until the resource is exhausted
Advantages	• Uses the NPV to measure the benefit • Allows projects to be ranked on value created per unit of resource consumed
Disadvantages	• Breaks down when there is more than one constraint • Requires careful attention to make sure the constrained resource is completely utilized

different decision rules used by his company when evaluating investments. We have demonstrated that while alternative decision rules may sometimes (or even often) agree with the NPV decision rule, only the NPV decision rule is always correct. This is because the NPV provides you with a dollar-value measure of the impact of the project on shareholder wealth. Thus, it is the only rule that is directly tied to your goal of maximizing shareholder wealth. Computing the IRR can be a useful supplement to the NPV because knowing the IRR allows you to gauge how sensitive your decision is to errors in your discount rate. And some decision metrics are much simpler to calculate, such as the payback period. However, you should never rely on an alternative rule to make investment decisions.

If you are employed by a firm that uses the IRR rule (or another rule) exclusively, our advice is to always calculate the NPV. If the two rules agree, you can feel comfortable reporting the IRR rule recommendation. If they do not agree, you should investigate why the IRR rule failed by using the concepts in this chapter. Once you have identified the problem, you can alert your superiors to it and perhaps persuade them to adopt the NPV rule.

MyFinanceLab

Here is what you should know after reading this chapter. MyFinanceLab will help you identify what you know, and where to go when you need to practice.

KEY POINTS AND EQUATIONS	KEY TERMS	ONLINE PRACTICE
8.1 The NPV Decision Rule • The net present value (NPV) of a project is $$PV(\text{Benefits}) - PV(\text{Costs}) \qquad (8.1)$$ • A good project is one with a positive net present value. • The NPV decision rule states that when choosing from among a set of alternatives, choose the one with the highest NPV. The NPV of a project is equivalent to the cash value today of the project. • Regardless of our preferences for cash today versus cash in the future, we should always first maximize NPV. We can then borrow or lend to shift cash flows through time and find our most preferred pattern of cash flows.	net present value (NPV), p. 228 NPV decision rule, p. 229	MyFinanceLab Study Plan 8.1 Financial Calculator Tutorial: Calculating the Net Present Value of a Series of Uneven Cash Flows
8.2 Using the NPV Rule • If your objective is to maximize wealth, the NPV rule always gives the correct answer. • The difference between the cost of capital and the IRR is the maximum amount of estimation error that can exist in the cost of capital estimate without altering the original decision.	internal rate of return (IRR), p. 232 NPV profile, p. 231	MyFinanceLab Study Plan 8.2 Using Excel: Making an NPV Profile

8.3 Alternative Decision Rules

- Payback investment rule: Calculate the amount of time it takes to pay back the initial investment (the payback period). If the payback period is less than a prespecified length of time, accept the project. Otherwise, turn it down.
- IRR investment rule: Take any investment opportunity whose IRR exceeds the opportunity cost of capital. Turn down any opportunity whose IRR is less than the opportunity cost of capital.
- The IRR rule may give the wrong answer if the cash flows have an up-front payment (negative investment). When there are multiple IRRs or the IRR does not exist, the IRR rule cannot be used.
- Project cash flows can be modified to eliminate the multiple IRR problem. The modified IRR is calculated based on these modified cash flows.

discounted payback rule, p. 235
internal rate of return (IRR) investment rule, p. 235
modified internal rate of return (MIRR), p. 239
payback investment rule, p. 234
payback period, p. 234

MyFinanceLab Study Plan 8.3

Interactive IRR Analysis

Financial Calculator Tutorial: Solving for the Internal Rate of Return

8.4 Choosing Between Projects

- When choosing among mutually exclusive investment opportunities, pick the opportunity with the highest NPV. Do not use IRR to choose among mutually exclusive investment opportunities.

mutually exclusive projects, p. 242

MyFinanceLab Study Plan 8.4

8.5 Evaluating Projects with Different Lives

- When choosing among projects with different lives, you need a standard basis of comparison. First, compute an annuity with an equivalent present value to the NPV of each project. Then the projects can be compared on their cost or value created *per year*.

equivalent annual annuity (EAA), p. 249

MyFinanceLab Study Plan 8.5

8.6 Choosing Among Projects When Resources Are Limited

- When choosing among projects competing for the same resource, rank the projects by their profitability indices and pick the set of projects with the highest profitability indices that can still be undertaken given the limited resource.

$$\text{Profitability Index} = \frac{\text{Value Created}}{\text{Resource Consumed}}$$
$$= \frac{NPV}{\text{Resource Consumed}} \quad (8.4)$$

profitability index (PI), p. 252

MyFinanceLab Study Plan 8.6

CRITICAL THINKING

1. What is the NPV rule?

2. How is the NPV rule related to the goal of maximizing shareholder wealth?

3. What is the intuition behind the payback rule? What are some of its drawbacks?

4. What is the intuition behind the IRR rule? What are some of its drawbacks?

5. Under what conditions will the IRR rule and the NPV rule give the same accept/reject decision?

6. When is it possible to have multiple IRRs?

7. How does the MIRR solve the problem of multiple IRRs?

8. Why is it generally a bad idea to use IRR to choose between mutually exclusive projects?

9. When should you use the equivalent annual annuity?

10. What is the intuition behind the profitability index?

PROBLEMS

All problems are available in MyFinanceLab. *The* [x] *icon indicates problems that are easier to solve using Excel and have data in an Excel format available in* MyFinanceLab. *An asterisk * indicates problems with a higher level of difficulty.*

The NPV Decision Rule

1. You have an opportunity to invest $50,000 now in return for $60,000 in one year. If your cost of capital is 8%, what is the NPV of this investment?

2. You have an opportunity to invest $100,000 now in return for $80,000 in one year and $30,000 in two years. If your cost of capital is 9%, what is the NPV of this investment?

3. Your storage firm has been offered $100,000 in one year to store some goods for one year. Assume your costs are $95,000, payable immediately, and the cost of capital is 8%. Should you take the contract?

4. You are preparing to produce some goods for sale. You will sell them in one year and you will incur costs of $80,000 immediately. If your cost of capital is 7%, what is the minimum dollar amount you need to expect to sell the goods for in order for this to be a non-negative NPV?

5. You run a construction firm. You have just won a contract to build a government office building. Building it will require an investment of $10 million today and $5 million in one year. The government will pay you $20 million in one year upon the building's completion. Assume the cost of capital is 10%.
   a. What is the NPV of this opportunity?
   b. How can your firm turn this NPV into cash today?

6. You have been offered a unique investment opportunity. If you invest $10,000 today, you will receive $500 one year from now, $1500 two years from now, and $10,000 ten years from now.
   a. What is the NPV of the opportunity if the cost of capital is 6% per year? Should you take the opportunity?
   b. What is the NPV of the opportunity if the cost of capital is 2% per year? Should you take it now?

7. Marian Plunket owns her own business and is considering an investment. If she undertakes the investment, it will pay $4000 at the end of each of the next three years. The opportunity requires an initial investment of $1000 plus an additional investment at the end of the second year of $5000. What is the NPV of this opportunity if the cost of capital is 2% per year? Should Marian take it?

Using the NPV Rule

8. Your factory has been offered a contract to produce a part for a new printer. The contract would be for three years and your cash flows from the contract would be $5 million per year. Your up-front setup costs to be ready to produce the part would

be $8 million. Your cost of capital for this contract is 8%.

a. What does the NPV rule say you should do?

b. If you take the contract, what will be the change in the value of your firm?

9. You are considering opening a new plant. The plant will cost $100 million up front and will take one year to build. After that, it is expected to produce profits of $30 million at the end of every year of production. The cash flows are expected to last forever. Calculate the NPV of this investment opportunity if your cost of capital is 8%. Should you make the investment? Calculate the IRR and use it to determine the maximum deviation allowable in the cost of capital estimate to leave the decision unchanged.

10. Bill Clinton reportedly was paid $10 million to write his book *My Life*. The book took three years to write. In the time he spent writing, Clinton could have been paid to make speeches. Given his popularity, assume that he could earn $8 million per year (paid at the end of the year) speaking instead of writing. Assume his cost of capital is 10% per year.

a. What is the NPV of agreeing to write the book (ignoring any royalty payments)?

b. Assume that, once the book was finished, it was expected to generate royalties of $5 million in the first year (paid at the end of the year) and these royalties were expected to decrease at a rate of 30% per year in perpetuity. What is the NPV of the book with the royalty payments?

*11. FastTrack Bikes, Inc., is thinking of developing a new composite road bike. Development will take six years and the cost is $200,000 per year. Once in production, the bike is expected to make $300,000 per year for 10 years. The cash inflows begin at the end of year 7.

Assuming the cost of capital is 10%:

a. Calculate the NPV of this investment opportunity. Should the company make the investment?

b. Calculate the IRR and use it to determine the maximum deviation allowable in the cost of capital estimate to leave the decision unchanged.

c. How long must development last to change the decision?

Assuming the cost of capital is 14%:

a. Calculate the NPV of this investment opportunity. Should the company make the investment?

b. How much must this cost of capital estimate deviate to change the decision?

c. How long must development last to change the decision?

12. OpenSeas, Inc., is evaluating the purchase of a new cruise ship. The ship will cost $500 million, and will operate for 20 years. OpenSeas expects annual cash flows from operating the ship to be $70 million and its cost of capital is 12%.

a. Prepare an NPV profile of the purchase.

b. Identify the IRR on the graph.

c. Should OpenSeas proceed with the purchase?

d. How far off could OpenSeas' cost of capital estimate be before your purchase decision would change?

13. You are CEO of Rivet Networks, maker of ultra-high performance network cards for gaming computers, and you are considering whether to launch a new product. The product, the Killer X3000, will cost $900,000 to develop upfront (year 0), and you expect revenues the first year of $800,000, growing to $1.5 million the second year, and then declining by 40% per year for the next 3 years before the product is fully obsolete. In years 1 through 5, you will have fixed costs associated with the product of $100,000 per year, and variable costs equal to 50% of revenues.

a. What are the cash flows for the project in years 0 through 5?
b. Plot the NPV profile for this investment using discount rates from 0% to 40% in 10% increments.
c. What is the project's NPV if the project's cost of capital is 10%?
d. Use the NPV profile to estimate the cost of capital at which the project would become unprofitable; that is, estimate the project's IRR.

Alternative Decision Rules

14. You are a real estate agent thinking of placing a sign advertising your services at a local bus stop. The sign will cost $5000 and will be posted for one year. You expect that it will generate additional free cash flow of $500 per month. What is the payback period?

 15. Does the IRR rule agree with the NPV rule in Problem 8?

 16. How many IRRs are there in part (a) of Problem 10? Does the IRR rule give the correct answer in this case?

 17. How many IRRs are there in part (b) of Problem 10? Does the IRR rule work in this case?

 18. Professor Wendy Smith has been offered the following deal: A law firm would like to retain her for an up-front payment of $50,000. In return, for the next year the firm would have access to eight hours of her time every month. Smith's rate is $550 per hour and her opportunity cost of capital is 15% per year. What does the IRR rule advise regarding this opportunity? What about the NPV rule?

 19. Innovation Company is thinking about marketing a new software product. Up-front costs to market and develop the product are $5 million. The product is expected to generate profits of $1 million per year for 10 years. The company will have to provide product support expected to cost $100,000 per year in perpetuity. Assume all profits and expenses occur at the end of the year.
a. What is the NPV of this investment if the cost of capital is 6%? Should the firm undertake the project? Repeat the analysis for discount rates of 2% and 11%.
b. How many IRRs does this investment opportunity have?
c. What does the IRR rule indicate about this investment?

20. You have 3 projects with the following cash flows:

Year	0	1	2	3	4
Project 1	−150	20	40	60	80
Project 2	−825	0	0	7000	−6500
Project 3	20	40	60	80	−245

a. For which of these projects is the IRR rule reliable?
b. Estimate the IRR for each project (to the nearest 1%).
c. What is the NPV of each project if the cost of capital is 5%? 20%? 50%?

 21. You own a coal mining company and are considering opening a new mine. The mine will cost $120 million to open. If this money is spent immediately, the mine will generate $20 million for the next 10 years. After that, the coal will run out and the site must be cleaned and maintained at environmental standards. The cleaning and maintenance are expected to cost $2 million per year in perpetuity. What does the IRR rule say about whether you should accept this opportunity? If the cost of capital is 8%, what does the NPV rule say?

22. Your firm is considering a project that will cost $4.55 million upfront, generate cash flows of $3.5 million per year for three years, and then have a cleanup and shutdown cost of $6 million in the fourth year.
   a. How many IRRs does this project have?
   b. Calculate a modified IRR for this project discounting the outflows and leaving the inflows unchanged. Assume a discount and compounding rate of 10%.
   c. Using the MIRR and a cost of capital of 10%, would you take the project?

23. You have just been offered a contract worth $1 million per year for five years. However, to take the contract, you will need to purchase some new equipment. Your discount rate for this project is 12%. You are still negotiating the purchase price of the equipment. What is the most you can pay for the equipment and not have a negative NPV?

*24. You are getting ready to start a new project that will incur some cleanup and shutdown costs when it is completed. The project costs $5.4 million up front and is expected to generate $1.1 million per year for 10 years and then have some shutdown costs in year 11. Use the MIRR approach to find the maximum shutdown costs you could incur and still meet your cost of capital of 15% on this project.

*25. You are considering investing in a new gold mine in South Africa. Gold in South Africa is buried very deep, so the mine will require an initial investment of $250 million. Once this investment is made, the mine is expected to produce revenues of $30 million per year for the next 20 years. It will cost $10 million per year to operate the mine. After 20 years, the gold will be depleted. The mine must then be stabilized on an ongoing basis, which will cost $5 million per year in perpetuity. Calculate the IRR of this investment. (*Hint*: Plot the NPV as a function of the discount rate.)

26. You are evaluating a project that will cost $500,000, but is expected to produce cash flows of $125,000 per year for 10 years, with the first cash flow in one year. Your cost of capital is 11% and your company's preferred payback period is three years or less.
   a. What is the payback period of this project?
   b. Should you take the project if you want to increase the value of the company?

27. You are considering making a movie. The movie is expected to cost $10 million upfront and take a year to produce. After that, it is expected to make $5 million in the year it is released and $2 million for the following four years. What is the payback period of this investment? If you require a payback period of two years, will you make the movie? Does the movie have positive NPV if the cost of capital is 10%?

Choosing Between Projects

28. You are choosing between two projects, but can only take one. The cash flows for the projects are given in the following table:

	0	1	2	3	4
A	−$50	25	20	20	15
B	−$100	20	40	50	60

   a. What are the IRRs of the two projects?
   b. If your discount rate is 5%, what are the NPVs of the two projects?
   c. Why do IRR and NPV rank the two projects differently?

29. You are deciding between two mutually exclusive investment opportunities. Both require the same initial investment of $10 million. Investment A will generate $2 million per year (starting at the end of the first year) in perpetuity. Investment B will generate $1.5 million at the end of the first year and its revenues will grow at 2% per year for every year after that.

a. Which investment has the higher IRR?
b. Which investment has the higher NPV when the cost of capital is 7%?
c. In this case, when does picking the higher IRR give the correct answer as to which investment is the better opportunity?

30. You are considering the following projects and can take only one. Your cost of capital is 11%.

	0	1	2	3	4
A	−100	25	30	40	50
B	−100	50	40	30	20

a. What is the NPV of each project at your cost of capital?
b. What is the IRR of each project?
c. At what cost of capital are you indifferent between the two projects?
d. What should you do?

31. You need a particular piece of equipment for your production process. An equipment-leasing company has offered to lease you the equipment for $10,000 per year if you sign a guaranteed five-year lease. The company would also maintain the equipment for you as part of the lease. Alternatively, you could buy and maintain the equipment yourself. The cash flows (in thousands) from doing so are listed below (the equipment has an economic life of five years). If your discount rate is 7%, what should you do?

0	1	2	3	4	5
−40	−2	−2	−2	−2	−2

Evaluating Projects with Different Lives

32. You are trying to decide between two mobile phone carriers. Carrier A requires you to pay $200 for the phone and monthly charges of $60 for 24 months. Carrier B wants you to pay $100 for the phone and monthly charges of $70 for 12 months. Assume you will keep replacing the phone after your contract expires. Your cost of capital is 4%. Based on cost alone, which carrier should you choose?

33. Gateway Tours is choosing between two bus models. One is more expensive to purchase and maintain, but lasts much longer than the other. Its discount rate is 11%. It plans to continue with one of the two models for the foreseeable future; which should it choose? Based on the costs of each model shown below, which should it choose?

Model	0	1	2	3	4	5 ...	7
Old Reliable	−200	−4	−4	−4	−4	−4 ...	−4
Short and Sweet	−100	−2	−2	−2	−2		

34. Hassle-Free Web is bidding to provide Web hosting services for Hotel Lisbon. Hotel Lisbon pays its current provider $10,000 per year for hosting its Web page, handling transactions, etc. Hassle-Free figures that it will need to purchase equipment worth $15,000 upfront and then spend $2000 per year on monitoring, updates, and bandwidth to provide the service for three years. If Hassle-Free's cost of capital is 10%, can it bid less than $10,000 per year to provide the service and still increase its value by doing so?

35. You have to buy a new copier. The cost of the copier is $2000, plus $400 per year in maintenance costs. The copier will last for five years. Alternatively, a local company offers to lease the copier to you and do the maintenance as well. If your discount rate is 6%, what is the most you would be willing to pay per year to lease the copier (your first lease payment is due in one year)?

Choosing Among Projects When Resources Are Limited

36. Fabulous Fabricators needs to decide how to allocate space in its production facility this year. It is considering the following contracts:

	NPV	Use of Facility
A	$2 million	100%
B	$1 million	60%
C	$1.5 million	40%

    a. What are the profitability indexes of the projects?
    b. What should Fabulous Fabricators do?

37. Kartman Corporation is evaluating four real estate investments. Management plans to buy the properties today and sell them three years from today. The annual discount rate for these investments is 15%. The following table summarizes the initial cost and the sale price in three years for each property:

	Cost Today	Sale Price in Year 3
Parkside Acres	$650,000	$1,150,000
Real Property Estates	800,000	1,400,000
Lost Lake Properties	650,000	1,050,000
Overlook	150,000	350,000

    Kartman has a total capital budget of $800,000 to invest in properties. Which properties should it choose?

38. Orchid Biotech Company is evaluating several development projects for experimental drugs. Although the cash flows are difficult to forecast, the company has come up with the following estimates of the initial capital requirements and NPVs for the projects. Given a wide variety of staffing needs, the company has also estimated the number of research scientists required for each development project (all cost values are given in millions of dollars).

Project Number	Initial Capital	Number of Research Scientists	NPV
I	$10	2	$10.1
II	15	3	19.0
III	15	4	22.0
IV	20	3	25.0
V	30	12	60.2

    a. Suppose that Orchid has a total capital budget of $60 million. How should it prioritize these projects?
    b. Suppose that Orchid currently has 12 research scientists and does not anticipate being able to hire more in the near future. How should Orchid prioritize these projects?

DATA CASE

You have just purchased a house for $500,000 that is located very close to the university you attend. You plan to put $100,000 down and borrow $400,000. You need to decide which mortgage deal to take. To find out what your choices are, go to www.bankrate.com and select the appropriate buttons to get a quote for a 30-year fixed rate mortgage on a new purchase (not a refinancing). Assume your FICO score is very high and you are looking for a zero point mortgage. Find the best coupon rate on a mortgage that requires paying no upfront fees or points.[9] We will refer to this mortgage as the no-fee mortgage and assume that the rate on this mortgage is your cost of capital.

You are going to make the decision about which mortgage to consider by calculating the NPV of switching from the no-fee mortgage to each of the top six mortgages listed (sorted by their coupon). To calculate the NPV of this decision, calculate the difference in payments today, and over the life of the mortgage, by subtracting the alternative mortgage payments from the no-fee mortgage payments and calculating the NPV. For good measure, calculate the IRR as well.[10] Assume that you will be living in the house for the next 30 years for certain and you will never repay the mortgage early. Which mortgage should you undertake? Do the NPV and IRR rules agree?

Next, assume that the bank will allow you to borrow any fees and points, so the loan amount will increase by these charges. Repeat the above calculations.

Finally, repeat the calculations assuming that you will repay the outstanding balance on the mortgage after 5 years, using the same cost of capital. What can you say about which mortgage you should choose if you have a long horizon versus a shorter horizon?

Of course, the choice of cost of capital will vary by individual. Because your cost of capital might be different to the one used above, for both horizons, pick the option with the largest NPV and plot the NPV profile.

---

[9]The mortgage coupon is listed in the *rate* field (*not* the *APR*) and is quoted as a monthly APR. Both fees and "points" refer to money that must be paid upfront. Fees are specified in dollars, while points refer to a percentage of the amount borrowed. So, a $1000 fee together with a 1% point implies that you must pay $400,000 \times 1\% + 1000 = \$5000$ upfront. This means that although the loan amount will be $400,000 you will actually only borrow $395,000 (so you need to put down an extra $5000).

[10]Hint: If you are having trouble calculating the IRR, make sure it exists by first plotting the NPV profile.

Index